when brooklyn was queer

when brooklyn was queer

hugh ryan

st. martin's press ≋ new york

www.stmartins.com

Designed by Steven Seighman

The Library of Congress Cataloging-in-Publication Data is available upon request.

ISBN 978-1-250-16991-4 (hardcover)
ISBN 978-1-250-16992-1 (ebook)

Our books may be purchased in bulk for promotional, educational, or business use. Please contact your local bookseller or the Macmillan Corporate and Premium Sales Department at 1-800-221-7945, extension 5442, or by email at MacmillanSpecialMarkets@macmillan.com.

First Edition: March 2019

10 9 8 7 6 5 4 3 2 1

To my Brooklyn family, Jason, Tim, April, Mori, & Lulu

contents

There will come a time, here in Brooklyn, and all over America, when nothing will be of more interest than authentic reminiscences of the past.

—WALT WHITMAN

when
brooklyn
was
queer

prologue: Brooklyn, Thanksgiving 1940

Arm in arm with Gypsy Rose Lee, Carson McCullers bursts out of the door of 7 Middagh Street and into the cool, sweet, smoky night. Somewhere nearby, a ship is coming into harbor, and its horn spills long, low notes that reverberate through the narrow blocks of Brooklyn Heights. Somewhere nearby, drunken sailors are laughing, sneaking out of the Navy Yard perhaps, or returning home from a day's leave spent whooping and wooing on the roller coasters at Coney Island. Somewhere nearby are some 2.7 million people—the teeming mass of Brooklyn; Brooklyn the Great, second city of the Empire, as some call it.

Anywhere else in the world, the two women would make an odd pair: the statuesque burlesque queen, and the gangly literary genius. Some say Carson dresses like a man; some say Gypsy secretly *is* one. They couldn't give a fig. In Brooklyn, they are best of friends, sisters in search of adventure, unable to resist the siren call of a fire alarm sounding, even though it's Thanksgiving and their house is filled with some of the most famous artists in the world, from the poet W. H. Auden to a good portion of the corps of the Russian ballet.

The two don't make it far from home before McCullers stops dead, smacked by a sudden revelation: she has figured out the central crux of her next book, the story that has been nagging at her all fall, which will soon become the novel *The Member of the Wedding*. She stops in the street, laughing, as Gypsy runs back to her, grabs her hand, and pulls her forward. This is the perfect moment; the perfect place; McCullers is the most perfect version of herself she will ever be. Their future is illimitable.

Except that in a year, they will both be gone from Brooklyn. In five, the very house they lived in—along with a good chunk of the block—will be destroyed. And in ten, Brooklyn itself will begin to shrink, collapsing inward after 150 years of unparalleled prosperity. The two women stand on a precipice, one that has nothing to do with the coming World War. Brooklyn as they know it—queer Brooklyn—is already under attack.

But tonight, there is a fire to be found, a party to return to, sherry to drink, and stories to tell. There is life to be lived. Brooklyn is waiting.

Arm in arm, they run.

introduction

In 1969—the year of the Stonewall Riots in New York City—Martin Boyce was just twenty-one years old, part of a pack of young, loud, unapologetic queens who hung out at the Stonewall Inn. The surrounding streets of the West Village were their stomping ground, the one area of the city they could lay claim to. Today, nearly a half century later, Boyce is telling me about those days as we sip cappuccinos and watch those same streets teem with affluent locals out for a walk on the first nice day of spring.

"The late sixties was the last hurrah of the turf situation in New York City," he says, his fluting voice now gravelly with age. "And it turned out that Christopher Street was *our* turf. We didn't even know until the riot occurred and we had to defend it."

Boyce is voluble and sweet, making his tales of assaults, arrests, and constant, casual harassment all the harder to hear. For every block he recalls another beating, for every neighborhood another gang. He tells me how queers learned to survive, and how that hard-won knowledge, which was literally beaten into his bones, made the Stonewall Riots possible.

"Anywhere you'd go, you'd have to be ready," he recalls with a sigh. "I was attacked in the Bronx, attacked in Brooklyn. Go to the movies? You'd be attacked. But whatever happened, we'd manage to meet up again, right in the vicinity and safe. That made us excellent urban guerrillas, because we knew how to break and reform. That kept the Stonewall Riots going for hours."

Days, actually. From June 28 to July 1, 1969, some of the most marginalized people in the country—the homeless, poor, sex workers, drug addicts, people of color, homos, dykes, queers, and queens—became an irrepressible force, fighting back against the routine police harassment they experienced. In that moment, they realized the Village was theirs.

"Nobody was against us, that's for certain, even if they weren't joining us." Boyce talks with his hands, driving the point home. "You could see it in their eyes: 'I can't do this, but do it for me.' And all the straight people that were trapped in it were guided out. Because it wasn't against straight people. It was against the police."

For nights on end, Boyce and his friends led the cops on a merry chase, smashing windows, throwing bricks, and rewriting the history of the world. Boyce tells me they knew it, all of them, almost instantly. Afterward, it was in the air. *Something* had changed.

"I remember going down the street, maybe four or five days after," he tells me. "I was *loud,* so they could tell what I was. And there was a sanitation man throwing bags into the back of the truck. He saw me, and he raised his fist in the power salute."

Boyce pauses for a moment, nodding emphatically to himself, looking at his hand unconsciously curled into a tight fist—memory made flesh. Around us, the clatter of cups and spoons, laptops and ringtones, fades away. I can feel him drifting backward in time, and when he speaks again, his voice is strained and quiet.

"Because a lot of people—the ones that were fair in their hearts and minds!— knew that we were really oppressed. To see *that* man . . . like *that* . . ."

For a while I think Boyce is done talking, overwhelmed by the memory. The seconds tick down on my digital recorder. Then suddenly he smirks, showing his teeth. "It was amazing."

These days, Boyce would remind you of nothing so much as a sweet gay Santa, but back then, he was a "scare queen," which meant he wore just enough makeup to "freak out the straights." From California to New York (and everywhere in between) it was people such as Boyce—those who couldn't or wouldn't hide; the ones black feminist scholar Alexis Pauline Gumbs calls "the never straight"—who acted as the foot soldiers of the gay revolution. Forever after, those three days in the summer of '69 have been cited as the birth of the modern gay, lesbian, bisexual, and transgender rights movement.

But I'm interested in what came before. If Stonewall represents the start of the modern gay movement, who (and where) were we before? Before Stonewall, before gay rights, before the word *gay* even meant anything other than "happy"?

And my eyes are set a few miles to the east. The island of Manhattan has always been one showy queen, her skyscrapers of sexual visibility casting long dark shadows over the benighted "outer boroughs." The intertwined stories of three neighborhoods—Greenwich Village, Chelsea, and Harlem—have come to stand in for the queer history of the city as a whole. But for the last six years, I've been talking to folks such as Boyce, asking them one big question:

What about Brooklyn?

"Brooklyn?" Boyce's head dips back, considering. He'd seen every part of the city, because his father was a taxi driver. I figured he could give me a good lay of the land. "Brooklyn had cachet. It was the only rival to Manhattan in hipness. Queens was nondescript. The Bronx was nonexistent to us. And Staten Island, of course, was meh. But Brooklyn! Brooklyn boys had the edge. They'd come from Kings Highway in a testosteronic show, with their DAs, and their cars polished to death, every amazing color."

Cliché as it is, my heart starts to beat faster. *Here we go,* I think.

But the boys, it turns out, were there for Boyce's sister, whose name "was dirt in Yorkville" because she dated them—good girls didn't go to Brooklyn back then. So much for my hopes for a gay(er) version of *Grease.*

Rarely, I've learned over the years, do people consider *queer, Brooklyn,* and *history* in the same sentence without a bit of prodding. Brooklyn has always been the "sub" to Manhattan's "urb," and most accounts of "New York's gay history" give it short shrift. Moreover, the stereotypical image of "Brooklynites" has always been one of tough broads and street-smart greasers, working-class men and women whose heterosexuality was as pronounced as their broad New York accents. Scratch that straight surface, however, and Brooklyn's queer history comes pouring out, full of poets, sailors, undercover cops dressed as sailors, brothels, sideshows, communes, rough trade, Nazi spies, trans men, dancers, machinists, pathbreakers, mythmakers, and more. And with every archive I riffle through, that "and more" becomes more, and more, and more.

But it's unusual that I get the chance to talk to someone who lived through some of the history I'm researching, since I'm mostly interested in the 111 years between 1855 and 1966—between when Walt Whitman published *Leaves of Grass* and when the US government shuttered the Brooklyn Navy Yard. Those years span the waterfront's explosive rise, its decades of prosperity, and its precipitous decline—and they coincide neatly with the emergence of our modern ideas of sexuality and gender identity, making it possible to chart one against the other. Boyce, born in 1948, with a direct connection to the most well-known moment in queer New York history, is a rare find. I nod encouragingly and he speeds up, memories coming quicker now.

"Brooklyn had a lore: the Dodgers. The language from the movies of the thirties. Murray the K's rock-and-roll show. Coney Island!"

Ah, infamous Coney Island: the most libidinous 442 acres in all of New York City, where Mabel Hampton, a black lesbian dancer, found her first real job in 1920. Home to the bathing pavilions where modernist poet Harold Norse had his sexual awakening. The spot where Jane Barnell performed as Madame Olga, the Bearded Lady. The place that most likely inspired Jimmie Monaco's wacky 1925 song "Masculine Women! Feminine Men!" If anywhere in New York City could be labeled definitively queer—not gay, not lesbian, not trans, but *queer;* odd and subversive and sexually different—it's Coney Island.

"Tell me about Coney," I prompt Boyce.

"Well . . ." He hesitates, grimacing. "That was a sexually permissive area. It had a name, you know? A reputation. *Anything* could happen at Coney Island. But!"

He stops short, his eyes wide with remembered anxiety.

"There was not one area of Coney Island that *we* could go to." He shakes his head. "It just wasn't ours. Even when all the queens got together—we'd go to the zoo, to the beach, to the museum—we never went to Coney Island. It was inviting trouble."

Another dead end, I think to myself.

Researching Brooklyn's queer history is a bit like playing a game of Whac-A-Mole: just when I think I know where it's going to pop up, it fakes me out. A queer moment in time fluoresces briefly, glows brightly, fades, and is forgotten. The further back you go, it seems, the briefer the shine. Without much in the way of community institutions or even social organizations to pass information around, queer life in Brooklyn, pre-Stonewall, was a many-splintered thing. And in the years before the words *homosexuality* and *heterosexuality* existed, that life was a very different experience. Some days, it feels as if I'm trying to complete a jigsaw puzzle without knowing what the final picture will look like. Plus, I don't know how many pieces there are, I'm pretty sure I'm missing a lot of them, and with every new piece I find, the others look a little different. For now, all I can do is keep collecting them and hope for some coherency later.

"So . . . what were the *gay* places in Brooklyn when you came out?" I ask.

Boyce gives a snorty little laugh. "There was a scene going on in Brooklyn, on the Promenade. A *local* scene," he clarifies dismissively. "It wasn't really hip enough to attract the Stonewall group. You went there once, just to know what it was."

I bite my tongue, wanting to let him talk, to hear what he has to say without prejudicing it with what I already know: that once upon a time, Brooklyn Heights—home of the Promenade—was one of the city's known queer neighborhoods, a fact few people remember (or were perhaps ever aware of). Hints linger, however. According to the US Census Bureau's most recent American Community Survey, the three New York City neighborhoods with the highest percentage of same-sex couples are Greenwich Village, Chelsea, and Brooklyn Heights. While the number of conventionally married gays is an imprecise stand-in for the actual size of the LGBT community in an area, it does suggest a long-term, settled community. But by Boyce's time, that community was almost entirely sub rosa, driven underground by conservative forces in the fifties and sixties, and overshadowed by Manhattan's wider, wilder scenes.

"How'd you hear about the Promenade?" I ask Boyce. This is the other part of my quest: to find out not just what people knew about Brooklyn, but *how* they knew it. Before schools taught it, televisions aired it, or books published it, how did people learn about gay life and gay history?

"The older queens." Boyce laughs. The word *obviously* hangs in the air, unspoken but strongly implied. "They'd relate a campy story at the bar, and then you'd get into what's *behind* the story." The funnier the queen, Boyce remembers, the more likely you were to listen.

The way Boyce uses *queen,* it cuts across a lot of modern labels, encompassing feminine gay men, drag queens, and transgender women. Another tricky thing about researching queer history is that our ideas about gender and sexuality have continually changed over the last 150 years, leading to a nearly endless string of forgotten terms such as *tribade, urning, gynander,* and *invert.* Other words have stayed in usage, but their meanings have radically changed, such as *bisexual,* which once meant roughly what we mean by *transgender* today. When you add in all the euphemisms, slang words, and legal categories, it becomes easy to miss (or misunderstand) queer history, even when it seems obvious. Because of this, in my research I use the catchall *queer,* similarly to the way Boyce uses *queen,* to refer to people whose sexuality or gender identity isn't conventional for their time, which helps me avoid projecting specific modern identities (such as *gay* or *transgender*) on folks for whom those ideas wouldn't necessarily have made a lot of sense.

After we chat for a little longer, it seems as if Boyce has run out of things to say. It's amazing how little of Brooklyn's rich, full, and complicated queer history has been passed down, even among queer people who were in the know. But I start asking about specific places, hoping to jog Boyce's memory.

The St. George Hotel, where the poet Hart Crane once cruised? "It wasn't a place you'd go, you know, but it was . . . *known*." Known as what, Boyce can't quite say, just that it was a place that existed on the queer map of the city he inherited one story at a time, a landmark with no history.

Sands Street? Boyce shrugs; the most infamous red-light district in Brooklyn, where Carson McCullers and W. H. Auden hung out with sailors and queens, means nothing to him.

The Brooklyn Navy Yard? "In decline, but famous in the past." He smiles and bites his lower lip. "Sailors." He nods conspiratorially.

The yard was decommissioned in 1966, the last in a series of crippling blows to Brooklyn's waterfront economy, so it makes sense that Boyce wouldn't know much about it. Yet perhaps no other single site in Brooklyn has contributed so much to its queer history. There, lesbians found work and economic freedom in the factories of World War II; gay men from all around the country were thrown together in close quarters during their naval service; and queer sex workers of all genders found ready customers and unpoliced streets upon which to ply their wares. This points to perhaps the one constant I've found in my research: early queer life flourished where there were jobs queer people could have. Those jobs were often low earning, low skilled, sometimes illegal, and frequently dangerous; but they paid. And often, they were along the waterfront—a pattern that holds true in Brooklyn *and* Manhattan (as well as in San Francisco, Boston, London, and most port cities where anyone's bothered to do the research).

Later, when Boyce is telling me about his time in the West Village (itself a waterfront neighborhood), he puts that connection into words.

"Whether Brooklyn or Manhattan, the waterfront is always the same," he tells me. "Cruisy. Dangerous. Lonely. Attractive in that noir way that a lot of gays like—as I do myself." He grins.

Long after our conversation ends, his words stay with me. Boyce is right: visit any major port city and you'll find sex along the waterfront, or at least a history of it, usually an unseemly one that no one wants to examine too closely. But "queer sex" and "queer community" are like smoke and fire—see one, and you can infer the other. After all, you can't have sex until you have two (or more) people who want the same thing.

Over and over as I've looked into Brooklyn's queer history, I've found that the trails leads back to the waterfront. It's true, as the gay liberation slogan says, that "we are everywhere"—but we're some places a whole hell of a lot more than we are others. Queer life in Brooklyn began by the water, and spread outward.

It's impossible to pinpoint an exact moment when that happened. Every true story starts in the middle, at the somewhat arbitrary point that the storyteller has chosen. But it is possible, in the sweep of history, to pick out moments that are emblematic, turning points after which something is definitively *there,* where it may or may not have been before.

And for my queer history of Brooklyn, that moment is the 1855 publication of Walt Whitman's masterwork, *Leaves of Grass.* In chapter 1, "From *Leaves of Grass* to the Brooklyn Bridge: The Rise of the Queer Waterfront, 1855–83," I intro- duce Brooklyn, which had become a major port city thanks to the opening of the Erie Canal in 1825. Whitman—and *Leaves of Grass*—stands in for an entire com- munity of white men who had sex with other men, who found one another along the waterfront as business boomed in the mid-1800s. However, the economic free- dom that the waterfront offered was more limited for women and black people in the nineteenth century, and I trace these exclusions as a way of showing how and why white men are often the earliest queer ancestors we can find. Queer women don't appear in this historical record until author and illustrator Mary Hallock Foote moved to Brooklyn Heights in the 1860s, and the earliest records of queer people of color date to the 1890s. However, by the time the Brooklyn Bridge opened in 1883, Brooklyn was already being described as "the second city of the Empire," after Manhattan (with which it would unite in 1898). Soon, queer people of all kinds would flock to its shores.

In chapter 2, "Becoming Visible, 1883–1910," I trace how the broader straight world slowly gained an awareness of these early queer pioneers, primarily via theaters and newspapers (both of which boomed in Brooklyn during the late nineteenth century). Performers such as Foley McKeever, Ada Dwyer, Ella Wesner, and Florence Hines were the most visible queer people of their day. Newspapers carried extensive reporting on their shows, their outfits, and their relationships.

However, journalists also introduced America to queer people in a much less wholesome fashion: through true-crime stories that both titillated and terrified "normal" Americans. Only people who visibly transgressed gender were considered truly "queer" in this period. A conventionally masculine man such as world-famous boxer Young Griffo could frequent gay bathhouses and be found guilty of sexually assaulting a twelve-year-old Coney Island boy and still be considered a "normal" man. However, as more and more queer people came to the attention of the general public, America would begin to define them as different, usually in regard to their gender, but also over this new idea of "homosexuality."

By 1910, a backlash began against the growing presence of queer people in America. In chapter 3, "Criminal Perverts, 1910–20," I chart the rise of three groups, all of who worked (sometimes together, sometimes in opposition) to exercise moral control over the future of Brooklyn: courts, doctors, and civilian reformers. These groups would teach America that there was such a thing as "homosexuality" and "heterosexuality," and that one was vastly superior to the other. Over the 1910s, they would try to define, contain, and control queerness and queer people—from sex workers such as Loop-the-Loop (perhaps the first explicitly "trans" woman in Brooklyn history), to queer-friendly bar owners such as Antonio Bellavicini and Robert Bonner. Although problematic, the records of these groups point to large numbers of queer people living in Brooklyn. Unfortunately, few of them had the ability, power, or necessary community to preserve their own histories, leaving us with only these inherently biased records to draw from.

However, by the 1920s, queer people had begun to find one another in dense enough numbers in Brooklyn that younger queers had elders to mentor them, and descendants to preserve their stories. In chapter 4, "A Growing World, 1920–30," I document this greatly expanded queer world—and a greatly expanded Brooklyn, as well. By the end of the decade, Brooklyn's population would outstrip Manhattan's for the first time. The subway would create a vastly more interconnected city, making Coney Island a pleasure ground for all of New York. For queer people such as dancer Mabel Hampton and poet Hart Crane, the 1920s were filled with excitement and potential, constantly ratcheting upward until the inevitable crash.

The Depression began the Brooklyn waterfront's long, slow skid into economic instability, as I chart in chapter 5, "The Beginning of the End, 1930–40." The end of Prohibition, the onset of film censorship via the Hays movie code, and early anticommunist government witch hunts would all imperil Brooklyn's queer communities, even as they continued to grow and expand. In the hyperbolic 1930s, bars on Sands Street would become famous the world over for their sexually permissive atmosphere, while arrests of gay men would tick steadily upward. From this point on begins a hard-and-fast separation between gay and straight worlds. However, the buildup to World War II would act as a stopgap for America's growing homophobia, while simultaneously helping to temporarily resuscitate Brooklyn's economy.

In chapter 6, "Brooklyn at War, 1940–45," I explore how the mobilization around the war created almost limitless possibilities for queer people. In the armed forces, millions of Americans were introduced to queerness (their own or others) for the first time. On the home front, Brooklyn would become a destination for a global antifascist queer intelligentsia, thanks in large part to an artist commune known as February House. In the factories of the war effort, women such as machinist Rusty Brown and welder Anne Moses had the chance to earn equal pay, wear pants, and be celebrated for traditionally unfeminine behaviors. However, the very vastness of this queer world would leave its denizens completely unprepared for the extreme clampdown on sexuality that began with the war's end.

After 1945, the story of Brooklyn's queer community is primarily one of diminution, separation, and persecution, as I show in chapter 7, "The Great Erasure, 1945–69." Not only was Brooklyn's wide queer world destroyed, but even the memory of it was erased. In part, this had to do with the larger shutdown of Brooklyn's waterfront, and the growth of the New York City suburbs, both of which starved city infrastructure and drove huge population shifts in Brooklyn. Although new queer institutions and communities would form after the Stonewall Riots in 1969, these were only dimly connected to the vast queer world that existed in Brooklyn before.

Today, Brooklyn is undoubtedly queer again; the borough is redolent with a queerness that is more diverse, more open, and more powerful than it has ever been. What better time to restore our queer past to its rightful place in the history of Brooklyn, the history of New York City, and the history of queer people everywhere. What follows in these pages is over one hundred and fifty years of Brooklyn's queer history—an incomplete record of a story that is still being written. *When Brooklyn Was Queer* charts that river and is part of its current.

1. From *Leaves of Grass* to the Brooklyn Bridge: The Rise of the Queer Waterfront, 1855–83

On the afternoon of July 4, 1855, Walter Whitman was a lithe but graying thirty-six-year-old hurrying through the busy streets of Brooklyn on his way to immortality. Most days he strolled leisurely through the hurly-burly crowds, stopping to chat with any strapping stevedore or intriguing young clerk who caught his eye, but today he moved with purpose. Nothing would put him off, not the flat gray sky of an incipient summer storm, nor the slippery surface of Brooklyn's cobblestoned streets, nor even the pleasure of raising a glass to America's birthday with some handsome man in a ramshackle sailor saloon. Whitman's destination? A two-story, redbrick printer's shop at the corner of Cranberry and Fulton Streets, run by the Rome

Walt Whitman in the engraved frontispiece from *Leaves of Grass,* by Samuel Hollyer, 1854.

brothers. He was picking up the very first printing of his first book of poetry, *Leaves of Grass.* All spring he'd worked in the convivial atmosphere of the shop, assembling the text, choosing the fonts, and even typesetting some of the pages himself. Now the book was done, and with it, he would etch two names on the ledger of history, forever linking their fame to each other: *Whitman* and *Brooklyn.*

Whitman was not yet known as a poet, or, really, as much of anything. The engraved frontispiece of *Leaves of Grass* shows a sturdy man with a trim graying beard. He wears a black hat but no belt; his gaze is direct; and his right fist sits jauntily on his hip. His demeanor has the air of a provocateur, as though he were about to cock an eyebrow and ask, "Well?" In an anonymous review of *Leaves of Grass* (almost certainly written by Whitman himself), he was described as being

> *of pure American breed, large and lusty—age thirty-six years, (1855,)—never once using medicine—never dressed in black, always dressed freely and clean in strong clothes neck open, shirt-collar flat and broad, countenance tawny transparent red, beard well-mottled with white, hair like hay after it has been mowed in the field and lies tossed and streaked—his physiology corroborating a rugged phrenology—a spirit that mixes cheerfully with the world—a person singularly beloved and looked toward, especially by young men and the illiterate.*[1]

And that love, according to *Leaves of Grass,* was amply returned.

Born on Long Island in 1819, Whitman was raised in Brooklyn and returned there at the age of twenty-six. As an adult, he bounced from job to job, including schoolteacher, journalist, publisher of an abolitionist paper, keeper of a print shop, and house builder. He liked long walks on the city's teeming streets and in Brooklyn's rural countryside and had a particular fondness for swimming naked in the streams, ponds, and beaches that dotted its landscape. He loved the opera, the ocean, and the ruddy young men who flooded the city looking for work. In the evenings, he liked to carouse at Pfaff's, a basement bar in Manhattan that was a candlelit version of CBGB—the hottest hangout for the city's most outré artists. But Whitman's early writings consisted mostly of dry editorials and the occasional stilted story. *Life and Adventures of Jack Engle,* which Whitman published in serial form in 1853, is fairly typical of his early output. It begins:

> *Punctually at half past 12, the noon-day sun shining flat on the pavement of Wall street, a youth with the pious name of Nathaniel, clapt upon his closely cropt head, a straw hat, for which he had that very morning given the sum of twenty-five cents, and announced his intention of going to his dinner.*[2]

Despite its having some pleasing rhythm—"clapt upon his closely cropt head"— no one would ever mistake Whitman for a novelist. His stories were too moralizing and fussy, and they dealt timidly with things of little importance. When that first copy of *Leaves of Grass* was printed, it would be as dissimilar to Whitman's other writings as it was to nearly *all* other writing at the time. It was new, brashly and brazenly so—a "barbaric yawp," as its creator termed it, written in free verse. At the time, most American poets wrote with formal meter and rhyme. By breaking with this tradition, Whitman rendered *Leaves of Grass* more conversational and accessible to a wide range of readers. With it, he answered a challenge from one of the foremost American writers of his day, Ralph Waldo Emerson, the transcendentalist author of "Self-Reliance." More than a decade earlier, Emerson had written an essay entitled "The Poet," which declared that America had produced no great poets as of yet. What defined this new genius according to Emerson?

> The poet has a new thought: he has a whole new experience to unfold; he will tell us how it was with him, and all men will be the richer in his fortune. For, the experience of each new age requires a new confession, and the world seems always waiting for its poet. . . .
>
> The poet is the Namer, or Language-maker, naming things sometimes after their appearance, sometimes after their essence, and giving to every one its own name and not another's. . . .
>
> I look in vain for the poet whom I describe. We do not, with sufficient plainness, or sufficient profoundness, address ourselves to life, nor dare we chaunt our own times and social circumstance. If we filled the day with bravery, we should not shrink from celebrating it. Time and nature yield us many gifts, but not yet the timely man, the new religion, the reconciler, whom all things await.[3]

Before 1855, no one would have guessed that the unprepossessing Walter Whitman from Huntington, Long Island, would be the poet for whom Emerson waited. Within just weeks of publication, however, Emerson would proclaim *Leaves of Grass* "the most extraordinary piece of wit and wisdom that America has yet contributed," full of "incomparable things said incomparably well." Many critics agreed, with the magazine *Life Illustrated* raving, "It is like no other book that ever was written."[4] But some saw a moral darkness in Whitman's work, "a degrading, beastly sensuality," as a reviewer in *The Criterion* called it.[5] Its poems celebrated the wondrous diversity of life in Brooklyn, the technological marvels of the nineteenth century, the natural beauty of America, and (for those in the know) love between men. It was so popular that Whitman printed a new version in 1856—and in 1860, '67, '71, '76, '81, '88, and '92.

Perhaps just as surprising as the sudden emergence of Whitman as a great poet was that he lived in Brooklyn. Although it was still a city in its own right—not yet a satellite borough to Manhattan—Brooklyn, like Whitman, had only just begun to come into its own. Originally spelled *Breukelen,* it was one of the six Dutch settlements created on the western edge of Long Island in the mid-1600s. At the turn of the nineteenth century, it was a farming hamlet of just six thousand residents, but by 1855, it had incorporated the nearby towns of Williamsburg and Bushwick to become an urban enclave of some two hundred thousand souls. According to Mayor George Hall, by annexing the other two towns, Brooklyn had become "the second city of the Empire," after Manhattan. Mayor Hall numbered among Brooklyn's virtues some nineteen thousand buildings, five hundred streets, thirty-seven hundred public lamps (twenty-six hundred of which used gas!), and eight and a half miles of industrious waterfront. Brooklyn possessed such incredible resources, wrote Mayor Hall, that no one could "set bounds on [its] future greatness."[6] After the publication of *Leaves of Grass,* the same could be said for Walt Whitman.

The pulsing heart of this new American city was the Fulton Ferry landing, just a few blocks from the Rome brothers' print shop, where dozens of steamboats hauled passengers and supplies in an endless loop between the sister cities, Brooklyn and Manhattan. Here, the sounds of lapping water and hungry gulls provided a constant backdrop to the polyglot shouts of sailors, the creaking of carriage wheels, and the heavy thuds of an endless stream of cargo being unloaded. Anyone looking for passage across the East River had to take the ferry, which made for unparalleled people-watching. Within just a few minutes, you could encounter wealthy Quaker women heading to Manhattan in horse-drawn carriages, Filipino cooks buying provisions for ships docked down in Red Hook, boisterous young sailors on leave from the navy, and tweed-suited titans of industry investigating their goods with monocled eyes. These variegated multitudes provided Whitman with an "impalpable sustenance," an endless chance to marvel at the greatness of the world.[7] Perhaps just as important, the ferry provided an endless chance to marvel at the greatness of young men.

Whitman immortalized the vitality of the Fulton Ferry landing in his poem "Crossing the Brooklyn Ferry," which contains perhaps the first description of cruising in American literature. Whitman wrote of loving those "who look back on me because I look'd forward to them"—a poetic invocation of the backward glance that is often the first step in the delicate business of expressing clandestine desire. Later in the poem, the object of that glance is made clear, as Whitman recalls the "loud voices of young men" hailing him in the streets, and how he

> *Felt their arms on my neck as I stood, or the negligent leaning of their flesh*
>   *against me as I sat,*
> *Saw many I loved in the street or ferry-boat or public assembly, yet never told them*
>   *a word*[8]

As surely as *Leaves of Grass* linked Whitman and Brooklyn for eternity, lines such as these indelibly connected Whitman to the generations of queer people who would come after him, people for whom urban life—Brooklyn life— provided the opportunity to express desires that were largely incompatible with the agrarian, family-based culture that predominated in America before the mid-nineteenth century. For the next hundred years, the development of Brooklyn would neatly track with the development of our modern ideas of sexuality. Whit-man stands like a beacon at the beginning of both—a beacon located squarely on the waterfront, the economic engine that powered Brooklyn. To understand queer Brooklyn, or Brooklyn at all, you have to start with the water.

Brooklyn's sudden transformation from farm town to "second city of the Em-pire" can be traced to one waterway in particular: the Erie Canal, which con-nected the upper Hudson River to Lake Erie, the gateway to the West. When the canal opened in 1825, it immediately redefined trade in America. According to *The Erie Canal: A Brief History,* "within 15 years of the Canal's opening, New York was the busiest port in America, moving tonnages greater than Boston, Baltimore and New Orleans combined."[9] The canal also redrew the map of the state: nearly every major modern city in New York today is along the route of the canal. As the terminus of this great trade, New York City was perhaps the single most impor-tant shipping location in the world. In just the year after the canal opened, five hundred new mercantile companies were launched in the city.[10]

There was just one problem: By the mid-1830s, the city's harbor was maxed out. Dense lower Manhattan simply had no room for the docks, warehouses, and other attendant industries that all of this new trade needed. Moreover, many of the piers were in poor condition, having gone unmaintained for years.[11] Land spec-ulators in Brooklyn rushed to fill this gap, starting in Red Hook (a neighborhood entirely along the waterfront, which is today mostly known for having NYC's only IKEA). According to Joseph Alexiou's *Gowanus: Brooklyn's Curious Canal,* one of the first groups to try to capitalize on the need for more shipping space was the Red Hook Building Company. In an internal memo from 1838, they wrote that the new shipping businesses coming to the city

> *cannot, with convenience, intermix with the shipping at the crowded docks of New York . . . they require space. They must have coal yards and warehouses in the immediate vicinity of their docks. Where shall they go? Where can they go but Brooklyn?*[12]

Unfortunately, their plan went nowhere, but soon the Atlantic Dock Company succeeded where the Red Hook Building Company had failed. In 1846, they turned forty-two acres of marshy Red Hook coastland into the Atlantic Docks, which included dozens of piers, bulkheads, docks, warehouses, and one of the first steam-powered grain elevators in America. The basin they created could house one hundred ships at a time, turning Brooklyn into an "international center of commerce."[13] The growth in trade created a bevy of new jobs, ranging from unskilled hauling to highly specialized shipbuilding. By the mid-1800s, Brooklyn was one of the leading manufacturers in the country for a wide range of products, from sugar, to rope, to white lead, to whiskey.[14]

This new industrial waterfront created the conditions that allowed queer lives to flourish in Brooklyn. As America transitioned away from a primarily farming economy, the extended family—once the main economic unit in the country—began to lose importance. New urban jobs allowed (some) people in Brooklyn to carve out separate space for themselves, far from their parents or anyone who knew them. Victorian culture mandated strict separations between men and women, meaning that most of these jobs were either all-male or all-female. Huge numbers of immigrants, mostly unaccompanied men, came to New York to meet this demand for laborers, creating large working-class bachelor subcultures where heterosexual sex (outside of prostitution) could be hard to find. The trading routes that created these jobs didn't just move goods, however; they also moved people and ideas—meaning that the average Brooklyn laborer had much greater exposure to other cultures (and their sexual mores) than did most other Americans. Many of these new Brooklyn residents were transient, living in the city only seasonally or for a few years at a time, enabling them to settle in these raucous neighborhoods with relative anonymity. Finally, since shipping and manufacturing were dirty endeavors, waterfront neighborhoods were often undesirable, inexpensive, and only lightly policed. One of the few drawbacks to Brooklyn cited by Mayor Hall in 1855 was that its police lacked the "qualifications and fitness for office."[15] Thus, Brooklyn's waterfront offered the density, privacy, diversity, and economic possibility that would allow queer people to find one another in ever-increasing numbers (though these freedoms would not be enjoyed equally by all queer people). The waterfront was no monolith, however, and different parts of it offered different opportunities, to different communities, in different eras. But by the time Walt Whitman published *Leaves of Grass,* the areas that offered the most support to the earliest queer communities in Brooklyn were already established neighborhoods drawing new residents from around the world.

A visitor to Brooklyn in 1855 would step off the ferry onto Old Fulton Street, which roughly bisected the city. To the east was low-lying Vinegar Hill, a working-class, dockside neighborhood with a large Irish population. The area was a warren of poorly constructed, tightly packed row houses and dirty businesses, filled with the sharp smells of varnish being manufactured and iron being smelted. Bootlegging was a major business in Vinegar Hill, from small-scale home distilleries making poteen, or Irish moonshine, to industrial-size whiskey and rum operations. These illegal establishments were so prominent that when the federal government tried to clamp down on them for tax purposes in 1870, it had to flood the neighborhood with more than two thousand soldiers, in a series of pitched battles known as the Whiskey Wars.[16]

Vinegar Hill was bordered to the south by Sands Street, an important thoroughfare that connected Old Fulton Street with the Brooklyn Navy Yard, which sat on the western edge of Vinegar Hill. The yard was the city's most important military base and the largest navy yard in the country, a sprawling complex that was home to innumerable sailors. Inaugurated in 1801 by President John Adams, the yard was a center for early American shipbuilding, military education, and technological innovation. In 1815, the first steam-powered warship, the USS *Fulton,* was built here, and the Naval Lyceum (the precursor to the US Naval Academy) was founded here in 1833. By Whitman's time, some six thousand men were employed in the Navy Yard's nearly two-hundred-acre campus.

If a visitor continued east, a few miles farther out was Weeksville, a small town

that was the only majority-black community in Brooklyn. By all accounts, Weeksville was a semirural enclave of "steep hills, deep valleys, and woodlands," which
was about ten minutes from the ferry via the Long Island Rail Road. Founded in
1838, by 1855 Weeksville had over five hundred residents (about 20 percent of
the entire black population of Brooklyn at the time). It served as "the center of
organized recreational activities for African-Americans from the entire region,"
according to Judith Wellman, author of *Brooklyn's Promised Land: The Free Black Community of Weeksville, New York*. Weeksville was "one of the two largest independent
free Black communities in the United States," a place where "people generally lived
in safety, supported themselves financially, educated their children . . . and set
up their own churches."[17] As one of the few majority-black areas in all of New
York City, it served as an incubator for black political and religious organizing
and a needed refuge in times of racial unrest and antiblack rioting. After a visitor
passed Weeksville, the rest of eastern Brooklyn was lightly settled farmland, still
crisscrossed with pastoral streams and woods, until one reached the newly incorporated town of Bushwick (formerly the Dutch town Boswjick).

If, on the other hand, a visitor disembarked from the ferry and followed Old
Fulton Street to the south, they would find the land quickly rising beneath them
to create high bluffs with panoramic Manhattan views. Just a few blocks into town
they would encounter the Rome brothers' print shop, one of the bustling businesses where the working waterfront edged into the more residential neighborhood of Brooklyn Heights. A few blocks farther south, wealthy families were
already building the Greek Revival–style town houses that earned the Heights
the label "America's first suburb."[18] The area on the other side of Old Fulton Street,
opposite Brooklyn Heights, would eventually be downtown Brooklyn, the city's
civic center.

Farther south still, the city gave way to the industrial basin of Red Hook and
the Gowanus Creek, an as-of-yet-unimportant inlet of the New York City harbor. Nearby were the gentle hills, streams, and farmland that would one day be
the neighborhoods of Park Slope and Sunset Park. Finally, a long carriage ride
south from Fulton Ferry would bring you to the oceanfront resorts of Coney
Island, which was primarily an escape for the middle class and the wealthy. Here,
hotels dotted the sandy ocean shores, giving the impression of a distant seaside
holiday just a few miles from the bustle of downtown Brooklyn.

For as long as these waterfront areas were economically successful (or until about the early 1950s), they enabled working-class people to create enclaves of queer life. These groupings were often small, sub rosa, isolated, and temporary, but they formed the nucleus for the later emergence of what we would recognize as gay communities. In the queer history of these areas, five waterfront jobs re-occur again and again: sailor, artist, sex worker, entertainer, and female factory worker. Each of these jobs had particular conditions that made them more avail-able or desirable to queer people. Sailors have always been a symbol of escape from small towns, and their long voyages, marked by single-sex isolation and exposure to different cultures around the world, provided great opportunity for sexual and gender experimentation. Artists were often given leeway to be "eccentric," and the Brooklyn waterfront drew them with its cheap rents (and—to be honest—with its cheap sailors). Sex workers (male, female, and transgender) had ready cli-ents, and few observers, in the dockside alleys and waterfront brothels of Vinegar Hill and Red Hook. Freaks and entertainers, particularly those who were gender nonconforming, found lucrative (if often exploitative) work in the vaudeville the-aters of downtown Brooklyn and the sideshows of Coney Island. Finally, in the lead-up to World War II, female factory workers broke gender stereotypes and provided lesbians with previously unimaginable freedoms.

Given the prevalence of these jobs in mid-nineteenth-century Brooklyn, it's unlikely that Walt Whitman was the first person to develop a queer community there. However, unlike those in the other jobs listed above, artists are often given a greater level of respect—and place in our cultural memory—than their incomes would otherwise generally afford them. Also, at a time when few people were inclined or encouraged to record their innermost thoughts, artists such as Whit-man were pushed to do so. Additionally, your average artist's behavior was (some-what) less policed than that of your average businessman, who had both customers and coworkers to worry about. In other words, artists had a *slightly* better chance of being able to live a queer life, a *slightly* better chance of recording that life, and a *slightly* better chance of having that record preserved. For all of these rea-sons, Whitman provides a good access point to the beginnings of queer life in Brooklyn.

One of the great things about Whitman is the tantalizing hints he left behind pointing to the existence of a subculture of working-class white men who loved other men. Many of these were laborers that he met while walking along the docks, or taking the ferry, or going for a bracing swim in the ocean. In his daybook,

Whitman kept lists of these men, mostly single-line entries commenting on their looks, personalities, and family relationships. A typical snippet from one such catalog, written around the time of *Leaves of Grass,* reads:

> Gus White (25) at Ferry with skeleton boat with Walt Baulsir—(5 ft 9
>   round—well built)
> Timothy Meighan (30) Irish, oranges, Fulton & Concord
> James Dalton (Engine-Williamsburgh)
> Charley Fisher (26) 5th av. (hurt, diseased, deprived)
> Ike (5th av.) 28—fat, drinks, rode "Fashion" in the great race
> Jack (4th av) tall slender, had the French pox [syphilis]

This particular list goes on for *over fifteen pages,* with almost no women included (and those that are mentioned are never physically described).[19] It's impossible to know how many of these men were receptive to advances Whitman made, but some of the entries certainly suggest they were, such as this one: "David Wilson night of Oct 11, '62, walking up from Middagh—slept with me—works in a blacksmith shop in Navy Yard."[20]

These were the "young men and the illiterate" whom Whitman was beloved by. They embodied his twin virtues of health and manly comradeship. *Leaves of Grass* was inspired by them, written for them, and often talked directly about them. Or as Whitman put it in "Song of Myself":

> *The young mechanic is closest to me, he knows me well,*
> *The woodman that takes his axe and jug with him shall take me with him all day,*
> *The farm-boy ploughing in the field feels good at the sound of my voice,*
> *In vessels that sail my words sail, I go with fishermen and seamen and love them.*

That love was not just platonic. Foremost among the "new experiences" that Whitman would chaunt and yawp into the American literary canon was the urban life of a man who loved other men, and who was able to bring together those similarly inclined. Men loving men was not something new, as Whitman was well aware from his studies in ancient Greek. But the idea that these men constituted a specific type of person, that they could define themselves by this love and carve out space to gather together as lovers of other men—what we would today call the idea of "being gay"—didn't yet exist in Whitman's world. The word *homosexual* wouldn't even be coined until 1868.

Leaves of Grass was written at the height of the Victorian era, which lasted from approximately 1840 to 1900. Socially, this was a relatively conservative time, but one that saw huge advances in industry and urbanization. During his life, Whitman witnessed the invention of everything from the telephone, to the photograph, to the flushing indoor toilet, to ice cream. Advances in farming, manufacturing, communication, and transportation enabled a vast population flux into cities around the country. In 1840, barely 10 percent of Americans lived in urban places; by 1900 that number had skyrocketed to 40 percent.[21]

According to Victorian morality, women and men inhabited complementary but separate worlds. Men were rational, active, and in the public eye; women were emotional, passive, and limited to the domestic sphere of family and home. Proper women were asexual and acted as a limiting force on the "animal instincts" of men. White Victorians saw all black men and women as inherently lesser; although New York State had abolished slavery by 1855, it was still the law of the land in many places. And even in free states such as New York, black people lived under tremendous constraints (legal and extralegal) on whom they could love, what jobs they could have, and where they could live. When *Leaves of Grass* was first printed, New York City's entire black population was around twelve thousand people.[22] Few whites—even those who opposed slavery, such as Whitman—believed in true racial equality.

Due to these divisions, New York was "an intensely homosocial city," according to the epic city history *Gotham*—a place where white men "clubbed, ate, drank, rioted, whored, paraded, and politicked together, clustered together in boarding-houses and boards of directors, [and] even slept together."[23] Aside from time with your own family, interactions between men and women were limited (particularly among the middle and upper classes). People of color lived mostly in small, segregated, and remote neighborhoods such as Weeksville, far from the economic and social centers of town. For Whitman, this meant that he lived in rooming houses that were full of white men; worked in print shops and newsrooms that were entirely staffed by white men; ate lunch in cheap oyster houses where the majority of patrons were white men; and in the evenings did his drinking and reveling in saloons that rarely admitted women or people of color.

It almost goes without saying that in a world so divided by sex (the identity), that sex (the act) was treated as a dangerous mystery. Sex education was mostly limited to what a child might observe among livestock or glean from older children (as it still is in many places today). Although Victorians are often remembered solely as prudes, they spent huge amounts of time considering and classifying kinds of sex. Sexual attraction to a person of the same sex was considered a disorder of gender, closer to what we today think of as "being transgender" than "being gay." Sexual acts between members of the same sex were stigmatized and lumped together with other nonprocreative forms of sex under the name *sodomy,* which could include anything from masturbation, to bestiality, to hetero- or homosexual oral sex. Legally, however, sodomy charges (sometimes called the crime against nature) were primarily used in cases of sexual assault, and not against consensual sex acts. At the time of the 1880 census, only sixty-three people were imprisoned on sodomy charges *in the entire country,* and only five of those in New York.[24] The idea that people had a fixed, inborn set of sexual desires that were permanent and could be used to classify humanity into groups was only just emerging among theorists in Europe. There was little agreed-upon language to even discuss those feelings.

As Ralph Waldo Emerson pointed out in his essay, the job of the poet is that of language-maker, the person who documents and names the new experiences of the times. What makes Whitman so memorable isn't his private desires, but his realization that those desires were shared by others, and his attempt to create or memorialize words, rituals, and experiences that these men shared—something he certainly could not have done in isolation. In *Leaves of Grass,* Whitman called these men his "comrades" or "camerados." Their affection for one another he dubbed "adhesiveness." To symbolize that love, he chose the simple calamus plant, a sturdy river reed with long vertical leaves and a protruding, phallic flower cone. Whitman wrote forty-five "Calamus poems" celebrating the love between men. He explicitly urged others to use the plant as a queer love token in Calamus #4, writing:

And here what I now draw from the water, wading in the pond-side,
(O here I last saw him that tenderly loves me—and returns again, never to
      separate from me,
And this, O this shall henceforth be the token of comrades—this calamus-root
      shall,

Interchange it, youths, with each other! Let none render it back!)

. . . . .

But what I drew from the water by the pond-side, that I reserve,

I will give of it—but only to them that love, as I myself am capable of loving.

Why did Whitman choose the calamus as his gift to "them that love, as I my-self am capable of loving"? Calamus was wild in Brooklyn, appearing in the very places where Whitman met his camerados. It grew on the banks of the streams where young farmers brought their livestock to drink; it dotted the marshy coast where sailors hunted for duck in between stints at sea; and it lined the secluded watering holes where salt-crusted stevedores went to wash off the day's labor. Its phallic shape was suggestive, but so were ears of corn, were it just a matter of form. But the calamus had an added bonus: its name was an allusion to the ancient Greek myth of a pair of young male lovers, Kalamos and Karpos, who died during a swimming competition. Whitman's Calamus poems comprise some of his most sensual and personal poetry. Over the next hundred years, this inclination to find "them that love, as I myself am capable of loving," was a con-sistent hallmark of early queer pioneers.

However, cruising the waterfront wasn't the only way that Whitman met other men. *Leaves of Grass* was not only a proclamation, it was an invitation: a love letter set afloat in the world to see who understood it and answered its call. The third poem in the book—"In Cabin'd Ships at Sea"—explicitly says this in its last stanza:

Then falter not, O book! Fulfil your destiny!

You, not a reminiscence of the land alone,

You too, as a lone bark, cleaving the ether—purpos'd I know

not whither—yet ever full of faith,

Consort to every ship that sails—sail you!

Bear forth to them, folded, my love—(Dear mariners! For you I fold it here, in

every leaf;)

Speed on, my Book! Spread your white sails, my little bark, athwart the imperious

waves!

Chant on—sail on—bear o'er the boundless blue, from me, to every shore,

This song for mariners and all their ships.

The ability to gather people to him with his words was one of the other qualities that Emerson enumerated a genius poet would possess, writing that "by truth and by his art . . . [he] will draw all men sooner or later."[25] This was certainly true for Whitman. In his lifetime, men such as Oscar Wilde and Edward Carpenter (an early English proponent of gay rights) flocked to Whitman's door, asking questions about the poet's sexuality, which he was loath to answer. Many later queer artists would be drawn to Brooklyn because of the city's association with Whitman. Hart Crane, the 1920s poet whose foremost muse was the Brooklyn Bridge, addressed Whitman and his legacy of "adhesiveness" directly in his poem "Cape Hatteras," writing, "O Walt!—Ascensions of thee hover in me now. . . . Thou bringest tally, and a pact, new bound / Of living brotherhood!" A decade later, modernist poets Chester Kallman and Harold Norse would cite both Whitman *and* Crane among the reasons they wanted to study at Brooklyn College. In the mid-twentieth century, playwright Tennessee Williams, editor George Davis, and novelist Carson McCullers were all inspired to move to Brooklyn partially because of their love for Crane and Whitman.

McCullers notwithstanding, however, this list of Whitman devotees makes one thing obvious. Whitman's appeal was primarily pitched to and received by queer people who were like him: white, male, cisgender artists. While Whitman professed a love of all people and believed in freedom and equality for men and women, black and white, he was rather disinterested in people who were *not* white men. He referred to black people as "darkeys" who were "superstitious, ignorant, [and] thievish," though "full of good nature,"[26] and he seemed surprised when women were interested in *Leaves of Grass,* since it was so from and for a male perspective.[27]

While Whitman's personal prejudices limited his appeal primarily to white men, larger structural forces also kept women and people of color away from Brooklyn's waterfront and its opportunities for exploring queer life (at least, they did for a while). Whitman wrote *Leaves of Grass* before the Civil War, and though slavery had been outlawed in New York in 1827, black communities were still isolated, small, and marginalized. Until 1940, Brooklyn's population never dipped below 96 percent white, and in 1855 it had just four thousand black residents total. The period immediately surrounding the Civil War was particularly harsh for New York City's black population, which declined steadily from 1840 to 1870. At this time "white supremacist ideology ruled the city," according to

Dr. Carla Peterson, author of *Black Gotham*.[28] Brooklyn was particularly bad. For example, in 1860 New York State contemplated a law granting universal male suffrage, which would have given all black men the right to vote with no property-ownership requirements. Statewide, only 38 percent of voters supported the measure—and in Brooklyn, that number dwindled to a pitiful 20 percent.[29] The *Brooklyn City News* was blunt in its racist disparagement of the law, suggesting that it would determine "whether ten or fifteen thousand sooty Negroes shall be raised" to equality with white men.[30] After the end of the Civil War in 1865, New York City's black population would again begin to rise, but Brooklyn would remain more conservative and less diverse than Manhattan.

This political disenfranchisement went hand in hand with economic barriers against people of color. Just as Brooklyn's waterfront started to grow, black people began to be pushed out of dockside jobs. In 1835, 14 percent of sailors on outbound ships from New York City were black; by 1866, that number would decline to 4.5 percent.[31] Even for black people who did find work in ships out of Brooklyn, many "found their options limited to occupations such as cooks or stewards," according to *Black Jacks,* a history of black sailors.[32] Certain waterfront jobs—such as longshoreman—were already dominated by the Irish, who often locked out black workers in an effort to use racism to help them assimilate into a city that was deeply suspicious of their poverty, lack of education, high birth rates, and Catholicism.[33] To many Americans, the Irish were barely white themselves. By keeping black people down, these new immigrants ensured they were not on society's lowest rung.

Understanding this legacy of racial exclusion is critical to understanding the development of queer history and community in Brooklyn. Although there undoubtedly were black people with queer desires in the city's early years, they don't show up in historical records until right before the beginning of the twentieth century. Even when they do, it's clear that Brooklyn was a more complicated space for early queer people of color. Many seemed to experience the city as an archipelago of safer spaces, dividing their time between its far-flung black neighborhoods, its burgeoning queer areas, and those places where the two overlapped (such as Harlem in the 1920s). Some found employment in majority-black neighborhoods, while living in tony Brooklyn Heights or densely packed Vinegar Hill. Others worked along the waterfront but lived in distant black communities such as Harlem or Weeksville.

It seems likely that the safety provided by Weeksville allowed residents to explore queer desires completely removed from the waterfront. Unfortunately, Weeksville's history is poorly known. The community was only rediscovered by historians in the 1960s, and records of and by residents are spotty at best. Brooklyn's major (white) newspapers rarely covered the town, and many of Weeksville's adults were illiterate. Thus they produced few written records of their own thoughts and experiences. Almost no documents from Weeksville predate the Civil War, and while two newspapers were founded in Weeksville, only one issue of one of them has ever been located. Aside from the fact that the majority of households in Weeksville were two-parent families, little is known about the sexual or romantic lives of its inhabitants.[34]

However, evidence suggests that queer black Brooklynites may have flourished in these gaps in our knowledge. Take, for instance, the experiences of writer and civil rights activist Alice Ruth Moore Dunbar Nelson. Born in 1875 in New Orleans, Nelson graduated from college at the age of seventeen and published her first book of short stories when she was just twenty. Nelson was active in the black women's uplift movement, which created an entire parallel world of volunteer-run social services for black communities and generally emphasized education and respectability as the proper path to equality. This work brought her to Brooklyn in 1895, as a teacher at PS 83, the public school in Weeksville. According to historian Judith Wellman, Weeksville was on the forefront of the national fight to desegregate schools in America, and PS 83 was "one of the first schools in the United States to hire both black and white teachers to teach both black and white students."[35] While teaching, Nelson lived in Brooklyn Heights with Victoria Earle Matthews, a leader in the uplift movement. Matthews was the founder of the White Rose Mission in Harlem, the first settlement house for black women in the city, where Nelson volunteered.

Little information survives from this early period of Nelson's life, except for her correspondence with the man she would briefly marry, author Paul Dunbar. However, thanks to Nelson's later letters and diaries, we know that she had intense, sometimes romantic relationships with other middle-class black women reformers dating back at least to the early 1900s.[36] For instance, in 1907, she worked in Delaware with black education reformer Edwina Kruse, who wrote passionate letters to Nelson declaring that "every thought of my life is for you, every throb of my heart is yours and yours alone."[37] Unfortunately, Nelson's diaries don't begin

until 1921, so we don't know how she felt about Kruse, or if she had similar relationships while living in Brooklyn. However, when she does write about her relationships with women in the 1920s, Nelson seems unsurprised, suggesting she had
prior same-sex experiences, perhaps with Edwina Kruse or even earlier. Certainly,
her letters from her time in Brooklyn show an ambitious, passionate woman wrestling with the restrictions of becoming a more traditional Victorian wife.

Although it's impossible to know how many other women were writing such
passionate letters, in many other ways Nelson was prototypical of women in the
mid-to-late 1800s, who were constrained by structural forces from living queer
lives. The Victorian cult of domesticity dictated that women were to stay in the
private sphere, away from public life. This kept white, American-born women
out of the labor market and meant that women of color and immigrant women
were often judged to be failed mothers, degenerates, or "fallen women" for having to work outside the home. Moreover, women's work was paid on the assump-
tion that women were primarily supported by a husband or a father, meaning
that an unskilled female laborer made fifty cents to two dollars a week (whereas
unskilled male laborers usually made around seven dollar a week).[38] This meant
they had less economic power, less privacy, and less opportunity to meet others
who might share their queer desires. Women were unable to vote until 1920, and
until 1848, married women could not legally own property. Few schools of higher
education admitted women (although those that did were important spaces for
women to explore same-sex desires). From entertainment to education, women
in the mid-1800s lived controlled lives that rarely allowed for the extensive writing, yawping, and queer-life building done by Whitman and other white men.

These racist and misogynist structural realities meant that even at its outset,
American queer life developed in splintered pockets that were already divided by
race, class, and gender. Although sexuality can create powerful, unexpected moments of connection and cross-cultural exchange, the economic opportunities that
initially allowed queer life to grow on the Brooklyn waterfront were primarily
limited to white men. However, while this slowed the development of queer communities of women and people of color (and the integration of white gay male
circles), it certainly didn't stop them.

Walt Whitman's time as the poet of Brooklyn ended with the outbreak of
the Civil War, when he went to Washington, DC, to volunteer as a nurse. Although
he returned frequently to visit, he never lived in Brooklyn again and spent most of

the end of the century in Camden, New Jersey. With the war's end in 1865, the queer history of Brooklyn's waterfront began to diversify. For people of color, the end of the war meant the end of de jure slavery, and an increase in self-determination, political power, mobility, and economic possibility. From 1870 on, the number of people of color living in Brooklyn would rise every decade. But the Civil War also had profound effects on white women. Some took part in the war as nurses, spies, or disguised soldiers, and many more had to take over the responsibilities of drafted husbands, fathers, and brothers (just as tens of thousands of Brooklyn women would during World War I, and hundreds of thousands would during World War II). Over thirty thousand Brooklyn men participated in the Civil War.[39] For the women who remained at home, maintaining the separate sphere mandated by Victorian morality was less important than keeping food on the table, and many went to work outside the home for the first time. It's no coincidence that the 1870 census was the first to ask about women's work, finding that 13.3 percent of women over the age of ten were gainfully employed.[40]

Slowly but surely, women were coming into the public sphere. Right around the end of the Civil War, the first evidence of a queer woman on Brooklyn's water-

front appears in the letters of Mary Hallock Foote. By the end of the nineteenth century, Foote would be famous for her stories and drawings of pioneer life in the American West. A contemporary critic named Foote one of the few great female artist-authors of the day, saying, "She produced better color effects with a pencil than some artists do with a brush."[41] Before her death in 1938 at the age of ninety-three, she would write or illustrate over thirty books, with evocative titles such as *The Chosen Valley* and *The Desert and the Sown*. But she got her start as an artist while living in Brooklyn, which is also when she met the great passion of her life, Helena de Kay Gilder.

Born in 1847 in upstate New York,

Photo of Mary Hallock Foote, date unknown. *(Photo courtesy of the Mary Hallock Foote Papers, M0115, Dept. of Special Collections, Stanford University Libraries, Stanford, Calif.)*

Foote was from a middle-class Quaker family that believed strongly in women's education. Her teachers noticed her artistic talents immediately. When she turned seventeen (in 1864), her aunt Sarah Walter Hallock insisted that her family send her to the School of Design for Women at Cooper Union. Cooper Union was a progressive, coeducational school in Manhattan, with separate day classes for women and night classes for men. One of the courses taught was wood engraving, which became Foote's specialty.[42]

Sketches and photos of Foote show a woman with bright big eyes, almost always looking modestly down and away, her dark hair piled in a loose twist on the top of her head. Images of Foote are rare, however, and she had a reputation for being a recluse. An article in the *Philadelphia Times* said that Foote "refused to let a curious public know anything of her personality" and that "her likeness has never appeared in print but once, and that was only after long and urgent persuasion."[43] Yet beneath that modesty was a woman of both great talent and great ambition, struggling with her place in a rapidly changing world.

While studying at Cooper, Foote lived with her aunt Sarah Walter Hallock in the well-heeled Quaker area of Brooklyn Heights, due south of the Rome brothers' print shop. By this point, a decade after the publication of *Leaves of Grass,* the Heights was the ritziest neighborhood in the growing city of Brooklyn. Its streets were dotted with Greek Revival mansions, three- and four-story town houses, and the light of flickering gas lamps in big glass globes. Brooklyn now had around four hundred thousand residents, and some, such as the Walters, were quite well-off. Their home was described as a "luxurious three-story house on Columbia Street," and Foote's room "offered a magnificent view" of the Brooklyn harbor.[44] The Walters were urbane sophisticates who frequently attended concerts, the theater, and large social events in both Manhattan and Brooklyn. Right before Mary Hallock Foote moved to the Heights, Brooklyn's first official theater was built not far from their home. Called the Park Theatre, this impressive, two-story edifice was made of imported Nova Scotia stone and nightly seated 1,250 people. Its domed ceiling featured frescoes depicting tragedy, comedy, painting, and music, while its first floor had two storefronts for shopping and a public lecture hall for community events. When it opened in 1863, *The Brooklyn Daily Eagle* proclaimed that the Park was "so beautiful, so conveniently located, and designed to meet so pressing a want, that we have no doubt it will flourish."[45] Along with the new Brooklyn City Hall (located just around the corner), the Park helped to define the area known today as downtown Brooklyn, the waterfront-adjacent neighborhood that was just east of Brooklyn Heights and just south of Vinegar Hill.

Most entertainment then were in rough venues that were men-only, but the Park allowed women into all of its shows and offered matinee musicals specifically designed for "ladies"—a sure sign of the increasingly public lives of women.[46] For its first eight years of operation, the theater was managed by a woman, Sarah Conway, whose husband owned the lease.[47] For ambitious young women such as Mary Hallock Foote, theaters such as the Park and schools such as Cooper Union harbingered a new era of possibility, one they would meet with both excitement and trepidation.

In winter 1866, Foote developed the most profound relationship of her life with fellow art student Helena de Kay Gilder. As Foote later described it, "Helena dawned on my nineteenth year like a rose pink winter sunrise, in the bare halls of Cooper, sweet and cold after her walk up from the ferry." According to *Mary Hallock Foote: Author-Illustrator of the American West,* "both then and years later, [Foote] called [Gilder] the first great passion of her life."[48]

Although not well remembered today, Gilder was an accomplished artist, writer, socialite, and reformer, as well as a founding member of both the Art Students League and the Society of American Artists. She received art instruction from and was painted by Winslow Homer, and her life was loosely fictionalized by both Henry James (in 1890's *The Tragic Muse*) and Wallace Stegner (who used Foote's and Gilder's letters to write his 1971 book, *Angle of Repose*). In Homer's *Portrait of Helena de Kay,* Gilder is shown dressed in all black, looking down, and holding a book—an unusual image for Homer, who rarely painted portraiture. However, he must have made an exception for Gilder, with whom he was rumored to be in love.[49]

Foote and Gilder were drawn together not only by their love of art but also by their chafing at gendered Victorian morality. In a letter to Gilder, Foote once wrote:

> I read in the Bible last night that a "meek and quiet spirit" is the only thing for a woman. But how can one ever do or be anything if meekness and quietness are the best things in life. I know plenty of women who have meekness but they have attained it only by giving up all hope or thought for themselves. I could not do that without giving up ambition too.[50]

Through their letters to each other, over more than forty years, a true picture of their intense relationship emerges. Yet not until the late twentieth century did historians began to take these kinds of sources seriously. Feminist author and historian Carroll Smith-Rosenberg wrote in her book *Disorderly Conduct* that reading Foote's letters in the 1970s "radically transformed [her] approach to women's history," by refocusing her scholarship on women's portrayals of their own lives. Without this kind of research, our understanding of historical events and attitudes is partial at best, and it becomes impossible to fully understand the ways in which anyone, male or female, made decisions and lived life. The standard approach to history, in which Smith-Rosenberg was trained, viewed the world through the lens of "great men" and their accomplishments, rendering women such as Foote, Gilder, and Nelson mostly invisible to historians—yet another reason why the queer history of women is still so little known today.

Just nineteen years old, away from her parents for the first time in her life, Foote threw herself headlong into her relationship with Gilder. Smith-Rosenberg describes their correspondence as being filled with "nights wrapped in each other's arms, the light of a full moon illuminating their pillow; of passionate kisses; of bathing and anointing each other's bodies." Foote wrote to Gilder that she wanted to "put my arms round my girl of all girls" and tell her that "I love her as wives do love their husbands, as friends who have taken each other for life—I believe in her as I believe in my God."[51] This kind of passionate relationship between middle- and upper-class white women was a hallmark of the late Victorian era, often referred to as a Boston marriage. These relationships trouble our modern ideas of sex and sexual identity. Often, it's hard to tell from the existing evidence the degree to which they had sexual components, making many scholars hesitant to discuss them as queer. Yet their intensity, their primary place in these women's lives, and their physical dimensions are undeniable. Many of these relationships lasted for decades or until the death of one of the partners. Depending on the women in question, they may or may not have fit our modern idea of what "lesbianism" looks like. Regardless, for all of the women in them, these were primary relationships of great importance. Forcing them to meet our definition of queer women's sexuality—one that focuses on sexual contact—ignores how queer these relationships already were, regardless of any sex involved. As Smith-Rosenberg writes:

The essential question is not whether these women had genital contact and
can therefore be defined as homosexual or heterosexual. The twentieth-century
tendency to view human love and sexuality within a dichotomized universe of
deviance and normality, genitality and platonic love, is alien to the emotions and
attitudes of the nineteenth century and fundamentally distorts the nature of these
women's emotional interaction.[52]

This is true; however, it's also true that the relationship between Foote and
Gilder was "fundamentally distorted" by Victorian gender roles, and their economic and social ramifications. Foote and Gilder may well have been having sex,
or perhaps they would have had sex if they had the privacy and space to do so. But
regardless of their sexual histories, it is unquestionable that their relationship was
powerfully constrained by the realities of life in late-Victorian America.

In many ways, Foote and Gilder subscribed to Victorian ideas about women,
despite pushing back when those same forces curtailed their ambitions. This tension between a kind of protofeminism and compliance with the cult of female
domesticity was evident throughout their lives. Gilder once told a journalist that
she hoped her that "none of her daughters will ever have any special talent," so
that they would never be tempted to neglect their families in pursuit of their
abilities—presumably a temptation she herself knew only too well.[53] When Foote
was invited to show her work in an exhibition that was also a fund-raiser for
women's suffrage, she tersely responded,

Dear Madam: I should not wish to exhibit my books or drawings as "woman's
work," as they are not put in the market on that basis; nor should I care to
contribute toward the campaign for municipal suffrage, not being entirely in
sympathy with it as a means towards the progress of woman.[54]

It might seem nonsensical for a woman of Foote's ambition and ability—a
woman who objected to her art being diminished by the label "woman's work"—
to not support suffrage, but there is a logic to it. The final clause in her short letter indicates that Foote supported "the progress of woman," but doubted that
pursuing the vote was the way to achieve it. This was in line with Victorian
gender ideologies, which saw electoral politics—as part of the public sphere—
as the domain of men. As Smith-Rosenberg points out, Victorian women inhab-

ited a "world of intimacy, love, and erotic passion . . . in which men made only a shadowy appearance."[55] This private women's world was the flip side of the homosocial public world of men that was enjoyed by the likes of Walt Whitman. While Foote wanted education, work, artistic recognition, and personal freedom, she still mourned the loss of her separate sphere. The separation of the sexes might have kept most women from having economic, social, and political freedom, but it was also a way of preserving the intense world of female relationships in which Foote had been raised.

Her views about gender were consistent with Foote's overall traditionalism, which resisted the social changes brought on by an increasingly modern world. As Christine Hill Smith wrote in *Social Class in the Writings of Mary Hallock Foote,* "nineteenth-century industrialization, immigration, [and] urbanization . . . had already begun to loosen barriers to social mobility. Mary Hallock Foote found this trend disturbing."[56] Foote and Gilder were in part united by that very urbanization—in the form of a city big enough to support a school for female artists—but as these trends accelerated, they threatened to tear apart the broader Victorian world that gave their relationship meaning and place. In the end, despite wanting to build a life together, both women would take a more traditional woman's role.

After leaving Cooper Union, Gilder joined a shared studio in Manhattan where other women artists worked, while Foote returned home to live with her family in upstate New York. In 1873, the two began to dream of opening their own studio for women and planned for Foote to live in Brooklyn while they created a place in Manhattan. However, this dream died quickly. Foote's family was displeased with the idea, and as she wrote to Gilder, "I never in my life persisted in anything that my Mother and the family didn't approve."[57] By the end of that year, Foote and Gilder were both engaged to men. While this forestalled their plans to create a life together, it by no means curtailed their powerful expressions of love. Even their husbands were well aware of the intensity of their relationship. In a sonnet entitled "Love's Jealousy," Gilder's husband wrote, "Of other men I know no jealousy / Nor of the maid who holds thee close, oh close."[58] A letter Foote sent congratulating him on the announcement of his engagement to Gilder, however, suggested that perhaps he should have had *some* jealousy: "Do you know sir, that until you came along I believe that she loved me almost as girls loved their lovers. I know I loved her so."[59]

What are historians to make of these letters? As Smith-Rosenberg points out,

"Had these women been writing to men, their letters would clearly fall within one of our post-Freudian conceptual categories—heterosexuality."[60] But for historical figures to be seen as homosexual we require a different, and higher, burden of proof: either explicit, verifiable sexual contact, or a degree of shame or fear about loving someone of the same sex, neither of which is present in this case. Neither Foote nor Gilder expresses any shame in their letters, just the enormous pressure of being pulled between multiple loves. Even as late as the 1920s, Foote's own daughter openly described the relationship between Foote and Gilder as having a "romance and a kind of glory like that the Greeks took in their epic friendships—Achilles and Patroclus" (a pair long associated with homo-erotic friendship).[61]

Paradoxically, this openness about their feelings has helped to make them invisible to modern historians, for whom queer love and shame are inseparable. But the very *appropriateness* of Foote and Gilder's behavior is what allowed them to profess their love as publicly as they did. Their ability to have an intense, passionate relationship rested in large part on their respectability: their whiteness, their class, their education, their commitment to the family and the home, and their eventual heterosexual marriages. Without these underpinnings, what was accepted as an intense but healthy relationship might well have been seen as abnormal or even pathological. Indeed, within just a few years, Victorian sexual morality would begin to give way to the emerging science of sexology, which saw these kinds of intense female-female relationships as suspect. In particular, friendships between women who were poor, "mannish," or vocal advocates for women's equality would be demonized as unnatural. By 1879, even Foote and Gilder began to worry about how their relationship was perceived by others. When Gilder had to send a letter via a relative of Foote's (who might presumably have had the chance to read the contents), she wrote, "We are too old and serious to let them see our weaknesses for each other, so read between the lines."[62]

What had changed by that time? For one thing, the idea of "homosexuality" had been named. As early as 1869, the word appeared in print in Germany, and the concept soon spread throughout Europe and into America. While the creation of the word itself is not of huge importance (other words, such as *uranian*, had been proposed before), in fact that *homosexuality* established a foothold in our language at this time suggests that it was defining something that people had begun to see, think about, and need a name for. Intense same-sex relationships, such as the one between Foote and Gilder, would soon become associated with the emerging idea of "the homosexual" as a person defined by this deviant sexual orientation. One unintended consequence of the demise of the idea of "separate spheres" was that it would slowly become less and less acceptable for women to spend too much time only with other women, and men to spend too much time only with other men. The emergence of the idea of homosexuality at this time can only be understood against the backdrop of this disappearing world of intense and socially sanctioned same-sex relationships.

It is impossible to say what Foote's and Gilder's lives would have been like if they had had the power to create the kind of artist space for women that they imagined, or to live together in Brooklyn. Would they have assembled around them, as Whitman did, "them that love, as I myself am capable of loving"? Perhaps so. Soon, women whose lives were closer to our modern ideas of lesbianism began to appear in Brooklyn. Some lived openly as queer women. Others used Victorian assumptions about women's asexuality and the appropriateness of intense friendships between women as a cover for their sexual and romantic relationships with one another. An uncountable number used the tried-and-true strategy of heterosexual marriage to hide their same-sex desires, or to enable them to enact those desires from a place of relative safety and financial security. Indeed, wife could almost be added to the list of waterfront jobs that were particularly attractive to queer women, since marriage (despite its many drawbacks) protected one's reputation, put food on the table, and was encouraged by the family, the government, and every other social institution of the day.

Whitman, Foote, and Gilder notwithstanding, however, Brooklyn itself was beginning to act as a magnet for queer people of all kinds. Around the country, a generation of queer pioneers was being born, not yet knowing that they would all one day congregate in Brooklyn. Some would make Brooklyn their permanent home, but many lived or worked there only briefly. Part of the story of Brooklyn— as with any city—is that it is often a temporary refugee, a place of finding oneself, or finding work, or finding love, before moving on to another location. For some queer people, moving was in and of itself a survival strategy, a way to always be just beyond the prying eyes of too nosy neighbors. If we imagine each of the queer lives this book will discuss as a single thread, Brooklyn is the place where they all momentarily knot together before shooting out again in every direction. Different forces drew each of these people to Brooklyn, but they were all connected by their need to make a living and their need to live safely—needs the waterfront was uniquely suited to meet.

As the mid-1800s came to a close, the Brooklyn waterfront was undergoing one of its most massive, singular moments of upheaval: the building of the Brooklyn Bridge, which took thousands of laborers nearly fifteen years to complete. Even before it was officially under construction, Brooklynites knew that the bridge would be a beacon that attracted people from around the world. The name for the structure was coined in a letter to the editor of *The Brooklyn Daily Eagle,* signed "E.P.D." and printed on January 25, 1867. It is one of the best examples of Brooklyn boosterism ever written:

> In America we have everything on a more magnificent scale than in the Old World. If then our rivers are wider, have we not a greater degree of enterprise and skill to be employed in erecting suitable structures across them? Let Europe boast of its towers, palaces and cathedrals—works of by-gone ages and questionable utility—but let New York and Brooklyn join in a work of art and real usefulness, so that for centuries to come, "Brooklyn Bridge" will be spoken of in the same category with Westminster Abbey or St. Paul's of London, The Cathedral at Antwerp, St. Peter's of Rome, and other celebrities.[63]

John and Washington Roebling, the engineers chosen to lead the project, were some of the best-regarded bridge builders of their day. John (the father) was born in rural Germany in 1806 and emigrated to the United States in 1831, landing in Pennsylvania. An engineering wunderkind, over the next thirty years he developed novel techniques that enabled his bridges to span longer distances, carry heavier loads, and, ultimately, last longer than those of his competitors. Around the world, the industrial revolution had spurred the creation of new kinds of manufacturing, new trade routes, and new modes of transportation, such as trains—all of which required upgrades in infrastructure. Moreover, during the Civil War, many older wooden bridges had been burned by soldiers on both sides. Thus, post-1865, American bridge building boomed, and the Roeblings were at its forefront.

When John Roebling died in the first year of construction on the Brooklyn Bridge, his son Washington took over. Although not the genius that his father was, Washington Roebling was well trained, incredibly focused, and a much nicer person, according to all contemporaneous reports. In 1855, while Walt Whitman was finishing *Leaves of Grass,* Roebling was in upstate New York, getting his degree at the Rensselaer Polytechnic Institute (RPI). As is true for many college students still today, at RPI he had his first encounter with queer people when a fellow student fell in love with him.

On an early morning in October 1856, Roebling—then just nineteen years old—returned to his room to find a letter, written in German, waiting on his table. In faint black ink, its delicate penmanship formed graceful, flowing sentences. Although its author skirted around his true subject, the letter stated that "one evening recently I unexpectedly asked you a question," which Roebling had answered evasively but kindly. The mysterious author explained "that something which appears only natural to me may perhaps appear incomprehensible or ridiculous to you" and repeated his question to Roebling, in writing: "Am I, of all the people you know, with the exception of your parents, brothers, and sisters, the one you love the most?"[64]

The writer begs Roebling to relieve his anxiety, to let him know the answer, and, regardless of what it is, to continue being his close friend. If Roebling cannot return his affections, the author assures him, "You will not have to suffer from me any longer." Unlike the intense protestations of love between Foote and Gilder, this correspondence has a palpable sense of shame. Were it typed in an email, it could be passed off as a modern letter (albeit one with exceptionally good punctuation). Like Whitman, this author seemed conscious of himself as a different type of person because of his sexual desires, although, unlike Whitman, he seems not to have found "them that love, as I myself am capable of loving."

Roebling kept the letter for the rest of his life, along with a second one that was written on Thanksgiving Day of the same year. In the later letter, Roebling's friend explains that he is going to take chloroform and leaves instructions for what Roebling should do if he overdoses: "Pour cold water over my head, then breath air from your mouth into my lungs, and if there is no success, go to Dr. Bontecon." If he dies, the letter continues, Roebling should "keep of my things whatever you like, it is all yours!" In a little note in his own writing below that message, Roebling recorded that his friend "staggered in, asking why I did not stay with him." Roebling also mentions another letter, which his friend took back, which contained only "an inventory of his property, together with some parting words of love."[65]

What is most fascinating is Roebling's response, which seems to have been loving, if not the reciprocated romance his friend desired. As his name is not

included on any of the messages, the exact fate of Roebling's friend would have
remained a mystery if not for a letter Roebling wrote to his wife, Emily, a decade
later, explaining that this friend was the only spirit he would ever want to contact through a séance. Roebling wrote to Emily:

> You have his picture with mine; he committed suicide because he loved me and I
> didn't sufficiently reciprocate his affection; I advised him to find someone like you for
> instance, but he always said no woman had sense enough to understand his love.[66]

It's tempting to read something into the word *sufficiently*. Same-sex desire has
always flourished in single-sex locations such as boarding schools, ships, prisons,
and brothels, much as situational heterosexuality has been practiced by many queer
people stuck in straight marriages or conservative social situations. But the specific
dimensions of Roebling's affections for this young man, whether they were erotic
or platonic, are irreparably lost. However, we can see that Roebling understood his
love for his friend to be of the same cloth as his friend's love for him; it is at most a
difference of quantity, not quality. The idea of "homosexuality" had not yet emerged
as a separate kind of male-male intimacy. What stands out from this story, aside
from Roebling's lack of shock or disgust, is the absence of any specific words for
this type of desire (or the men who profess it). It is often assumed that the history
of American sexuality is one of linear progress, moving from a time of benighted
homophobia to our present-day enlightenment. However, the further back one
looks, the more it seems to be a story of incoherence before intolerance, of "not
knowing" before "not accepting." The increasing urbanization of America in the
mid-1800s allowed more queer people to begin leading queer lives, and to see each
other doing so, and thus to conceptualize what it meant to be queer in the first
place. It would take the straight world a while to catch up, but by the late 1800s, as
the Victorian era began to wind down, the concept of "sexuality" was becoming a
hot-button issue among doctors, politicians, and moral reformers. In 1886, New
York State would become the second state in the country to take its vaguely worded
statute about "the crime against nature" and define it explicitly as covering anyone
who "carnally knows any male or female person by the anus or the mouth."[67] Although not precisely aimed at queer people, by writing specific sexual acts into the
code of law, this change set the stage for the intense policing of queer sexuality that
would develop in the twentieth century.

The world was changing, and Brooklyn was changing along with it. During the critical years when this modern idea of sexuality was being created, starting in the mid-1800s, modern Brooklyn was also being created. The same forces of urbanization and globalization, the industrial economy, the tensions between religion and science, the changing definitions of the family, the struggle for abolition and equal rights for women—all of these helped to define Brooklyn, and queerness, contemporaneously. And the pace of those changes was only speeding up, accelerated by people such as Whitman, Foote, Gilder, and even Roebling.

Roebling would nearly give his life to help make Brooklyn the city we know today. The Brooklyn Bridge was one of the first structures built in America using sunken caissons—large hollow structures dropped to the bottom of the river that trapped air for laborers to breathe while building the supports of the bridge. The tremendous atmospheric pressure in these conditions exposed many of the men to the bends, a crippling condition that occurs when someone moves from a high-pressure environment to a low-pressure environment too quickly. The bends incapacitated Roebling for many years. With great help from his wife, Emily, he directed the final stages of the bridge's construction by looking out the window of his apartment at 110 Columbia Heights—the same small building where some forty years in the future, the gay poet Hart Crane would live and write his magnum opus, *The Bridge,* as part of an artist commune created by the little-remembered gay Brooklyn socialite Hamilton Easter Field.

When the Brooklyn Bridge finally opened in 1883, no other single feat of engineering had had—or would have—as big an impact on the city's future. The editors of *The Brooklyn Daily Eagle* called it a "a triumph for the civilization of our century" and said that "thousands will come here to live who would have gone elsewhere had there been no other means of reaching our shores than *by the ferryboats* [emphasis mine]."[68] One can almost feel the writer grasping his pearls at the mere mention of the suddenly old-fashioned ferries. On its first open day, more than 150,000 people walked across the Brooklyn Bridge. Within a year, it would see an average of 37,000 people crossing *every day,* and when the trains opened, they would bring an additional 9 million people across it annually.[69]

But the bridge didn't just allow for greatly increased traffic between Brooklyn and Manhattan; it also lived up to the hopes of the anonymous *Brooklyn Daily Eagle* letter writer E.P.D. and gave Brooklyn an architectural masterpiece that put it on the map as surely as did Whitman's *Leaves of Grass*. Historians often mention the two in the same breath. In his prodigious tome *The Great Bridge,* author David McCullough wrote that this

> was to be something much more than a large bridge over an important river. It was to be one of history's great connecting works, symbolic of the new age, like the Atlantic cable, the Suez Canal, and the transcontinental railroad. "Lo, Soul, seest thou not God's purpose from the first?" wrote Walt Whitman at about this time. "The earth be spann'd, connected by networks . . . the lands welded together."[70]

Brooklyn was a real city now; a rival to Manhattan (although like many great rivalries, this one would soon end in a wedding, as the two cities would finally unite right before the dawn of the twentieth century). From some six thousand people in 1800, to two hundred thousand in 1855 when Whitman wrote *Leaves of Grass,* Brooklyn had grown to hold over six hundred thousand people by the time the bridge opened in 1883.

Signs that a new century was approaching were everywhere. The separate spheres of public men and domestic women were beginning to fall apart. According to nightlife historian Lewis Erenberg, this period saw a general "reorientation

Rendering of photo of Lower Fulton Street and Ferry (c.1880). (*Photo courtesy of the Brooklyn Eagle Photographs—Brooklyn Public Library—Brooklyn Collection.*)

away from the confinement, restrictions, and conventions of . . . the code of gentility."[71] As the social rules of the Victorian era broke down, a new heyday for nightlife dawned across America. For the upper class, the city developed "legitimate drama," which often imported actors from Europe to perform in stage plays, while in saloons, the working class enjoyed shows made of rough, sexualized variety acts. And for the vast middle ground "clean variety" presented less sexual acts in more refined, mixed-sex venues. In dance halls, theaters, and dime museums around Brooklyn and Manhattan, these new entertainments provided the chance for the sexes and the social classes to mix, while simultaneously helping to define American culture. Although women were still expected to be accompanied by men, they had greatly expanded social opportunities compared to just a few decades prior. The archetype of the New Woman, who wanted education, suffrage, and a place in public life, would soon sweep the country. A vast and diverse public was being constructed, one that had space for the multitudinous communities drawn to New York City—including queer people, who would both participate in and become a subject of this new public life.

In Brooklyn, the first most visible manifestations of this new culture were in the theaters and music halls of downtown Brooklyn and Coney Island. These venues attracted new visitors to Brooklyn and changed the tenor of the neighborhoods in which they were situated. They helped to usher in an era of celebrities whose lives—including their sexual lives—would be discussed, dissected, emulated, and scorned by Americans from Brooklyn to Biloxi to Berkeley. The venues also provided employment for a whole new generation of queer Brooklynites, particularly women and gender-nonconforming people.

For those who couldn't make it to these performances, newspapers around the country would provide extended coverage of the lives, loves, and perversions of the American stage. They also introduced the country to queer people via scandalous true-crime coverage, always a sure bet for selling newspapers.

The end of the nineteenth century and the beginning of the twentieth was *the* period in which our shared public understanding of queerness took shape, primarily via these early institutions of mass culture. If the first period in the queer history of Brooklyn was primarily about queer people discovering themselves, the next would be marked by queer people discovering one another, and in turn being discovered by straight America.

2. Becoming Visible, 1883–1910

The funeral of Foley McKeever—aka the Great Ricardo—was a big affair for the little Church of St. Agnes. Located in south Brooklyn, in 1883 the church was a temporary wooden structure that hardly presaged the beautiful limestone-and-stained-glass building that would eventually take its place. It had been built recently to serve the large Irish (and growing Italian) working-class population of the neighborhood, which was sandwiched between residential Brooklyn Heights and commercial downtown Brooklyn to the north, and industrial Red Hook to the south and west. By the 1880s, all three neighborhoods had far outgrown the boundaries that contained them in the time of Walt Whitman, knitting together Brooklyn's disparate patchwork towns into one densely interconnected urban fabric.

The northern area was growing in large part due to the Brooklyn Bridge, which made it an even more attractive locale for businesses and city dwellers looking to escape the press of Manhattan. But the growth of Red Hook had been enabled by a much smaller feat of engineering: the conversion of the bucolic Gowanus Creek—an inlet of the New York harbor that wended more than a mile inland; a skinny crooked finger of water pointing north to the Navy Yard—into the fetid Gowanus Canal, an industrial waterway used by a bevy of new manufacturers making everything from soap to flour to coal gas. The canal opened in 1869, and by 1883, more than a hundred ships passed through it every day. It also served as an open-air sewer for the rapidly expanding working-class neighborhood that is today Carroll Gardens; according to an 1877 report, it carried some "9,187 pounds of feces and 10,682 gallons of urine . . . on average, every day."[1] With the right wind, the stench would surely have reached the little church on the corner of

Hoyt and DeGraw Streets, where McKeever's body lay on the morning of Friday, November 2, 1883.

McKeever was a small Irish-American man with a powerful soprano voice that earned him frequent comparisons to the opera diva Adelina Patti. But McKeever made his living in a much less reputable (if, arguably, more popular) form of musical entertainment: he was one of the "monarchs of minstrelsy," a female impersonator who did "burnt cork burlesques," aka blackface send-ups of popular operas.[2] Or as one of his obituaries bluntly put it, he was "a man who made a living by his effeminacy."[3] I say one of his obituaries because McKeever was so famous, when he died of Bright's disease at the age of thirty-four, newspapers from Vermont to Louisiana all decried the loss of "one of the sweetest singers in the business."[4]

His funeral must have been quite the spectacle in a working-class area such as south Brooklyn. According to his obituaries, McKeever was buried in a "pure white grave cloth" and laid in a casket lined with thick black brocade. His body was surrounded by sprays of white and red roses from the members of the San Francisco Minstrels, the troupe he had performed with for the last eleven years. A broken shaft of white flowers, perhaps symbolizing a life cut short, was laid atop the casket by the janitor who worked for the troupe; in it, she had picked out the words AT REST in red roses.[5] The ceremony was presided over by three Catholic priests and attended by McKeever's mother (also a Brooklyn resident), and by his "intimate friend," Francis Patrick Glassey.[6] Glassey was also a drag queen in blackface, who performed under the name The Only Leon. If you squint hard enough, there might be the dim outline of a romantic tragedy hidden in McKeever's obituary: in the fall of 1883, the San Francisco Minstrels had added Glassey to the cast, allowing the two stars to briefly perform on the same bill for the first time ever.

Late-Victorian America viewed performers such as Glassey and McKeever with a gimlet eye—not because they were female impersonators, nor because they did blackface (a common form of entertainment, particularly in places such as Brooklyn that had few actual black residents), but because they worked on the stage. The theatrical world of this time was large and roughly bifurcated. For the upper class, there was "legitimate drama," which were full-length plays, often featuring imported European actors. For everyone else, there were evenings of varied performances, which could include everything from blackface drag, to a one-act play, to yodeling. These mixed shows were known by various names, including variety (which was the earliest and roughest of these performances), minstrelsy (which were performances by white people in blackface), and, eventually, vaudeville (which was also known as clean variety) and burlesque (which was sexualized variety, or what remained of the grittiest original variety shows after vaudeville became popular). A life in any of these professions was associated with sin, prostitution, alcoholism, and sundry immorality, as Father Duffy—one of the three priests at McKeever's funeral—addressed in his sermon. According to one journalist, Father Duffy

> *said that people imagined following a public life was inconsistent with the life of a Christian, but he believed that was a mistake. A man could be as good a Christian in public life as out of it. Although the dead actor had led a public life and been constantly subjected to all the temptations inseparable from his profession he was a good Christian at heart, and one of his greatest virtues was his great love for his mother.*[7]

McKeever's last performance was in *X-Seltzer,* a mock of the popular ballet *Excelsior,* which extolled the wonders of modern technology. McKeever played "Electricity, a giddy fairy"—an apt role, because if audiences might have applied any word to a feminine man such as McKeever, it would probably have been *fairy.*[8] People who transgressed gender were the most visible early queer pioneers. There still weren't common words for masculine men who were attracted to other men (such as Walt Whitman), or feminine women attracted to other women (such as Mary Hallock Foote), but McKeever was of a recognizable type: if not a fairy, he might be called an *invert,* a word that connoted his "inverted" gender, although that term was known to few people at the time of McKeever's funeral. It was coined in an 1873 essay by English writer J. A. Symonds, a devotee of Walt Whitman's, which was printed in a tiny run of ten copies the same year McKeever died. *Invert* and *inversion* would be the first popular scientific terms for "queerness" in America. Although Symonds intended *sexual inversion* to mean something similar to what we mean today by *homosexuality,* both *invert* and *fairy* were inexact categories that combined and contained our modern ideas of homosexuality, being transgender, and being intersex. Sexologists, primarily in Europe, were only just beginning to name and elucidate these as separate identities. In the twentieth century, educating America about gender and sexuality would become the province of scientists, doctors, psychologists, lawyers, politicians, and moral reformers, but in the late nineteenth century, Americans were most likely to encounter queer people on the stage.

Many theatrical acts presented broad stereotypes of the people that made up the country—the drunken Irish "Paddy"; the stingy Jewish "Yid"; the dumb Southern "darkie"; the shallow, trendy "dandy"; or the bawdy, ridiculous "fairy"—and by so doing, taught Americans who Americans were, in a biased and simplified way. These portrayals would become more complex and nuanced only as those individuals being stereotyped gained social power and began to create their own characterizations and theatrical spectacles (a process that is still happening today, particularly for black and transgender Americans). But at a time before television, movies, or even radio, these traveling entertainments *were* America's mass culture. They spread new ideas, introduced far-flung communities to different kinds of people, and provided the arena in which "good" and "bad," "modern" and "passé" were debated. By bringing the same shows to every corner of the continent, they stitched the country together. They also employed a whole lot of people, not just performers, but everyone from literal Victorian street urchins used as errand boys, to widows and unmarried women who cleaned the theaters, to flashy barkers and advance men who got the crowds excited. Manhattan was the epicenter of theater in America, particularly variety; by virtue of proximity, Brooklyn couldn't help being the moon to its sun—a smaller celestial body, but still one that ruled the sky. Performers often lived in Brooklyn (when not on the road); the best shows all played Brooklyn since they were already coming to Manhattan; and Brooklynites had easy local access if they wanted to get involved in showbiz themselves.

Compared to Manhattan, Brooklyn was slow to establish a theatrical scene. The first venues in either borough were the "free and easies," where a saloon owner (or perhaps a member of his family) would sing or tell stories at his bar one or two nights a week. These saloons were for men only and gained popularity as Brooklyn industrialized in the early 1800s. Single men needed places to socialize other than cramped shared tenements. Workers needed to find a way to replace the comradeship of older master-apprentice relationships, which had been displaced by the anonymized routines of factory labor. Saloons took on these roles—any many more. They occupied a much more central place in society than do bars or restaurants today. According to George Chauncey's *Gay New York*, saloons

> served as informal labor exchanges . . . cashed paychecks, and made loans to men
> who had little access to banks . . . provided such basic amenities as drinking
> water and toilet facilities to men who lived in tenements . . . and became virtual
> "working-men's clubs," where poor men could escape crowded tenements, get a
> cheap meal, discuss politics and other affairs of the day, and in a variety of ways
> sustain their native cultural traditions.[9]

Over time, some of these evolved into concert saloons, which were like bars with large halls attached, sometimes capable of holding upward of two hundred men. Saloon owners began to hire professional entertainers—the first variety acts—as well as "pretty waiter girls," who sold refreshments and were often assumed (rightly or wrongly) to be for sale themselves. According to Timothy Gilfoyle's encyclopedic tome *City of Eros: New York City, Prostitution, and the Commercialization of Sex, 1790–1920*, in the mid-nineteenth century "courtesans worked in the foremost theaters, concert halls, and hotels" throughout New York.[10] The "third-tier," which referred to the cheapest seats in a theater, was a common venue for johns to meet sex workers. By the late 1800s, "prostitution was an important sexual outlet for American men in both the working and middle classes, and prostitutes were well integrated into New York's working-class neighborhoods."[11] This integration of sex work with daily life was directly related to the city's increasing urbanization. More work required more workers, who were generally single young men. A good percentage of these were transient or immigrant and hoped to marry once they returned home. Living as many of these men did in bachelor subcultures, sex workers (and other men) represented their sole sexual outlets. Indeed, some areas of Brooklyn such as Williamsburg—which was also an industrial neighborhood along the waterfront, to the far north of the Brooklyn Bridge—have much less visible queer history in part because the communities that settled those areas (predominantly Germans and Eastern European Jews) were more likely to emigrate to America in full family units, and with greater overall parity in the proportion of men to women. But for Italian and Irish immigrant men in the 1800s, saloons were a place to meet sex workers (and other men).

In these sweaty, sawdust-strewn venues, men weren't afraid to throw rotten food at the stage if they didn't like the show, or to pick a fight with a man next to them if they didn't like his face. In Brooklyn, the first such venue was Burtis' Varieties, which opened in 1859 just two blocks from the Rome brothers' print shop where Walt Whitman typeset *Leaves of Grass*. Entrance was a dime, a seat in the orchestra cost twenty cents, and most evenings, between one hundred and 150 men packed themselves into the hall, which had a wooden floor and a low raised stage for performances at one end. As would be the case in minstrel, variety, and vaudeville shows for the next fifty years, the acts were a mixture of dancers, comedians, singers, and actors. They also featured more specialized entertainments, such as performers who removed a horse's teeth using gunpowder, and what were known as *tableaux vivants:* groups of living statues (mostly played by women) who posed as famous works of art, giving the men in the audience a rare chance to ogle at the female form. According to variety historian Gillian Rodger, in these places "men bonded by expressing their shared admiration for women and taking pleasure in watching women."[12]

These venues were considered some of the most disreputable, sin-soaked joints in the city. In the words of one New York journalist, concert saloons were

> nothing but public nuisances in the disguise of places of public amusement, and are no better and no worse than the filthy places in our back streets where abandoned women barter body and soul for a present subsistence, and putrescent men initiate the unsophisticated into the mysteries and miseries of a depraved social system. In a word, these saloons are a living pestilence in our midst, far more to be dreaded than the small pox or yellow fever. They are moral charnel houses, full of the untainted atmosphere of ghastly corruption.[13]

One presumes the journalist didn't like the show.

Concert saloons, while important in the development of the theater in America generally, never got much of a foothold in Brooklyn. During their heyday in the 1850s, most Brooklynites tended to visit Manhattan for their amusements. By 1862, there were only three such venues in Brooklyn, and if they ever showed drag acts, they never advertised them. That year, New York State passed the Concert Saloon Law, which required all venues that showed performances to get a license. Licenses were refused to any place that sold alcohol in the theater or

employed female waitstaff. The fees and fines levied under this new law funded
the Society for the Reformation of Juvenile Delinquents, one of the earliest and
most powerful urban moral-reform organizations in the city, which saw theaters as sites of potential corruption, particularly for the young.

All three concert saloons in Brooklyn promptly folded after passage of the law.
Although the Park Theatre, offering "legitimate drama" to the middle and upper
classes, would open the next year, in 1863, the entertainment scene in Brooklyn
was generally depressed by the Civil War, and by a brief economic downturn that
the city entered shortly thereafter. In search of new audiences—and pushed by
the law—variety began to tack toward the socially acceptable, both in the acts it
showed and the venues it showed them in. New spaces offering "clean variety,"
suitable for women and families, began to proliferate. These acts would eventually be called vaudeville, to distinguish them from disreputable, sexual variety
acts, which were only suitable for men. Women would no longer stay (content-
edly or impatiently) at home while their brothers and husbands enjoyed nightlife
on their own.

By 1882, one journalist would expressly link Brooklyn's rise as an entertainment destination to its status as a major port:

> With many local advantages in her favor, with a real preponderance of manufac-
> turers and shipping interests to back her, Brooklyn . . . has now actually entered
> into competition in regard to the luxuries and conveniences of metropolitan
> existence . . . the practice of going to New York in search of theatrical recreation
> has ceased.[14]

At this time male and female impersonators first became popular on the variety stage. Particularly as the world of separate spheres for the sexes began to collapse, artists that played with gender became more and more in demand. As
loose, public women and flashy, oversexed dudes became cause for popular concern, they also served as fodder for comic relief. In the late-Victorian era, cross-
sexed caricatures of these social archetypes could be found with increasing
regularity in the two main entertainment districts in Brooklyn, both of which
were on the waterfront: one stretching from the Brooklyn Bridge down along Old
Fulton Street, where downtown Brooklyn and Brooklyn Heights overlapped, and
one all the way to the south, in Coney Island.

In 1862, the year the Concert Saloon Law went into effect, only a single drag act was advertised in *The Brooklyn Daily Eagle*—Master Eddie, "the Celebrated Danseuse and Female Impersonator," who performed at Hooley's Opera House near the Brooklyn Bridge.[15] But in 1889, a Brooklyn theatergoer would have had the option of checking out the female impersonators Crowley at Hyde & Behman's or Gus Mills at the Lee Avenue Theater, and male impersonators Little Nell at the Standard Museum, Maggie Trainer at the Everett Assembly Rooms, La Petite Annie at the Smithsonian Hall, or the reigning king of male impersonators, Ella Wesner, at either the West Brighton Hotel in Coney Island, or at the Gaiety Theater in downtown Brooklyn.

By this time, Brooklyn had more than fifty theatrical venues, nearly half of which were located in the Old Fulton Street area, the dividing line between posh Brooklyn Heights and commercial downtown Brooklyn.[16] And that wasn't counting the many private clubs that hired entertainments for their members, or the legions of saloons that still provided the cheapest, roughest, and most tawdry entertainments, advertised only by word of mouth.

The Gaiety was one of the most storied theaters in Brooklyn—or at least its building was. Located on Old Fulton Street in the shadow of the Brooklyn Bridge, the impressive three-story edifice had begun life as a church, before becoming an armory, then a large minstrelsy hall called Hooley's Opera House, then a "clean" variety and minstrelsy hall named Hyde & Behman's, then an eccentric home for curios and performances known as the Standard Museum, before finally getting reimagined as the Gaiety in August 1889. "England's favorite and America's pride,"[17] the male impersonator Ella Wesner, performed there for a run that September, then again in October, showing both her popularity—to be asked back so soon—and her extended relationship with Brooklyn, where she would perform regularly, live for many years, and eventually be buried in Evergreen Cemetery in male attire (in her 1917 obituary, *The New York Times* simply noted that "throughout her life Miss Wesner had preferred man's apparel.")[18]

Promotional card for Ella Wesner, produced by Little Beauties Cigarettes. (*Photo courtesy of the collection of Gillian Rodger.*)

Born in Philadelphia around 1841, Wesner was

one of the premier acts of her day. She came from a variety family and got her start at the age of nine doing ballet with her mother and sisters (her father, Charles Wesner, was in and out of jail for passing bad checks). Although it might seem surprising today, at the time ballet was incredibly popular in rough concert saloons, as it was the rare theatrical form where women outnumbered men and often performed wearing revealing outfits of tights and knee-length skirts. Some time in the 1860s, Wesner switched to male impersonations, which made her a star. By her heyday in the 1880s, she was earning over $200 per week (an eye-popping $5,200 a week in today's money) and was one of the rare women to have her own variety troupe, known as Wesner's Coterie.

In the working-class world in which she got her start, to a large degree Wesner performed and was accepted as just another dandy. As Gillian Rodger points out in her history of American variety theater, *Champagne Charlie and Pretty Jemima,* "variety audiences accepted male impersonators as exceptional . . . there was a place within working-class culture for strong assertive women."[19] For a variety of reasons, the working class in New York City at this time was more accepting than the upper classes of gender deviations, premarital sexual relationships, and non-procreative sex. Skewed gender ratios made "appropriate" sexual relationships less possible in working-class immigrant communities; a lack of property made inheritance and paternity less important; and a lack of privacy made sexual and gender variations more visible. Deviant sexualities and genders were still judged, but they also had an acknowledged place in many of these communities.

By 1889, Wesner had worked her way up the ladder and was performing at some of the most upper-crust variety theaters in the city. A patron at one of Wesner's performances at the Gaiety that year would have been greeted at the doors by uniformed attendants, dressed in the billowing red pants and short blue jacket of the French Zouaves, or soldiers stationed in North Africa. Inside the doors, light chamber music would be playing in the promenade, a grand lobby fitted up with the latest fad—electrical lighting, which had only just been invented by Thomas Edison in 1880. For fifty cents, patrons could have one of the best seats in the house in the front of the orchestra, or for a dime they could stand in the dress circle on the upper floor. The managers promised "to give the best kind of vaudeville amusements and to cater chiefly to families," indicating that they probably brooked no (obvious) sex workers (and likely, no unescorted women at all), no shouting at the stage, and no drinking in the theater.[20]

As a star, Wesner probably closed out the first act of the show, after the French Martinette Brothers did their acrobatic floor routine, but before the "comic opera" *Olivette*, which made up the whole of the second act. Taking the stage, Wesner would be dressed as one of her iconic male characters: most likely a send-up of the flashy, well-dressed dandies of the day, but perhaps a stuffy old Victorian sea captain, or a drunken Irishman, if she wanted to switch things up. Her dark hair was always closely cropped, exposing her strong jaw and deep-set eyes, and in her publicity photos, she liked to wear a fez or a men's cap. To start the show with a shock, she might have stepped out smoking a cigarette—she was paid by the Little Beauties Cigarette company to hawk its products from the stage, and she may well have distributed the promotional cards they made for her as she prepared to sing her first number. (The cigarette business had recently undergone huge technological improvements, and the resultant increase in competition had created a cottage industry producing racy images of actresses to include with the products. According to Amy Werbel's history of obscenity in the United States, *Lust on Trial*, many of these cards "depicted women wearing men's dress . . . [bringing] copious images of gender-bending women to the attention of male consumers.)[21]

Once the applause died down, Wesner would probably have launched into one of her songs. She tended to sing comic pieces imported from English concert halls, such as the drinking ballad "Hi! Waiter, a Dozen More Bottles," whose first verse goes:

Lovely woman was made to be loved,
To be fondled and courted and kissed;
And the fellows who've never made love to a girl,
Well, they don't know what fun they have missed.
I'm a fellow, who's up on the times,
Just the boy for a lark or a spree
There's a chap that's dead stuck on women and wine,
You can bet your old boots that it's me.[22]

As with the Great Ricardo, audiences and reviewers seemed to have little problem with Ella Wesner's gender-deviant ways onstage. She was praised for offering top-to-toe looks that didn't simply use tailored, masculine-esque clothing to show off her female form (as some other, less classy drag acts were accused of doing). Particularly in the earliest part of her career, when her audiences were almost entirely men, this praise sometimes had a Sapphic overtone. When she performed in San Francisco, a local reviewer remarked that if women were allowed in the venues where Wesner performed, "they would all fall in love."[23]

Offstage, her queer ways received slightly more scrutiny, but nowhere near as much opprobrium as might be imagined. In the mid-1870s, Wesner conducted a highly public love affair with Helen Josephine "Josie" Mansfield, a minor actress whose zaftig appeal made her much more in demand off the stage than on it. Mansfield achieved notoriety in 1872 when one of her wealthy lovers (Ned Stokes, director of the Brooklyn Oil Refinery Company) shot another (financier Jim Fisk) at the Grand Central Hotel. During the resulting murder trial, Wesner and Mansfield connected and attracted the attention of the Victorian paparazzi, who reported on their whereabouts regularly. Soon, Mansfield began accompanying Wesner on local tours in the New York City area. In August 1872, according to the Oswego (N.Y.) *Daily Palladium,* "Josie had been following the troupe for two months or more, having joined it, or rather Miss Wesner, at Pittsburgh. Since that, she has never been out of the society of the latter."[24] A few months later, the pair eloped to Paris, where they established a salon at the Café American and "had all the Parisian gallants at their feet."[25]

Most newspapers seemed unsure how to describe the relationship between the two women. The *Chicago Tribune* was the most negative, alleging the two were rumored to have an "unnatural attachment."[26] Oddly enough, this was mentioned in just the final line of an article suggesting that a Chicago businessman had recently left his family to move to Paris to be with Wesner. A fuller, yet still conflicting description of Wesner and Mansfield's relationship was offered by a reporter from *The Rochester (N.Y.) Democrat,* who wrote:

> It appears that Mansfield had taken a singular fancy to the society of Miss Wesner, had arrived at Buffalo closely veiled, and sought an interview with Ella. . . . The cause of the companionship between the two is not a fancy of Josie's, but of Miss Wesner's—at least, that is the explanation we have heard. . . . The relationship between them is certainly a singular one. We have alluded to the matter not because of its importance, but simply to settle a question which our exchanges are asking relative to the whereabouts of Fisk's notorious mistress. If they want to know where she is, they have simply to notice where Ella Wesner is playing.[27]

Here is a perfect encapsulation of the public view of these women and their same-sex desires in the late 1800s: confusingly caught somewhere between an unimportant "singular fancy" and a sinister "unnatural attachment." The world of Mary Hallock Foote and Helena de Kay Gilder—where women were seen as asexual, cloistered creatures whose relationships with one another didn't disturb the ruling social order—was fast disintegrating. As women took on more public roles and began to be seen as sexual beings, their behavior with each other came under increased scrutiny. Masculine dress, excessive attachment to other women, and interest in education or suffrage would soon be seen as signs of a woman's potential inversion. Notably, despite the fact that *Mansfield* was following Wesner around, newspapers tended to identify Wesner as the aggressor or pursuer in the relationship. Wesner's gender presentation made her queer, and while Mansfield's attraction to her was unusual, it at least fit the proper pattern of a feminine woman attracted to a masculine person. In the straight Victorian mind, women such as Mansfield were often thought to be experiencing a normal crush that was encouraged or taken advantage of by an invert, or perhaps they contained some latent seeds of inversion deep inside them, which were brought out by the presence of a woman such as Wesner—but they were not themselves queer in the same way as those who openly transgressed gender.

Few late-Victorian male impersonators had their lives documented as thoroughly as Wesner, which makes it hard to say anything definitive about their gender identities or sexual orientations. Many were married to men, which doesn't preclude same-sex attractions or transgender identities, but certainly doesn't suggest them either. At times, these marriages were clearly ones of convenience. Yet the simple fact of a marriage is often used to presume the heterosexuality of historical figures. In truth, queer women married men for all kinds of reasons, ranging from economic necessity, to sexual attraction, to social pressure, to desire to form a family, to "lavender marriages" where both members were queer.

However, if little is known about most white male impersonators, even less is known about black women who worked in drag in the late 1800s. But at least a few—such as Alberta "Bert" Whitman and Florence Hines—achieved notoriety in their time. Most of these women worked exclusively in all-black minstrel shows, which rarely received extensive coverage in the largely white mainstream papers (unlike white performers in blackface—such as Foley McKeever—who performed similar routines to great acclaim). But Hines had a particularly impressive career, which brought her mentions in newspapers around the country from the 1890s up to the 1920s. In 1892, a Kansas reviewer described her as "perfection itself" and wrote that "improvement on Florence Hines' part is out of the question,"[28] while a reviewer from St. Paul, Minnesota, raved that Hines was "one of the best male impersonators on the vaudeville stage."[29] Brooklyn audiences were first introduced to Hines when she rolled into Flynn's Concert Hall in Coney Island with *The Creole Show* in 1894. (By 1896, Brooklyn would have over 3,600 bars, some of which showed entertainments, openly flouting the now rarely enforced Concert Saloon Law. By comparison, Philadelphia, a similar-size city, had fewer than 1,400 saloons, and Boston had a mere 666.[30] The moral panic over "pretty waiter girls" and rough manly amusements thirty years before no doubt seemed quaint to Brooklynites at the end of the century, and saloon entertainments were no longer something that engendered jeremiads in the press.)

If the entertainments on offer in north Brooklyn skewed toward the high-class tastes of suburbanites from Brooklyn Heights and visiting Manhattan Brahmins, those lining the beaches of Coney Island were firmly for the working class. Coney's time as a wealthy escape from the city came to an end with the increasing ease of public transit in Brooklyn in the late 1800s. Although a few high-class hotels still clustered on the far west side of the island, the vast majority of Coney's amusements were pitched at the working class. As Kathy Peiss explains in her book *Cheap Amusements,* by the turn of the century as many as half a million people could be found at Coney Island every day. Working-class visitors particularly enjoyed the "free dancing pavilions and bathing beaches, where they reveled in such indecorous behaviors as screaming and chasing through crowds."[31]

Coney was where rules broke down; where young heterosexuals, bored by the prim and proper courting done by their parents, participated in the new world of "dating," sneaking away to spend their hoarded pennies on rented bathing suits, cheap beer, polka pavilions, fortune-tellers, games of chance, sideshow hokum, and perhaps some canoodling on the sandy dunes after dark. Its three iconic amusement parks—Dreamland, Luna Park, and Steeplechase Park—wouldn't open for a few more years, but it was still the place where New Yorkers came to see all that was new and exciting in the world of fun.

Thus, Coney Island was the perfect location for *The Creole Show,* an important piece of largely forgotten American theater history, which "set the trend for African-American performance on the legitimate musical stage," according to *Tap*

Roots: The Early History of Tap Dancing.[32] *The Creole Show* toured for five straight years, primarily in front of working-class audiences up and down the Eastern Seaboard. It was one of the earliest shows to feature a large cast of women of color (sixteen in all).[33] These women weren't just burlesque beauties, but each had her own solo talent that she performed during the show. For Florence Hines, this was male impersonation. Hines was cast in the central role of the show, the interlocutor or master of ceremonies—a role that almost always went to a man. Perhaps most important, *The Creole Show* abandoned the stereotypical Southern mytho-historical-plantation setting of minstrelsy and set their performance in a modern world of black performers. According to the historian of black performance Marvin McAllister, *The Creole Show* was "a major outlet for black artists interested in . . . developing a comedic tradition that was racially grounded but not riddled with stereotyping."[34]

Flynn's Concert Hall regularly featured black acts and was both geographically and temperamentally at the lower-middle end of Coney Island entertainments. It was just two blocks west of "the Gut," the cheapest, meanest streets of Coney, where gangsters gambled and loose women danced the cancan, showing scandalous bare ankles with every chorus-line kick. And it was a long way east of the West Brighton Hotel, a resort for the wealthy where Ella Wesner occasionally performed. Flynn's had recently survived one of the city's perennial "cleanup" operations, which had shuttered more than a dozen other halls and saloons on Coney earlier in 1894. Still, it was the kind of place that made local headlines when a "colored soubrette" attacked patrons with a chair.[35] Men in the audience commonly begged women to show some ankle and heckled performers with shouts of "Oh, come off! That's too tame" and "Give us something lively-like!"[36] With slavery still a recent memory, in a city that was extremely white (the proportion of black residents in Brooklyn having actually fallen between 1880 and 1890, to a measly 1.3 percent), when both actresses and black women were assumed to be hypersexual and almost constitutionally incapable of saying no, it must not have been an easy room for a queer black female performer.

Hines's act was likely quite similar to that of Ella Wesner or other contemporary white male impersonators. Reviewers in *The Colored American* often compared her favorably with the most popular white drag acts of the day.[37] An article in the *Indianapolis Freeman* mentioned that she "leaped into fame" by "rousing the galleries of the country nightly with her bibulous song 'Hi Waiter! A Dozen More Bottles'"—

the song Wesner also performed regularly.[38] However, some of the meaning shifted when Hines donned her wide-lapelled jacket, waistcoat, trousers, cane, and bowler hat. Black variety entertainers "did not simply mimic the cross-dressing perfor- mances of white actors and actresses," according to Kathleen Casey, author of *Cross-Dressers and Race-Crossers.*[39] Whereas white male impersonators used the dandy to mock modern masculinity, black drag acts also used the dandy as a way to resist the degraded depictions of black men, and overly sexualized images of black women, that were popular onstage with white audiences and performers. The dandy character allowed these women to claim not just any masculine identity, but one that was well-off and thoroughly modern—as opposed to the benighted, slow- witted "mammies" or slutty "Jezebels" they were often forced to play.

Like Wesner, Hines was so in demand that she was able to work in venues that catered to black audiences, to working-class white audiences, and (eventu- ally) to well-off white families. Even more than white women in entertainment, black female performers were assumed to have loose morals and be inherently sexually provocative; that Hines performed in family-friendly white venues sug- gests the great reach of her popularity. Yet unlike Wesner, Hines seemed to have no personal publicity materials (or at least none that have been kept in archival collections), and few profiles of her in newspapers. For years, she "commanded the largest salary paid to a colored female performer"; today, I can locate only a single photo of her.[40] According to two articles in *The Chicago Defender,* Hines was either permanently incapacitated in 1906, or she left male impersonation when Prohibition passed in 1920 and became a preacher. Either way, a woman claim- ing to be her daughter wrote in to tell *The Defender* that Hines had died in March 1924.[41]

However, Hines's time in *The Creole Show* does provide one tantalizing sugges- tion into her queer life beyond the stage. While performing in Cincinnati, Ohio, in 1892, Hines got into a physical fight with one of her costars, a singer named Marie Roberts, with whom she performed a duet act. When it was reported in *The Cincinnati Enquirer,* the journalist heavily implied that the two were lovers, writing that "the utmost intimacy has existed between the two women for the past year, their marked devotion being not only noticeable but a subject of com- ment among their associates on the stage."[42] Those comments have, unfortu- nately, been lost to history, but the suggestion of a relationship between the two is obvious.

Both Wesner and Hines came up through the world of working-class variety, but New York City's "legitimate" theater scene—the world of upper-class plays that gained prominence at the dawn of the twentieth century and eventually evolved into Broadway—also provided employment for queer people. At a time when only the most gender variant were read as queer, being conventionally gendered allowed some of these performers to conduct fairly public same-sex relationships.

So it was for Ada Dwyer, a Mormon actress who was born in Salt Lake City when it was still a horse-and-buggy pioneer town in 1863 (right around the time Ella Wesner began performing as a male impersonator). Her father was a wealthy bookstore owner and her mother a local actress, and they fought hard to ensure that Dwyer received an education. "There was never a teacher of elocution, or

Photograph of Ada Dwyer and Eleanor Robson in a 1906 production of *Nurse Marjorie*. (*Photo courtesy of the Robinson Locke Collection, NAFR+. Billy Rose Theatre Division, The New York Public Library for the Performing Arts.*)

any foreign language, that came to Utah in pioneers days, that my father did not have me take lessons from," she later told reporters. From her father, she may also have learned a tolerant attitude toward sexual diversity; in 1913, he was censored by Mormon church elders for "teaching young men that sodomy and kindred vices are not sins."[43]

By the age of twelve, Dwyer had begun performing, and around the age of twenty, she accepted a three-year engagement with the show *Puddin' Head Wilson,* which took her around the world, before it eventually landed in New York City sometime around 1890.[44] Pictures of the day reveal Dwyer as a round-faced, fashionably dressed woman with strong eyebrows and thick dark hair.

Dwyer quickly signed on with one of Brooklyn's leading theatrical troupes, Cora Tanner's Company, which was based out of the New Park Theatre in Brooklyn. The New Park, on Fulton Street, was a reincarnation of Brooklyn's first legitimate theater, the Park (which Mary Hallock Foote might well have visited). By 1890, when it was taken over by Cora Tanner's husband, William Sinn, the Park was no longer the shining jewel of Brooklyn's performance venues. Fulton Street was now a booming commercial district, chockablock with theaters, so Sinn spared no expense in making the New Park stand out: "Moorish tiles" in the lobby, newfangled electric lights throughout the building, and twelve box seats for the most elite patrons. The new building used iron in place of wood for many structural elements, giving it a lighter, airier, more modern feel—similar to the cast-iron manufacturing buildings that were going up across the East River in SoHo.[45]

In 1893, Dwyer married another member of the company, the British *enfant terrible* Harold Russell, in a private ceremony at the New Park. A number things suggest this was a marriage of convenience or, at most, a short-lived flirtation with heterosexuality on Dwyer's part. For two popular actors, their marriage received surprisingly little attention, getting just a squib line in a few papers. Life together was brief for the two. As the *Utah Historical Quarterly* circumspectly noted, "After a week-long honeymoon, the newlyweds returned to their separate careers."[46] A year later, they had a daughter, Lorna, who was raised by Dwyer's family in Utah. On a handful of occasions over the next decade, the married couple were mentioned as being together in Salt Lake City, most likely visiting their daughter, but they otherwise toured and lived separately.

Russell had a bad-boy reputation that he may have been trying to rehabilitate through marriage to a popular actress. In 1884, he'd been hauled into court by a former fiancée who was trying to recoup some $200 she'd lent his family; in 1890, he was arrested after starting a brawl in a Manhattan hotel at four on a Sunday morning. As one reporter put it in discussing that incident, Russell "always solicited a spat" when drunk.[47] When he was younger, Russell was something of a heartthrob, but by the 1890s, his reviews tended toward faint praise (such as "earnest and conscientious")[48] or downright condemnations, such as "Harold Russell is not a convincing leading man, but he looks nice."[49]

By the end of the 1890s, Russell and Dwyer stopped being linked in the press, and Dwyer mostly returned to using her maiden name. Although Russell lived at least until 1920, the two led completely separate lives by that point. In a three-page, first-person autobiography published in 1928 in *The Juvenile Instructor*, a magazine for children, Dwyer devoted all of four sentences to their relationship, stating:

> Fate brought me in a play in which Harold Russell, a famed actor of the day, was also appearing. . . . A romance followed and "Mrs. Russell" was added to my name off stage. We were very happy and a daughter, Lorna, was born. Later death took Mr. Russell and for many years I have been a widow.[50]

While it was technically true that Dwyer was Russell's widow (the pair never divorced), Dwyer spent most of her life in two intense same-sex relationships. In 1901, she appeared in a flop called *A Gentleman of France*. The leading lady in that production was a British actress, Eleanor Robson; for the next ten years, the two would be inseparable, appearing together in at least a half dozen touring shows.

Their connection did not go unnoticed by the press. When *The Dawn of To-morrow* opened in October 1909, an entire article dedicated to their devotion to each other appeared in the *Evening News* of Wilkes-Barre, Pennsylvania. As the journalist put it:

> Between Miss Robson and Miss Dwyer exists a friendship that is almost unique among people of the theater. . . . These two actresses live together while in New York, room together on the road, and travel together throughout vacation time. No one who knows them would think of inviting one anywhere without the other.[51]

Because of Dwyer's marriage, and because both women were conventionally feminine in their public appearance, their relationship received no criticism in the press. Much like Mary Hallock Foote and Helena de Kay Gilder, their propriety offered them protection. Although Dwyer and Robson parted in 1910, Dwyer would go on to have another such Boston marriage (this time actually *in* Boston), with the poet Amy Lowell. Lowell would dedicate her most erotic poetry to Dwyer and bequeath her entire estate to her as well. After Lowell's death, Dwyer devoted her life to ensuring that Lowell's poetry and memory stayed in the public eye.

In all likelihood, Dwyer and Robson's public reception benefited from the rise of the "star system" in the theater around this time. Under the star system, managers of high-profile actors started to take care of their clients' reputations as well as their bookings. Dwyer and Robson's press might have been scrubbed of any salacious gossip before it reached audiences. Their shared manager, Charles Frohman, was one of the most powerful men in the theater and could easily have pulled strings on their behalf.

According to theater historian Helen Deborah Lewis, this lack of public opprobrium hid Dwyer—and other "lesbianlike" popular actresses in the theater at that time—from the eyes of modern queer historians. As she wrote in her PhD dissertation, "Friends, Beloveds, and Companions: The Shadow Life of the Fin-de-Siècle American Lesbian Actress":

> For the actresses at the fin de siècle, the decision to live with another woman and then congregate with others like them did not make or break their careers. . . . There has been very little historical analysis of these actresses by theatre historians or gay and lesbian scholars because these women worked in and for the mainstream commercial theatre and were, for all intents and purposes, accepted.[52]

Dwyer and Robson are just two of the actresses Lewis examines, along with Johnstone Bennett and Elsie de Wolfe (as well as de Wolfe's partner, theatrical agent Elisabeth Marbury). All of these women worked in legitimate theaters throughout New York City. Yet because of their constant touring schedules, it is hard to connect any of them to a permanent location—another reason why their sexuality may have evaded public censure or later historical recognition. However, aside from Dwyer's time at the New Park Theatre, another piece of evidence points to Brooklyn as an important locus in the international world these women inhabited: *The Stone Wall*, a pseudonymous autobiography written by "Mary Casal." Published in 1930, *The Stone Wall* is the frank story of a New England lesbian who was born in 1864 (one year after Ada Dwyer's birth in Utah), and it shows how visibly queer women onstage had an outsize effect on queer women offstage.

Although she uses neither the words *homosexual* nor *lesbian,* Casal's book is one of the earliest self-reported records we have of a woman in America who understood herself as a type of person defined by her sexuality (and not her gender). It appeared in print just two years after Radclyffe Hall's groundbreaking lesbian roman à clef, *The Well of Loneliness,* was published in England. In *The Stone Wall,* Casal argued for greater honesty and sexual education for children, believing that it would help both those who were sexually different, and those who survived childhood sexual abuse. "The time is coming," she wrote, "when man's love for man and woman's love for woman will be studied and understood as it never has been in the past."[53] With her book, Casal hoped to help usher in that moment.

The true identities of Mary Casal and the women of her circle have been a mystery since the book's publication by Eyncourt Press in Chicago. However, thanks to the pioneering scholarship of historian Sherry Ann Darling, it is now known that Casal was actually Ruth Fuller Field, "the ninth and last child of Joseph and Lydia Fuller, the niece of painter George Fuller, and part of a large extended family of musicians and artists in Deerfield, Massachusetts."[54]

Born on a farm, Field was a studious yet active tomboy in her early years. At the age of twelve (around 1876), she lived for a summer in Boston, where she met her first girlfriend. Field wrote rapturously about their "many nights together, always in loving embrace, repeating all the little love sayings, and sleeping in each other's arms, perfectly happy." However, despite this and other romantic and sexual interactions with women throughout her teen years and early twenties, Field believed herself to be the only woman "like her" in the world. She went so far as to get married in an effort to fit in, writing, "It certainly was not sexual desire that led me to the altar . . . but in my ignorance I supposed I was the only woman who did not possess this desire." However, after two difficult miscarriages, Field and her husband divorced quietly. Field eventually became a businesswoman, a writer, a schoolteacher, personal secretary to heiress Helen Jay Gould, and an inventor of small toys for kids. This last job brought her to New York City, sometime around the turn of the twentieth century, where she met her girlfriend of many years, Emma Altman.

One evening around 1900, Altman and Field attended the opening night of a new light comedy in Manhattan, whose starring role was played by a masculine young actress who specialized in cross-dressed parts and quick costume changes—almost certainly Johnstone Bennett, one of the "lesbianlike" actresses discussed by historian Helen Lewis. Bennett was then starring in the farce *A Female Drummer*. Born in France in 1870, Bennett was a star from the age of fifteen who managed to jump from the world of variety to the legitimate stage. She played mostly comic roles or character parts because, as she put it, "I cannot play anything else. As a soubrette I would be a dismal failure. I could not do tragedy if I tried, and there you are."[55] An orphan three times over, Bennett's life seemed like a story from one of her own plays, a rags-to-riches tale of an immigrant hitting it big in America. She worked for Charles Frohman, the same powerful theatrical impresario who managed Ada Dwyer and Eleanor Robson. Tragically, however, Bennett died at thirty-six from tuberculosis.

Like Ella Wesner before her, Bennett made no effort to hide her masculine ways, which were endlessly commented on in the press. As early as 1893, *The Brooklyn Daily Eagle* devoted an entire column to her tailored, menswear-adjacent looks, claiming that she inspired an army of emulators, whom the paper called "tailor made girls."[56] From the moment she walked onstage, Field and Altman felt a shock of recognition. Dressed in their own smart tailored suits, the pair returned to the play night after night and eventually sent flowers to Bennett. One night near the end of the show's run, Bennett invited them backstage, changing their lives forever.

When the pair arrived at her dressing room, Bennett was already slipping into one of her own suits, which was most likely similar to one she'd worn in Buffalo earlier that year: a dark gray striped skirt combined with a bright plaid waistcoat that had big brass buttons, all topped off with a sporty white ascot, "fastened with a tiny gold pin."[57] The moment of recognition felt by Field seemed to go both ways, or at least Bennett dropped some serious clues about her personal life within the first few minutes of their meeting. She introduced another actress as her "best girl" and broke out cigarettes for the little foursome—a vulgar, mannish habit in a woman, according to late-Victorian society. Still, Field and Altman didn't believe she was "like them" until the day they escorted her to Grand Central to catch the train to San Francisco, where *A Female Drummer* was headed next. As they bid their goodbyes, a histrionic young woman appeared, begging Bennett to stay. To Field's confusion, Bennett asked them to take care of the girl for the night and escort her to a friend's party in Brooklyn. "That seemed easy," thought Field, "as easy as a trip to Brooklyn could ever be!"

Soon, they arrived at the home of a woman they called Phil, short for "Philosopher," whom historian Sherry Ann Darling has identified as the outlandish Vittoria Cremers. Here it is worth quoting Field at length:

> Upon arriving we were presented to a most astonishing personality—a little woman with short, black hair tinged with gray, wearing heavy white silk pajamas, smoking, and very hospitable. She had the most charming manners and beautiful but very piercing hazel eyes. She looked us through, and I knew at once that she too knew! I was impelled at first to seize my [Emma] and run, for I did not want to think that there was anyone else in the world who knew of love such as ours. . . .
>
> At last, and too late, did I find that I was not a creature apart as I had always felt.[58]

Of all the people Field writes about in *The Stone Wall,* Cremers is the strangest and least verifiable. She was (or claimed to be) connected to Italian nobility; British aristocracy; the NYPD; the leaders of the Theosophical spiritualist movement; the so-called "wickedest man in the world," satanist Aleister Crowley; the famous nineteenth-century diva Sarah Bernhardt; and the serial killer Jack the Ripper.

What *is* known about Cremers? She was born sometime around 1859, most likely in Pisa, Italy, to an Italian father and a British mother. Early in her life, Cremers emigrated to New York, where she worked at a theater magazine called *Stage Gazette,* which specialized in "handsome pictures of pretty actresses and pretty pictures of handsome actors."[59] This may well have been how she met Sarah Bernhardt, with whom she claimed to have had a long-standing affair. Although Cremers is not mentioned by name in Bernhardt's autobiography, *My Double Life,* a brief, tantalizing mention is made of a journalist who sounds like Cremers. In Bernhardt's description of her first encounter with the New York City press in 1880, she wrote, "A female reporter in a tailor-made skirt, with her hair cut short, asked me in a clear, sweet voice, 'Are you a Jewess-Catholic-Protestant-Mohammedan-Buddhist-Atheist-Zoroaster-Theist-or-Deist?'"[60] This could well have been Cremers, who had a passion for theology and occult practices. As well, almost all accounts of Cremers mention her short hair and her penchant for tailored clothing.

A few years after Bernhardt's American tour, in November 1886, Cremers married the incredibly wealthy Baron Louis Cremers, "the son of Russia's Rothschild, the great St. Petersburg banker, whose wealth is at least $40,000,000."[61] In later years, Cremers would tell Aleister Crowley that this was done on a bet to prove she could have a sexual relationship with a man. When the two separated, just a little more than a year after being married, Baron Cremers told newspapers:

> We were only a couple of weeks married when she told me that she could not possibly love any man. About the same time I began to learn that prior to our marriage my wife had displayed an extraordinary infatuation for actresses . . . and had been in the habit of going out in boy's clothes to see the town. An illustrated account of some of her exploits was printed in a Saturday serial. . . .
>
> When she told me of her peculiar temperament I replied that if such were unfortunately the case, still, although it would be a calamity to me, so long as she loyally adhered to me, and did nothing to discredit my family or myself, I should accept such share of friendly feeling and gratitude as she could give me.[62]

Spoiler alert: it didn't work out.

By the time Field and Altman met Cremers around 1900, she had established her home in Brooklyn as something of a clubhouse for queer women in the theater. This suggests a much earlier and more sizable network of queer women than is usually recognized in American history. As highly visible women of independent means, who visited most large and midsize cities, and who were given leave to be single and eccentric, actresses such as Bennett were uniquely positioned to connect the disparate communities of queer women in early twentieth-century America. Over the next few years, Field and Altman would visit Cremers often in Brooklyn, and the three would even travel together throughout Europe. That moment of recognition that struck Field upon seeing Johnstone Bennett in *A Female Drummer* ushered her into a world of women *like her,* one she'd never realized existed.

However, queer people weren't the only ones beginning to notice and comment on other queers. Field mentioned in her book that Cremers not only dressed in a masculine fashion, but occasionally even wore *pants* in public, and that she was frequently harassed because of it. When Ella Wesner got her start, women weren't even allowed in the venues where she performed, so newspapers were fine with suggesting that they emulate her, or that they might even be attracted to her. But Johnstone Bennett's "tailor made girls" were much more problematic because women now had greater freedom to actually follow her example. The 1890s saw the emergence of the *New Woman,* a term that was coined by feminist author Sarah Grand in 1894. Compared to her predecessors, the New Woman was much more likely to go to college, work outside the home, remain single (and childless) until later in life, and take an active role in civic organizations. By 1900, nearly 350,000 women worked outside the home in New York City.[63] The *Detroit Free Press* addressed these women at the conclusion of an article about Bennett's masculine garb, writing, "The average woman who tries to assume the masculine in dress or bearing makes a piteous yet ludicrous object of herself."[64]

Newspapers were one of the main places where these gender transgressions were discussed. By the start of the twentieth century, papers had joined the theater as a bastion of America's mass culture. In 1880, America had some nine hundred daily papers; by 1900, they numbered well over two thousand. Many of them carried syndicated content from the biggest publishers, ensuring that news from places such as Brooklyn reached towns around the nation. These papers covered the comings and goings of performers such as Ella Wesner, allowing average Americans a glimpse at life as a very different kind of woman. But queer people also routinely made their pages under darker circumstances: as grist for the mill of true-crime stories, which set hearts racing, warned Americans about the dangers of modern life, and—most important—sold an awful lot of ink. These stories generally reinforced existing notions that regardless of their sexual or romantic behavior, people were only queer if they flagrantly violated gender norms.

In 1892, America was fascinated by the case of Alice Mitchell and Freda Ward, two wealthy white teenagers from Memphis, Tennessee. The two were in love and made plans to elope; when Ward changed her mind, a devastated Mitchell shot her with a revolver in broad daylight on a public street. Newspapers couldn't print articles about the two fast enough. In columns from Brooklyn to New Orleans, debate raged over their relationship. Much was made about how Mitchell asked Ward to call her Al and planned to be the groom when they married. Despite the pair's ongoing relationship, Mitchell would become associated with predatory lesbianism, while Ward came to symbolize the dangers queer people held for normal Americans. Or as *The Brooklyn Daily Eagle* once summarized the case, "The two girls had been close and intimate friends and Alice had developed a strange and unnatural fondness for her girl friend."[65]

This consensus of opinion wasn't born overnight. Through Mitchell's trial (and its resulting newspaper coverage), Americans discussed what their relationship meant and what had caused it. The resulting columns portray a country not so much ignorant of same-sex love as unsure about it. For instance, on the same day in July 1892, *The Brooklyn Daily Eagle* carried two columns about the murder. In one, a "medical expert" testified, "There was a mutual love between them as between male and female." He explained that "such cases are rare," but not unnatural, and that he found "no evidence of depravity" in the two.[66]

In a separate piece, a different author weighed in, suggesting that relationships between women were more frequent—and dangerous—than most people knew:

> *The relations between the two girls are by no means so uncommon as supposed.*
> *The deleterious effect of the English public school on the boy is equaled if not*
> *surpassed by that which brings the young woman to the foot of the tree of*
> *knowledge in this country, an effect brought about in any large community of*
> *girls, no matter where.*[67]

A host of the tropes that would soon come to define homosexuality are woven through these two short sentences: that it was the same experience for both men and women; that it was "deleterious"; that it was vaguely foreign and upperclass; that it wasn't an inborn, permanent, and fixed orientation, but rather something that was caused by negative experiences; that spending too much time with only men or only women could be dangerous (particularly for the young); and that one of the signs and causes of deviant sexuality was a desire for things that were improper for your gender, such as women's education.

Properly gendered behavior also insulated men from being considered queer, even if they were known to have sexual relations with other men (or boys). In 1896, New York City society was shocked by the case of the notorious Australian prizefighter Alfred Griffiths—aka Young Griffo—who pleaded guilty to raping a twelve-year-old boy in his training gym on Coney Island. Although Griffo was tried for sodomy, papers around the country downplayed the nature of the assault and reiterated Griffo's skill and success as a pugilist, the manliest of athletes. At his sentencing, when he received a slap on the wrist of one year in the penitentiary, the judge said from the bench:

I consider you one of the best professional boxers in the world. . . . It is a pity you cannot leave liquor alone. . . . I don't think you are vicious, but careless and full of animal life. You are without sufficient self-control to restrain yourself.[68]

The idea that even the most proper men were full of violent, animal desires was common in the Victorian era. So long as a man was masculine, sex with other men could sometimes be excused as a spontaneous, explosive release of male energy that had nowhere else to go. It wasn't something to be celebrated, but it didn't define someone as being a different *kind* of person. Who you wanted to have sex with was one component in your larger ability to conform to proper gendered behavior—not the defining line between homosexuality and heterosexuality that we treat it as today.

After 1910, however, that line would be drawn more and more sharply with every passing year. Queer people were coming into focus. In the nineteenth century, the people I've described were like scattered data points on an unlabeled chart: notable, but not understandable. But by the start of the Progressive Era, enough information had accumulated for the larger straight world to begin to develop theories about queer people. Doctors examined the bodies of queer people to understand the origins of their degeneracy. Moral reformers stumbled across queer people while trying to control the depravity of the poor and realized they represented a discrete moral threat all their own. They joined ranks with police, lawyers, and lawmakers, who were also beginning to look for ways to punish queer people specifically for their sexuality. All told, if the nineteenth century was about noticing queer people, the twentieth century would be about controlling them.

Twentieth-century Brooklyn—the city—was also a new and different animal. In 1898, Brooklyn merged with Manhattan, Staten Island, The Bronx, and Queens, to form New York City. According to the *New York World,* at the stroke of midnight on January 1, 1898, "the old year and the old cities were dead. The new year and the new city, the magnificent New York, with her 3.5 million people, were born."[69] By 1900, 1.1 million of those people would live in Brooklyn, and by 1910, that number would hit 1.6 million. The sleepy Dutch town of Breukelen was no more. It had been obliterated by a century of progress, industrialization, and rapid growth, and more was still to come.

3. Criminal Perverts, 1910–20

The official declaration that Brooklyn and Manhattan were now one city had far-reaching and slow-moving consequences, as two of America's foremost metropolitan centers worked to knit their civic institutions together. So it was that the Brooklyn City Prison—generally known as the Raymond Street Jail—wasn't turned over to the new New York City Department of Correction until 1908, a full decade after the cities were joined. When it was built in 1838, at the corner of Willoughby and Raymond Streets (in the area known today as Fort Greene), the prison was a declaration of Brooklyn's aspirations to greatness, writ in limestone and human misery. Modeled after the Bastille in Paris, it was built to imprison upward of four hundred people at a time. One famous—and likely apocryphal—story holds that when the jail was constructed, the builders forgot to include a front door; an apt metaphor for the way prisoners were treated. A women's auxiliary, known as the Annex, which held around forty people, was added the next year.

When the jail was built, there wasn't much to the neighborhood, which was nestled between downtown Brooklyn and the lightly unsettled area where the town of Weeksville would soon be. There had been a Revolutionary War–era fort, but it was decommissioned in 1815. Prominent Brooklynites, including the editor of *The Brooklyn Daily Eagle* (the still unknown Walter Whitman), pushed for the land to be turned into Brooklyn's first official park. In 1848, thirty acres were designated for that purpose. The jail and the new Washington Park (known today as Fort Greene Park) were separated by just a single block of empty land. The small residential part of the neighborhood was mostly laborers who worked in shipbuilding, predominantly at the Navy Yard. By the end of the nineteenth century, the area was home to about half of Brooklyn's small black population (as is still true today, correctional facilities are much more likely to be found in black neighborhoods than in white ones). With every year, Brooklyn stretched farther to the east, incorporating large farms and small towns as it went. By the early 1900s, the areas of Bedford, East New York, Crown Heights, and Flatbush would all be growing Brooklyn neighborhoods.

Not much changed at the Raymond Street Jail over this first seventy years of its existence. The small exercise yard was surrounded by thick stone walls some twenty-four feet high, and four iron gates stood between the imprisoned men and the outside world (five, if you counted the one on their cells). Inside, the men were kept in a long open room, which had two rows of metal cages stacked four high. When it was taken over by the Department of Correction in 1908, inspectors said:

> *Males were confined in dark, smelling cells with no light whatever, except that furnished from a flicker of a candle, a luxury to be enjoyed by those who had the means to procure this and at an exorbitant price. The odor arising from the cells was almost unbearable.*[1]

This was because the city refused to spend money on cleaning services. As the prisoners held at the Raymond Street Jail were all awaiting trial (a period that could last up to six months), they were technically considered innocent, which meant the Department of Correction couldn't compel them into forced prison-labor cleaning crews. As a result, the men's jail was perennially filthy.

The women's Annex was cleaner and brighter, with the women kept in separate rooms off central hallways, but it was "above all a wretched fire trap."[2] Conditions were so bad that when the NYC Department of Correction took over, they immediately tore down and rebuilt it, while they merely renovated the men's jail. Although these changes made some improvements (for instance, making it harder for imprisoned people to commit suicide by jumping off the roof), postrenovation the men's jail was still condemned as a dank, dreadful place where prisoners spent the entire night in darkness, leaning against the bars to catch a glimmer of lantern light from the guards' rooms. By 1911, some twenty thousand men passed through its cramped metal cages every year.[3] Smuggled drugs, particularly heroin and cocaine, were a constant problem. Still, newspapers argued, this was an improvement over how it had been in the past, when it was "dirty, ill managed, the prisoners were starved, [and] it was dark and filthy and worse than anything in Siberia."[4] As for the women's prison, cleaner didn't necessarily mean safer or more compassionate. A 1904 newspaper report strongly suggested that two of the guards had sexually assaulted an imprisoned woman in one of the bathrooms.[5] In 1909, a report by the Women's Prison Association complained that "insane women are turned loose in the corridors," even though magistrates now had the option to send them to charity institutions instead.[6] Concern for the delicacy of womanhood, it seems, ended where the doors of the jail began.

Although prisons are rarely considered a queer space—except in the context of disturbing jokes about sexual assault—they are as intimately connected with queer people as any other physical locations in American history, particularly in the twentieth century. Queer people were sent to jail for specifically queer crimes (such as cross-dressing and sodomy), and queer people picked up on other charges were often given lengthier sentences because of their sexuality or gender presentation. Imprisoned queer people lived under constant surveillance, making it more likely that straight people (from doctors to wardens to other imprisoned people) would notice their existence. And like all other single-sex institutions, jails provided space for people to explore same-sex desires that they might never have recognized or had the chance to engage with in the outside world. Thus, in the first decades of the twentieth century, as doctors, lawmakers, and moral reform organizations began to explicitly focus on sexuality, prisons such as the Raymond Street Jail would become queerer and queerer spaces. And in the year 1910, a shocking trial would see two Brooklyn men held in the jail for months on charges of obscenity, sodomy, and first-degree murder.

It all began when seventeen-year-old James Vickers landed in New York City in the waning days of December 1909. At the age of fourteen, Vickers had left his home in Philadelphia to work for three years as a fireman on an ocean freighter, and he hoped to find similar work in the docks of Brooklyn. The blue-eyed, brown-haired Vickers was short but powerfully built, standing just five feet tall and weighing 150 pounds. For a little while, he found a place to stay in the Bowery, a notorious slum in lower Manhattan. Around Christmas Day, he wrote his mother and stepfather with the exciting news that he "had fallen in with two men in Brooklyn who were going to give him a good home."[7] Those men were James Hagaman, a painter of some small renown who lived in Brooklyn Heights, and the architect Emerson Colburn, who lived in the area of Brooklyn known as East New

York, a growing residential neighborhood to the east of what had once been Weeksville (which had now been rebranded as suburban Crown Heights). Around this
time, despite a warning from his stepfather to be "extremely careful about the
friends he had made in New York," Vickers moved in with Colburn.[8] On New
Year's Day, he was found raped and murdered, his naked body sprawled on a di-
van in Colburn's spare room.

Hagaman and Colburn were quickly arrested and charged with sodomy and
first-degree murder. The pair claimed they had discovered Vickers unconscious
and called a doctor, but he died before the physician arrived. Evidence against
them mounted swiftly, however: a coroner testified that the boy had been dead
for at least three hours before the doctor was called; Colburn had a black eye,
which he first claimed was from boxing, but then admitted had come from Vickers; and the two seemed generally incapable of keeping their stories straight, each
claiming they had last seen Vickers at different times on different days. Within a
few weeks, it would come to light that Colburn had previously sexually assaulted
a fifteen-year-old Brooklyn boy in 1904. The final nail in his coffin appears to have
been the discovery of obscene photos, made by Hagaman, in Colburn's home,
along with a list of the names and addresses of some two hundred other sailors.
Presumably these were men they'd also met along Brooklyn's waterfront, like
Vickers.

Obscenity charges were a big deal at the time and were frequently used against
makers of pornography, publishers of "indecent" novels, sexual-health educators,
people who performed abortions, theaters, and—increasingly—anyone looking
to provide the general public with information on queer people. The most powerful censor in the country was Brooklyn postal inspector Anthony Comstock,
who successfully lobbied Congress to pass in 1873 a law banning the shipping of
"obscene, lewd, or lascivious" materials through the mail. This law was one of
those most frequently used against queer people, along with sodomy, masquerade, and disorderly conduct charges. Under the auspices of his organization, the
New York Society for the Suppression of Vice, Comstock wielded obscenity
charges like a weapon against those he viewed as moral degenerates. It's not unlikely that he or one of his acolytes had a hand in the Vickers case.

Faced with an additional felony obscenity charge (on which he would almost
certainly be found guilty), Hagaman quickly turned against Colburn, who was
convicted of sodomy and murder in the first degree. Colburn was sentenced to

sixteen years in jail, and in exchange for his testimony, Hagaman received a light sentence of eleven months in the workhouse.

The case of James Vickers represents a transitional moment in our understanding of sodomy. Sodomy has come to be synonymous with consensual sex between men, but for most of American history, it was a broad concept that contained many kinds of nonprocreative sexual activity, performed by both men and women. Before World War II, the legal charge of sodomy was one step removed from rape, and "prosecutions were generally against aggressive men deriving sexual pleasure from a weaker person, usually a boy, girl, woman, animal, or ward."[9] Starting in the time of Young Griffo, the boxer, sodomy prosecutions became more common in New York City because of the work of the Society for the Prevention of Cruelty to Children (SPCC). Often referred to just as "the Cruelty," for their habit of taking children away from working-class parents for relatively minor infractions, the SPCC breathed new life into New York's antisodomy laws by using them to prosecute adult men who abused male children. As George Chauncey documented, there were twenty-two sodomy prosecutions in New York City between 1796 and 1873, but starting in the 1880s, "the number of prosecutions increased dramatically . . . [and] at least 40 percent—and up to 90 percent—of the cases prosecuted each year were initiated at the complaint of the SPCC."[10] This was fully in keeping with earlier uses of the law as an anti-sexual-assault measure, but by focusing *only* on male-male sexual assaults (and not male-female assaults that didn't involve vaginal penetration, bestiality, etc.), they would help to redefine sodomy, in the eyes of the public, as synonymous with homosexuality—and homosexuality as synonymous with pedophilia.

As was true with Young Griffo, neither Colburn nor Hagaman were ever identified as "homosexuals" or even "fairies" in newspapers or court reports. However, the court repeatedly referred to Vickers as a "catamite," a Renaissance term for the younger, passive partner in a sexual relationship.[11] This suggests that even in a case of rape, being penetrated could compromise a man's heterosexuality, while an act of sexual assault—even against another man—might not. Broadly, the court was more interested in Hagaman's and Colburn's other sexual crimes than their sexual identities, because in as much as the courts were interested in sex, it was as a form of violence. Over the 1910s, however, a triumvirate of powerful forces would work together to punish and control consensual same-sex and cross-gender desires. Sodomy prosecutions would continue, but more and more of them would target consensual sex between men, and proportionally fewer would focus on sexually violent cases like that of Emerson Colburn and James Hagaman. Medical professionals, legal experts, and civilian reformers would begin to make the case that queerness was directly linked with criminality and mental illness; that existing legal tools were inefficient or ill-suited to prosecuting criminal identities (as opposed to criminal acts); and that the entire future of the "white race" was imperiled by creeping hordes of black people and queers.

While the motives and conclusions of these doctors, lawmakers, and antivice organizers are biased and often self-serving, their work provides a vast (if problematic) archive of information about queer people in America at the start of the twentieth century. Many of these investigators published their results in medical journals or were connected to powerful institutions that generated reams of forms, annual reports, and internal memos. These, in turn, made their way into growing civic institutions, such as libraries and municipal archives, which preserved them for future study. This is yet another way in which urbanization helped to make queer lives visible to future generations.

Before turning to these records, it is important to consider a few things. First, this information reflects only those queer people who came to the attention of these more powerful groups, not *all* queer people. Second, these sources are not neutral records of events as they happened; rather, they were created by people who were already actively invested in containing and controlling queer desires. Finally, it shouldn't be assumed that just because queer people were participating in these interactions that they were necessarily telling the truth. Even in situations that weren't clearly coercive, such as a patient talking freely to a doctor, queer people might, for many reasons, have shaded or dispensed with the truth entirely. Part of the difficult work of researching queer history is balancing this asymmetrical record, and paying attention to what queer people said and did, not just what was said and done to them. Many of these records might best be understood as recordings of what straight people knew, thought, assumed, or did about queer people, rather than being directly about queer lives.

Despite these caveats, these kinds of documents are an incomparable resource to historians of sexuality. They contain information that would otherwise have gone completely unrecorded—such as the earliest record of an explicitly transgender person in Brooklyn, a sex worker who went by the name Loop-the-Loop.

Loop-the-Loop was a young white trans woman from "the slums of Brooklyn,"

Photograph of Loop-the-Loop (c.1917), taken by Dr. R. W. Shufeldt and published in the *American Journal of Urology and Sexology*. (*Photo courtesy of the New York Academy of Medicine Library.*)

who was born on April 23, 1883 (just a few months before the death of the Great Ricardo). She was tall for her day—five feet eight inches—and slender, with wavy dark brown hair that she often tucked under a blond wig. Her eyes were blue, her teeth bright white, and when she was fourteen (in 1897), she'd had her ears pierced. She'd adopted her name from the popular Coney Island roller coaster, which had opened in 1901 and was one of the first to turn its riders completely upside down. She was an orphan, and she lived with a woman who acted as her guardian. Quick-witted, perceptive, and talkative, she had a meager education; though she could read English, she couldn't write it well.[12]

How then do we know so much about Loop? On multiple instances, starting in 1906 and continuing at least until 1916, she was examined by Dr. Robert Wilson Shufeldt, who would publish his interactions with her in a 1917 journal article entitled "The Biography of a Passive Pederast."

As well as being a medical doctor, Shufeldt was an army lieutenant, prolific author, passenger pigeon enthusiast, photographer, grave robber, sexologist, blackmailer, and virulent racist who believed that inversion and miscegenation were leading America to white racial suicide. He saw his work on sexuality as a means of saving humanity, and in particular saving the white race from a slow, etiolated death by attrition. When Shufeldt wasn't writing about "passive pederasts" such as Loop, he devoted his time to publishing books with titles such as *America's Greatest Problem: The Negro* and *The Negro: A Menace to American Civilization*. However, these weren't two separate topics that caught his interest; rather, they were both part of his belief in the science of eugenics.

Early twentieth-century medical science was dominated by the eugenics movement, which believed social problems were rooted in deviant bodies and inheritable traits. This movement reached its apogee with the sadistic, anti-Semitic science of the Holocaust, which has allowed us to conveniently forget the power and prevalence of the eugenics movement in America. Just as people of color, women, and queer people were gaining social power and becoming visible, eugenic science would be trotted out to prove that black people were less human, women were less intelligent, and queer people were a biological dead end that threatened to contaminate good (white) Americans. The same doctors who would define "the homosexual" as a biological class unto itself would also define "the pickpocket" that way, and "the woman who is erotically stimulated by hat pins" as well. Today, it seems natural to view homosexuality this way, and ridiculous to think that being a pickpocket might be a hereditary, biologically defined class. But this is the biased, thoroughly unscientific swamp from which our modern ideas about sexuality arose.

As a eugenicist, Shufeldt's interest in Loop was twofold. One, Shufeldt wanted to define what it meant to be a "contrary sexed male," primarily in terms of Loop's physiology, but also to some degree in terms of her lifestyle. Two, Shufeldt wanted to show that her degeneracy could be read from, and was defined by, her body. Sigmund Freud's system of psychoanalysis, and his ideas about sexuality residing in the human mind, only reached American shores in 1909. It would take long decades before they would supplant eugenic ideas about the body as our dominant way of understanding sexuality (and personality in general). For this reason, Shufeldt's article, although ten pages long, barely contains any insights into what Loop thought or how she was raised. But it *does* meticulously diagram her body, including multiple nude photos. Loop's body, not her mind, was where her problems lay.

A surprisingly large number of body parts could communicate unwholesome or downright psychopathic personality traits, according to Shufeldt. Loop's facial features were "coarse" and "of a criminal cast." Her "thin, non-sensuous lips" were inconclusive, but suggested she was more of a decisive kind of person than a weak one. Overall, Shufeldt judged that her face lacked "every expression indicative of truth, refinement, or good moral purpose." Although Loop informed the doctor that she had breasts, Shufeldt said he could see no evidence of *gynocomastia,* the technical term for the development of breasts in someone who was judged to be male at birth. This was a good thing for Loop, Shufeldt believed, as gynocomastia "is in evidence sometimes in criminals." Tellingly, although she could sing soprano, Loop could not whistle—a deficit that was at the time a commonly accepted indicator of inversion. Overall, Shufeldt judged her to be a "nervous, loquacious, foul-mouthed and foul-minded 'fairy' of the most degraded slums of a multi-millioned city."[13]

Loop made her living as a sex worker, and more specifically, as a streetwalker in Brooklyn. Digest this thought and all it implies for a moment: as early as 1906, in some areas of Brooklyn a trans woman could be out on the street, soliciting for sex, with an active clientele. When Shufeldt pressed her about how these men reacted to such things as her body hair, Loop simply shrugged and said, "Most of the boys don't mind it."

According to her own statements, Loop was sexually aggressive and had a high libido. She seemed to delight in telling Shufeldt outlandish stories from her sexual exploits, which began at least by the age of sixteen (in 1899), when she was "constantly in the company of men whom [she] sought as paramours." You can almost hear the good doctor's virtuous panic when he wrote:

> [She] informed me that on one occasion [she] had satisfied as many as forty men in twenty-four hours, and that on the 21st of July, 1906, no fewer than twenty-three men copulated with [her] (immissio penis in anum), one immediately after the other, each producing ejaculation during the act; this took place in a room in Brooklyn.

During their last meeting before Shufeldt wrote his article, Loop brought along her boyfriend of several years, a musician whom Shufeldt described as "an intelligent young man, of about twenty-four years of age." Shufeldt seemed disinterested in him, aside from being slightly shocked that he was so "cool, collected, and respectful." This was most likely because Shufeldt judged him to be heterosexual (but seduced or tricked by Loop), or at most an "acquired invert," whose body was likely to lack the usual tells that Shufeldt was looking for in a "congenital invert" such as Loop.

Acquired inverts, in this developing schema of sexuality, were those who mostly conformed to traditional gender roles. Their attraction to members of the same sex was assumed to be brought on by a lack of appropriate sex objects, coerced by a congenital invert, or was a sign of their utter dissolution and/or insanity. (Josie Mansfield, the lover of Ella Wesner, would have been seen as an acquired invert.) Because acquired inverts did not fit well into an understanding of sexuality that rested on gender and visible bodily signs of inversion, eugenicists tended to ignore these men and women. Shufeldt was willing to accept that some normal-seeming men might, after drinking, have sex with a woman such as Loop, but for a nice young lad to talk openly about a relationship with such a person was disarming. Even as doctors such as Shufeldt were laying the groundwork for our modern idea of homosexuality, they couldn't see it themselves. Had Shufeldt investigated the young man with the thoroughness with which he examined Loop, he might well have been forced to confront the biased limitations of his science—and so he didn't.

What incensed Shufeldt most about Loop was not her body or her sex life, but rather, her complete openness about being who she was. "Lost to every sense of shame," Shufeldt wrote, Loop answered his invasive questioning "as though [she] were talking about the rearing of fancy pigeons."

Loop told Shufeldt that she was, in our modern terms, intersex (meaning her body had a mixture of typically male and female characteristics), and that she had previously been pregnant. Shufeldt disputed this with his medical examinations, which were so thorough they bordered on being a cavity search. It's impossible to know what to make of Loop's assertions. Did she truly believe herself to be intersex? Was this an elaborate camp put on by a fairy out to have some fun with a serious doctor? Or was she attempting to tell Shufeldt what she thought he wanted to hear, to get him to validate her identity (as many trans people are still forced to do with therapists and doctors today)? The answers to these questions remain unknowable, but the questions are important to highlight because we have no insight into them from Loop's point of view. She had her own motivations for allowing herself to be studied and may not have been entirely truthful with Shufeldt.

Aside from her claim to be intersex, in only one other matter did Shufeldt question Loop's story: when she told him that she had never been arrested—"something I am very much inclined to doubt," he noted in his article. Loop pushed back and offered to give Shufeldt a nighttime tour of the Brooklyn streets where she worked. "Fifty cents or a dollar will buy off any cop," she told him, "and that from dark to daylight. We all do it."

How tantalizing are those last four words—who is the *we*? Aside from bribing the cops, what exactly did they *all* do, where did they do it, whom did they do it with, and how many of them were there? These questions either went unasked, or Shufeldt deemed the answers not worth recording.

However, Loop was not the only trans person in New York who came under Shufeldt's microscope. In 1918, a year after he wrote about Loop, his photographs of a trans woman named Jennie June were published in the book *Autobiography of an Androgyne*. This book was the first in a three-volume biographical series written by June, who obscured the facts of her life so well that to this day no historian has been able to identify her. Unlike Loop, June was highly educated and had access to both wealth and doctors on a more even footing. Much like Ruth Fuller Field, June wanted to share her story with sexologists (and eventually laypeople) to promote a greater understanding of inversion. Her first volume was completed around 1899, but it took her nearly twenty years to find a willing publisher—primarily because of anti-obscenity crusader Anthony Comstock. According to June, upon being given a copy of her book, Comstock told her that he would never allow it to be widely distributed. To get around him, *Autobiography of an Androgyne* was offered for sale via the *Medico-Legal Journal,* with a note stating it was "sold only to physicians, lawyers, legislators, psychologists, and sociologists." Queerness was now the provenance of powerful men.

Autobiography of an Androgyne reveals a wide world of "fairies" having sexual relationships with men, mostly working-class white men who both accepted Jennie June as a trans woman and also frequently resorted to violence, extortion, and blackmail against her. In the first chapter, she offers an interesting etymology of the word *fairy*:

> *It probably originated on sailing vessels of olden times when voyages often lasted for months. While the crew was either actually or prospectively suffering acutely from the absence of the female of the species, one of their number would unexpectedly betray an inclination to supply her place. Looked upon as a fairy gift or godsend, such individual would be referred to as "the fairy."*[14]

It's impossible to know how apocryphal this story is, but it again highlights the connection between sailors and queer sexuality, as well as a kind of male sexual flexibility whose existence is routinely denied today.

June met men mostly in saloons and on the streets in less reputable areas of Manhattan, including the Bowery and (as she calls it) the "14th Street rialto," which is today the area near Union Square. She also frequented nearby military forts, which she referred to as being "outside the city," but by which she probably meant in the outer boroughs. June mentions both College Point and Whitestone in Queens, but sadly, whether she ventured out to Brooklyn is impossible to say. However, the larger worlds in which both she and Loop moved were likely fairly similar and overlapping. Although June came from an upper-middle-class background and knew some other inverts of her own social strata, most of her public life as a fairy was spent in working-class areas, much like the "slums of Brooklyn" where Loop lived and worked. June's books provide rare, first-person insight into how trans women were received in these spaces. Here, for instance, is her reminiscence of a typical night spent at an at-home tenement party:

> With half a score of adolescents and two or three young women, an evening would be spent in some humble two-room apartment. Everybody was exceedingly happy, and I perhaps the happiest of all, sitting now in one young man's lap, and now in that of another. And how we all did sing! The young men petted and babied me more than they did any of the girls, and even right before the eyes of the girls. The latter were not jealous of me, especially because I was the one who financed these parties. . . . The girls thought nothing strange of me, as the nature of fairies was well known to them. I wish it understood, however, that these gatherings were no more indecent than a children's party in the best social stratum. Even these knights of Mulberry Street had their sense of decency. At these home parties, extreme intimacies were allowed only in private. The only refreshment was beer, the three-quart pail passing around the room from mouth to mouth, and being repeatedly sent out to be refilled.

June estimated that two-thirds of the young men in these neighborhoods would, under the proper conditions, be attracted to a woman such as her. Most of the men with whom June had relationships did not seem to think that their own identities were threatened or changed in any way by desiring her. She might not have been the kind of woman they were used to, but she was a woman, and they were men, and so the natural order of gender went undisturbed in their eyes. Today, we function on something of a "one-drop rule" when it comes to male sexuality: any amount of sexual experience with or attraction to another man, or to a gender-nonconforming person, defines you as being queer. But in the early 1900s, that was far from a settled way of thinking. In *Gay New York*, George Chauncey characterizes the place of fairies in working-class cultures in New York as being similar to that reserved for sex workers (perhaps in part this is because both fairies and sex workers first came to popular attention inside the same bawdy saloons). This identification afforded them an understandable role in the community: "The fairy's sexual aggressiveness in [her] solicitation of men was certainly inconsistent with the sexual passivity expected of a respectable woman, but it was entirely in keeping with the sexual character ascribed to tough girls and prostitutes."[15] This connection between brassy women and fairies would be celebrated in the 1910s by such performers as the Brooklyn-born Mae West, whose stage persona was said to be inspired by popular vaudeville drag queens such as Bert Savoy and Julian Eltinge—another way in which the theater, sex work, and queer identity have always been interrelated.

However, the fact that queer people occupied this place in working-class culture allowed upper-class sexologists and reformers to dismiss them as inherently degraded. June wrote her book so that the experts in her readership would be "moved to say a kind word for any of the despised and oppressed step-children of Nature—the sexually abnormal by birth." But her life story would also be used to vilify queer people of all kinds, particularly the men who had sex with her.

June got her book sold by having it prefaced, edited, and verified by Dr. Alfred W. Herzog, the publisher of the *Medico-Legal Journal*. Despite finding the book "nauseating," and believing it lacked "any scientific value," Herzog agreed to publish it largely unedited as a kind of exposé of the one of dark corners of modern life.[16] He seemed to genuinely pity June and to have some general sympathy for the people we would today define as transgender. But it was a complicated, patronizing kind of sympathy.

In his introduction, Herzog perfectly captured the shifting (and shifty) understanding of queerness that was emerging in the 1910s. He explained to his readers that "if a male feels sexual desire for another male, or a female for another female, they are called sexually inverted or homosexual." He mentioned Freud's theory that all people are born bisexual, but contended (with no explanation) that this condition was established "anatomically," not just psychologically. He laid out three possible routes to adult inversion: the born invert such as Jennie June, who was both transgender and intersex; the acquired invert, who is inducted into inversion in childhood (again, connecting adult homosexuality with pedophilia); and finally, a kind of indiscriminate or forced inversion that is caused by a normal man's being full of vice and sensuality (and possibly insanity) that has no outlet. From this standpoint, Herzog argued for a complicated legal approach to queerness, which basically was to allow trans women such as Jennie June to live freely, because it was their nature, but to work to prevent or punish all other forms of queerness. He ends his disquisition on a muddied note, showing just how unclear all of these identities were, even to so-called experts such as Herzog. Going back on his definition of the homosexual quoted above, he wrote that a trans woman such as Jennie June "is a homosexualist, because he feels like a woman and to him all male persons belong to the opposite sex. . . . He is born an androgyne . . . a male person with female ways."

Herzog's introduction marks an intermediate point in our understanding of queerness, one that's not yet our modern ideas of sexuality and gender identity, but gestures in those directions. We can see that Herzog had begun to locate sexuality in the mind as well as in the body, and to separate homosexuality from being transgender—sort of.

A trans woman such as June made sense to Herzog: she desired men, acted in a feminine manner, and even had parts of her body that Herzog decreed to be more female than male. But masculine men who desired other men or trans women such as June were a strange and dangerous hybrid of gendered impulses. In Herzog's eyes, this made them either crazy or utterly debauched and immoral. Sexuality was still understood as a function of gender, and at least June wanted to have an appropriate gender identity: feminine, attracted to men, and with an acceptably female body. But the masculine working-class men who wanted June not only broke those rules, they seemed entirely unconcerned with them. In this, *Autobiography of an Androgyne* highlights a fascinating disjunction in early American understandings of queerness: June's manly working-class lovers saw themselves as sexually normal, whereas her upper-class doctors saw their desires as not only abnormal, but downright dangerous to the fabric of society.

June herself mostly agreed with the classifications laid out by Herzog (if not the antipathy that animated them), but with one main point of differentiation: instead of seeing herself as "a male person with female ways," June defined inverts such as herself as having a "female brain in a *female* body" that had "various abnormal developments along the line of male structure." Like Loop-the-Loop, June actively pushed back against the scientists who were seeking to define her existence, even while she cooperated with them.

Transgender men from this period wrote no comparable documents; however, the prosecution of one Elizabeth Trondle for "masquerading in men's clothes" in 1913 captured Brooklyn's imagination and made headlines across the country. Cross-dressing arrests were not uncommon in this period, but Trondle's outspoken and unrepentant thoughts on gender were so outlandish that newspapers across the country quoted them at length, allowing us some unique access to his thoughts.

Trondle's brief time as a cause célèbre began when he was arrested in the back room of a saloon while "masquerading in male attire, smoking cigarettes, and drinking with men."[17] Like James Hagaman and Emerson Colburn, he was confined at the Raymond Street Jail while on trial, and his case was heard in the courthouse on Adams Street, which was located just a few blocks from where Mary Hallock Foote once lived in Brooklyn Heights.

Trondle claimed to be twenty-four, and an orphan, but a court probation officer asserted that he was seventeen and had family in the Richmond Hill neighborhood of Queens. Apparently, this was not the first time he'd been in trouble with the judicial system. He had a tattoo on his forearm, which he said was from his time working as a sailor on a ship named Dixie. Given the time period, he most certainly did not work under the name Elizabeth Trondle, but whatever name he did use went unrecorded—as is often the case in historical records on people who crossed genders. But the papers did report that Trondle's family had written him off as "incorrigible,"[18] and that he had little contact with them.

At the time of his arrest, Trondle was wearing a "natty blue serge suit and trousers, with silk hose and tan oxfords." A boy's cap covered his closely shorn hair.[19] Repeatedly offered other clothing by the police, he refused to change, asserting, "They can't make me wear it if I don't want to, and I won't wear them, so there."[20] He also refused to give his birth name and, when pressed, said that he would rather be sent to a reformatory than submit to the court's wishes. "I've always been more boy than girl," he told reporters on the steps of the courthouse.[21]

His plan, he informed Magistrate Voorhees during his arraignment, was to write to President Woodrow Wilson and request permission to wear men's clothing. He was inspired by the case of Dr. Mary Walker, a physician, spy, and abolitionist who had received special dispensation to wear trousers after becoming the first female surgeon employed by the US Army (during the Civil War). To this day, Dr. Walker is the only woman ever to receive the Medal of Honor. Until her death in 1919, she traveled the country lecturing about dress reform, suffrage for women, and temperance. She was known to visit Brooklyn, and Trondle might have heard her speak or have at least read about her visits in the newspapers, which covered Dr. Walker's comings and goings closely.

During his first night in the Raymond Street Jail, Trondle composed a short letter to President Wilson, which he shared with the court the next day:

> *Dear Mr. Wilson—I am a woman in trouble and I want my rights. It is no crime for a female to wear male attire, and yet I have been arrested here in Brooklyn for doing it. I want a permit from you or some one else to wear the costume I have adopted. I am tired of being kicked around and abused and poorly paid. If I can appear as a man and do man's work, I shall be more respected, better paid and happier. Won't you please see what can be done for me?*[22]

Newspapers around the country, from Texas to Kentucky to Rhode Island, printed the letter and some short details on Trondle's case, taking Trondle from local news to nationwide infamy overnight.

Like Loop-the-Loop and Jennie June, Trondle was unapologetic about his desires and pushed back against the structures that attempted to control or thwart them. However, perhaps because Trondle was seen as a woman, neither the courts nor the police brought up inversion, homosexuality, or other terms relating to queerness. Unlike Loop or June, who used the word *fairy* to describe themselves, Trondle didn't seem to have specific words for his identity (or at least not ones he said out loud). Information about "female" sexuality and gender transgression were not then widely available to the general public. This was just beginning to change— the same year that Trondle was arrested, an optometrist and typeface designer named Douglas McMurtrie began publishing a series of articles on sexual inversion in women, primarily based on the experiences of his friend Ruth Fuller Field and the queer actresses of her circle. Trondle certainly didn't have access to those publications, but as his case wore on, others would soon bring sexology and queerness into the discussion—both to defend *and* condemn Trondle's actions.

But first, what are we to make of Trondle's various assertions to being a boy and being a woman, and why did I choose to use male pronouns for him? On its face, the economic explanation—that he was simply passing as a man to get gainful employment—seems a sufficient answer. However, Trondle's family was well-off, and at seventeen, he probably wouldn't have needed to work *if* he had been on good terms with them. Trondle reported at least one previous incident of running away and living as a boy (when he worked as a sailor and got a tattoo), suggesting that his gender identity was an ongoing issue. Trondle likely had no examples of transgender men to pattern his desires on, but he did know the story of Dr. Mary Walker, who claimed a female identity and said that she needed to wear pants because they made her job as a doctor easier. Asserting an economic rationale for his actions may have acted as a cover for Trondle's transgender identity, while simultaneously providing the slim possibility that the president might grant him permission to live as he desired.

People arrested for cross-dressing often gave work-related explanations. When Christine Becrens, who worked as a maid, was arrested for dressing as a woman (as she had been doing for almost a decade), she told the Brooklyn court, "I cannot get work as a gentleman, so I dress as a lady."[23] Similarly, when vaudeville performer Gus Seib was arrested for dressing as a man, Seib told the judge he "would be unable to obtain work as a woman."[24] In both Seib's and Becrens's cases, it seems that while they cross-dressed to gain employment, they did so in part because their gender presentation was already so at odds with what was expected of them. This might also have been true for Trondle, as reporters were quick to note his deep voice and masculine mannerisms.

Although Magistrate Voorhees urged Trondle to wear women's clothes if he expected any kind of "consideration" from the court (a suggestion Trondle pointedly ignored), Voorhees was also swayed by Trondle's arguments.[25] Upon arraignment, Voorhees told the arresting officer, "It is no crime for a woman to dress in any attire she desires unless to commit a crime."[26]

This was a correct—although infrequently expressed—interpretation of New York state law, which made it a crime to wear a mask or costume *only* while attempting to commit another crime. The statute was based on an older law that was enacted in 1845 as a way to prosecute upstate New York farmers who rioted and fought off tax collectors while dressed in faux–Native American garments. However, in the late 1800s and early 1900s, the masquerade law was often used as an imprecise but effective method of prosecuting inverts. (Interestingly, the law would be revived again some one hundred years later to prosecute Occupy Wall Street protesters.)[27]

This was yet another way in which the early 1900s were a transitional period for queer people in America: after the public had begun to recognize and name our existence, but before the legal system had had a chance to devise methods of enforcement and prosecution targeted at us. Instead, a patchwork of laws against vagrancy, disorderly conduct, solicitation, obscenity, prostitution, and being a public nuisance were pressed into service as necessary.

When the original charge failed to stick, Trondle's probation officer returned with a new one: "associating with idle and vicious persons."[28] More important, this new charge was overseen by a new magistrate who was much less sympathetic to Trondle's case. The original judge, Voorhees, had a reputation for not being tough enough; in 1918, moral reformers in the Committee of Fourteen (an antiprostitution society that was just beginning to worry about queer people in New York City) wrote letters to the city government complaining about the lax sentences he doled out.[29] When the new magistrate sentenced Trondle to three years at the Bedford Hills Reformatory for Women in upstate New York, he made clear that the new charge was simply a useful pretense. "I sent her to the Bedford Reformatory," he told papers, "because I believe she is a moral pervert. No girl would dress in men's clothing unless she is twisted in her moral viewpoint."[30] The word *pervert* did not have a specifically queer meaning at this time, but like *sodomy,* it was used to suggest a range of deviant sexual behaviors that included inversion. Although our legal system hadn't yet been rewritten to prosecute queerness directly, the magistrate's desire to do so is evident in this case. Even though Trondle's style of dress was legal, it marked him as a degenerate person—a moral pervert—who needed to be put away.

Trondle's case has a curious codicil. The day after his sentence was reported, a letter from Brooklyn resident Otto Spengler was published in multiple papers around New York City, arguing in support of Trondle's right to wear men's clothing. There "have been and no doubt always shall be persons of either sex whose inborn impulse will tend to dressing in the attire of the opposite sex," Spengler wrote. These "naturally timid" individuals "dread anything like public exposure," but "freedom in matters of dress means life and death to them."[31] To back up these assertions, Spengler cited the two most influential European sexologists, Magnus Hirschfeld and Richard von Krafft-Ebing, whose work inspired the entire American field of sexology.

Spengler knew all of this from firsthand experience. The same year that Trondle was arrested, a New York City gynecologist named Bernard Talmey presented a paper to the New York Society of Medical Jurisprudence on the cases of five "transvestites" that he had met through his practice; Spengler was one of them. A married German immigrant and parent of three, Spengler preferred the name Othilie, which is what she used when corresponding with a wide variety of other transgender individuals around the world. Some of these people would make up the source material for Talmey's article "Transvestitism: A Contribution to the Study of the Psychology of Sex," which he published in 1914 in the *New York Medical Journal*. In it, Talmey attempted to disentangle what we would call being transgender (which he, following in the footsteps of Magnus Hirschfeld, referred to as transvestitism) from being gay; he specifically mentions excluding someone who was "homosexually inclined" from the study.[32]

Showing the growing influence of psychiatric theories of sexuality, Talmey wrote that transvestitism was "one of the newest discovered anomalies . . . where the sole psychosexual anomaly consisted in the desire for cross-dressing." However, this didn't stop Talmey from repeatedly suggesting that most of the people in the article might actually have been homosexual as well. Talmey wrote that Spengler "has no homosexual inclinations, but rather a profound repugnance to homosexual relationship . . . still he seems to want a man before whom he could expose the charms of his own person and who would kiss and caress him."[33] That desire, however, is not expressed by Spengler herself anywhere in her direct quotes, which suggests that Talmey may have been putting his own interpretation on her impulses. Much like Dr. R. W. Shufeldt, Talmey found homosexuality disgusting; it was a "morbid sex state of gross somatic experiences . . . emanat[ing] from the crude powerful sensation of sex." Transvestitism, on the other hand, he thought primarily an aesthetic desire for femininity, which explained why "the anomaly is found mostly in individuals possessing the so called artistic temperament."

Spengler was not only out to other queer people and to Talmey; her entire family knew and accepted her identity. Her youngest daughter referred to her as "papa-lady," and she shared lingerie with her wife.[34] She also corresponded with Dr. Mary Walker, whom Trondle had cited as his inspiration for the idea to write to President Wilson. Talmey's article is perhaps most fascinating because it documents how connected queer people were becoming. Sexologists such as Talmey depended upon these preexisting networks to fuel their work, much as Ruth Fuller Field made Douglas McMurtrie's writing on lesbianism possible, by introducing him to the wide world of women from whom he drew his observations (which included Field herself, as well as Johnstone Bennett, Vittoria Cremers, and Field's

girlfriend Emma Altman). Over the next two decades, Spengler would participate in sexological research studies of all kinds, and we will return to her experiences again in the 1930s, when she partook in one of the most groundbreaking
studies of queer people ever attempted, undertaken by the Committee for the
Study of Sex Variants. For now, though, her public defense of Trondle shows
the extent to which queer people were beginning to actively find, recognize,
and organize with one another.

The discussions around Trondle's case make it clear the idea of queerness in
women was becoming public knowledge that was both medicalized and stigmatized in ways that it simply wasn't when Ella Wesner and Florence Hines were
performing in theaters not far from the Adams Street Courthouse. This was part
of a larger trend that was concerned with the rebellious sexuality of young women
in general in the 1910s. The same Freudian theories of psychosexual development
that began to shift discussions of queer sexuality from the body to the mind were
also producing profound shifts in how teenage *heterosexuality* was viewed. Adoles-
cence began to be seen as a time when teenagers needed to be assisted in order to
reach proper emotional development. Those girls who failed to do so (prostitutes,
lesbians, and others) were often labeled feebleminded, insane, or psychologically
damaged. Increasingly, their minds, not just their bodies, were seen as broken—
although that damage could still be divined from looking at their physical makeup.
Adolescents like Trondle, who seemed inclined to go down a bad path, were increasingly brought under the thumb of the state—via the courts—who in turn
handed them over to the emerging medicalized world of "mental hygiene" workers, such as the women who ran the Bedford Hills reformatory.

Medical and legal professionals made up two of the three pillars upon which
the emerging regulation of queer sexualities was being built. The third? Civilian
morality organizations. Trondle's case shows the difficulties of attempting to prosecute queer people through the courts in the early 1900s. However, there was an
active world of extrajudicial antivice organizations in New York City which dated
all the way back to the Society for the Reformation of Juvenile Delinquents (the
organization funded by the Concert Saloon Law). These groups were happy to
step in and take up the slack. One of the most powerful was the Committee of
Fourteen (so-called for its fourteen founding members), which formed in 1905
to shut down what were known as "Raines Law hotels."

Raines Law was an 1896 state statute that banned the sale of alcohol on Sundays. As Sunday was the day most working-class men had off, this was an early form of pro-temperance social control, aimed at reforming the drinking habits of the poor. Tellingly, hotels with more than ten rooms were exempted from the law, meaning that traveling gentlemen could still partake as they saw fit. Saloon owners soon began to take advantage of this loophole by carving up their second floors or public halls into small rentable rooms. By 1900, Brooklyn had some 1,664 official hotels.[35] Sex work, which had been driven out of the theaters by earlier waves of reformers, relocated to these Raines Law hotels. These spaces also facilitated sex between unmarried heterosexual couples by providing cheap, easily accessible semiprivate space, which was rare in this time of crowded tenement living. Here again, the lines between sex work, casual sex, and dating blurred easily. Women who had premarital sex for pleasure at Raines Law hotels were just as likely to be arrested for prostitution as were women who *actually* exchanged sex for money.

To combat this new scourge, leading businessmen, clergy, socialites, doctors, judges, and politicians formed the Committee of Fourteen in 1905. By 1911, Brooklyn had such an active nightlife scene that it became the only borough with its own specific auxiliary branch of the committee. This branch worked primarily in two neighborhoods. The first was the waterfront district closest to Manhattan, from the Brooklyn Navy Yard in the east, down along Sands Street to the City Hall area (where the New Park Theatre stood) and over to Columbia Heights, the street that bordered the water on the western edge of Brooklyn Heights. The committee often referred to this area as "the Adams Street tenderloin district," and it encompassed parts or all of the neighborhoods we now know as Dumbo, Vinegar Hill, downtown Brooklyn, and Brooklyn Heights.[36] The other area that had a particularly active underworld sex trade? Coney Island, whose reputation as a hedonistic playground had only grown since the days of Florence Hines. According to Timothy Gilfoyle, the historian of prostitution, in the early 1900s these two neighborhoods were "synonymous with commercial sex."[37]

Two important inaugural figures in the Committee of Fourteen's Brooklyn auxiliary were the husband-and-wife pair Sarah Truslow and Robert Latou Dickinson. Truslow was a steely-eyed social reformer who also founded the first YWCA in Brooklyn; Dickinson was a doctor specializing in gynecology and maternal health. Both were born and bred Brooklynites who grew up in the downtown waterfront area. Truslow remained active with the Committee of Fourteen for over twenty years, until it shut down in 1932. Dickinson's involvement was briefer, but his experiences with the committee would spark an interest in queer and deviant sexualities, which would eventually lead him to help organize the Committee for the Study of Sex Variants (who would in turn examine Othilie Spengler in the 1930s).

These reform-minded upper-class men and women sought to bring their social power to bear against immoral activities in a variety of ways. Most directly, they employed informants who visited saloons throughout the five boroughs looking for unescorted women, prostitutes, pimps, degenerates, fairies, mixed-race socializing; hotels that rented rooms to unmarried couples; and saloons that served alcohol on Sundays, to men in uniform or without licenses. When they found these violations, they contacted the brewers connected to the saloons. Most saloons were "tied shops," which meant they worked with a single alcohol supplier.[38] These breweries usually owned the bars that sold their products or had a controlling interest in them, but the bars were run by local managers, who applied for a state liquor license to do so. By shaming them or threatening legal action, the Committee of Fourteen forced breweries to withdraw their imprimatur from saloons the committee considered to be operating immorally. If the committee felt it had enough evidence to charge a saloon operator with actual criminal activity, it worked directly with the police (though those collaborations were often fraught, with the police viewing the committee members somewhere between helpful informants and moralizing zealots). Finally, the committee also heavily lobbied for laws that made it easier to arrest people for vagrancy, prostitution, solicitation, disorderly conduct, and the keeping of a disorderly house. (This phrase referred to any dwelling that was considered a public nuisance, be it brothel, private club, or simply a raucous home.) The law, they realized, was slow to change, but they could be nimble, following vice however it tried to escape the widening net of police repression.

In this, they were startlingly effective. By 1912, they had reduced the number of Raines Law hotels in Brooklyn to just three hundred, shuttering or driving underground more than thirteen hundred establishments in just seven years. In their success, the committee saw the opportunity to expand further. In an annual report issued in January 1912, Chairman Frederick Whitin wrote that the committee had "become conscious of the need of a much larger work which must be done."[39] From this point on, the committee would combat *any* sexual vice in *any* commercial venue. This broader purview set them on a direct collision course with some of the earliest queer public institutions in Brooklyn: bars that served queer men around World War I.

In July 1914, just a year after Elizabeth Trondle was arrested, the "Great War" began with the assassination of Archduke Ferdinand of Austria. World War II is often cited as the moment when many men and women, uprooted from their homes and thrown together in single-sex barracks and factories, became cognizant of queerness (their own and others). But World War I had just as profound an effect on the lives of many gay men and lesbians, if on a smaller scale. Margot Canaday, in her book, *The Straight State,* argues that World War II was when "military officials developed and implemented a policy solution to deal with what they learned about perversion during World War I."[40] Many people, not just in the army, were learning about homosexuality around this time. In the lead-up to World War I, *The New York Times* printed the word *homosexual* for the first time, in an article by playwright George Bernard Shaw. Shaw was a pacifist (and at times a vocal proponent of sexual rights), but in the final paragraphs of his article, he made it clear that didn't mean he approved of decadent German society. Instead of war, he wrote, we needed "to trust to the march of Democracy" to condemn such institutions as "the forty tolerated homosexual brothels of Berlin . . . [to] the dustbin."[41] The war did little to Berlin's queer subculture, which would flourish during the Weimar Republic of the 1920s. But it *would* prompt extensive collaboration among the Committee of Fourteen, the police, and the military, which led to the first recorded legal action against a gay bar in Brooklyn.

Through a deal proffered by Chairman Whitin, the committee functioned as the "eyes and ears" of the military police at training camps throughout the Northeast, from Atlantic City, to Philadelphia, to Brooklyn.[42] The committee was well aware that the war was causing an uptick in homosexual activity, which they blamed on "the great influx of sailors."[43] Chairman Whitin was blunt in his belief that homosexuality "has been an evil among sea-faring men from time immemorial."[44] Thanks to the Navy Yard, Brooklyn was flooded with sailors throughout World War I. At the start of the war, the yard was already the largest in the country, employing some five thousand men on its massive, hundred-plus-acre campus. By the time the war ended in 1918, its rolls would swell to some twenty thousand, according to labor historian John Strobo. As a result, the Navy Yard area would be "flooded with young men, far from home and lonely."[45] One Committee of Fourteen investigator described the area as being overrun with rowdy sailors and loose women. In a report about street conditions on a random Wednesday evening, he wrote:

It seems to me that the sailors were sex mad. A number of the sailors were with other men walking arm in arm, and on one dark street I saw a sailor and a man kissing each other. I saw a few sailors enter one of the hotels with these men, who I judged to be perverts, and register for rooms. It looked like an exhibition of mail [sic] perversion showing itself in the absence of girls or the difficulty of finding them. Some of the sailors told me that they might be able to get a girl if they went "up-town" but it was too far up and they were too drunk to go way up there.[46]

Instead, many of these men found comfort with one another in the saloons, hotels, and alleys of Brooklyn's waterfront. In turn, the Committee of Fourteen found them.

On the evening of January 14, 1916, Antonio Bellavicini went to work at a nameless saloon at 32 Sands Street, about halfway between the Brooklyn Bridge and the Navy Yard. Located on the corner of Adams Street, two steps down from

Photograph of 32 Sands Street in the year 1913, three years before it was raided by the police and the Committee of Fourteen for serving homosexuals. (*Photo courtesy of the Brooklyn Historical Society. W.J. Mullen, [32 Sands St], 1911, photographic print, v1973.2.34; Brooklyn Historical Society.*)

the sidewalk, this saloon was in the shadow of one of the elevated trains that pre-figured the subway. Sands Street had a reputation as one of the worst streets in Brooklyn, where tattoo parlors and cheap chop-suey joints catered to sailors and sex workers all night long. Despite being a bitterly cold January night, with temperatures expected to dip into the teens,[47] the saloon was busy with sailors and civilians out for fun on a Friday. Unbeknownst to its patrons, the bar had been under the watchful eye of the Committee of Fourteen for "three or four weeks" because it was "frequented by degenerates."[48] According to the committee's records, it was a "resort of male perverts, catering to sailors," one of the first they had come across in Brooklyn.[49] Under intense pressure to preserve the moral standing of the military during wartime, the committee was eager to shut the saloon down.

However, there was a problem: it was not illegal for homosexuals to gather in public, nor for bars to serve them. The year before, the committee had success-fully worked with a Brooklyn assemblyman to amend the vagrancy law so that police no longer needed to prove that a woman exchanged sex for money, just that she was loitering with the intent of encouraging lewdness. This much lower standard of evidence allowed the police to arrest virtually any woman they deemed immoral. A "prostitute," in their eyes, was no longer a woman who accepted money for sex, she was a degraded person who could be jailed for who she *was*, not for what she had done. But when it came to homosexuals, the law still revolved around sodomy, disorderly conduct, creating a public nuisance, and masquerading in clothing of the opposite sex—all specific, actionable activities that the police could be called upon to prove in court. If they were going to raid a bar such as 32 Sands Street, they needed to catch its patrons committing one of those offenses.

On that cold January night, they used a novel strategy to do so: the police disguised Officer Harry Saunders in a US Navy sailor uniform and sent him into the bar on an entrapment exercise. If any of the patrons hit on him, they could be arrested for disorderly conduct.

Around 10:00 p.m., Officer Saunders entered the bar and ordered a beer. Al-most immediately, three men at a nearby table called out to him, saying, "Sailor, dear, come over and drink with us." After a second round of beers, Officer Saunders asked why the men had called him over. A man named John Meehan responded by inviting Saunders to 170 Schermerhorn Street. "If you will come down there," he offered, "we will suck your cock." Meehan assured Saunders that everyone in the bar—some ten or twelve individuals, plus Bellavicini, the bartender—were "all the same." After three men at another table also hit on Saunders, he dropped a quarter on the bar for his drinks, then promptly arrested all six men who had spoken to him (and Bellavicini). The entire raid took about fifteen minutes.

All six patrons were convicted of disorderly conduct, a misdemeanor, and sentenced to six months in the workhouse. Had the police contented themselves with this, the case of 32 Sands Street would have been lost to the view of historians, since these arrests generated no publicity and no trials, and the charge was no different from what other men might have gotten for public intoxication. But in this case, the police, most likely at the urging of the Committee of Fourteen, overstepped their bounds and arrested Antonio Bellavicini for keeping a disorderly house. On February 1, Bellavicini was tried, convicted, and sentenced to three months in the workhouse. Unlike the other men, Bellavicini—a married, thirty-four-year-old, Italian-immigrant father of five—fought back. He hired a lawyer named John J. McGinniss and appealed his case. The resulting trial transcripts were preserved by the New York State Court of Special Sessions, and they are a gold mine of information for the historian attempting to reconstruct New York City's early, incoherent attempts to police homosexuality.

Bellavicini's appeal rested on three points. One, that he hadn't heard the men talking with Officer Saunders and therefore could not be expected to have known they were committing an offense. Two, that even *if* those men had said what Saunders accused them of, that was an isolated incident and the law around keeping a disorderly house required repeated, flagrant disorderly conduct. Three, that it was impossible for any judge to issue a fair ruling in a case related to homosexuality because "the character of the charge awakened their innate hostility to such vice as was alleged, created an irremovable bias in their minds and suppressed their judicial temperament."[50] The court, unsurprisingly, was not sympathetic to this last line of defense, but it at least considered the other two.

During Bellavicini's appeal, the three police officers involved in the raid suddenly shifted their stories in an attempt to undermine his defense. Now, they said, the men in the saloon had all been wearing makeup and carrying powder puffs. Moreover, two sailors were sitting on the laps of other men in the back room of the saloon. These details had never been mentioned earlier. Even if Bellavicini hadn't heard the solicitation, the district attorney argued, he should have been able to tell that these men were degenerates by the way they dressed and acted. These behaviors inherently created a public nuisance, which meant Bellavicini was guilty of keeping a disorderly house. Multiple other men, including a sailor stationed at the Navy Yard, testified that no one wore makeup, and that only one person—other than Saunders—was in a sailor's uniform in the saloon that night. The district attorney attacked their credibility in his cross-examination. In particular, he went after the sailor who testified that no other sailors were in the bar, and no men with "blackened eyebrows" or "rouged cheeks" either. The DA attempted to destroy the sailor's trustworthiness as a witness by tricking him into admitting that he could not name the master of arms on his ship, then telling the judges that the position of master of arms had been abolished by the navy. When Saunders's attorney objected and requested an adjournment for time to show that ships still employed masters of arms, the judges brushed him off.

Bellavicini lost his appeal, though two of the judges were persuaded by his arguments. Judge Stapleton, in writing the court's dissent, said, "Although there is competent evidence of an isolated, indecent or obscene act . . . there is no evidence that painted men with effeminate voices resorted there with the knowledge of defendant." The lead three judges, however, ignored this issue entirely, basing their verdict on police testimony that they had had the place under observation for weeks. What happened that night, the judges reasoned, was less important than the ongoing events that had attracted police interest to the saloon in the first place—even though no testimony or evidence from the trial related to those weeks of observation. Bellavicini was sentenced to three months in the workhouse for keeping a "place of public resort at which the decency, peace, and comfort of the neighborhood were disturbed."[51] After that, Bellavicini disappeared from public records entirely.

Slowly, the state was inching toward an understanding that homosexuality was an identity, not a set of actions, and that the mere existence of queer people in public was dangerous to the community—much like the existence of immoral women. In the cases of Elizabeth Trondle and 32 Sands Street, we can see the police bumping up against the limitations of the law, which had been written to deal with criminal behaviors, not criminal classes of people. Reform organizations such as the Committee of Fourteen would be essential in getting legislators to amend the necessary laws to account for this emerging new understanding of sexuality. It had taken the reformers nearly a decade to change the laws defining prostitution; it would take a little longer to change the laws regarding homo-sexuality. But they would ultimately succeed in the 1920s, as the Committee of Fourteen was nothing if not diligent. However, Bellavicini's case also shows the extent to which the police were able to bend existing laws into service when it came to criminalizing queer people. More pointed legislation would make this job easier, but it wasn't strictly necessary, as Bellavicini unfortunately discovered. Ultimately, what mattered was not whether he had broken the law (as the police were fully capable of manufacturing whatever evidence was necessary), but whether he was considered a priori guilty because of who (or what) he was. In other words, the law lagged behind social understandings of right and wrong.

For their part, the committee was overjoyed that they were able to help "get the perverts" at 32 Sands Street, and Chairman Whitin personally sent a note to the acting police commissioner congratulating Officer Saunders on his undercover work.[52] Whitin also wrote to the head of the State Excise Department in Albany, which oversaw liquor licenses, to ensure that 32 Sands Street was shut down for good.

Throughout the 1910s, similar raids appear to have been conducted by the po-lice and the Committee of Fourteen, but because they generated no trials, there is almost no information about them. For instance, a small note in the commit-tee's files relates to a similar case in 1913, where the police, in cooperation with the military, also used an officer dressed as a sailor to entrap men drinking at 36 Myrtle Avenue, a saloon-hotel "used by male perverts."[53] Since no one challenged these arrests, they generated no other paper trail—although someone in the com-mittee did scratch an angry message in pencil at the bottom of the page to note that using a sailor uniform in this way was in "flat disregard" of federal law and should be discontinued. A few years later, in a list the police shared with the com-mittee on August 23, 1915, it's noted that the Commercial Hotel, located in downtown Brooklyn at 254 Fulton Street, was a "meeting place for degenerates." The undated notes of one of the committee's paid informants briefly mentions a saloon at 1120 Myrtle Avenue in Brooklyn, where a man named Harry, "said to be a fairy," performed women's songs in an effeminate voice and manner.[54] But there's little other information about any of these places.

Of slightly more interest is the case of Bonner's Saloon, located not far from 32 Sands Street and the Navy Yard. In 1910, Bonner was listed in the US census as being a single, twenty-five-year-old black man from North Carolina who was

living across the street from his saloon, which was on the second floor of a nondescript building on Myrtle Avenue. Bonner was the rare black bar operator who
came to the committee's attention. In their reports, the committee noted that it
was hard for them to gain access to establishments for people of color, since almost all of their investigators were white, and they devoted little resources toward
policing the bars and neighborhoods where people of color congregated (another
reason why the queer history of people of color in Brooklyn lacks records).

The earliest public mention of Bonner's Saloon is a newspaper report from
1910, when a card game gone wrong led to a shoot-out; Bonner killed the gun-
man and was acquitted for self-defense.[55] Two years later, the police attempted
to frame the saloon for illegally serving alcohol on Sunday, but the case was dismissed for lack of evidence, with The Brooklyn Daily Eagle going so far as to call
the police a "strong arm squad."[56] However, by 1913, the Committee of Fourteen crowed in their bulletin that they had succeeded in having the place shut down
and reopened under new ownership, though just how they did so is a mystery.[57]

Clearly, Bonner's was a thorn in their side. But why exactly? Two reports from
committee investigators suggest some answers. In a visit in 1912, the investigator noted that the "tone" of the saloon was actually "above the other places observed." Although the bar was playing ragtime—a distinctly black style of music
that was considered racy and sexual—it was not "out of the ordinary or vulgar."
This was in sharp contrast to the supposed immorality the investigator observed.
He seemed particularly upset by the bar's distinctly interracial clientele. He
saw black men drinking with white women (three of who, he noted, seemed to
be there expressly to "solicit colored fellows"), and white men hanging out with
black women (who were having a "very big and loud time"). Later, when
two black women came to sit with him, he inferred that they were prostitutes
because they invited him home with them after he purchased a round of drinks.
All unescorted women in bars were generally assumed by the committee to be
prostitutes, or at least prostitute-adjacent, but black women came in for particularly harsh scrutiny.

In a separate, undated report, a different investigator commented with
horror that blacks and whites at Bonner's were "mixed in with each other like
hash." This investigator also noticed another kind of immorality: "the presence of
fairies." Fairies, he explained, were "a very effeminate type of man." As in the
case of 32 Sands Street, the mere existence of gay men in public was seen as an

indicator of criminality. "Whether or not they were soliciting trade I cannot say positively," the investigator wrote, "but I am not willing to give them the benefit of the doubt."[58]

(The term *trade,* as used here, was a common way of referring to the customers of sex workers, which would later be extended to refer to any masculine and/ or straight-identified men who had sex with men. Just as fairies were seen as equivalent to prostitutes, the men who slept with them were considered the same as johns.)

Although they may seem only slightly related, fears about "race mixing" and queer people were intimately connected, flip sides of the same eugenic coin. Both fears, ultimately, were about preserving the "white race." Black people represented an external threat to whiteness; queer people represented an internal one. After emancipation, white scientists, lawmakers, and doctors saw a looming threat of extinction, through the degeneration of white bloodlines via interracial relationships on the one hand, and through sterility and enervation via homosexuality on the other. Because these were ultimately sexual issues, it's no wonder that American sexology, even more so than its European counterpart, was deeply racist. Some of the same eugenic scientists who were defining "homosexuality" in this era were also (re)defining whiteness, primarily by promoting the idea that black people were both a physical and existential threat to the so-called white race. They argued that ethnic differences among Europeans were nothing when compared to the differences between whites and blacks. Whiteness at this time was a less unified identity, with much being made over intra-European ethnic divisions. Irish people, southern Italians, and Jews of European descent were only tentatively considered white by most New Yorkers. Only once larger numbers of black Americans moved to the city during the 1920s did whiteness come to be understood as the pan-European identity it is today (and still today, European-descended Jews are often viewed as racially other). Sexologists would be integral to this unification of the "white race."

The 1910s were still a very white time in Brooklyn's history; marginal gains had been made in the population of people of color around 1900, but by 1910, Brooklyn was once again 98.54 percent people of European descent, according to the US census—about the same percentage as Staten Island, slightly whiter than Manhattan, and a little less white than the Bronx or Queens. In real numbers, this meant some 22,000 black people in Brooklyn; 1,000 people of Asian descent;

146 people listed as "other"; an uncounted number of Latinx people; and 1.6 million whites.[59]

R. W. Shufeldt, the doctor who photographed Jennie June and Loop-the-Loop, was prototypical of the doctors involved in racist American sexology. In his 1915 book, *America's Greatest Problem: The Negro,* he argued at length that "the black races of mankind came nearer the anthropoid apes than any of the white races did."[60] In Shufeldt's view, black men were violent rapists, and black women were licentious, promiscuous, and purposefully trying to seduce white men. Or as he put it:

> *It is the aim and highest ambition of the negresses to have children by white men,*
> *for the reason that such children, by the superior intelligence coming from their*
> *white fathers, will command better positions when they grow up than the pure*
> *blacks, and in so doing will powerfully further the interests, political and*
> *otherwise, of the African population in this country.*[61]

Shufeldt believed that white perverts were helpless before their "sexual disability." He argued therefore that homosexuality, pederasty, sodomy, and transvestitism (among other "disorders") should not be criminalized. Instead, he believed in a dystopian future like that which Aldous Huxley would soon describe in *Brave New World.* Only science, Shufeldt thought, could save white people from queers:

> *We will continue to breed millions of sexual perverts and inverts—psychopathic*
> *types—just so long as any ignorant priest, justice of the peace or other party, is*
> *permitted to give people permission to breed them, that is, without the would-be*
> *parents having first been examined by a competent medical expert.*[62]

In other words, to prevent homosexuality, it was necessary to more closely police *heterosexuality,* which was work that doctors such as Shufeldt and reformers such as the Committee of Fourteen were more than happy to take on. Throughout the 1910s, a series of state laws were introduced with the aim of controlling reproduction—and thereby saving the white race. In both 1910 and 1913, New York State tried to pass a law requiring that couples obtain a physician's certificate before getting married, as Shufeldt wanted, although it failed both times. In 1912, the Committee of Fourteen worked with doctors to pass the McClellan-

Brush Bill, which empowered a three-person board of medical experts to examine and sterilize "the feebleminded, idiotic, epileptic, and a certain class of criminals confined to state institutions." In their bulletin, the committee noted that similar legislation had already been passed in Indiana, Connecticut, New Jersey, California, and Michigan.[63] Throughout the decade, as previously discussed, the committee also pushed for stricter laws regarding heterosexual prostitution. None of these laws directly addressed queer people or desires, but preventing the birth of "sexual perverts and inverts" was an explicit goal of the men and women who created these laws. Just as queer people were becoming more connected, a parallel and increasingly tight web of sexual control was being woven among doctors, the police, and upper-class moral reformers.

During this period, psychological and medical experts became intimately involved in the criminal justice system at every level, from running reform institutions such as Bedford Hills, to testifying as expert witnesses in cases such as the murder of James Vickers, to sitting on parole boards, to performing studies on incarcerated people. From these newfound positions of power, they attempted to enact their eugenic ideas about sexuality and race. Elizabeth Trondle and Antonio Bellavicini had been prosecuted using inexact laws that were not created to police sexuality; over the next two decades, the triumvirate of police, doctors, and moral reformers would create laws and policies that *explicitly* targeted queer people.

By July 1919, the Committee of Fourteen was well aware of the growing queer community and the limits of the law. In one of their regular internal bulletins, they wrote that "the number of convictions for degeneracy was very much larger than here reported," but that without better legal tracking, it was "impossible to learn the number of such cases."[64]

At the same time, however, it was becoming increasingly possible to live a queer life in America, in New York City, and in Brooklyn. Attempts to repress sexuality were becoming more complicated and powerful precisely because queerness was becoming more common and well known. The scattered moments of queer sexuality that had existed in earlier decades had begun to coalesce into a critical mass. The idea of a "gay man" or a "lesbian woman" had become thinkable in America in a way that it simply wasn't before this time. Brooklyn's next crop of queers would in many ways share our current understanding of sexuality as a fixed part of one's psychological makeup, which was distinct from, but related to, gender. Perhaps the critical difference between this new generation of queer people and those who came before them, however, is that queer people post-1920 found one another in dense enough numbers that their stories have been preserved not just by doctors or court transcripts, but by their own words as shared with other queer people. The private lesbian theater circles of Ada Dwyer and Johnstone Bennett, the transgender networks of Othilie Spengler and Loop-the-Loop, and the small-time saloons run by Antonio Bellavicini and Robert Bonner were the precursors to a more robust and self-organized queer world that would grow in the 1920s and 1930s.

Brooklyn was also changing. From 1900 to 1920, the borough nearly doubled in size, until it was home to more than two million people. Although the original waterfront—the downtown area nearest Manhattan—would remain important, the booming population meant that other areas of Brooklyn were developing the kind of urban density that allowed queer life to flourish. Moreover, during the 1910s, the New York City subway finally penetrated Brooklyn in a meaningful way. Previously, the borough's mass transit had been a patchwork of trolley cars, elevated trains, horse-drawn omnibuses, ferries, and sloops. Starting with the Brooklyn Loop Lines (which opened in 1913), subway cars were sent over the bridges and into downtown Brooklyn for the first time.

These initial lines made the Brooklyn waterfront *more* attractive to potential residents and businesses, by making them less remote. A number of artists would leave Greenwich Village for Brooklyn Heights in the 1920s, cementing its reputation as Brooklyn's bohemian enclave. However, the subway also contained within it the seeds of the waterfront's downturn. In the latter half of the 1910s, new subways would be built to connect these first Loop Lines to other areas of Brooklyn, as well as to Queens and Manhattan. This was a conscious attempt to reorganize the city's population and reduce the density of areas such as lower Manhattan and downtown Brooklyn. Within a decade of the first subway's coming to Brooklyn, seven more lines crossing the East River would begin operation. Laborers who once needed to live near the water to be near work could now easily move into farther-flung parts of the city.

All of New York was suddenly vastly more connected than it had ever been. Thanks to the subway, in the coming decades, a queer Brooklynite would be able to loaf about at a bathhouse on Coney Island, get a drink at a saloon in Greenwich Village, stop by a rent party in Harlem, and then cruise for sailors at the Brooklyn Navy Yard, before easily returning to his apartment in Brooklyn Heights. Prior to this, all commuters had to stop at the edge of the East River and switch from one mode of conveyance to another, but the subway allowed for one continuous ride. Soon, people would not only not need to live near the waterfront, they would no longer have to stop there at all.

However, the subway didn't just connect preexisting queer spaces; it also created them. The subways accidentally provided a vast network of sexual hot spots for queer men, in their public bathrooms. If subway cars were like packed clubs, tossing New Yorkers against one another millions of times a day, then the men's room was decidedly the after party. The subways are a perfect metaphor for queer life in the Roaring Twenties: new, exciting, fast, vast, and growing.

4. A Growing World, 1920–30

The skies over southern Brooklyn were overcast on Saturday, May 1, 1920, which put a damper on the massive crowds that were expected at Coney Island that day. Still, a new era dawned that morning at "the people's playground." Nothing had changed on the island itself: the two huge amusement parks, Luna and Steeple-chase, still stood like siren sisters luring city residents to the ocean; the miles of beach still offered what felt like unlimited outdoor space to those who dwelled in New York's cramped tenement apartments; and the hundreds of saloons, bath-houses, hotels, tattoo parlors, music halls, dime museums, and other attractions still served hedonism in as many flavors as the mind could dream up.

But something more profound and less visible had changed, transforming Coney Island overnight into "the Nickel Empire." After protracted wrangling be-tween various companies and city agencies, the price of a subway ride to Coney Island was finally lowered from ten cents to five, the same amount it cost to go to any other station in the rapidly expanding subway system. *The Brooklyn Daily Eagle* crowed that a new "epoch in the history of transit in Brooklyn was starting."[1] By the end of June, the *Eagle* would announce that some 350,000 New Yorkers had visited Coney Island on one particularly nice Saturday.[2] In August, 450,000 would arrive in one day.[3] And the numbers kept climbing; at particularly busy times over the next few years, "as many as a million people poured in during a single day," meaning that about a third of the city's entire population could be found somewhere on Coney Island's meager 442 acres.[4] By the end of the decade, Clark Kinnaird would use his nationally syndicated Diary of a New Yorker col-umn to bash Coney Island for its overcrowding, writing, "It isn't news unless half a million pack into the series of amusement parks which comprise 'Coney,' and at least 50 children are lost."[5]

The nickel fare accelerated both growth and change at Coney Island. Originally it was a distant seaside excursion spot for the city's elite, but as Brooklyn became more navigable in the late 1800s, New Yorkers of all classes rushed to enjoy its salt breezes and sandy beaches. However, much as in downtown Brooklyn, the first working- and middle-class venues, such as the joints where Florence Hines performed, primarily served white men. Coney wouldn't be a beacon for all New Yorkers until the very end of the nineteenth century. In 1897, George Tilyou opened Steeplechase Park, the first of the island's iconic amusement parks. Luna Park was built next, in 1903, and Dreamland appeared in 1904 (only to disappear in a tragic fire in 1911). These parks featured exciting new automated technology, vast rainbows of electric lights, roller coasters, tunnels of love, a profusion of new foods, and, perhaps most important, a social opportunity that men and women could enjoy together. The parks consciously catered to middle- and working-class consumers, marketing themselves as "family-friendly" areas where people of all classes, ethnicities, and races could mix, while not being far removed from the "freer sexual expression of the dance halls, beaches, and boardwalk."[6] In

Portrait of dancer Mabel Hampton (c.1920). (*Photo courtesy of the Lesbian Herstory Educational Foundation, Mabel Hampton Collection.*)

1919, the construction of the West End Terminal—a massive train depot capable of handling the hundreds of thousands of passengers from the four subway lines that began serving Coney Island in the 1910s—set the stage for Coney's busiest era, which coincided neatly with the Roaring Twenties. World War I was over, and Americans were ready to celebrate. Coney Island, where cheap pleasures reigned supreme, was the place to do so.

On May 2, 1920—one day after the new fare was inaugurated—Mabel Hampton turned seventeen. Hampton was petite, pretty, and originally from

North Carolina. Shortly after she was born, her mother died under suspicious circumstances, and Hampton was raised by her grandmother. When she died in 1910, the then seven-year-old Hampton was sent north to live with an aunt and uncle in Manhattan, where she would become an entertainer and fixture in the burgeoning queer scenes developing in Harlem, Greenwich Village, and Coney Island. In many ways, her experiences are emblematic of the best parts of the Roaring Twenties, at least in regard to queer life in New York City.

Hampton was an early part of a nationwide demographic shift called the Great Migration. After Reconstruction, Southern black communities saw most of the meager power they had gained post–Civil War destroyed by the imposition of Jim Crow laws. In response, many headed North and West looking for better jobs and living conditions. According to Kevin Mumford, author of *Interzones: Black/White Sex Districts in Chicago and New York in the Early Twentieth Century,* "between 1910 and 1920 the black population of New York increased by 66 percent, and from 1920 to 1930 it expanded by 115 percent, from roughly 153,000 to more than 327,000 black residents."[7] From this point on, the black population in New York City would increase steadily, giving rise to the Harlem Renaissance and the image of the New Negro: empowered, educated, and dedicated to the black community. At the start of the 1920s, Brooklyn's population was still more than 98 percent white, and it would remain significantly whiter than Manhattan until the 1970s. However, the changing racial and ethnic composition of the city as a whole meant that vastly more people of color were now traveling through Brooklyn regularly—many of them, like Mabel Hampton, on their way to Coney Island.

Like many migrant girls, Hampton had a difficult time upon first arriving in New York. Her aunt and uncle were poor, and her uncle sexually and physically abused Hampton repeatedly. Not long after she arrived, at the age of eight, Hampton ran away. Not knowing where to go, she let the flow of the crowds in Greenwich Village lead her to the subway, which she'd never before seen. A friendly older woman, mistaking her for the daughter of an acquaintance, gave Hampton a nickel and told her to go home to Harlem, which was just becoming the fast-beating heart of the city's black community. Hampton got on the first train that came and eventually found herself across the Hudson River in Jersey City, where she was taken in by a working-class black family in a mixed neighborhood. Hampton feigned ignorance of everything—where she was from, her last name, where her aunt and uncle could be found—and eventually this new family adopted her.

She would stay in Jersey City with them until right around 1920, when she would begin doing domestic work for Manhattan families.

Seventeen, making her own money, and living on and off in Harlem, before long Hampton found her way to Coney Island, which changed her life forever. As she recalled many years later while being interviewed by Joan Nestle and Deb Edel, the founders of the Lesbian Herstory Archives:

> *The making of me? It's that one woman in Coney Island. I can't right now recall her name, but she is the beginning of me being a lesbian. I was no more than about seventeen, eighteen years old. I fell in love with her. I didn't know I fell in love, but I did.*[8]

The hours of taped interviews between Hampton, Nestle, and Edel are an unparalleled archive of information about queer women in early-twentieth-century New York. Nestle and Edel began recording Hampton in the late seventies and continued almost up until her death in 1989. The resulting tapes contain a unique, wide-ranging, and occasionally contradictory wealth of information for historians interested in black lesbian life. While Hampton's experiences cannot stand in for all black queer women in New York City, the wide-ranging world she describes hints at the multiplicity of lives these women made for themselves (and with one another).

The first time she visited Coney, Hampton was living in a three-room basement apartment in Harlem with a friend named Mildred Mitchell and her mother, Miss Mitchell. Mildred was a dancer, and she had the idea that the two should get work performing in a sideshow. Miss Mitchell, eager to keep an eye on the two young girls, joined the show as a cook. The troupe consisted of between six and fifteen other black women who wore "velvet suits," did choreographed dance routines, and sang popular songs of the day. Hampton recalled that she sang the 1922 hit song "My Buddy." In photographs, the troupe is pictured rehearsing on the beach in front of Henderson's Music Hall, an elegant and storied Coney Island venue that was then on its last legs. It's possible they performed there, as its stage was home to many cabarets and concerts, but Hampton never specified a venue, saying only that she danced "in the sideshow."

The troupe must have performed during the day; Hampton recalled that they ate breakfast together, and that most nights she took the subway home around

6:00 p.m. One evening during their supper, she noticed a "tall, light-brown-skinned woman . . . [who] had to have been in her thirties."[9] The woman was visiting with a group of Mildred's friends from "somewhere West." Throughout dinner, the two made eyes at each other, although Hampton looked away every time she realized the woman knew she was watching. Hampton had fooled around with other women before, mostly friends with whom she was living, but this was different. "Her look shot through me like electricity," Hampton later told Joan Nestle.

Over breakfast the next morning, the eye games continued—so much so that Miss Mitchell even noticed. "I tried to keep my eyes off her, but she was like a magnet," Hampton recalled. After breakfast, the woman intercepted Hampton and invited her to go on a walk when rehearsal was over.

Once they were alone, the woman wasted no time. "When I look at you, it thrills you, don't it?"

Hampton blushed and stammered, "Yes, I think so."

"That's all right," the woman said kindly. "You can't help with that. But I have to go so I don't ruin your life. . . . I'm a lesbian, and I'm married."

That was the moment, Hampton says, when she learned the word *lesbian*. "I said to myself, 'Well, if that's what it is, I'm already in it!'" Never one to be easily dissuaded, Hampton convinced the woman that while she might be young, she knew what she wanted. So she asked Miss Mitchell, Mildred's mother, if she could spend the night with her new acquaintance.

Miss Mitchell looked appraisingly at the woman. "She knew exactly what it was," Hampton told Nestle years later. In part, Hampton suspected this was because Miss Mitchell *also* knew that Hampton and Mildred occasionally fooled around. Miss Mitchell made the woman swear that she wouldn't "mess up Mabel," then gave the pair her blessing.[10]

Of her one night with this mysterious older woman, Hampton would say only, "She taught me quite a few things. I knew some of them, but she taught me the rest."[11] The next morning, the woman announced over breakfast that she had to return home. Already, she seemed worried that she had broken her promise to Miss Mitchell, that she had inculcated something in Hampton that would ruin her. But Hampton is clear on the tapes that the woman only helped her to name and understand feelings she already had.

Over the twentieth century, "coming out" to an older, wiser queer person would become one of the defining experiences of being queer. The phrase *coming out* is derived from debutante culture, and it once referred exclusively to being brought out into gay society (as opposed to our modern usage, which is more about proclaiming your sexual identity to the straight world). But Hampton's generation is the first group for whom this experience was widely possible. For the first time, queer people such as Hampton had an avuncular older generation to educate them, and a younger generation to preserve and pass on their stories. This represents a new stage in queer history. First, individual queer people kept their own stories, often privately or in code. Then, the larger straight world began to write about queer lives, often pejoratively and in limited venues that presented them as anomalies to be studied. Now, a wider community of queer people were beginning to share their experiences with one another and preserve them for future generations. This changed not just the quantity of available information, but the quality, enabling historians to get a closer, more personal understanding of what it meant to be queer in these times.

Hampton met many other queer women, black and white, married and single, while she worked at Coney Island. Once, a married black woman took Hampton home in the middle of the day, only to have her husband arrive unexpectedly. Hampton was forced to hide under the bed while he peppered his wife with questions as to why she was home—and naked—in the middle of the afternoon. Eventually, when the pair went downstairs to make lunch, Hampton grabbed her clothes and sneaked out through a side door.

Slowly, Hampton settled into the role of *stud,* a popular term among queer black women that was analogous to being the butch in a butch-femme couple. "You had to be very careful," she recalled. "In those years you had fun behind closed doors, but you'd go like you were going to work." She and other studs would bring suitcases to parties so they could change into trousers when they arrived—it would have been too dangerous, Hampton said, to dress that way on the streets. Although many women did not identify as either a butch or a femme, and some moved between the two roles throughout their lives, the butch-femme paradigm in lesbian relationships would become dominant in the years leading up to World War II.

Yet despite the need for subterfuge, Hampton was tapped into a large lesbian network. "I had so many different girlfriends it wasn't funny," she told Nestle and Edel. Throughout the Roaring Twenties and into the early thirties, Hampton said,

"You'd go out, have a ball, spend the night somewhere, and have another ball." Her circle of friends was almost exclusively lesbian and bisexual women, though she occasionally befriended queer men at parties. Much as Walt Whitman serves as an indicator of the existence of queer white working-class men in Brooklyn in the mid-1800s, Hampton's oral history suggests large, parallel networks of white and black queer women, which sometimes overlapped. Her queer life was expansive, happening all around New York and even out in Jersey City, but the three main centers of action were Harlem, Greenwich Village, and Coney Island. While most of the black lesbians Hampton knew had at-home parties (often called buffet flats) up in Harlem, the white women were more likely to go to bars or clubs—often down in Greenwich Village—that were lesbian owned or lesbian friendly. "White folks can get into places where you can't," Hampton told Nestle during her interviews. "They'd take me to nice clubs and I'd meet all the women I wanted to meet."[12]

In Harlem, Hampton was quickly immersed in the world of A'Lelia Walker, the glamorous patron of many of the queer voices of the Harlem Renaissance, whom Langston Hughes dubbed "the joy goddess of Harlem."[13] Walker was the daughter of Madam C. J. Walker, who was born in Louisiana in 1867, just after the end of the Civil War. The first freeborn child in a formerly enslaved family, Madam Walker founded an incredible business empire selling hair and skin products for black women. By the early 1900s, she was the richest black woman in America. Her daughter, A'Lelia, was her only heir, and while never the business genius that her mother was, A'Lelia was the recognized queen of Harlem's bohemian scene. Over six feet tall and strikingly handsome, A'Lelia often strode the streets of Sugar Hill carrying a riding crop and wearing a bejeweled turban.[14] She named her home on West 136th Street the Dark Tower, after the poem of the same name by Countee Cullen, a queer black poet to whom Walker served as a patron. Her parties were epic, as likely to include visiting Scandinavian royalty as they were a bootlegger from Vinegar Hill. The first time Mabel Hampton went, she was ushered through a warren of rooms by a butler, who instructed her to remove her gray sheath dress and short white fur coat, before bringing her and her girlfriend to a sumptuous ballroom filled with pillows, low tables bearing fruit and wine, and dozens of nude or nearly nude partygoers. As Hampton described the night to Joan Nestle and Deb Edel:

There was men and women, women and women, and men and men. And they were
all on the pillows and [if] they wanted to do anything, they go ahead and do it.
Then—now, you'd call it dope, but I didn't realize what it was then. . . . So we
had a lovely time. Stayed all night. Until three or four the next day. And everyone
did whatever they wanted to do. Some of them did one thing and some of them did
the other thing. Nobody paid anybody else any attention. . . . There was girls
there with no clothes on. They served me with food. It was marvelous.[15]

On other nights, Hampton socialized in the burgeoning (white) queer public
scene miles to the south of Harlem, in Greenwich Village. The first official spot
run by and for queer women in New York City was Eve Addams' Tea Room, which
opened in 1925 on MacDougal Street. A sign on the front door read MEN ARE
ADMITTED, BUT NOT WELCOME. It lasted only a year before its owner, Polish immigrant Eva Kotchever, was arrested for obscenity and keeping a disorderly house
and eventually deported. But other spots catering to queer women would appear
in the late twenties and thirties, many of them literally in the shadows—beneath
the elevated trains, which ran through lower Manhattan. Gay bars catering to
men also appeared around the same time, some up by Times Square, while others were also downtown under the elevated trains. At the same time that the
nickel fare was inaugurated, Prohibition was enacted, with profound although
unexpected long-term effects on gay bars. By making all bars illegal, and all bar
patrons criminals, it leveled the playing field between queer and straight venues.
For the same reason, Prohibition also helped normalize the presence of women
in most drinking establishments. The criminalization of the recreational choices
of straight white men—which made their establishments just as subject to raids
as those that catered to queers or sex workers—helped queer and queer-friendly
venues proliferate throughout New York City in the late 1920s and early 1930s.
The enacting of Prohibition also cut the legs out from groups such as the Committee of Fourteen, in two ways: because they had "succeeded" in outlawing alcohol, they found it harder to raise money for their work, and because public
saloons had transformed into hidden speakeasies, that work had become all the
harder to do.

Later in the twenties, Hampton left Coney behind for bigger, better-known
stages. She performed at such venerable institutions as the Garden of Joy and the

Lafayette Theater, which were central to the booming black art scene at the heart of the Harlem Renaissance. She befriended some of the crème de la crème of the city's queer black society, including comedian Jackie "Moms" Mabley, entertainer Gladys Bentley, and the singer Ethel Waters and her girlfriend, dancer Ethel Williams. Although Hampton never lived in Brooklyn, her life shows the intimate connections that existed between queer worlds in different parts of the city. The subway that made Coney Island more accessible also made the entire city smaller, closer, and more interconnected. Harlem, just as much as Coney Island, would be transformed by it. The combination of a growing black population and available, easy transportation turned Harlem into both the biggest black neighborhood *and* the hottest nightlife destination in the city. According to Kevin Mumford, "Before the late 1910s Harlem was neither a popular nightspot nor a common destination of tourism; even among New Yorkers it was not notable in the ways that Times Square or Broadway had become."[16] Over the 1920s, however, it would become known for its drag balls, jazz clubs, and speakeasies. Many venues catered to black New Yorkers; others, to rich white New Yorkers who were interested in "slumming"; and a few provided legitimately mixed space where black and white patrons mingled. Although Coney Island helped Hampton start her life as both a lesbian and a performer, she would spend most of her time in Harlem.

Life in the theater wasn't all parties and sunshine. Hampton didn't love dancing, she says on the tapes; it was simply a job that was available to her as a young black woman with an eighth-grade education. Most of the other queer women she knew worked either in factories or in show business. The money was never great, and sexual abuse at the hands of club owners and patrons was common. "Every place I worked," Hampton told Nestle, "some man would feel my pussy and I'd have to leave that job."[17]

In 1924, a few years after she started dancing at Coney Island, Hampton was arrested in a "setup" for prostitution and sent to the Bedford Hills Reformatory for Women—the same institution where Elizabeth Trondle had been sent a few years earlier. This was a not-uncommon experience for black women in New York City. Not only were they prejudged as more criminal and sexual than their white counterparts, but their higher rates of employment and the greater gender imbalance in the black population also meant that they were more likely to be out on the streets unaccompanied by men. To groups such as the police and the Committee of Fourteen, those facts alone were enough to arrest a woman for prostitution. As historian LaShawn Harris wrote in her book, *Sex Workers, Psychics, and Numbers Runners: Black Women in New York City's Underground Economy,* "Whether strolling city streets with friends, visiting a relative's apartment, renting rooms to boarders, or operating legitimate businesses, black women faced police harassment and were arrested and convicted for a number of crimes, including possession of numbers slips, loitering and vagrancy, and prostitution."[18] Black lesbians, who were even less likely to be accompanied by men than black straight women, were at even greater danger for this kind of police abuse.

According to Hampton, she and her friend Viola met a man at a cabaret who bought them a soda and offered to treat them to a night out. Most likely, he was a police informant; when he arrived to pick them up at the apartment in Harlem where Hampton was working as a live-in domestic, the police were right behind him. From the very beginning, even in her statements to the social workers at Bedford Hills, Hampton maintained that she was framed. Thanks to the low legal bar in prostitution cases (established by the Committee of Fourteen), Hampton was convicted on thin evidence and sentenced to three years in Bedford Hills. The magistrate in her case, Judge Jean Norris, was the first female magistrate in New York City history, and she was known to judge both prostitution cases, and cases involving black women, harshly. In over five thousand cases, and especially in prostitution-related arrests of black women, Norris handed down 40 percent more convictions than other magistrates.[19] Eventually, she would be removed from office for her prejudicial rulings. However, the discrimination black women faced in the legal system in New York went far beyond one bad apple. According to Cheryl Hicks, author of *Talk with You Like a Woman: African American Women, Justice, and Reform in New York, 1890–1935,* compared to convicted white women, black women were less likely to receive probation, were accepted by fewer of the charity homes that took in troubled women, and were—like Mabel Hampton—more likely to be sent straight to Bedford Hills on their first arrest.

Both New York City and the country as a whole were becoming much more interconnected, meaning that more black women, such as Mabel Hampton, were in the city, spending all or part of their days outside of predominantly black neighborhoods—a vulnerable and precarious situation that made them easy targets for the police. White reform organizations such as the Committee of Fourteen were unperturbed by the disproportionate arrests and convictions of black women. In discussing prostitution arrests in an internal bulletin dated June 5,

1922, the committee wrote, "The high proportion of convictions of negroes was not unanticipated . . . [and] the proportion of negro defendants, is . . . four times the proper proportion."[20] No efforts to investigate or change these statistics were suggested or pursued, leaving black women with few sources of support inside the criminal justice system. Black women's reform organizations, such as the White Rose Mission in Harlem (where Alice Dunbar Nelson had volunteered in the 1890s), offered some assistance, but lacked the funding to help the many young black women who needed their services. Moreover, many of these organizations worked under a theory of racial uplift and judged working-class and criminally involved black women harshly. Some saw these women as holding back the entire race, while others took a paternalistic view that reduced poor black women to near children who could not be trusted to make good life choices. A black lesbian dancer, arrested for prostitution, did not make an obvious candidate for their help.

While queer black women were thus often at the mercy of a justiceless justice system, they also found ways to use that system to their benefit. Hampton was adept at marshaling the resources available to her through Bedford Hills. Her case files show that she quickly befriended both residents and staff and was considered a model inmate. After being released early on a work program, she voluntarily returned to Bedford because the conditions she was working under were exploitative and the family was impossible to please. A few months later, in 1927, Hampton was released from Bedford for good. However, she still found ways to use her connection to Bedford to her advantage. When a white family refused to pay her an appropriate wage, she got the staff of Bedford Hills to intercede on her behalf and demand a raise.

Although she was somewhat loath to discuss it on tape, Hampton had sexual relationships with several other residents during her time at Bedford. The staff were well aware that some of the girls in their care were romantically and sexually entangled; they worried mostly about young white women pursuing young black women. This relatively open approach to same-sex sexuality was most likely due to the first director of the institution, a lesbian reformer and sex researcher named Katharine Bement Davis. In 1929, Davis would publish a remarkable study on the sex lives of women. Out of 1,200 college-educated participants, Davis found that 605 had "intense emotional relations" with other women. For 234 of those women, the relationship included mutual masturbation or "other physical expressions recognized as sexual." For an additional 78, those relationships were not physical, but the women in them recognized them "as sexual in character" while they were happening.[21] Put more plainly, over a quarter of the women Davis interviewed admitted to having relationships with other women that were sexual in nature, if not always in deed. Although Davis left Bedford before Hampton arrived, her modern attitude toward sexuality permeated the administrative culture, creating a surprisingly open space for exploring lesbian desire.

After leaving Bedford for good in 1927, Hampton mostly stopped performing. That year, she sang "My Buddy" in the funeral procession for Florence Mills, the black cabaret star known as the Queen of Happiness. But within a few years, she began primarily relying on domestic work for her income and would for the rest of her life. Even after she stopped performing, however, Coney Island remained a popular destination with Hampton and her circle of queer women. "We'd hang out, go out on the beach . . . under the boardwalk, we'd have a ball!"[22] In 1932, she met the love of her life, Lillian Foster, and they remained together until Lillian's death in 1978. We know all of this thanks to Hampton's constant cultivation of a circle of queer women, and thus it's no surprise that she was an integral part of the founding of the Lesbian Herstory Archives in 1974. A decade later, in 1984, Hampton addressed the crowds at New York City's LGBT Pride Parade to say:

> I, Mabel Hampton, have been a lesbian all my life, for eighty-two years, and I am proud of myself and my people. I would like all my people to be free in this country and all over the world, my gay people and my black people.[23]

The next year, at the age of eighty-three, Mabel Hampton's decades of organizing were recognized when she was named grand marshal of the New York City Pride Parade. Four years later, while living with Joan Nestle, she died of pneumonia. Her papers and effects are preserved at the Lesbian Herstory Archives in Park Slope, Brooklyn.

Hampton's experience shows how Coney Island's sexually charged atmosphere allowed for the exploration of queer desires. But one aspect of Coney was queer by design: the freak shows, where gender-nonconforming and intersex people were both celebrated and exploited. Bearded women were among the most common of these performers, but other acts also explicitly played with gender, such as "half-and-halfs," who were said to be half-man, half-woman, and "animal girls" or "missing links," which is what bearded women of color were called. According to Ward Hall, a gay man who got his start in the circus in the early 1940s, these acts were sometimes performed by people who were actually intersex, but they were also done by effeminate men and masculine women whose gender presentations were already so at odds with what the audience expected that they believed them to be physically intersex as well.

By at least the late 1800s, bearded women were performing at Coney Island. Madame Myers, known as the "queen of the bearded ladies," toured the United States with a number of different sideshows between 1870 and 1910, and Coney Island was one of her regular stops. She would have been but one of the many acts, including Ella Wesner and Florence Hines, who were making a living by exposing Americans to the wide world of gender variance. According to an article written in 1879, Myers was "a handsome girl" of twenty-five, whose beard began to grow after the birth of her first child, when she was seventeen.[24] Her contemporaries, who also performed on and off at Coney, included Annie Jones, Miss Leo Hernandez (aka the Spanish Bearded Lady), and Madame Lyons.

Unfortunately, little is known about most of these women. Many changed their names when they joined the circus, then changed them again when their routine had grown stale and they wanted to reinvent themselves. Little of their personal lives was ever documented, and what information does exist usually comes from their professional biographies, which were designed to titillate audiences and are highly suspect. Jean Carroll, for example, made her life in the sideshow by selling a pamphlet entitled "How I Became the Tattoo Queen," which explained that she had once been the bearded woman at Coney Island, but had shaved for the love of a man who would not marry her otherwise. In love with the circus—and having no other way to support herself—Carroll became the tattooed woman, a role she would perform on and off at Coney Island up until the 1960s. However, while there is ample evidence that Carroll worked as a tattooed woman, there's no evidence that she ever had a beard.[25] Tattooed women were considered so strange and unfeminine that they usually invented these kinds of elaborate backstories to entertain their audiences and explain their origins.

One Coney Island bearded woman whose life was relatively well documented, however, was Lady Olga Roderick—aka Jane Barnell, from Wilmington, North

Coney Island bearded lady Jane
Barnell and husband, date unknown.
*(Photo courtesy of the collection of David
Denholtz.)*

Carolina. Her story shows the complicated life of
exploitation and empowerment that many *freaks*
(her preferred word) experienced in the sideshow. Born in 1871, Barnell said that she began
growing a beard at the age of two and was sold to
the circus by her mother at the age of four. A year
later, she was rescued by her father and returned
to North Carolina to live with her grandmother,
who was Catawban (a small part of the much-
larger Sioux Nation). At age twenty-one, she returned to circus work, launching a spectacular
career that spanned some six decades.

According to Edo McCullough, author of
Good Old Coney Island, Barnell was "the most celebrated" and "widely traveled" bearded woman
of her day. Barnell had many names and backstories in her career, but her favorite way to be
introduced was:

*It gives me great pleasure at this time to introduce a little woman who comes to us
from an aristocratic plantation in the Old South and who is recognized by the
finest doctors, physicians, and medical men as the foremost unquestioned and
authentic female Bearded Lady in medical history. Ladies and gentlemen, Lady
Olga!*[26]

McCullough places Barnell at Coney Island starting in the 1930s, but she was
actually performing there at least as early as 1926, the year Zip the Pinhead died.
Zip was one of the most famous sideshow performers of all time, and accounts of
his death and burial include Lady Olga among the other performers with him at
Coney Island.[27]

How do we know so much about Barnell? In 1932, Barnell was cast in the cult
horror film *Freaks,* which made her a national sensation. Newspapers around the
country reported on her beauty tips for women with beards, which included "never
use too hot a curling iron," "wash the beard in warm milk once a week," and "avoid
eating Chinese noodles."[28] Almost a decade later, in 1940, Barnell would again

capture the public's interest, when writer Joseph Mitchell profiled her for *The New Yorker.*

According to Mitchell, Barnell liked working at Coney Island a little better than she did most places because "that salt air is good for her asthma" and "she has a high regard for the buttered roasting ear corn that is sold in stands down there."[29] As with most coverage of bearded women, Mitchell made a big deal of Barnell's four marriages. Reporters and managers often went to great pains to establish the heterosexuality and femininity of bearded women, as a way to contain their gender nonconformity and render them less threatening or "queer." However, Barnell herself seemed to have no interest in letting viewers into her personal life. Mitchell describes Barnell's usual turn on the sideshow platform thusly:

> *Miss Barnell is rather austere. To discourage people from getting familiar, she never smiles. She dresses conservatively, usually wearing a plain black evening gown. "I like nice clothes, but there's no use wasting money," she says. "People don't notice anything but my old beard." She despises pity and avoids looking into the eyes of the people in her audiences; like most freaks, she has cultivated a blank, unseeing stare. When people look as if they feel sorry for her, especially women, it makes her want to throw something. She does not sell photographs of herself as many sideshow performers do and does not welcome questions from spectators. She will answer specific questions about her beard as graciously as possible, but when someone becomes inquisitive about her private life—"You ever been married?" is the most frequent query—she gives the questioner an icy look or says quietly, "None of your business."*

Barnell preferred the company of other freaks and lived with them whenever possible, either on the road or in special boardinghouses where they all congregated. She saw herself and was treated as one of the "aristocrats of the sideshow world," because of her beard. As she explained to Mitchell, the economy of the sideshow was divided into three tiers. At the lowest level were novelty acts—reformed criminals, once-famous sports figures, war heroes, etc. Young Griffo, the boxer, became one late in life. These acts were only profitable for as long as the public remembered who they were. In the middle rung were "made freaks," such as tattooed women, sword swallowers, or geeks who bit the heads off live animals. These performers had to have some level of skill or uniqueness, but they were still replaceable. The pinnacle of the sideshow were the "born freaks," people whose unique bodies titillated audiences and could not be re-created: rubber boys, alligator girls, conjoined twins, bearded women, etc. Their acts were often exploitative, and some—such as Barnell herself—were forced into circus work, but within the sideshow, they were treated like the royalty they often claimed to be.

Barnell started her career as Princess Olga, a name that suggested both royal and foreign lineage. At various times, her barkers claimed that she was born in Budapest, Paris, Moscow, and Shanghai. This was an easy way to add mystique to a show, and many sideshow performers similarly embellished their biographies. Foreign parentage was a useful story because it not only made them more interesting, it also reassured good American audiences that they were biologically and culturally superior. When Coney Island sideshow impresario Samuel Gumpertz was asked why so many freaks came from outside the United States, he gave an explicitly eugenic answer: "The probable explanation is that the marriage laws are not as rigid as in the Western countries. There, very near relatives are frequently permitted to marry, and as a result deformities and shrunken bodies and freaks in human makeups occur."[30]

In truth, most performers were American, and a good portion of those who were foreign-born were either survivors of human trafficking or were otherwise forced into performing. Around 1881, the performer Krao, for example, was taken from her home in Siam (now Laos) at the age of four by Guillermo Antonio Farini, who would adopt her and be her manager until the early 1900s. In different versions of the story, Farini kidnapped her, or rescued her from kidnappers, or was given her by the king of Siam. Regardless, it seems unlikely that her start on the stage was consensual. Krao spent decades being exhibited as (and eventually, exhibiting herself as) "the Missing Link." Women of color with hypertrichosis (the technical term for "excess" hair) were never exhibited as bearded women. Instead, like Krao, they performed as missing links or animal girls. White women with beards could still qualify as women—especially if they talked about their marriages, dressed in a conventionally feminine way, and exhibited proper womanly decorum (at least onstage). But for women of color, who were already considered masculine, unattractive, and animalistic, having a beard pushed them outside the category of human entirely.

There is no evidence that Barnell saw herself as connected to any kind of larger community of people who transgressed gender, although her preference for living with sideshow performers probably stems from the same forces that drew other kinds of queer people together. But the public presence of bearded women, half-and-halfs, and other sideshow acts that played with gender contributed to a generally queer atmosphere at Coney Island. Like Ella Wesner and Florence Hines before her, Barnell's stage presence constituted a public acknowledgment of queerness that was relatively nonthreatening to most Americans.

In 1926, James Monaco cowrote a song about such gender transgressors, possibly inspired by his time as a piano player on Coney Island. Called "Masculine Women! Feminine Men!," the song's gently ribbing tone suggested that playing with gender was strange, but also part of modern life. Its lyrics begin:

Hey hey women are going mad, today
Hey hey fellers are just as bad, I'll say
Go anywhere, just stand and stare
You'll say they're bugs when you
look at the clothes they wear
Masculine Women Feminine Men
which is the rooster which is the hen
It's hard to tell 'em apart today

The song goes on to catalog gender transgressions among family members, girlfriends, and even royalty, turning queerness from a scary part of modern life into a strange, funny, but ultimately relatable way of being—much as getting to know the freaks at Coney Island would surely have. Additionally, in the 1920s, an androgynous look for women was popularized by flappers, who bobbed their hair and cultivated "masculine" habits such as smoking and driving. With the passage of the Nineteenth Amendment in 1920—giving women the right to vote—many believed that the last vestiges of separation between the sexes would finally collapse entirely. No wonder "Masculine Women! Feminine Men!" would be a minor success in the latter part of the decade, getting recorded by multiple artists.

Feminine men—and gay men in general—already had a definite place at Coney Island. By at least 1910, female impersonators were the main attraction at some saloons at Coney, which we know because a young Jimmy Durante got his start in one called Diamond Tony's. As Durante described it, "At our place and Jack's [another Coney Island saloon], the entertainers were all boys who danced together and lisped. They called themselves Edna May and Leslie Carter and Big Tess and things like that."[31] However, Durante makes clear that while gay men were on the stage, they were not in the audience. Like many clubs that featured drag acts in the early part of the twentieth century, Diamond Tony's was a straight bar. "Outside of the queer entertainers, our place was no different from most of the others," Durante wrote. "The usual number of girls hung out there, and the customers were mostly on the level; that is to say, they were not interested in our entertainers any more than they would have been in the freaks that filled the Surf Avenue sidewalks."

However, by the 1920s, at least one kind of establishment at Coney attracted large queer male crowds: the public bathhouses, which became increasingly popular once the subway reached the beach.

New York City's oldest bathhouses date back to the 1850s. These grand institutions were privately run, located in Manhattan, mostly catered to the upper and middle classes, and functioned as social clubs as well as bathing pavilions. In the 1890s a push began to create city-run, municipal public baths that were free or low cost, to promote bathing in working-class districts, where private bathrooms were still rare. Reformers also worked to popularize the idea of bathing as essential to physical and moral health. By the early 1910s, Brooklyn had seven such bathhouses, mostly clustered around the working waterfront that bordered the East River.[32]

The bathhouses at Coney Island were something of a hybrid of these two kinds of institutions. They were privately run, but catered mostly to the working class. They served both social and hygienic roles. One of their primary functions was to rent bathing suits to city residents. Not only did few people own a bathing suit, but up until the late 1930s wearing bathing suits on city streets was prohibited, meaning you had to change somewhere at Coney. According to Michael Immerso's Coney Island: The People's Playground, by 1930,

> there were more than thirty bathing establishments to select from. Large bathhouses such as Steeplechase Baths, Ward's, and Washington Baths charged about fifty cents for a locker and provided amenities such as a pool, handball court, punching bags, and a sunbathing deck. Raven Hall, one of the oldest, had a

picnic grove and dance pavilion. Silver's Bath and Stauch's were known for their
steam baths, which were popular with Russian and Jewish patrons. Less prestigious
establishments with fewer amenities charged as little as fifteen cents. Bathhouses
were one more link to the city's poorer neighborhoods, where public baths were
familiar institutions. Community solidarity was transferred to many of Coney
Island's bathing establishments, which gained a loyal following among a particu-
lar neighborhood group. [33]

Like the rest of Coney, these bathhouses had their heyday in the 1920s. Although most served men, women, and families, a decidedly masculine culture
grew up around some of these facilities. Certain bathhouses, such as Stauch's and
the Washington Baths, would become particularly popular with gay men.

The Washington Baths was one of the swankier places on the island, located
on the beach at Twenty-first Street, on the western side of Coney. The giant two-
story edifice was built around a central pool, like a hidden courtyard, accessed
through a series of arches on the boardwalk. One block away, the baths had an
annex with a saltwater pool, a bright pink stucco building with three-foot me-
dallions featuring the head of King Neptune repeated along the walls. By at least
1929, the Washington Baths had a dedicated gay clientele, as the owners discovered to their chagrin on a balmy afternoon in the second week of August. As a
publicity stunt, they had organized a male beauty contest, which was to be judged
by singer Rudy Vallee, film star Carroll Nye, and Broadway actress Beryl Halley.
Over twenty-five men competed, and a large crowd turned out to watch. Perhaps tipped off as to what was about to unfold, Vallee skipped the engagement at
the last minute and sent his sister, Sobbie, to judge instead. Organizers realized
the event was not going to be what they expected when the audience turned
out to be mostly men. Soon, effeminate male contestants began "tripping across
the front of the platform," parading past the scandalized judges. The publicity
manager for the event cautioned the judges not to vote for a contestant with
"paint and powder on." The manager had already instructed four contestants to
take all their makeup off, but it was no use; almost all of the beauty kings were
gay, and no amount of scrubbing their faces could hide it. *Variety* magazine reported that the most difficult part of the competition became "picking a male beaut
who wasn't a floozie."[34] The word "floozie" once again connected effeminate men
to brassy, sexually forward women, much as they were in Jennie June's day.

Interestingly enough, the women in the audience—described as "Coney Island dowagers"—seemed to have no problem with the gay male contestants, including the one who participated in full drag and the "pretty guy who pranced
before the camera and threw kisses to the audience." When Beryl Halley pointed
out that these women had chosen "all the beauts with mascara on their eyelashes,"
Sobbie yelled at them, "Ladies, don't you know those boys are awful floozies?"
The women persisted in their choices, even as Vallee's sister explained plaintively
that it was "a question of the sanctity of the home." Nye finally instructed the
women to choose only "a man who is tattooed or hairy," assuming that they must
be straight, but even that method seemed to fail. Finally, the judges discovered
that a contestant was married to one of the "Coney Island dowagers" and awarded
him first place. The other three prizes went to "brawny looking chaps who were
not much to look at." Their work done, "the fatigued judges fled before the disappointed beauts burst into tears."

Although little other evidence points to the presence of gay men at Coney
Island around this time, the size of the crowd, the number of contestants, their
comfort at being campy in public, and the nonreaction of the Coney Island na-
tives strongly suggests that this was not the first or only time gay men had gathered at the Washington Baths. Over the next few decades, that bathhouse would
become a popular cruising spot for gay men, and we will return to it again in the
1940s and '50s. Any institution that provided gender-segregated, semiclothed privacy (whether bathhouse, public bathroom, reformatory, jail, or boarding
school) was likely to be a magnet for same-sex sexual activity—which New York
City police and civilian crusaders began to understand in the 1920s.

During and immediately after World War I, the number of arrests for "degeneracy" (aka soliciting for sexual activity, or cruising) skyrocketed. According
to the Committee of Fourteen, in both 1918 and 1919, degeneracy cases increased
50 percent over the year before. But even that was a low estimate because, as they
noted in their bulletin, police "reports do not contain detailed figures of cases of
degeneracy."[35] Men were still being arrested for the more general charge of disorderly conduct. In cases where convictions were made, these men were sent to
be fingerprinted, and only then were they marked as degenerates. (The crimi-
nologist who invented fingerprinting, Henry P. DeForest, was also the doctor who
first sent Loop-the-Loop to see R. W. Shufeldt. Criminology, like sexology, started
from a belief that degeneracy could be read in the body, so it's no surprise that

the same scientists would practice both.) Starting in 1920, the Committee of Four-teen began writing proposed changes to the disorderly conduct law, breaking it into multiple subsections. By so doing, the committee hoped to track both de-generates and men who frequented female sex workers more closely.

In 1921, using the records of the Fingerprint Bureau, the committee released an internal report entitled "Sexual Perversion Cases in New York City Courts, 1916–1921."[36] At the start of that period, they found 92 cases of degeneracy. By 1920, that number had increased over 700 percent, to a whopping 756 cases. They also noted that 89 percent of all men arrested on degeneracy charges were eventually convicted—"a percentage much above the average of convictions for all offences."

Not only were men who had sex with men more likely to be convicted than other offenders, men of color who had sex with other men were more likely to be convicted than white men. In their report, the committee broke convictions down into eight racial categories. Five of these categories were what we would today call white or Caucasian people: Anglo-Saxon (English), Latin (French, Span-ish, Italian, and other Mediterranean-descended people), Teutonic (German and Northern European), Scandinavian (Swedish, Danish, etc.), and Slavs (Eastern European). The other three categories were Near East (Middle Eastern), Orients (Asian), and Negroes (black). White people accounted for 89 percent of degen-eracy arrests, Middle Eastern people 4 percent, black people 6 percent, and people of Asian descent just 1 percent. At the time, New York City's population was around 97 percent white. The Committee of Fourteen documented their own lack of informants of color, and the unwillingness of the police to pursue vice cases in primarily black neighborhoods, yet despite both these limiting factors, men of color were still being arrested in higher-than-expected numbers. Whiteness was not yet the consolidated identity we know it as today, but it still offered some pro-tection from police abuse.

Regardless of the race of the men involved, the committee believed that two factors contributed to this rise in degeneracy cases. When considered together, their two arguments highlight the changing understanding of sexuality. The first cause they pointed to was their own success. By driving heterosexual prostitu-tion further underground, they believed they had opened the door for degener-acy to take its place. This belief was in line with older ways of thinking, such as that of the judge who sentenced Young Griffo, which saw same-sex sexual con-tact as a substitute for heterosexual sex under certain conditions. Homosexuality wasn't a permanent and fixed identity defined by the gender of your partner; instead it was an action that almost any man might undertake if the circumstances were right.

This probably had some influence, the Committee of Fourteen conceded, but not as much as World War I. During the war, "American boys undoubtedly became familiar with perverse practices while in France or while at sea and to some extent while in the large cities of their own country," they wrote. The idea that homosexuality was something that you learned or were inducted into was the committee's great fear. "The pervert, not deeming his acts unnatural, is constantly seeking converts to his practices," they wrote. "Figures indicate that their efforts are successful. This makes the situation a serious one requiring consideration and special action" (emphasis in the original). The idea of the predatory homosexual, out to recruit innocent "American boys" into his way of life, was taking hold. Sex acts between men were no longer discrete disgusting activities, they were the gateway to becoming a specific type of person—the homosexual. An invert was obvious from his or her contrary gender presentation, but anyone could be a homosexual, including war heroes. Now that the idea of sexual orientation was spreading, same-sex sexual contact between gender-normative men had higher stakes and needed to be policed more heavily. The committee quickly took up that work.

However, they noted problems with their World War I theory. In particular, 63 percent of the arrests they studied were of men over the age of thirty, making it unlikely that they were "boys" who had been corrupted by immoral foreigners, desperate sailors, or wicked urbanites. Many of them were probably too old to have served in World War I. The war still contributed to the rising tally of degeneracy arrests by bringing large numbers of men together in urban centers, but it is unlikely that these men *learned* to be gay while serving as young soldiers. Yet while they noted this contradiction, the committee made no efforts to account for it or adjust their theories.

In the pages of the committee's report were two pieces of information that might have helped them to understand the rise in degeneracy cases. First, they noted that certain policemen were responsible for most of the convictions. These officers worked in a small number of locations, mostly near Herald Square, Times Square, Union Square, Madison Square Park, and Columbus Circle. What did all of these places have in common? They were transportation hubs that were frequented by men of all kinds, making them easy places to cruise without drawing attention. Neither laborer nor businessman, sailor nor painter, would stick out if he was seen lingering in these places. The second, and arguably more important piece of information, was *where* in those areas the arrests were taking place: "chiefly motion picture theaters and subway toilets." Both were recent additions to the city's landscape. The pattern of these arrests suggested that rather than learning a new vice from somewhere far away, or using homosexuality to compensate for a lack of access to heterosexual sex, men were suddenly finding that spaces to solicit for homosexual sex were widely available—another way in which the queer world was expanding with the urbanization of New York.

And find sex they did. Although the exact numbers fluctuate, over the next twenty-five years, degeneracy arrests steadily increased throughout New York City. By the end of the 1920s, over one thousand men would be arrested annually—most while soliciting (or having) sex in a subway bathroom. The number of arrests in Brooklyn was generally low (a few dozen per year at most), but men from all five boroughs were regularly arrested in Manhattan. In 1945, the arrest count hit two thousand for the first time. In 1947, when over thirty-one hundred men were arrested for degeneracy, the Magistrate's Report would note that "the basis of the charge in all cases is overt homosexual activity in a public place, usually a subway or theater, toilet or park."[37] The subway provided easy connection between nascent "gayborhoods" such as Harlem, Greenwich Village, Coney Island, and the Brooklyn Navy Yard, while simultaneously creating hundreds of small, private, male-only spaces where men disrobed together. The city probably couldn't have designed a better way to promote gay sex if it had tried.

We know all of this because in 1923 the Committee of Fourteen successfully fought for the passage of the Schackno Bill, which divided disorderly conduct into ten subsections. Subsection DC-8 made it a misdemeanor for any man to "frequent or loiter about any public place soliciting men for the purpose of committing a crime against nature or other lewdness."[38] For the first time in New York City history, the law specifically criminalized consensual same-sex activity. More dangerously, it criminalized any man that the police decided was *looking* for same-sex activity. The law was so broad that homosexual men (or any man who *seemed* homosexual) could now be arrested simply for being in public. Much like the prostitute, the homosexual was now a moral danger regardless of whether he was actually committing a sexual act. No longer would the police need to falsify evidence or entrap men into soliciting sex (though both practices would continue).

Curiously, however, while this was the Committee of Fourteen's explicit goal in changing the disorderly conduct law, it seems the police and the courts had different ideas about the Schackno Bill. In describing the changes to the law in its annual report for 1923, the Magistrate's Court barely mentioned the prosecution of sexual activity. Instead, its focus was on the way in which the bill provided for increased oversight and prosecution of pickpockets. While this might seem laughable today, at the time eugenicists viewed being a pickpocket as a biological, inheritable, and permanent condition—nearly identically to the way they viewed homosexuality. In the court's 1923 annual report, Chief City Magistrate William McAdoo wrote:

> As a biological proposition, I believe with eminent psychologists that this species of rascals are emotionally deficient, ill balanced in physical brain and incurable thieves who ought to be in continuous custodial care and not running in and out of jails and penitentiary, but in establishments where they could lead useful and improving lives.[39]

As draconian as it might sound today, the chief magistrate of the City of New York wanted to institutionalize pickpockets for life. In subsequent annual reports, only two types of disorderly conduct arrests were tracked specifically: pickpockets (or "jostlers") and degenerates (aka homosexuals). The other eight subsections of the law were tracked together as disorderly conduct cases. At every step of the judicial process, men arrested for degeneracy received harsher treatment than other cases. They were less likely to be discharged and more likely to be convicted, and when they were convicted, they received larger fines and longer sentences at the workhouse. Even "incurable thieves" such as pickpockets received better treatment (although only marginally).

By providing the city with explicit yearly data on the (increasing) numbers of men soliciting for sex, the Schackno Bill set the stage for all future crackdowns on homosexuality. Before you can effectively regulate a behavior, you have to be able to define, locate, and track it. In the coming decades, in an effort to regulate gay male sex, New York City would try everything from mass arrests to a first-of-its-kind program that sent men convicted of degeneracy to therapists in-

Photo of poet Hart Crane (c. 1920). (*Photo courtesy of the Richard W. Rychtarik/Hart Crane Papers; MSS 103; box 1; folder 3; Fales Library and Special Collections.*)

stead of jails—none of which would have been possible without the Schackno Bill.

We know little about most of the men who were arrested as degenerates in the 1920s. While the law established a way to track arrests, it didn't define what should happen to these men after arrest, or how/if records of their arrests should be kept in perpetuity. Since disorderly conduct was a misdemeanor, these arrests almost never led to trials or stories in the press. However, the exploits of one of Brooklyn's most famous early twentieth-century residents can give us some insight into the world of subway cruising (and waterfront cruising. And bathhouse cruising. And speakeasy cruising. And . . . you get the picture).

The poet Hart Crane was born just a few months shy of the start of the century, on July 21, 1899, in Garrettsville, Ohio. He was seventeen when he first landed in New York City, in the middle of World War I. A high school dropout from a wealthy and tempestuous family, he didn't stay long. Within a few months, Crane moved to Cleveland, where he worked a variety of jobs, some for the war effort, some as an "adman" and copywriter, and some for his father, a self-made millionaire who built a large candy company (in part by licensing a new ring-shaped candy known as Life Savers). In 1923, the year the Schackno Bill was passed, Crane returned to New York City, now a poet of some growing renown, ready to shed his Midwestern roots and roar his way into the 1920s. During this period he would produce his most renowned work, *The Bridge,* an epic six-part poem whose central image was the Brooklyn Bridge, a structure he revered. In many ways, Crane—with his love of jazz and gin, his outsize personality, his sui generis genius, his ever increasingly frantic life, and his early death—exemplifies the rise and tragic fall of the entire decade.

Even as a young man, Crane's eyes seemed always hooded, with tired circles beneath. His thick dark hair leaped away from his temples in a great upright shock, though he would go gray (the exact color of a seagull, according to friends) while still in his twenties. His personality was boisterous, oversize, and equal parts entertaining and irritating. Crane made friends nearly as easily as he lost them, and at one point or another he counted among his admirers many of the leading men of American arts and letters, including Eugene O'Neill, Malcolm Cowley, Waldo Frank, Charlie Chaplin, Walker Evans, E. E. Cummings, John Dos Passos, William Carlos Williams, and Alfred Stieglitz. His relationships with female artists were more fraught; although he counted some (such as Caroline Gordon) as friends, in his letters he routinely dismissed and diminished female poets such as Marianne Moore, Harriet Monroe, and Edna St. Vincent Millay. Although he left behind just two slim volumes of poetry when he died at the age of thirty-two, his extensive correspondence gives us insight into his life. Crane's letters show how having queer peers can crucially change the way in which a historical figure is remembered. In his introduction to Crane's collected correspondence, Langdon Hammer wrote, "There are obvious differences between his letters to straight and gay friends, manifest in idiom and tone as much as in what is said."[40] Crane's letters to his gay peers contain more camp, more frank sexual discussion, and more honest pathos. As is true for Mabel Hampton, part of the reason we know so much about Crane is because of these other queer people who preserved his legacy in letters.

From childhood on, Crane was resolute about two things: his homosexuality and his poetry. At the age of six he declared that he would be a poet. Upon first arriving in New York at seventeen, he wrote to his father, "I have powers, which, if correctly balanced, will enable me to mount to extraordinary latitudes."[41] Although he was right about his literary abilities, Crane never achieved balance of any kind. His poetry seemed to thrive on a hectic, herky-jerky life full of tremendous highs and suicidal lows. He wrote best (or at least most often) when drunk. He had a habit of sneaking away from parties to write in a side room, the Victrola blaring as he did. His poetry was dense and imagistic, but also highly rhythmic; he often said he was looking for a way to translate jazz into words.

Crane had sexual experiences with men dating back to his midadolescence. Like Walt Whitman before him, Crane had a fondness for sailors, laborers, and other working-class men. This fascination rested on many pillars: the frisson of excitement that came with class-jumping or slumming, the unlikeliness of running into anyone he knew in the saloons where these men gathered, his own sense of shame around not living up to a certain standard of masculinity, and the greater degree of acceptance of male-male sexual activity that prevailed in some working-class neighborhoods. At the age of nineteen, he came out to his friend and fellow literary young Turk Gorham Munson in a letter, writing, "This 'affair' that I have been having, has been the most intense and satisfactory one of my whole life, and I am all broken up at the thought of leaving him. Yes, the last word will jolt you."[42]

While Crane was open about his desires with most of the people in his life, he rightly feared how he would be perceived because of it. As part of the first generation to grow up with the concept of homosexuality, Crane worked hard to present himself as a straight-seeming, gender-conforming man. As his friend the poet Samuel Loveman recalled:

> He confided to me . . . that he had so practiced the art of camouflaging and hiding anything that might possibly be construed as feminine in his makeup—[hence] the long and somewhat ponderous, swaggering stride, his inveterate cigar-smoking, the Whitmanesque habit of wearing expensive but extremely comfortable and easy "crash" clothes—what had once been assumed actually became a part of him.[43]

Some of his contemporaries were put off by Crane's queerness, such as poet William Carlos Williams, who admitted that while he admired Crane's writing, he avoided him because he was a "crude homo" and "cock sucker."[44] Others, such as the author Yvor Winters, liked Crane personally but believed that his sexuality precluded him from writing poetry that could speak to most people—or as Winters put it in a damning review that ended their friendship, Crane was "temperamentally unable to understand a very wide range of experience"[45] and was thus limited in what he could produce upon the page.

By the age of twenty-three, when Crane was preparing for his return to New York, he realized that being out put him in a precarious economic position. "I discover I have been all-too easy all along in letting out announcements of my sexual predilections," he wrote to his friend Munson on March 2, 1923. "When you're dead it doesn't matter, and this statement proves my immunity from any 'shame' about it. But I find the ordinary business of 'earning a living' entirely too stringent to want to add any prejudices against me of that nature in the minds of any publicans and sinners."[46] He urged Munson to be discreet on Crane's behalf, but discretion was never among Crane's strengths himself.

Crane had already begun to conceptualize his masterwork, *The Bridge,* before he returned to the city. In another letter to Munson, he described the poem as "a mystical synthesis of 'America,'" and the idea of the bridge metaphor itself as a "symbol of our constructive future, our unique identity."[47] Crane explicitly saw himself carrying on the legacy of Walt Whitman and wanted *The Bridge* to combine the hopeful, epic lyricism of *Leaves of Grass* with the ultramodern poetics of T. S. Eliot (whom Crane found depressing and nihilistic, though prodigiously talented). *The Bridge* was conceived at a moment when Crane's America was full of hope: the war was over, the economy was booming, the twenties were roaring, and gay life was beginning to find public expression. Crane's poem would contain all of that, by telling the history of the continent, from the birth of Pocahontas to the construction of the subway. The anchoring metaphor would be the Brooklyn Bridge, that towering symbol of New York City (the beloved center of the modernist movement in art and literature), which was built during the last flowering of Victorian Romanticism. It "bridged" both worlds—and both boroughs—as Crane hoped his writing would. Similarly, he hoped his writing would also bridge the queer and straight worlds, offering queer love—only slightly disguised—as an experience with which any reader might identify.

As he worked on the poem, Crane wrote, "I begin to feel myself directly connected to Whitman."[48] Part of this connection rested on his desire for the same kind of "adhesive brotherhood" that Whitman had tried to chaunt and yawp into existence some seventy years prior. Sections of *The Bridge* are love poems, and Crane was determined (in part) to show that there was space for queer love in the American mythos, *and* that queer love could create a universal metaphor with which all people could identify. In the fourth section of *The Bridge,* "Cape Hatteras," Crane invoked Whitman by name, writing:

> *O Walt!——Ascensions of thee hover in me now*
> *As thou at junctions elegiac, there, of speed*
> *With vast eternity, dost wield the rebound seed!*

. . . .

. . . O, upward from the dead
Thou bringest tally, and a pact, new bound
Of living brotherhood!
. . . .
. . . thy wand
Has beat a song, O Walt,——there and beyond!
And this, thine other hand, upon my heart

As the last verse makes clear, Crane's connection to this living brotherhood, and to Whitman, is sexual. Whitman's one hand might be on his heart, but the other is firmly on his wand. As they would be for many, queer love, Walt Whitman, and Brooklyn were intimately connected in Crane's cosmology.

It was queer love that brought Crane to Brooklyn, early in 1924. Emil Opffer was a Danish sailor and journalist, with blond hair, blue eyes, and a "generous and gregarious disposition."[49] He volunteered occasionally at the storied Provincetown Playhouse in Greenwich Village (where Eugene O'Neill's plays were first staged), which is probably how he entered Crane's social circle. He was a few years older than Crane, and he was calm where Crane was tempestuous, quiet where Crane was loud, and easy where Crane was difficult. Opffer worked on commercial ships that traveled from Brooklyn down to South America, and sometimes to California. His father had been a journalist of some renown in Norway, but now lived in Brooklyn Heights, where he was the editor of *Nordlyset,* a paper that served the two-hundred-thousand-strong Danish community in the city.

Opffer was, without a doubt, the love of Crane's life and the muse that inspired some of his most beautiful poetry. Soon after they met, Crane wrote a rapturous letter to a friend about being with Opffer, describing "the ecstasy of walking hand in hand across the most beautiful bridge of the world, the cables enclosing us and pulling us upward in such a dance as I have never walked and never can walk with another."[50] In Opffer, Crane found that sexual brotherhood he longed for, and he immortalized their relationship in the poetic sequence he called "Voyages." The name references Opffer's travels, but these journeys were also sexual ones, as part 3 of "Voyages" makes clear:

Past whirling pillars and lithe pediments,
Light wrestling there incessantly with light,

Star kissing star through wave on wave unto
Your body rocking!
And where death, if shed,
Presumes no carnage, but this single change,——
Upon the steep floor flung from dawn to dawn
The silken skilled transmemberment of song;
Permit me voyage, love, into your hands . . .

The first four lines describe an intense sexual encounter ("body rocking") be-tween two men (the "whirling pillars" and "lithe pediments"). "Death" here refers to *la petite mort*—literally, "a little death," but also French slang for orgasm—after which the lovers' clothes are found flung to the floor. Then, after a short break, the lovers begin their sexual voyage again. Although Crane was often criti-cized (rightfully) for his oblique and incomprehensible poetry, Opffer inspired some of his most eloquent and readable lines.

When the two were first introduced, Opffer was living with his mother and stepfather in Manhattan (when not out at sea); however, Crane's tendency to show up at his door at three in the morning soon led to a rift with his family. "I have to lead my life as best I can," Opffer told his stepfather. "I don't want to give up Hart's friendship. After my dreary life at sea, I need some fun."[51]

Crane was bouncing around apartments in Greenwich Village, spending money he didn't have and wearing thin the hospitality of friends. He needed somewhere from which to write *The Bridge*. Opffer proposed a solution that would help them both: they would move into the building where Opffer's father lived, in Brook-lyn Heights. Opffer's father (also named Emil) lived in a kind of commune founded by artist and patron Hamilton Easter Field and his adopted son, sculptor Robert Laurent (who was rumored to have also been Field's lover).

Field came from Brooklyn royalty. According to his peers, he was "tall and dark-haired, Byronic in appearance, bohemian by temperament, and said to be homosexual."[52] In 1845, his grandfather built the family home, called the Field Mansion, at 106 Columbia Heights, as well a number of other buildings on the block, which were collectively referred to as Quaker Row. Field was born there in 1873 and spent most of his young life in Brooklyn, except for a semester at Harvard and a few years studying art in Europe. By 1905, he had returned home and become a painter of small renown. When he had his first exhibition in Man-

Photo of Columbia Heights (c. 1920), facing North toward the Brooklyn Bridge. Hart Crane, Emil Opffer, and Hamilton Easter Field all lived at 110 Columbia Heights. (*Photo courtesy of the Brooklyn Eagle Photographs—Brooklyn Public Library—Brooklyn Collection.*)

hattan's Clausen Gallery in March of that year, *The Brooklyn Daily Eagle* called him "the Height's first artist who promises to make an important name for himself."[53] Over the next seventeen years, he would turn his corner of Brooklyn into a celebrated destination for artists and art enthusiasts. Beginning in 1912, he hosted numerous exhibitions in his home, which he dubbed the Ardsley Studio. In 1916, he bought two other buildings on Quaker Row, including 110 Columbia Heights— the building where Washington Roebling had lived while completing the Brooklyn Bridge. Field turned all three buildings into an art school and commune, which he called the Ardsley School. There, he showed a stunning variety of work, from historic Japanese prints to cutting-edge cubist paintings and sculptures.

The three houses of the Ardsley School were "connected on the basement and parlour floors, with an art school situated in the basement; the upper stories were residential."[54] Field had previously established an art school in Ogunquit, Maine, which played host to famous queer artists such as Marsden Hartley, but Field decamped to Brooklyn in part because the Maine locals found him so strange. In an interview given many decades later, Field's close friend Lloyd Goodrich attributed part of this less than warm reception to Field's being "fundamentally . . . a homosexual."[55] Field continued to run an art school in Ogunquit during the summers, but throughout the 1910s and into the 1920s he primarily lived in Brooklyn, where he found a welcoming home. His presence there would entice a wide variety of admirers to cross the East River. William Henry Fox, the director of the Brooklyn Museum, described Field as playing constant host to "distinguished strangers from overseas, 'Society folks,' artists, musicians, writers . . . and on one occasion I saw in his parlors an East Indian princess."[56]

The Brooklyn Daily Eagle considered Field the epitome of a local boy done good; when he died, the paper wrote, "Among the men who have identified Brooklyn with the higher spirit of art in America and in the world, not one had a keener art sense, or so much of capacity for intelligent and sympathetic criticism, as Hamilton Easter Field." In fact, he would review art exhibitions for The Eagle for a number of years before he founded his own influential journal, The Arts, in 1919, which The Eagle called "perhaps the most progressive, certainly the most authoritative, [journal] in the country."[57] He took seriously his role as a booster of Brooklyn and its artists; not only was Field the founder of the organization the Salons of America, he was also the president of the Brooklyn Society of Artists, the director of the Independent Society of Artists, a member of the executive committee for Modern Artists of America, and a member in good standing of the Brooklyn Water Color Society. Although many critics lamented that he never lived up to his natural talent as a painter, Field was unsurpassed as a patron.

Sculptor Robert Laurent was one of many talented artists that Field found in his frequent trips around the world. Laurent was twelve when Field discovered him in France and became his patron. Although he was frequently described as Field's adopted son, there seems to have been no formal adoption arrangement between them. The two were virtually inseparable (even after Laurent married sometime around 1918). When Field died of pneumonia in 1922, he left everything to Laurent, "a life long friend, with whom he lived," as one obituary put it.[58]

Laurent continued the tradition of renting out inexpensive rooms to artists and writers, although the Ardsley School seems to have died with Field. It's unclear how well Hart Crane knew Laurent, or if he ever met Field, since Crane moved to Columbia Heights two years after Field died. However, many other art luminaries passed through the buildings in those years. The author John Dos Passos lived there while Crane and Opffer were in residence, and it's possible that this influenced the sympathetic gay character he included in his novel *Manhattan Transfer*. Other famous residents included visual artists Yasuo Kuniyoshi, Adelaide Lawson, Katherine Schmidt, and Stefan Hirsch (who would quite coincidentally be one of the last people to see Crane alive).

For Crane, the move to Columbia Heights had the mark of providence. Not only would he be living in the same building as Opffer, whom he nicknamed Goldilocks and Phoebus Apollo, but he would literally be in the shadow of the Brooklyn Bridge, in a building directly connected to its history. Emil Opffer Sr. actually lived in Washington Roebling's old room. "That window is where I would be most remembered of all," Crane wrote rapturously to his friend Waldo Frank.[59] When Opffer Sr. died during minor surgery a few months after the pair moved in, Crane took over his room and described the view to his mother:

> *Everytime one looks at the harbor and the NY skyline across the river it is quite different, and the range of atmospheric effects is endless. But at twilight on a foggy evening, such as it was at this time, it is beyond description. Gradually the lights in the enormously tall buildings begin to flicker through the mist. There was a great cloud enveloping the top of the Woolworth tower, while below, in the river, were streaming reflections of myriad lights, continually being crossed by the twinkling mast and deck lights of little tugs scudding along, freight rafts, and occasional liners starting outward. Look far to your left toward Staten Island and there is the statue of Liberty, with that remarkable lamp of hers that makes her seen for miles. And up at the right Brooklyn Bridge, the most superb piece of construction in the modern world, I'm sure, with strings of light crossing it like glowing worms as the Ls and surface cars pass each other going and coming. It is particularly fine to feel the greatest city in the world from enough distance, as I do here, to see its larger proportions.[60]*

Other artists were also beginning to notice the charms of Brooklyn Heights. Like Greenwich Village and Harlem, the neighborhood was increasingly being recognized as a "bohemian" enclave. In 1921, syndicated national journalist Frederic Haskin wrote a column entitled "Bohemia's Moving Day," in which he opined, "With the Village growing less artistic and more expensive every day, the artists are scattering in all directions. . . . A large group has taken up its abode in the former aristocratic Brooklyn Heights . . . [which] so closely resembles Greenwich Village in every way."[61] This would only become more true in the coming decades, as another columnist from 1921, this time in *The Brooklyn Daily Eagle*, predicted:

> *The time is not far off when every other basement along Remsen St. [in Brooklyn Heights] is to be converted into a low-roofed, bare-table café, a la "Romany Marie's" of Greenwich Village fame, where be-sandaled, bare-legged, bob-headed maids, in smocks, will sip cool drinks and gaze soulfully into the eyes of their artist lovers seated opposite at the tables.*[62]

Crane loved the area so much that he urged his friends to move there, such as poet Samuel Loveman, who had been Crane's close companion since their time in Cleveland. "I want you to live near me," he told Loveman. "Brooklyn Heights is one of the loveliest places in the whole world. . . . You will never care to live elsewhere, and wherever I may be, I shall always return to you."[63] In case that wasn't enough enticement, he also promised Loveman that the neighborhood was full of sailors. Loveman, in turn, convinced others, such as publisher George Kirk and cult horror writer H. P. Lovecraft, to move to the Heights as well.

The constancy that Crane promised Loveman, however, wasn't in his nature. Crane left Brooklyn Heights many times over the next few years—for Patterson, New Jersey; for California; for Cuba. Whenever money became tight (which was often, since Crane never held down a job for long), Crane moved on, always convinced that in the next place he would be able to finish *The Bridge*. In 1924, he hoped to win the Dial Award, a prestigious prize that would provide him enough support to work on the poem for a year. Although he had published a few poems in *The Dial*, he stood no chance of receiving the award, as he had yet to publish a book. Instead, the award went to Marianne Moore, the poet who would be the editor of *The Dial* for the rest of the 1920s. *The Dial* was the most respected of the pack of "little magazines" where serious writers such as Crane and Moore were publishing their work. It helped to launch literary modernism in America, which was filled with linguistic experimentation, psychological and scientific insights, and a rejection of the staid, traditional, or the overly romantic. As editor, Moore was more supportive of Crane's work than most, but he bristled at her edits to his poems, and their relationship was never strong. Crane referred to her dismissively as "the Right Reverend Miss Mountjoy" in his letters, and Moore found Crane's impenetrability and lack of lucidity to be a detriment to his poetry. Although they both lived in Brooklyn at different times, they were never friends.

The Bridge, which Crane had once estimated would take about a year to write, ended up taking nearly six years, almost right up until his death. His constant movement, which he hoped would stimulate his creativity (or at least provide less difficult circumstances in which to exercise that creativity) drained him, and by at least 1925 his friends were beginning to worry about his serious drinking problem.

Crane was unreliable in his sexual relationships as well. Despite his love for Opffer, they broke up a little more than a year after they got together. As Loveman recalled:

> *The inevitable happened. His friend [Opffer] returning unexpectedly one evening to their apartment at 110 Columbia Heights, encountered Hart's stupid betrayal. There was no explosion, except Hart's ineffectual hammering protestations and attempt at an explanation—then silence. The friendship was resumed; their love never.*[64]

Opffer would continue to sail out of New York, and in the 1930s, he had a brief relationship with experimental author and filmmaker James Broughton, before he moved back to Denmark and married a woman. Toward the end of his life, when a curious historian tracked him down, Opffer seemed reluctant to discuss Crane. Opffer had kept none of their letters, and he "repeatedly stated that his relationship with Crane is now so far back in time that he regards it as something very distant and something he is completely finished with."[65] He characterized it only as a friendship, and one that was more intense on Crane's part than his.

Although Loveman wrote nothing about the man at the crux of Crane's betrayal, there were many possibilities. Most of Crane's sexual partners went unnamed and unrecorded, but he told his friends about a few of the more serious ones: there was Bob Stewart, a sailor from Alabama stationed on the USS *Milwaukee;* Alfredo, a young Cuban sailor that Crane met in Havana and kept in touch with ever after; and Jack Fitzin, another sailor, this time encountered while on shore leave from the navy in Brooklyn. Crane's surviving letters are full of tales of "flying back to Brooklyn with a wild Irish red-headed sailor of the Coast Guard, who introduced me to a lot of coffee dens and cousys on Sands Street, and then took me to some kind of opium den way off God knows where."[66] Crane loved to cruise, and in Brooklyn Heights he had a lot of cruising grounds to choose from. The area between the base of the Brooklyn Bridge and the Sands Street entrance to the Navy Yard (which sailors called Tattoo Row) was a dangerous erotic playground whose reputation for debauchery had only increased since the days when Robert Bonner and Antonio Bellavicini ran their saloons. Sands Street was so synonymous with the gay sex trade that when Charles Demuth painted a watercolor of a businessman picking up two sailors there, he simply entitled it On "That" Street, certain that his audience would know which street he was referencing. In Crane's time, not only was the area home to bars, sailors, and dimly lit alleyways, the Heights also had a new cruising ground: the Clark Street subway station.

When it opened in 1919, the Clark Street subway station extended express service from Times Square into Brooklyn for the first time, doubling the system's entire Manhattan-to-Brooklyn capacity. The entrance was built at the intersection of Henry and Clark Streets, right beneath the infamous St. George Hotel. Opened in 1885, the St. George was once the largest hotel in the country, and it continued to expand up into the 1930s. Both Loveman and Crane would live at the hotel for short periods in the twenties. Given its proximity to the Brooklyn Navy Yard, it was the go-to spot for visiting naval officers and well-off enlisted men. By at least the late 1920s, the subway station had a cruisy reputation, and the hotel was a notorious gay rendezvous point up through the 1960s (and one of the only gay places in Brooklyn that Martin Boyce, the Stonewall veteran, learned about from older queens). When discussing why Loveman liked Brooklyn Heights so much, Crane asserted it was because of "the attractions of the St. George subway station!"[67] However, Crane himself wasn't above finding momentary pleasure underground. In "The Tunnel," a section of The Bridge that focused on the subway, Crane wrote that love was "a burnt match skating in a urinal."[68] According to critic Robert Martin, this part of the poem represents "a sexual encounter in a subway men's room . . . [where] love, even in its most reduced, transitory form of anonymous sexual encounter, is an experience of regeneration."[69] Crane referred to both his sexual encounters and his poetry writing as ecstasies, and early in his career, each seemed to fuel the other. However, as he got older, he seemed to find more time for cruising, carousing, drinking, and fighting, and less and less time for love and poetry. Once, his lovers had been his inspiration, his "reasons to believe in God"; but by 1927, they were merely "sources of fond, amusing anecdotes."[70] The genius that he had once sensed in himself was a combination of youth and talent, and as the former faded, he began to doubt the latter as well.

By the end of the decade, Crane—like the rest of the world—seemed to be on a manic roller coaster he couldn't escape. Friends described him as bloated, irritable, unfocused, alcoholic, and erratic. He was arrested somewhere in Brooklyn on charges that were quickly dropped (most likely soliciting); he met Emil for a few days in California, but the two were badly beaten and robbed by a group of sailors; he begged for money from his family, but his father's business had collapsed and his relationship with his mother had turned increasingly toxic. Crane's final address in Brooklyn, where he lived while finishing *The Bridge* in 1929, was a basement apartment at 190 Columbia Heights. Many years later, his friend Edward Dahlberg wrote:

> He lived in a one-room apartment, somewhat beneath the sidewalk, with a gallon of whiskey on the floor next to his cot, and a pile of Sophie Tucker records for his Victrola. Though not yet thirty years old, his hair was the color of a seagull. In the daytime he was deeply pooled in mouldy sleep, and at night he ran about Red Hook, the libidinous docks of Tarshish in Brooklyn, soliciting the favors of sailors.
>
> Many times Crane had been beaten by seamen; on one occasion, living on Columbia Heights hard by his iron seraph, the Brooklyn Bridge, he complained to me that a young man whom he thought had the milk-white shoulders of Pelops (I am paraphrasing Christopher Marlowe, Hart Crane's demigod) had stolen his clothes and forsaken him. He was sorely wounded by this ill hap, but, as I have said, when he was not humiliated, or had not drunk hyssop in some waterfront pot-house, he was unable to achieve that Apollonian composure which he needed to enable him to sit at a table—a poet's guillotine—and write.[71]

Right around the time that Crane finally marshaled his "Apollonian composure" and completed *The Bridge*, his life—and the world at large—were thrown into chaos. On Tuesday, October 29, 1929, the stock market experienced the epic crash that ushered in the Great Depression. *The Bridge* was set to be published in an expensive, limited-edition printing done through Black Sun Press, a boutique publishing house owned by Crane's friends Harry and Caresse Crosby. Harry Crosby was the scion of a rich banking family from Boston; a few weeks after Black Tuesday, he shot himself and his mistress in the head while Crane and Caresse were waiting for him at the theater. Publication of *The Bridge* was delayed, and although it eventually went forward, Crane had lost one of his staunchest supporters (and one of the few people in his life who had the capacity and desire to rescue him financially when needed).

Today, *The Bridge* is considered a modern masterpiece, but critics' reviews at the time were mixed. A number of writers whom Crane considered close friends, such as Yvor Winters and Allen Tate, panned the book unexpectedly. Winters, in particular, went in deep, saying it had "no logical exposition of ideas," and that Crane, as a writer, was "disintegrating." Winters seemed to suggest that Crane's sexuality was the source of the problem, writing that Crane was developing "a sentimental leniency towards his vices . . . instead of understanding them and eliminating them." The one thing the book demonstrated clearly, Winters felt, was "the impossibility of getting anywhere with the Whitmanian inspiration."[72]

The world no longer seemed to have a place for a poet interested in romantic epics filled with love, myth, and transcendence. The magazines where Crane had once published his work, such as *The Dial* and *Secession,* were now either gone or only interested in political writing. The Roaring Twenties had come to a screaming stop. In a letter to Waldo Frank, who had remained his close friend since the late 1910s, Crane wearily wrote:

> These are bewildering times for everyone, I suppose. I can't muster much of anything to say to anyone. I seem to have lost the faculty to even feel tension. A bad sign, I'm sure. When they all get it decided, Capitalism or Communism, then I'll probably be able to resume a few intensities; meanwhile there seems to be no sap in anything. . . . Maybe I'm only a disappointed romantic, after all."[73]

In 1930, Crane received an unexpected lifeline: a Guggenheim Fellowship worth $2,000. Crane moved to Mexico City, where he thought he could make the money last longer, but he found himself unable to write. His drinking became constant, he was repeatedly arrested, and Guggenheim called him the most troubled and troublesome fellow they had ever had. While he was in Mexico, his father died suddenly. Crane was left a yearly inheritance in his father's will, but his company was so underwater that it was never paid out. Crane's friend Peggy Cowley was also in Mexico City, divorcing her husband, Malcolm—a friend and long-standing supporter of Crane's, one of the few he had left in the literary world. In the last months of his life, Crane proposed to Cowley and bragged that she had succeeded in changing him, where so many women had failed before. In early 1932, as the pair were sailing back to New York City, Crane allegedly attempted an affair with a sailor on board their ship. Whatever passed between them, Crane ended up badly beaten and locked in his cabin. The next morning, he informed his fiancée, Cowley, that he was "utterly disgraced." Calmly, he proceeded to the deck of the ship, where his old neighbor at 110 Columbia Heights, the painter Stefan Hirsch, suddenly caught sight of him looking "generally battered." Without saying a word, Crane walked quickly to the ship's railing, took off his coat, folded it carefully, and threw himself overboard. He was spotted once, "swimming strongly," and then was gone.[74]

In response to a mutual friend who asked about Crane's motivations, Cowley wrote that she could add "practically nothing" to what was already known, except that "he was depressed before leaving Mexico about finances."[75] Despite his wealthy background and critical success, Crane lived most of his life on the edge of bankruptcy and died that way as well, no doubt also worn down by his increasing estrangement from his friends, his drinking, and his fears about the future.

Without a will, or any kind of legally binding relationship with Cowley, Crane's personal effects and literary estate went to his mother, Grace. Although they were inseparable when he was young, Crane and his mother had long since become estranged. The pair seemed made from the same cloth, both hyperbolic, excitable, and always looking for someone to take care of them. Grace was determined to control Crane's legacy, often brutally so. Always uncomfortable with her son's sexuality, she tried her best to erase that part of him. When she discovered pornography, sexually explicit writings, and letters from Crane's many lovers, "there was nothing for it but destruction . . . to eliminate all the cycles of correspondence which had any bearing on her son's sexual temper. . . . She appears to have destroyed all the correspondence sent by Harry Candee, Wilbur Underwood, Emil Opffer, Jack Fitzin, and any unlettered sailor who had struggled to express feelings and desires for which he never knew a name." Perhaps the saddest of all was the case of Bob Stewart, the Alabama navy man who, according to Grace, sent Crane more letters than any other correspondent in his life, "all of which seem to be trying to convince Hart that he still loves him."[76]

The surviving copies of Crane's letters give us only a tiny taste of what was lost. While Crane himself is obviously in no danger of being forgotten, the men he loved—working class, unknown, and poorly educated—lost one of the few repositories of their thoughts and feelings regarding queer sexuality. Everything from their names, to how they made sense of their desires, to the bars they frequented, is gone. But Crane succeeded in one thing: he established himself as the literary and sexual descendant of Walt Whitman. For the generation of queer people—particularly white men—who would come after him, Brooklyn Heights now held a special luster. Brooklyn as a whole, too, was gaining in popularity. In 1929, budding author Parker Tyler (who would write a scandalous gay novel entitled *The Young and Evil* just a few years later) encountered a campy gay waiter in a restaurant in Brooklyn Heights. Tyler was so tickled by their interaction, and what he learned about the neighborhood, that he immediately wrote to friends to say, "Brooklyn is wide open and N.Y. should be notified of its existence."[77]

A flurry of queer poets would soon move to the area. Some, such as the austere Marianne Moore, would decamp from Greenwich Village, as journalists had predicted earlier in the decade. Others were native Brooklynites, such as the comfortably middle-class Chester Kallman and the working-class son of Lithuanian immigrants Harold Norse. During the "pansy craze" of the early thirties, queer life would become ever more visible—and ever more policed. The end of Prohibition in 1933 set the stage for police raids and Mafia control over queer bars, which would extend up to the Stonewall Riots and beyond. Sands Street would go from squalid sailor hangout to the hottest spot for slumming Manhattan socialites. For the first time in America, queer people would take control over sexological research, but their groundbreaking work would be plagued with infighting, homophobia, misogyny, intellectual theft, and government repression. And as the Great Depression bled into the start of World War II, Brooklyn College, founded in 1930, would become a hotbed of sexual, literary, and political radicalism, less than a half mile from 110 Columbia Heights.

5. The Beginning of the End, 1930–40

In some ways, the thirties are the beginning of modern Brooklyn. The borough's population hit 2.5 million in 1930, and it's stayed near that mark ever since. Although Manhattanites would mock Brooklyn residents as "bridge and tunnel" visitors who were still technically not part of "the city," Brooklyn was now bigger than Manhattan for the first time, with some seven hundred thousand more residents, and Brooklyn's black population would double over the decade, bringing the borough closer to the multiethnic enclave it is known as today.

Physically, too, Brooklyn was entering its modern incarnation. The subway now connected Brooklyn to every other part of New York City (aside from Staten Island). The twenties had seen a boom in skyscraper and high-rise construction along the Brooklyn waterfront, but that ended in 1929, right after the creation of the Williamsburgh Savings Bank Tower in downtown Brooklyn. One of the borough's most recognizable landmarks, the Bank Tower is a domed art deco skyscraper that thrusts priapically into the sky, with clock faces that can be seen throughout the neighborhood. Shortly after it opened, Black Tuesday wiped out some $14 billion from the New York Stock Exchange ($199 billion in today's money), decimating a wide swath of US industries, from housing to manufacturing. Impoverished families were unable to buy homes, so throughout the thirties, Brooklyn saw a major downturn in residential construction, which eventually led to extreme housing shortages after World War II—one of the prime factors for the suburbanization of New York in the 1950s, which *again* reduced demand for construction in Brooklyn. Thus, post-1930, Brooklyn's skyline would stay largely the same for decades, with its newest and tallest buildings all sharing a unified art deco style. The Bank Tower would remain Brooklyn's tallest building for the next eighty years.

Even before the stock market crash, there were signs that the Roaring Twenties were grinding to a hoarse whisper. The decade's artistic byword was *modern-ism,* a celebration of all things new and untraditional, but the movement splintered as the thirties rolled in and political concerns began to trump stylistic ones. In literature, modernism had largely been supported and spread by a host of "little magazines," which published and employed the likes of Hart Crane, Marianne Moore, John Dos Passos, T. S. Eliot, E. E. Cummings, Ezra Pound, and Amy Low-ell (girlfriend of the actress Ada Dwyer). Few of these publications survived the twenties, and even most of the holdouts didn't last through the first years of the Great Depression. *The Little Review, Secession, Broom, Contact,* and *The Dial* had all stopped publishing by the time the stock market crashed; *Pagany, Hound & Horn,* and *This Quarter* folded soon after.

Of those magazines, *The Dial* was arguably the most famous and most impor-tant. When it published its last issue in July 1929, it was eulogized in newspapers from Minneapolis to Nashville. One reporter wrote upon its passing, "Brilliant edi-tors gathered some of the finest thought of the period in its pages. . . . It will be necessary for most of us to subscribe to three magazines to replace it."[1] During the last five years of its existence, *The Dial* was almost entirely steered by one bril-liant, yet unassuming woman (and her mother): the poet Marianne Moore. Within a few months of *The Dial*'s demise, Moore would leave Greenwich Village for an apartment at 260 Cumberland Street in Brooklyn, where she would live for the next thirty-six years.

Redheaded and slight, Moore stood five feet four inches and at times weighed less than eighty pounds, yet she was one of the lions of modernism: a bold writer, a tough editor, and a scintillating conversationalist, despite her reflexive mod-esty. T. S. Eliot called her "one of those few who have done the language some service in my lifetime."[2] Aside from poetry, she also wrote book reviews, trans-lations, essays, a novel, a play, and the liner notes for Muhammad Ali's 1963 spoken-word album, *I Am the Greatest!* Before her death in 1972, Moore won nearly every imaginable writing award, including the Pulitzer, the National Book Award, the Robert Frost Medal, a Guggenheim Fellowship, the Bollingen Prize, and over a dozen honorary degrees.

For queer historians, Moore's life provides a wealth of information that adds up to no definitive conclusions. Hart Crane's nickname for her, "the Right Rev-erend Miss Mountjoy," was a jab at her austere life and sexless public persona. Moore had no known sexual or romantic relationships as an adult and lived with her mother (often sharing a bed) for almost her entire life. Indeed, had the labels been available to her, Moore might well have identified as asexual or a-romantic, since most of her recorded thoughts about sex, marriage, and children range from modest disavowal to downright repugnance. According to biographer Linda Leavell, "Marianne showed no more sexual interest in women than she did in men." In her poetry, "never does she long for a lover's embrace. . . . She comes to distrust unifying metaphor as much as she does romantic love."[3]

However, despite the enduring mystery of her own sexual desires (or disinterests), what is inarguable is that Moore lived the vast majority of her long life in a queer milieu, and that her home in Brooklyn hosted some of the most famous queer artists of the mid-twentieth century. Moore may well be the first prominent American to have been largely raised by a queer couple. Moore's father was institutionalized with schizophrenia in 1887, right before Moore was born. When Moore was thirteen, in 1900, her mother, Mary, began the most significant relationship of her life, with Mary Norcross. Norcross was the youngest daughter of the Moores' neighbors in Carlisle, Pennsylvania. When Mary Moore and Mary Norcross met, Norcross was twenty-five, a fresh-faced graduate of Bryn Mawr who tended to wear old-fashioned brown petticoats (for which Marianne gave her the nicknames Ruffles and Beaver). Mary Moore was a thirty-eight-year-old teacher and mother of two. Yet despite the thirteen-year age gap, the two women fell in love almost immediately. Their letters show a caring, romantic, and erotic relationship. While traveling in 1904, Mary Norcross envisioned the next time the two would be together, writing, "Think of having each other at night and all through the day for a whole month, Darling! I've never been so starved."[4] Their relationship spanned the next eleven years, and Norcross remained close to the family even after the two women broke up.

Norcross encouraged Marianne Moore to study at Bryn Mawr, starting in 1905. Not only did Moore begin her career as a writer while there, she also met many other queer women in its manicured lawns and high Gothic halls. The school was overseen by Dean Carey Thomas, who lived on campus with her partner, Mary Garrett. Moore was close to two of her English professors, Lucy Martin Donnelly and Katherine Fullerton, who were also a couple. And although they wouldn't become friends until after college, Moore first met queer modernist poet Hilda Doolittle (better known as H.D.) while both were Bryn Mawr students.

At Bryn Mawr, Moore expressed her most romantic feelings, in a series of "crushes" on other students. Romances between students were expected at Bryn Mawr; students even wrote a daily roundup of "bird news," a gossip column that covered older students and their admirers (who were colloquially called birds). Moore was no exception, and over the years she developed strong feelings for a series of other students. She told her mother, brother, and Mary Norcross about them in her voluminous letters home. Of one she wrote, "I have liked her ever since last November, but never would have said as I can now, 'She can have me any time she wants me.'" About another, a senior when Moore was a freshman, she wrote, "I'd give anything but my family's health and happiness to have her 'fond on me.'" Moore's most serious crush was on Peggy James, the niece of author Henry James, whom Moore greatly admired. Peggy James, she wrote, was "exactly like a wild horse—Too beautiful to leave unbroken, and yet too perverse not to make you want to swear." Unfortunately for Moore, James liked her only a little and didn't "feel any terrific excitement" over her.[5]

Nothing indicates that any of these relationships, although intense and erotic, were sexual. Aside from her feelings for Peggy James, Moore's infatuations were all fairly short-lived. What is most suggestive about these feelings is not their existence, but their quick passing. Although some scholars have read Moore as a closeted lesbian, her crushes actually seem to belie that notion. Moore had a supportive family of queer women, older role models for happy same-sex couples, and an environment that treated relationships between women as normal and healthy. She obviously had little problem discussing her intense feelings for other women, but those feelings seemed to fade quickly. When it came to sex, she seemed less closeted and more disinterested. As an adult, Moore attracted a wide array of suitors, male and female, all of whom she worked assiduously to dissuade. At least three lesbian heiresses served as patrons to Moore: British author Bryher (heir to the Ellerman shipbuilding fortune); Boston socialite Katherine Jones (whose family owned fruit plantations in Jamaica); and Louise Crane (heir to the Crane paper fortune). While Moore valued all three as friends and occasionally allowed them to provide her with money, food, or clothing, she shut down any attempts at flirtation or romantic entanglements (although her mother encouraged them). Displaying the degree to which psychology was becoming the dominant way to understand sexuality, a frustrated Bryher referred to Moore as "a case of arrested emotional development."[6]

Without a doubt, Moore's closest relationships were with her mother and brother who was called Warner. The three kept up an intense correspondence throughout their entire lives, and aside from a brief period during college and immediately after, Moore and her mother always lived together. Interestingly, Moore (at her own insistence) was usually referred to with male pronouns within the family. Whether this speaks to a transgender identity, a lack of interest in typically "feminine" behaviors, or an over-identification with her brother (as some scholars have argued) is unknowable. But it adds further fuel to the image of Moore as a queer and gender-transgressing figure—if not specifically a lesbian, bisexual, or transgender one.

As a poet, Moore was one of the first imagists, who were antiromantic modernist writers and used precise language to draw detailed pictures, which were often metaphorical or symbolic in ways the poems suggested but did not unpack at length. Moore drew many of her images from science, nature, and museum exhibitions. Take, for instance, the start of one of her most famous poems, "The Pangolin," which minutely describes that variety of Asian anteater:

> Another armored animal-scale
> lapping scale with spruce-cone regularity until they
> form the uninterrupted central
> tail row! This near artichoke with head and legs and
> grit-equipped gizzard[7]

As "The Pangolin" demonstrates, modernists played with meter and rhyme—or else abandoned them entirely. The resulting poems were far removed (in both form and content) from the epics, odes, and sonnets that were popular in earlier decades.

Unlike Hart Crane, who achieved almost immediate success with his late-adolescent poems, Moore labored for nearly six years after college without publishing more than a handful of pieces. However, by the 1920s she was finally recognized as a major new poetic voice, although because of the difficulty of her writing, she was often called a poet's poet, and her work wouldn't sell widely until much later. When she won the prestigious Dial Award in 1924 (beating out Hart Crane), she was working as a librarian to afford the tiny apartment she shared with her mother in Greenwich Village; the prize was awarded to allow her to work "untroubled by financial considerations."[8]

Immediately after winning, Moore joined *The Dial*'s staff as acting editor. She was soon making nearly all editorial decisions, with assistance from her mother, one of the few people whose opinions Moore valued. As an editor, Moore championed the works of T. S. Eliot, Ezra Pound, W. B. Yeats, Alyse Gregory, James Joyce, and many others. For five years, from 1924 to 1929, she helped steer the course of modernism in America. Moore loved her position, and although she was only paid to work part-time, she worked on *The Dial* six days a week, often until midnight. But her work came at a steep personal price: despite being "at the height of her creative powers when she took over *The Dial*," she published no new poetry of her own during her five-year tenure as editor.[9] As a result, although she at first viewed leaving Greenwich Village as an exile, her first decade in Brooklyn would be one of the most fecund periods of her life.

In Brooklyn, the air was cleaner, the neighborhood was quieter, and Moore had fewer demands on her time (although she always maintained an active literary and artistic life). In an essay entitled "The Plums of Curiosity," Moore described her new life in Brooklyn thusly:

> An atmosphere of privacy with a touch of diffidence prevailed, as when a neighbor in calling costume, furred jacket, veil, and kid gloves would emerge from a four-story house to visit the meat-market. Anonymity without social or professional duties, after the conflicting pressures of our life in New York, was welcome.[10]

Moore and her mother lived in a fourth-floor apartment, chosen by her older brother, Warner, who was stationed as a chaplain at the Brooklyn Navy Yard and wanted them close to him. Although in Fort Greene, a little removed from the water, the apartment was still close enough to the docks that Moore's mother complained that the "silt from the coal-burning smokestacks along Brooklyn's waterfront could soon cover a freshly made bed."[11]

That would not be true for much longer. Unbeknownst to anyone in 1929, Brooklyn was in its last year as a truly thriving industrial zone, when its waterfront was still a critical nexus for international trade. The Great Depression would soon decimate much of Brooklyn's economy. However, even had the stock market never crashed, another threat was slowly leaching into the borough, transforming both its economic and physical worlds: automobiles. Cross-country shipping over land radically redrew the lines of trade in America, diminishing

Brooklyn's importance to the country as a whole. Inside the borough, neighborhoods were being torn apart to make room for ever-widening streets, mostly pushed by the ruthless city planner Robert Moses. One of his earliest city street projects was the four-lane Gowanus Expressway, which smashed through the neighborhoods of Gowanus and Sunset Park and helped to isolate the waterfront and was "obsolete almost immediately" because it lacked details (such as shoulders) that were necessary for car traffic.[12] More than one hundred businesses were closed and twelve hundred families evicted to build the highway—and this was just a tiny taste of what Moses would do to New York City post–World War II. Access roads such as the Gowanus Expressway were the crucial arteries that allowed suburbanization to transform America in the fifties, by creating easy commutes for now-far-flung workers. Brooklyn was becoming dominated by cars, as was the entire country. According to the Federal Highway Authority, in 1920 a little more than 8 million cars were on the road in the US; by 1930 that number had more than tripled, to 23 million.[13] And one in every ten of those vehicles was located in New York State.[14]

Most likely, one of those cars—perhaps a hired hack or a Model T owned by a friend—brought Marianne Moore and her mother across the Brooklyn Bridge to their new life in Fort Greene. There, Moore entered into a "prolific five-year period during which [she published] two new books of poetry and some of her finest reviews and essays."[15] She also hosted a who's who of queer cultural luminaries out of her Brooklyn apartment, with frequent visitors including publisher Monroe Wheeler, novelist Glenway Wescott, photographer George Platt Lynes, the poets Hilda Doolittle and W. H. Auden, and the English heiress Bryher. Moore's mother loved hosting these distinguished guests and "preferred the company of homosexuals to that of heterosexuals."[16]

Many have speculated that Mary Moore kept a stranglehold on her daughter's life and affections. While the pair were inseparable, and Moore allowed her mother's health and needs to dictate her own travel and work schedules, the poet was also clear that having her mother so close not only allowed her to write, but also pushed her to create the best work she could. Her biographer Linda Leavell described Moore's complex relationship with her mother as having "*hindered* her to *succeed* as a writer," meaning it held her back, but that that very impediment was also necessary for her success.[17]

A few years after moving to Brooklyn, in March 1934, Moore began mentoring one of the most famous poets of the mid-twentieth century: Elizabeth Bishop. Moore was introduced to Bishop via a friend from Moore's college days at Bryn Mawr, who was now the librarian at Vassar, where Bishop was an undergraduate. In turn, Bishop introduced Moore to Louise Crane, a fellow Vassar student who was also a philanthropist and Bishop's first serious girlfriend. Crane would be a valued friend and patron to both Moore and Bishop throughout their lives, and Bishop and Crane would be frequent visitors to Moore's home in Brooklyn. Aside from poetry, Bishop and Moore bonded over their difficult family circumstances: Bishop's mother had been institutionalized when she was young, much as had Moore's father.

According to Moore biographer Linda Leavell, for many years "Bishop took her poems to Marianne's apartment to ask for advice."[18] After an afternoon at the zoo or the theater, Moore and Bishop would return to Moore's small, cluttered Brooklyn apartment to discuss writing (sometimes with Moore's mother present as well). It is easy to picture these two diminutive giants of poetry in the back of a taxi arriving at the squat yellow brick building with the "two mothballs in front," as Moore described the gaslights to drivers. The walls of her apartment's narrow central hallway were lined with books, pictures, and gifts from friends. A set of carpenter's tools, which Moore used to build shelves, hung by her kitchen door. She'd also installed a trapeze in the doorway that led to the living room, which she used for exercise. Piles of new books were always on the floor, surrounding unique and expensive gifts, such as the bronze bust of Moore that had been given to her by the sculptor Gaston Lachaise. Big bay windows looked out on the Brooklyn street below, letting in the light and giving Moore and Bishop a place to gather and look over Bishop's carefully written poems.

An interest in everything—old and new, books and tools, trapeze and Lachaise—was a defining aspect of Moore's life and of her poetry. Her Brooklyn apartment, more than any other home she ever had, was the distillation of all of these elements. Moore would remain in Brooklyn throughout the thirties—and the forties, fifties, and into the sixties. She lived in Brooklyn when her mother died in 1947, and when she won the Pulitzer Prize in 1951. She published some seventeen books during her time in Fort Greene, earning her the moniker "the poet of Brooklyn." As she got older, her verses became less dense, her poetic structures less demanding, and her topics more topical, such as 1961's "Baseball and Writing," which begins:

Fanaticism? No. Writing is exciting
and baseball is like writing.
  You can never tell with either
    how it will go
    or what you will do;[19]

This new poetic lightness resulted in a sudden burst of popularity for the aging Moore. She was photographed for a *Life* magazine spread, although she disliked most of the photos, except for one that showed her holding a baseball bat while smiling at three confused small boys. Her signature look—a tricorn hat and a dark capelet—was now so out of style that it was amusingly kooky, not just old-fashioned or severe. Her new writing was seen as approachable, and her older (as much as it was remembered) was seen as canonical. As years passed, Moore became a symbol of a bygone era of literary greatness. She would only leave Brooklyn in the last decade of her life, when economic distress and shortsighted urban planning blighted her neighborhood—part of the larger downfall of Brooklyn's working waterfront, which helped to destroy and erase the area's queer community as a whole.

Like Walt Whitman and Hart Crane before her, Moore helped to cement the idea of Brooklyn as a poetic destination. One of the last poems she ever wrote was an ode to both Brooklyn and Crane. "Granite and Steel," the title poem of her last book of new work, is directly in conversation with Crane's writing. Not only is the title drawn from *The Bridge,* but she quotes Crane directly in the poem's third stanza:

"O path amid the stars
crossed by the seagull's wing!"
"O radiance that doth inherit me!"
—affirming inter-acting harmony!
Untried expedient, untried; then tried;
way out; way in; romantic passageway
first seen by the eye of the mind,
then by the eye. O steel! O stone!

The first two lines of the final stanza refer to the construction of the bridge, a crossing that went untried until John and Washington Roebling made it possible. But they can also be read as describing Moore's own experience of the bridge—that untried expedient, which was at first a way out of Greenwich Village, but would become a way in, a "romantic passageway" taken by the many eager artists who flowed across the East River to knock upon the poet's door. A few years before she left Brooklyn for good in 1966, Moore wrote of her adopted home, "Brooklyn has given me pleasure, has helped to educate me; has afforded me, in fact, the kind of tame excitement on which I thrive."[20]

Although there are no records of lesbian bars or other gathering places for queer women in Brooklyn at this time, evidence is ample that individual queer women, such as Moore, were also finding their own "tame excitement" on Brooklyn's waterfront. This follows a pattern with queer neighborhoods in general, which often cater initially (and primarily) to men and develop institutions for women only later. This renders the lesbian and bisexual pioneers of so-called gayborhoods relatively invisible to historians. Yet they helped create the early queer density necessary for these areas to thrive.

In Brooklyn, these pioneers included women such as Jerre Kalbas, who was born in Harlem in 1918 and moved to Brooklyn Heights sometime in the late thirties to live with her lover, Patty Storm. Storm and her mother shared an apartment in a rooming house on Hicks Street. Storm worked as a ballroom dancer, and Kalbas was an electrician, welder, and jewelry smith. Kalbas recalled that at the time she "walked like a truck driver," and Patty helped her femme up to get work, going so far as to buy her a purse so she would stop carrying her money and cigarettes in a brown paper bag. Before World War II depleted the city of working-age men, even factories weren't open to women who seemed too masculine.

Most of the gay and lesbian venues the two women visited were in Manhattan, but Kalbas recalled that they "had a lot of gay friends" in the area, and that a restaurant down the block in the Heights was known for having a gay clientele.[21] But Kalbas and Storm didn't stay long in Brooklyn. Shortly after Kalbas moved in, the mobilization for World War II began, and the pair left New York for California, where they would find jobs on a ship working for the war effort.

Around the same time, a trio of women came to Brooklyn to make an unusual purchase. Their leader was Dorothy Bennett, a solidly built woman in her late twenties with short dark wavy hair and a penchant for button-down shirts. Bennett was an assistant astronomy curator at the American Museum of Natural History, who would go on to live a long and storied life (mostly outside of New

York). She not only created and edited the Little Golden Books series for children, but she also wrote multiple books of her own, mentored the Nobel Prize–winning physicist Roy Glauber, and eventually moved to Berkeley, California, where she worked as a museum anthropologist and lived for four decades with her "close companion," Rosamund Gardner.[22]

On a sunny summer day in 1936, Dottie (as Bennett was called) brought her roommates Ruhe and Gibby out to the Gowanus Canal to buy a sixty-foot barge that they christened *The Barnacle*. In the fifty years since the funeral of the Great Ricardo, the Gowanus had only gotten muddier, murkier, and more polluted. Today in New York State, water is defined as unswimmable if it has more than 24 bacteria per cubic centimeter; according to Brooklyn historian Joseph Alexiou, in 1908 parts of the Gowanus were found to have 625,000 bacteria per cubic centimeter.[23] Over the 1930s, a variety of factors would diminish the canal's importance as a working waterway. First, the Depression hit the industries clustered around the canal hard, closing many of its factories. Second, what shipping remained was being done out of larger and larger boats, which couldn't pass through the narrow, shallow canal. Third, the spread of electric light and heating had greatly reduced the call for manufactured gas and coal, two of the biggest industries in the area. Finally, as mentioned before, early efforts to convert New York City into a car-friendly metropolis had cut the canal off from the rest of Brooklyn. While World War II would provide the city with a needed economic reprieve, looking backward, the decline of the canal was like a canary in a coal mine, signaling bad things for all of Brooklyn's working waterfront. By the time Bennett and her friends arrived in 1936, the Gowanus was well on its way to becoming an abandoned Brooklyn backwater, which was most likely why *The Barnacle* was for sale in the first place.

According to writer Amy Sohn, the three women "spent the remainder of the summer restoring [*The Barnacle*] with the help of the junkies, drunks, and captains they met on the canal of the canal, as well as their bohemian friends from Greenwich Village"—yet another connection between the Village and bohemian Brooklyn.[24] Despite the smell of the canal, the women considered this an ideal summer, tucked away from the concerns of the larger world on their own private adventure. The trio didn't stay long in Brooklyn, though, as the water was too fetid to provide the kind of private idyll they had imagined. After a year of repairs and a few months living on board, they had *The Barnacle* towed to Long Island, where they would host parties and have weekend getaways up into the 1940s.

The histories of early female gayborhood residents such as Bennett and Kalbas are often forgotten, but one group is even less visible in the early stories of gayborhoods: those who never identified publicly as queer at all. Not far from where *The Barnacle* was moored, an unlikely source was making his own evocative entries into Brooklyn's queer waterfront history. Edward Casey came to Brooklyn to attend Pratt Institute after World War I and never left the borough again. He was originally from upstate New York, but little is known about Casey's life, except that he was a married high school art teacher and devoted Catholic. Yet throughout the 1930s, he created beautiful, detailed canvases that featured large groups of naked men horsing around on Brooklyn's shoreline, such as his watercolor painting *Stevedores Bathing Under the Brooklyn Bridge,* which depicts dozens of black and white men toweling off in the bridge's shadow. Today, the painting is housed at Green-Wood Cemetery in Brooklyn, where Casey is buried. The intense homoeroticism of his private paintings seems at odds with the quiet, married, heterosexual life that is evident from the few contemporaneous news clippings that mention his name. While his sexual identity is unknown, his paintings are either evidence of easily observable homoerotic practices among Brooklyn men, or evocations of private fantasies. Either way, they gorgeously demonstrate appreciation for masculine beauty.

Moore, Kalbas, Bennett, and Casey might have found *tame* excitement in Brooklyn, but for many other visitors in the 1930s, Brooklyn was a party destination. In particular, post–World War I the area near the Brooklyn Navy Yard became synonymous with nightlife. Slumming Manhattanites could find titillation and a sense of the exotic there, much as in Harlem. Sailors had a reputation for loose morals, rough excitements, and international experience. When New Yorkers wanted to find sailors, they headed across the East River to the Brooklyn Navy Yard, right where Antonio Bellavicini had been busted for serving gay men in his saloon twenty years earlier.

By now, however, the police weren't the only ones keeping watch on gay bars. Throughout the 1920s and '30s, a national magazine called *Broadway Brevities* advertised itself as "America's First National Tabloid Weekly." It specialized in sex scandals and thinly veiled gossip, with tawdry headlines and bawdy comics screaming off every page. "Sex Torture Bared—Whips, Thumbscrews, Handcuffs Found by Dicks in Raid on Immoral Establishment" read a typical cover story from 1932. While it was far from a legitimate news source, in one respect *Broadway Brevities* had every other publication in America beat: when it came to reporting on queer life, no one else wrote as prolifically or as accurately. Although its articles were disapproving and salacious, the writers of *Broadway Brevities* clearly had intimate knowledge of New York City's queer scene. In *Gay New York*, George Chauncey wrote that *Brevities* had a "remarkable familiarity with gay slang," and that it was "the one paper that delighted in identifying the haunts of even the most discreet gay men"—including the haunts of gay men in Brooklyn.[25]

In November 1931, *Broadway Brevities*' back-cover story was explicitly about gay Brooklyn. Under the headline "Third Sex Plague Spreads Anew! Sissies Permeate Sublime Social Strata as Film Stars and Broadwayites Go Gay," a subhead read, "Brooklyn Navy Yard Center of Flagrant Camping for Gobs and Society Slummers."[26] *Gob* was slang for "enlisted sailor," and the article was a tell-all exposé on queer celebrities and the bars they cruised. This was the era of the "pansy craze," when it was fashionable to have dishy, effeminate gay men in Hollywood films, and when hip straight people began visiting drag reviews and gay cafés in larger numbers. Both of these trends are evident in the 1932 film *Call Her Savage*, in which Clara Bow's character was romanced by a man who took her to a café in Greenwich Village where "only wild poets and anarchists eat." There, they watched a musical number performed by a pair of campy queer waiters. According to *Broadway Brevities*, the bars of the Navy Yard were another common stop for the era's pansy-crazed socialites.

In particular, the article described the scene at Frank's Place, a gay bar "just back of the Navy Yard," which had been repeatedly raided and reopened. The author wrote:

> *The average citizen would scarcely believe his eyes had he been transported there as recently as the late spring, when the "fleet was last in." Night after night, but especially on Saturdays and Sundays, anywhere from fifty to seventy-five sailors were there, and anywhere from fifty to a hundred men and boys, with painted faces and dyed tresses, singing and dancing. "High Society" dropped in, on "slumming" tours, of course. One recognized Mons. T——, the Scandinavian whose portrait*

has graced the society publications, and Adolphe D———, rich and fashionable,
whose brother married the widow of one of the outstanding millionaires of America.

As the piece continues, it becomes clear that the author is very familiar with the bar. He describes the hostesses, a pair of drag queens named Violet and Blossom, as having their own "special following" thanks to their "elaborate drags." Interestingly, from this point on, male and female impersonators almost exclusively used professional names of the gender they performed under. This was a sea change from the time of the Great Ricardo and Florence Hines and perhaps indicates that the impersonators were less concerned with, or capable of, projecting a traditionally gendered image offstage.

At Frank's Place, the *Brevities* author picked up rumors from sailors from California, who talked about the "star who likes them 'salty and sea-going,'" and the one who owned an antique store to conceal his faggy interest in period décor. Later in the article, the author discusses a variety of gay men and their lives in Brooklyn, from "Frank M——," who has "an elaborate abode in Brooklyn" and "occasionally cultivates the society of some pretty actresses" to throw off suspicion about his homosexuality, to "another and much younger actor, one who still earns good money," but also "makes frequent trips to the vicinity of the Navy Yard Y.M.C.A., in Sands Street."

Overall, the piece makes it clear that a high-end gay scene in Brooklyn was directly connected to a network of gay nightlife around the city and country. According to a gay New York City resident named Thomas Painter (who provided Alfred Kinsey with a wealth of anecdotal information about gay New York during the 1940s and '50s), "from Brooklyn to Harlem there were a score of bars catering exclusively to homosexuals and their prostitutes."[27]

By the mid-1930s, thanks to the decreased size of the military between the two world wars and the end of Prohibition in 1933, the neighborhood around the Navy Yard lost some of its rough edges—but it retained its gay clientele. In 1935, *The Brooklyn Daily Eagle* devoted an entire article to not-so-subtly suggesting that something about Sands Street was queer. "Sinful Sands Street Really Just a Sissy," ran the headline. If that wasn't clear enough, the subhead explained that the "Picturesque Brooklyn Thoroughfare" was "like Greenwich Village," which had been the epicenter of the pansy craze. The neighborhood was "cosmopolitan," filled with "brightly-lighted bars" and "strolling sailors." On the weekends, "crowds of expensively-clad men and women from the five boroughs and from out-of-town roll down Sands Street in luxurious automobiles, and seek the excitement and glamour they've heard about, in the bars, the one cabaret, and in the passing characters on the street."[28]

That one cabaret was Tony's Square Bar, which serviced sailors and their admirers throughout the 1930s and well into the '40s and '50s. Tony's was just "a couple of hundred yards" from the Sands Street entrance to the Navy Yard and had a sign on the door that read NO MINORS UNDER 20 ALLOWED (in response to which one journalist wryly noted, "Minors age rapidly in Sands Street").[29] Inside, the bar was painted in a dark-red-and-black-checkerboard pattern, which confused the eye (and hid any unsightly stains from the evening's entertainment). At one end of the room was a small, triangular-shaped balcony, where a band nightly performed jazz and torch-song favorites. One journalist derisively wrote that tourists had to "cross the ocean and pay guides" to find European cafés that had an atmosphere quite so "shivery."

By 1939, *The Brooklyn Daily Eagle*'s nightlife columnist would go so far as to refer to Sands Street as "The Navy's Broadway" and called out Tony's as the bar from which he had "never come away disappointed." The manager of Tony's told him that when the navy was in town, the bar's orchestra started going at noon and went all night.[30] That same year, Kinsey's informant Thomas Painter included Tony's on a list of "Homosexual Resorts in New York City, as of May 1939." He listed the clientele as "Navy sailors and homosexuals." In small script under his description of Tony's, Painter listed "another bar near by, the same"[31]—possibly Frank's Place or another queer sailor bar in the area.

Who were the slumming Manhattanites out cruising for gobs at these bars? They were men such as Lincoln Kirstein, who cofounded the New York City Ballet in 1948 and was one of the cultural leaders of postwar New York. On April 18, 1932, a twenty-five-year-old Kirstein wrote in his diary that he and some friends had attempted to go to Frank's Place, but discovered it had recently been raided. After talking to a sailor at the YMCA, they ended up at another speakeasy nearby, "a dive full of sailors and a few tarts," which was filled with "crepe paper decorations as the place had only opened."[32] The unnamed sailor from the YMCA (whom Kirstein described as "sweet hot subservient") accompanied them. As well, Kirstein brought along his friend Sergei Eisenstein, the famous

Russian director who had just finished his film *¡Que viva México!* and whose queer sexuality was an open secret that the Russian government tried to suppress.

After a little while at the bar, "a very large, very drunk and quite attractive gob shuffled across the room and started being offensive" to Kirstein and his friends. At first, he seemed annoyed that they were slumming, but he was soon persuaded to take a seat and join them in a round. Suddenly, Kirstein wrote, the sailor "got a perfect idea: 'we'll all put a dollar on the table and then we'll all jerk off, until the first guy that comes picks up the pot.'" Despite Kirstein's attempts to dissuade him, the sailor's "erection grew under his pants," until one of the "tarts" intervened to make certain he wasn't bothering the group, after which Kirstein and friends hightailed it back to Manhattan.

Bars such as Frank's Place and Tony's—where gay and straight worlds mixed—appeared and disappeared throughout the next few decades, but two changes that occurred in the mid-1930s set gay bars on a path to being smaller, more dangerous, and more insular: the end of Prohibition and the beginning of the movie code.

In 1933, Prohibition was officially repealed, once again drawing a thin blue line between straight bars and their queer counterparts. Mixed queer-straight venues would slowly begin to disappear, as the law encouraged straight people to avoid (still illegal) gay bars, and to keep queer people out of straight establishments (to prevent them from being raided). In *Gay New York*, George Chauncey called this "the most significant step in the campaign to exclude the gay world from the public sphere."[33] Once there were safer options, the appeal of slumming in dangerous queer bars quickly cooled. As legal drinking establishments pushed out those that were controlled by organized crime (which had greatly expanded during Prohibition), the Mafia maintained a stranglehold on gay bars. In large part, this was thanks to the New York State Liquor Authority (SLA), which was created in 1934 to regulate drinking establishments. "While the legislature did not specifically prohibit bars from serving homosexuals," Chauncey wrote in *Gay New York*, "the SLA made it clear from the beginning that it interpreted the statute to mandate such a prohibition. The simple presence of lesbians or gay men, prostitutes, gamblers, or other 'undesirables,' it contended, made an establishment disorderly."[34] In essence, the SLA was continuing the work of the Committee of Fourteen, but now with the entire power of the government behind it. Pushed into the shadows, gay bars became a staple among mob-owned and mob-protected businesses (which remained true into the 1990s). More than any other single factor, the repeal of Prohibition created the seedy, underground world of gay bars that came to the fore after World War II.

Simultaneously, in June 1934, the Motion Picture Production Code (aka the Hays Code) was suddenly given new teeth. When it was written in 1927, the Hays Code banned films from exploring a long list of subjects, including "any inference of sex perversion," "any licentious or suggestive nudity," "miscegenation," and "sympathy for criminals" (including homosexuals).[35] The code was drafted by two prominent Catholics, a Jesuit priest named Daniel Lord and a layman named Martin Quigley, which explained some of the other rules, such as the prohibition of any ridicule of the clergy.

At first, the code was routinely flouted. Little money was put toward oversight, and the people tasked with enforcing the code found it prudish and censorial. However, that changed in 1934, when all films were required to obtain a certificate of approval from the newly created Production Code Administration (PCA) before they could be released. The PCA was headed by Joseph Breen, another prominent Catholic, who demanded dogmatic adherence to the Hays Code before he would approve a film. The pansy craze, which presented America with a vision of queer people as odd and unusual but also harmless and exciting, was over. Even in vaudeville, where queer people had an established presence dating back to the mid-1800s, they were now persona non grata; in 1931, the RKO vaudeville circuit banned performers from using the words *fairy* or *pansy* in their acts.[36] Largely in response to the gains in public representation queer people had made during the progressive 1920s, they were now being driven out of most American mass culture. In the late 1930s, this antihomosexual panic would begin to spread to government institutions, and post–World War II, American culture would increasingly be filled with images of homosexuals as violent psychopaths and pathetic failures.

Other forms of entertainment also faced increased regulation in New York City at the end of the 1930s. The vestiges of variety's early, bawdy roots clung to life as burlesque. Although today burlesque is synonymous with stripping, in the 1930s it was a small but still-active live-theater scene where sexualized forms of classic variety acts (dance, comedy, music, etc.) ruled the day. Although burlesque venues primarily catered to heterosexual men, they still created space for queer people. Queer women worked in these venues, as did drag performers of all kinds;

lesbianism—or at least the suggestion of it—was a frequent part of the show. But in 1937, newspaper coverage of a string of lurid sex crimes convinced reform-minded Mayor Fiorello La Guardia that burlesque was a blight on the city's soul. La Guardia placed a former theater producer, Paul Moss, in charge of licensing theatrical venues, with explicit instructions to shut down burlesque. At the start of Moss's tenure, fourteen theaters in the city produced only burlesque; he shuttered all of them and pursued burlesque acts when they performed in so-called legitimate theaters as well. According to the *New York Daily News,* "more than 2,000 girls, stagehands, musicians and ticket sellers were put out on the street" by Moss's campaign.[37] The word *burlesque* was banned from theater marquees, and yet another space where queer and straight worlds overlapped was erased from the city's landscape.

Thus almost overnight, queer people were removed from straight movies, straight people disappeared from queer bars, and the final remnants of vaudeville's sexually permissive edges were filed down. As the prosperity of the twenties gave way to the poverty of the thirties, all kinds of experimentation—from literary to sexual—became less enticing, exacerbating the conservative retrenchment that always follows periods of intense social progress. Moreover, the increasing racial diversity of cities around the United States (including New York) fueled white-supremacist fears, which were channeled into (and empowered by) eugenic doctors and organizations. Although the repression of queer sexuality was rarely the primary goal of these institutions, it was certainly on the agenda.

This physical separation was accompanied by a psychological one, as the idea of sexual orientation took hold in popular culture. For most of the nineteenth and early-twentieth centuries, being gender variant was the primary marker of sexual difference, and the actual sexual history of a man or a woman mattered less than how well he or she conformed to an idea of masculinity or femininity. Sexuality, as a concept separate from gender, didn't exist. But Sigmund Freud's ideas about psychoanalysis made huge gains on American soil throughout the 1910s and '20s, introducing the idea of psychosexual motivations—hidden sexual aspects of our personalities that drive many of our other behaviors. Freud visited America in 1909, and psychoanalytic organizations opened immediately in his wake; in 1910, the Psychopathological Association was founded in Washington, DC, and the next year it was joined by the New York Psychoanalytic Society, which was followed in 1914 by the American Psychoanalytic Association in Baltimore.

Although it took a few decades for their theories to spread beyond their nascent profession, by the 1930s these theories were becoming the dominant way to understand sexuality and gender in America. Thanks in large part to psychiatry, the world was increasingly divided between homosexuals and heterosexuals, and while gender normativity still mattered, Americans were coming to understand that a deviant sexual nature could lurk within the most manly man or feminine woman. The need to actively define oneself as straight, and police any activities that might imply queerness—from going to a gay bar, to enjoying a movie with gay characters, to having any sexual contact with a person of the same sex— became paramount. As historian of sexuality Jennifer Terry points out, "Although homosexuality was talked about more openly in New York during the 1930s than it had been previously, popular and police attitudes toward it tended to be more vicious and condemnatory than they had been in the 1920s."[38] This trend would continue post–World War II, leading queer and straight people to inhabit increasingly separate worlds.

Yet even as gay and straight life were separating, an unprecedented assemblage of queer people and straight medical professionals were coming together in NYC to launch a vast research project called the Committee for the Study of Sex Variants (CSSV). Over the next thirty years, the project would splinter into many different groups, but along the way it would interview hundreds of queer people, publish an important treatise on queer sexuality, attempt to create a secret gay espionage ring during World War II, and help launch the first ever alternatives-to-detention program for men arrested for having gay sex in public places. But it all started in 1931, when a young lesbian named Jan Gay traveled to Berlin to study with Magnus Hirschfeld, the foremost sex researcher in the world at the time and an early proponent of gay rights.

Born Helen Reitman in 1902, Jan Gay was a journalist, professional nudist, and children's book author who attended the University of Chicago. At the age of twenty-five, she took the last name Gay, as did her girlfriend, Zhenya Gay. According to her half sister, Gay was an old family name, but the significance of the choice was obvious.[39] Ostensibly, Gay went to Germany to study the organized nudism movement, and upon returning to America, she would write a book (*On Going Naked*) and open a nudist resort (the Out-of-Doors Club in Highland, New York). According to newspaper accounts from the time, Gay was "the leader of nudism in New York,"[40] who "apparently cuts her own hair" and is "a little dandy."[41]

Photos show a strikingly handsome woman with short dark hair, an athletic frame, and an intense gaze.

However, Gay traveled to Berlin with an ulterior motive: she wanted to understand female homosexuality. She had already begun collecting case histories from lesbians, detailing their lives, their sexual practices, and their families. She visited Hirschfeld to learn how he, as a professional sex researcher, conducted his voluminous interviews. She would use a modified version of his questions to collect information from some three hundred lesbians, mostly in New York, Berlin, and Paris.

Gay hoped to publish her research, and to establish an organization for the study of homosexuality, à la Hirschfeld's Institute of Sex Research. However, as a young woman with no formal medical or scientific training, she needed to find a partner who could legitimate her work. Around 1933, she contacted a venerable scion of Brooklyn, the now seventy-two-year-old obstetrician Robert Latou Dickinson. Although he and his wife, Sarah Truslow, had continued to work with the Brooklyn auxiliary of the Committee of Fourteen for decades, they had recently left Brooklyn for Manhattan, and for most of the previous ten years Dickinson's energies had gone toward the National Committee on Maternal Health (NCMH), which he founded in 1923. As part of his work with the NCMH, Dickinson used his five-thousand-plus case files on female patients (primarily from Brooklyn) to write two books on women's sexual health: *A Thousand Marriages* (1933) and *The Single Woman* (1934). A planned third volume, looking at married and single women combined, was never completed.

The white-haired patriarch of a large family, Dickinson was not interested in the sex lives of women for purely educational reasons; he wanted to promote heterosexual marriage, which he believed was endangered by the pressures of modern life. Unlike many physicians of his time, however, Dickinson believed that sexual pleasure for women was crucial to a healthy union. As he wrote in the introduction to *The Single Woman*, since 1890 he had believed that "sex desire is not sin; that the sex parts are not shame parts (*Schamtheile*); and that autoerotism is apparently natural and rarely physically harmful."[42] He approached lesbianism in much the same vein: while it was not a priori wrong or evil, it represented a threat to (or at best, a distraction from) heterosexual marriage, which was the ideal. In *The Single Woman*, Dickinson defined homosexuality as "a transient attempt" to ape heterosexual love with someone of the same sex, whether or not sexual contact was involved. However, he made it clear that he respected his queer female patients. He wrote that they tended to have good health, steady employment, and appearance and social class "above the average." None of the women were involved in pedophilic relationships, he noted, and all of their relationships had emotional, not just sexual, components. Furthermore, he said that none of his queer patients wanted to be men, but that they did tend to have absent fathers and maladjusted mothers and perhaps distrusted heterosexual family formations for that reason.[43]

To a young lesbian such as Gay, this attitude would have been refreshingly forward thinking, as it didn't present lesbians as psychotics, men trapped in women's bodies, or feebleminded idiots, and it paid more attention to their mental and emotional states than to the shapes of their bodies. Today, talking about missing fathers and unstable mothers seems pejorative, but at the time Freudian theories of sexual development were relatively progressive, in that they didn't present homosexuals as some kind of in-between, inverted, or third sex. Dickinson's medical training in the late 1800s emphasized those kinds of eugenic beliefs, as is obvious in his case notes, in which he frequently tried to deduce a woman's sexual history and identity from the shape, size, and plasticity of her vagina. Yet his writings show that he was willing to keep up with advancements in the field (such as psychology), which may have attracted Gay's attention.

Gay might also have met Dickinson through his coauthor on both of his books, Lura Beam. Beam worked closely with Dickinson for over a decade. It's likely that some of Dickinson's progressive ideas about sexuality came from Beam, who was primarily a lesbian and spent most of her life in a relationship with Louise Stevens Bryant, a social reformer who served on maternal-health committees with Dickinson. According to a sexual-history interview that Alfred Kinsey did with Dickinson sometime in the 1930s, Dickinson had a long-standing affair with a secretary who was primarily a lesbian——either Beam or Bryant. According to Kinsey's notes, Dickinson described the woman as "vigorous, widely experienced in very active homosexuality, [but] she enjoyed men as much." The relationship "lasted years" and was wildly passionate for both of them. Dickinson said they would have sex "at an instant's notice on a chair, or all night with three sessions, [giving] her several strong orgasms and he would have one or more."[44]

According to historian Jennifer Terry, in 1933 Dickinson "tried unsuccessfully to get the Committee on Maternal Health to sponsor a study of 'sexual inversion' under the guidance of Jan Gay and a young gay man named Thomas

Painter" (the same Painter who would go on to work with Alfred Kinsey).[45] Two years later, Dickinson and Gay decided to start their own group, which they called the Committee for the Study of Sex Variants. Dickinson invited a wide range of experts to join them, including psychologists, physicians, social workers, anthropologists, and officials in the state penal system. The committee included some prominent Brooklynites, such as August Witzel, a psychologist from Brooklyn State Hospital. In an informal way, it also included several queer people who would be instrumental in legitimating the CSSV within queer circles, enabling it to recruit a wide array of research subjects. This was different from many previous studies, which often focused on inmates, psychiatric patients, or isolated individuals who were already receiving treatment for their sexuality or gender variance.

Thomas Painter was one of the committee's "inside men." Born in 1905, Painter was the dissipated heir of a well-off New York City family. Like Jan Gay, he was also working on a book, a sprawling, never-published two-volume look at male prostitutes (his prime interest in life). According to his papers at the Kinsey Institute, Painter and Gay met first, and she introduced him to Dickinson. Painter described Dickinson as a "militant liberal" who pushed Painter to pursue his research, "though the work that I had done at the time scarcely warranted it." Although Painter worked closely with the CSSV for a number of years, in his private notes he described them as "a sorry crew" who were "exploiting the old idealist," Dickinson. He described Jan Gay as "the dominant type," who used homosexual men "as stooges, messenger boys and furniture movers." As one might guess from that description, he and Gay had a prickly relationship, and they didn't appear to be close (for instance, Painter thought her last name was Goldberg). However, when she wasn't trying to get him to become a nudist, Painter described Gay as "pleasant, intelligent, and agreeable."[46]

Aside from Gay, Painter, and Dickinson, the two most important individuals to join the committee—and the ones who accomplished the majority of the work done under its auspices—were two New Yorkers named George Henry and Alfred Gross. George Henry was a psychologist who worked at the Payne Whitney Psychiatric Clinic at New York Hospital, and who had previously conducted research on incarcerated "psychopathic homosexuals."[47] Alfred Gross was a defrocked Episcopalian priest who worked with Henry, and who was interested in this research because of his own homosexuality. Gross conducted most of the interviews done by the committee, although this was kept from the rest of the

CSSV and the Payne Whitney Clinic, all of who believed Dr. Henry was the primary investigator. Had the truth been known, it's unlikely the CSSV would have been able to pursue their work. Decades later, Gross told people that they "used each other," and that he pushed their work in directions that Henry either did not know about or turned "a blind eye" to.[48]

The active participation of queer people at every stage of this study, from formulation to execution, distinguished it from previous American sexuality research. But it also created tension within the group. Over all, the CSSV was divided into two subtly separate factions: the heterosexual scientists, who were sympathetic to the plight of queer people but primarily saw their work as a first step toward preventing or curing homosexuality; and the queer laypeople, who believed this work would help heterosexuals understand queer people *and* help queer people receive the care and study they needed.

However, despite the best efforts of Gay, Painter, and Gross, the committee's work was steeped in homophobic and eugenic assumptions about sexuality. Henry suggested that the CSSV conduct their study out of the Payne Whitney Psychiatric Clinic, where he worked. In his initial proposal to the clinic, he stated that the CSSV study would begin with one hundred secured subjects, fifty men and fifty women, all obtained "through the agency of Miss Jan Gay."[49] The inclusion of men and women, as well as people of all races, further differentiates the CSSV study from previous efforts and highlights that sexuality was beginning to be understood as a characteristic that could be examined on its own, separate from gender or race.

Henry's proposal framed homosexuality as a threat to heterosexuality and society broadly; in his words:

Since homosexuality is a form of arrested psychosexual development which seriously interferes with reproduction and leads to personality conflicts often ending in mental illness and many other forms of tragedy, its causes, methods of prevention and the ways in which those already distorted may be aided in achieving a socially acceptable adjustment should be studied with the greatest care.

In one convoluted sentence, Henry captured the thoughts of the entire committee: his own interest in psychosexual development; Dickinson's belief in an embattled heterosexuality; and (at the very end), Gay, Painter, and Gross's hopes to help other queer people find "socially acceptable adjustment." Although it doesn't mention race, as the entire committee was white, the proposal's framing of homosexuality as endangering reproduction carries overtones of Dr. R. W. Shufeldt's concerns about preserving the "white race."

The Payne Whitney Clinic accepted Henry's proposal, and from 1935 to 1943, the CSSV interviewed an incredible number of queer people in their offices. Just from '35 to '37 alone, for example, they saw eighty-four patients who submitted to incredibly thorough interviews, mapping out their family histories (with an eye toward homosexuality, narcissism, and psychiatric problems), their life stories, their sexual experiences (in incredible detail), and their thoughts on the future. They also underwent intensive medical study, which included X-rays, physicals, the taking of semen samples, and internal vaginal examinations so invasive they would definitely be illegal today. They pursued physical data that seem esoteric and strange to a modern reader, such as cataloging the "thickness and angularity of the cranium" in each patient.[50] The committee collected such a variety of data because one of their initial questions was whether sexuality could more easily be deduced from the body or the mind. Dickinson urged what we might call a "eugenics 2.0" approach, which argued that sexuality might not reside in the body directly, but that a life of homosexuality, or even a homosexual orientation that went unconsummated, left evidence that could be read via physical examinations. He believed gay men would have bodies more like women's (and vice versa), and that lesbians would have larger, tougher, and more responsive vaginal areas than their heterosexual counterparts. Dr. Henry, on the other hand, came from a post-Freudian mentality, which believed that sexuality was mostly caused by adverse childhood experiences and preexisting pathological leanings and was more likely to be divulged via psychiatric techniques than by physical exams. According to Jennifer Terry, "by the end, both Dickinson and Henry realized that one could not determine whether an individual was a sex variant or not merely by looking at his or her body."[51] Although the idea that you can tell a person's sexuality just by looking at them has never gone away, the research of the CSSV would help to push most future legitimate sexuality studies in a firmly Freudian direction.

Around 1940, the CSSV began preparing its research for publication, choosing forty men and forty women for discussion in a two-volume book entitled *Sex Variants*. The introduction to the book was a hodgepodge of tolerance and homophobia. This research was important because "the sex offender must be studied if progress in the prevention as well as in the treatment of sexual maladjustment is to be achieved."[52] Yet at the same time, "it is clearly evident that a homosexual is being punished by society largely because he is a homosexual rather than because of an actual offense he has committed. . . . [He] becomes the symbol of iniquity to his enemies and he is promptly and automatically purged by his former friends." Dr. Henry wrote that "no two homosexuals are alike," which sounds positive until he continued, "Homosexuality is associated with an almost endless variety and complexity of human problems." Overall, Sex Variants has a tragic air of missed opportunity to it. Thanks to their queer insiders, the experts of the CSSV were given an unvarnished look into the difficulties that queer people faced in America in the 1930s. However, thanks to their preexisting prejudices, the committee members continually interpreted what they saw as evidence that homosexuality itself was pathological and damaging—but also often incurable, and therefore deserving of pity more than punishment.

One of the people examined by the committee was none other than Othilie Spengler, the trans woman who had come to the defense of Elizabeth Trondle. In Sex Variants, the committee spent over ten pages meticulously diagramming her body, her life story, and her family history. The committee appreciated her "interest in promoting a more tolerant attitude toward transvestites" and how she was "ready at any time to present [herself] for study and examination." Since her time being studied by sexologist Bernard Talmey, Spengler's life had been difficult; her wife had left her (despite her in-laws wanting them to remain together, even knowing she was transgender), and her children had become much less accepting as they grew older. The committee was cold toward her, calling her a "caricature" and a "hermit," and saying that she "dwell[ed] in a world of classical fantasy," while taking pains to highlight the squalid nature of her home. But they also managed to capture her many attempts at advocacy for herself and other trans people: working with prominent sexologists; petitioning the police for the right to wear dresses in public; writing to other trans people around the world; joining a club for lesbians in Berlin; and even taking hormones and agreeing to an experimental procedure in which X-rays were applied to her testicles to render her sterile. They also recorded the thing that would make her most famous: during and immediately after World War I, Spengler compiled a four-hundred volume history of the war, told entirely through newspaper clippings. Originally housed at the New-York Historical Society, it now resides in the Library of Congress.

By the time *Sex Variants* came out, Thomas Painter had quit his involvement with the CSSV, as had Jan Gay (who may have been forced out after recruiting subjects). Although the introduction to *Sex Variants* recognized that "the general plan of approach embodied in this project was first laid before the members of the Committee by Miss Jan Gay," she was given no authorship credit, and her years of independent research were viewed as preliminary to the real study. The book listed none of the queer members of the CSSV as part of the official committee. Although Thomas Painter respected Dr. Dickinson, Painter's notes for Alfred Kinsey savaged Gross and Henry and their work:

> [*Gross*] *was Dr. George Henry's stooge and man-of-all-work. . . . Henry has a hold on him somehow, and uses it, like a ring in his nose. Gross has a lot on Henry, too, I feel, and I picture them as a couple of evil beings—a magician and gnome—snidely running a half legitimate racket on the public ignorance of homosexuality. Gross admits Henry is a cold-blooded, mercenary phoney [sic]—but his position with Henry is one where he can play big shot and petty tyrant to a lot of frightened, helpless, dependent homosexuals and ex-convicts—and does, and enjoys it immensely.*[53]

Painter had to fight the pair to reclaim his manuscript on male prostitutes, and to prevent it from being absorbed into the CSSV's official reports. In his notes at the Kinsey Institute, Painter wrote that he "had to raise hell to get it back." Afterward, Painter gave the manuscript to Kinsey, who preserved the entire book in his files.[54]

Sadly, Jan Gay's own manuscript was completely incorporated into *Sex Variants,* and no extant copy has ever been found, leaving it impossible to say how much of the work of this first incarnation of the CSSV was hers. Undoubtedly, the committee would not have existed without her. Over the 1930s, she developed a severe drinking problem and, according to a few sources, moved to Mexico to dry out. There, she became an expert on US–Latin American foreign relations, and she continued to be a lifelong proponent of nudism, but her experience with the CSSV seemed to have destroyed her interest in studying sexuality. In the mid-1940s, she contacted Alfred Kinsey, who proclaimed to have been inspired by the CSSV to conduct his own sexuality work. Unasked, he wrote that she could "very definitely help on this research."[55] A few years later, as Gay was preparing an application for a Guggenheim Fellowship to analyze the work of Alcoholics

Anonymous, she contacted Kinsey again to ask for a reference. His terse response seems to have been their final communication:

I am not the person to recommend you. . . . I met you once for a short time and know nothing more about you than general hearsay. I know nothing of your specific scientific training and have had no opportunity to observe you in scientific work.[56]

Over and over, Jan Gay's pioneering research was seen as good enough to further the careers of men with advanced degrees, but never good enough to stand on its own. Today, she is perhaps the most important, most forgotten footnote in the history of American sexuality studies.

In 1930—the year before Jan Gay made her pilgrimage to meet Magnus Hirschfeld in Germany—a very different kind of educational experiment launched in downtown Brooklyn: Brooklyn College. This was not the first institute of higher education in the borough. It was created from the merger of two earlier schools, both of which were satellites of Manhattan campuses. But from its beginning, Brooklyn College was a new educational experiment. It was the first public, coeducational liberal arts college in all of New York City, and as a municipally funded institution, it was basically free for all city high school graduates. It was often compared—favorably—to the top colleges in America. An adage at the time went, "While not every student at Brooklyn College would have been accepted into Harvard, at least half of the students in Harvard would not have qualified for Brooklyn."[57] As one alumna from the class of 1934 remembered, "We were the children of peddlers, tailors, first-chance Americans, and everybody pointed to the city colleges and said, 'This is your opportunity, take it.'"[58]

Most schools in America did not share this egalitarian approach to their student bodies. Just two years before Brooklyn College opened, the dean of Yale's medical school wrote in a letter that the admissions office should "never admit more than five Jews, take only two Italian Catholics, and take no blacks at all."[59] In this, Yale was no racist, anti-Semitic outlier; the leaders of many major universities sat on the boards of eugenics organizations (with such ghastly names as the American Breeder's Association), which encouraged white supremacy, anti-Semitism, and biological determinism.

Brooklyn College was the mongrel upstart in this purebred field. It opened with approximately ten thousand students, about equally divided between men and women. Even though Brooklyn's black population was still small, the school was integrated, and it was noted for its large number of Jewish students. (New York City as a whole was then about one-third people of Jewish descent, including many new refugees from Germany, Eastern Europe, and the USSR.) The school prided itself on community involvement, educational achievement, and a progressive vision for society. Thus, it's no surprise that it attracted many queer people to both its faculty and student body from day one. However, as the decade wore on, its radical roots would make it an easy target for conservative anticommunist activists, whose purges would provide an early blueprint for Senator Joseph McCarthy's Red Scare in the 1950s.

Opening a new school immediately after the start of the Depression could not have been easy. For the first seven years of its existence, the college's "campus" consisted of a scattering of repurposed sites in downtown Brooklyn, including three floors of a squat brick commercial building on Joralemon Street, and an evening annex inside a boys' high school. The original school song, "These Are Not Towers of Marble," celebrated the school's humble origins and was written by Robert Friend, a gay Jewish poet who was among the first students to grace its grubby halls.[60] A stooped, owlish young man, Friend was a closeted radical during his days at Brooklyn and would only come into his own—erotically and literarily—after leaving the city, first for a stint teaching English in Puerto Rico and Panama, and then eventually to Israel (where he fled to escape the Red Scare). But even in his first book of poetry, 1941's *Shadow on the Sun*, Friend's sexuality could be deduced from such poems as "Meaning," which read in part:

> This love is solitary that will die this death;
> it weeps on your breast, gathers loneliness
> of all men who at the self-same hour
> lying behind dark shades in a rotting house
> shut out the light of history, shut out that love[61]

All around the college's campus were signs of the worsening Depression: unemployed men wearing their suits to go sit in the park outside Brooklyn's City Hall so their families wouldn't know they had lost their jobs; shoeless children begging for change outside the entrance to every subway; entire families waiting in line at the Salvation Army for a handout. Encampments of homeless people, all named for President Hoover, sprung up around the country. In Brooklyn Heights, a "Hoover City" was located between Henry and Clinton Streets, where the homes were just "makeshift shacks built of packing boxes, scrap iron and barrel staves," some of them with small vegetable plots tilled into the city's polluted soil.[62]

Still, it was by all accounts an exciting time to be in downtown Brooklyn. The borough's population had exploded in the 1920s, so that distant neighborhoods such as Flatbush and Park Slope had become the new suburbs to downtown Brooklyn's urban center. Busy Brooklyn families could now take an elevated train to their homegrown department store, Abraham & Straus (which had just completed an $8 million expansion of their flagship space on Fulton Street), and buy everything from lingerie to gardening shears. As the Depression was forcing stores across America to fold, A&S instituted an across-the-board 10 percent salary reduction and was thereby able to stay open and avoid laying off a single employee. For the new American transplant craving a taste of home, downtown Brooklyn's specialty grocers offered everything from gefilte fish to *platanos*. But the neighborhood's shining jewels were its glorious new movie palaces, which offered a whole evening of fantasy for just a single quarter. By 1930, downtown Brooklyn was home to five of these newfangled temples of amusement, all clustered within spitting distance of Brooklyn College. After slipping out of class in some anonymous office building full of peeling plaster and rusting pipes, a student could easily find her way to the Paramount Theater, sashay through the ornate three-story, vaulted, art deco lobby, and join four thousand other avid moviegoers in its gilded baroque auditorium.

For some students, the college's downtown location also held other, more esoteric delights. The swarthy, diminutive Beatnik poet Harold Norse was born in Brooklyn in 1916 and raised in one of the large Jewish ghet-

Photo of Brooklyn College student and Beat poet Harold Norse (c. 1931). (*Photo courtesy of the collection of Todd Swindell.*)

tos that had sprung up down by Coney Island. One of his earliest sexual memories was staring down from his narrow tenement window at the naked Italian boys horsing around in the showers of the nearby municipal bathhouse, "bodies glistening in the sun . . . flicking wet towels on bare butts."[63] But not until he enrolled at Brooklyn College in the midthirties would he finally be "cured" of his virginity (as he put it).

The son of an impoverished Lithuanian single mother, Norse wrote in his autobiography, "Today an unwed mother and her bastard raise no brows. But when I was born we were untouchables."[64] Norse was the very definition of the gifted child of the striving class that Brooklyn College wanted to attract. However, while Norse went to the college to get an education, it wasn't the kind you received in a classroom. As he recalled many years later:

> If our "campus" consisted of city streets, only a few blocks away lay an area venerable for its literary tradition: Brooklyn Heights. . . . There in 1855 Walt Whitman hand-set the first edition of Leaves of Grass on Cranberry Street; in the 1920s on Columbia Heights Thomas Wolfe wrote Look Homeward, Angel, and a few doors away Hart Crane conceived and wrote sections of The Bridge. . . . If spirit of place means anything, a case can be made for a literary line of succession that links Whitman, Wolfe, and Crane in a family of rhapsodic, visionary writers established there. I had found my literary place. There was another link, the manly love of comrades (even about the lofty head of Wolfe hovered hushed rumors)—the "adhesiveness" of brotherly love, as Whitman called it. My initiation into this brotherhood began there.[65]

Specifically, his initiation began at the hands of one of his teachers, a young Communist activist and English-literature professor, David McKelvy White.

The son of the governor of Ohio, White had a patrician upbringing, which included an undergraduate degree from Princeton and a master's from Columbia. Tall, skinny, balding, and bespectacled, White looked like your standard-issue 1930s nerd, but beneath his placid exterior beat a militant heart. In 1926, in between schooling, he taught briefly at Lafayette College in Easton, Pennsylvania. The head of the English department there described him as a "homo-sexualist" who lived openly with his "male wife."[66] According to historian Matt Young, White was out to his family from an early age, which is perhaps why several contemporaries described him as "a great disappointment to his father."[67] To Norse, White was an "aesthete," as well as an "idealist," "an unfailing gentleman," and "a fervent Communist."[68] The ranks of the Communist Party were swelling at this time in America. Not only was the USSR seen as one of the strongest voices pushing back against Hitler, but the American Communist Party took a strong progressive line on issues of race, class, and religion. The party also strongly supported domestic government intervention to provide relief from the Great Depression. That, as well as its anti-anti-Semite politics, made the party incredibly popular in Brooklyn, and particularly at Brooklyn College.

White was among the first instructors in Brooklyn College's English department, and he was the faculty adviser to the men's student lit magazine, which is how he met Norse. At first, he hired Norse to organize his extensive record collection and tried to "drop a hairpin" (as the saying went) about his sexuality by playing contemporary camp classics when Norse came over: "There Are Fairies at the Bottom of Our Garden," by Beatrice Lillie; "Mad About the Boy," by Noël Coward; and "Falling in Love Again," by Marlene Dietrich. Seventeen and scared, Norse was oblivious, so White tried harder and invited him to go swimming at the St. George Hotel—perhaps the most elegant cruising ground in all of Brooklyn's history. The vast, Olympic-size saltwater pool was surrounded by deep emerald green tiles, a

The St. George Hotel, a popular Brooklyn cruising ground, in 1943.
(*Photo courtesy of the Irving I. Underhill photograph collection—Brooklyn Museum/Brooklyn Public Library—Brooklyn Collection.*)

completely mirrored ceiling, large art deco mosaics on the walls, and—at one end—a two-story waterfall. In the thirties, men's bathing suits tended toward tight, high-waisted shorts, sometimes with a stretchy top, and the muscular, pouty-lipped Norse must have gotten a lot of attention in his. "You have a fine figure," White told him one night. "Why do you hide it?" Norse was beginning to have an inkling into the truth of White's interest in him, but he believed that a "respectable" man such as White "didn't have such thoughts." It would take White a full year of dinners at the St. George before he and Norse finally consummated their relationship.

However, this was sometime around 1936, and the global conflagration that was leading to World War II soon separated Norse and White. White was increasingly active in the local chapter of the Communist Party, which also included many other faculty members. According to Bernard Grebanier, another English-literature professor at Brooklyn (and according to Harold Norse, a closeted homosexual), White was recruited to join the party by Marxist philosopher Howard Selsam. As Grebanier described it years later in an interview:

> Even sex was used as a way to draw people in. One man, who was the son of a governor in the middle west, was very very plainly a homosexual, living with another man at the college, and he developed a crush on Selsam. Now Selsam was perfectly straight, but seeing this he encouraged the man's feelings. . . . And as soon as he became a member, Selsam stepped on him like a steamroller.[69]

Grebanier was himself a member of the party, although he would later claim to have joined reluctantly and only because the party was working to improve life at the college, and he felt it would have been unfair to benefit without taking part. According to Grebanier, White's new boyfriend, Murray Young, quickly joined the party as well. Young was *also* an instructor in the English department at Brooklyn College, and the two lived together on Columbia Heights, just a block from Hamilton Easter Field's old home where Hart Crane used to write.

(The Communist Party in the thirties also attracted queer women in Brooklyn, such as labor activists Eva Kollisch and Gerry Faier. However, the party was militant in its promotion of women's heterosexuality, as Kollisch documented in her book, *Girl in Movement*. Young women were encouraged to wed, so that if and when their husbands went off to fight fascism, they could receive government subsidies that could be donated back to the party. Kollisch described feeling "blackmailed" into marriage, as if the movement and matrimony were one and the same for women.[70] Both Faier and Kollisch would only realize their queer desires after leaving the party, post–World War II.)

Despite the party's rather coercive approach to sexuality, White was firmly committed to the cause. In 1937, he walked off his job at Brooklyn College midsemester to become a machine gunner with the Loyalists fighting against the fascist rebellion of General Francisco Franco in Spain; two years later he was back in Brooklyn, now a national spokesperson for the fight against fascism and the promise of Communism. But as Americans became increasingly worried about Hitler, and dependent on government support to survive the Depression, White's criticisms of the United States and their allies—"the so-called democratic governments of Great Britain and France and even of the United States [which] are branded with the blood of the Spanish people"—resonated less and less with America's political mood.[71] Unsurprisingly, Brooklyn College refused to hire him back. Then, in 1939, as White was helping to release a report that praised Stalin and condemned the United States, Russia signed a surprise nonaggression pact with Hitler. What good feeling the American Communist Party had garnered over the rest of the decade for their progressive politics was destroyed overnight. Only the most fervent—such as White—stayed involved.

Regardless of their parting ways, White cited his experiences at Brooklyn College as the reason he fought in Spain. "Eight years ago I wouldn't have thought of going over," he told a reporter from the *Cincinnati Enquirer*. "Teaching in a municipal college strengthened my interest in democracy."[72] Unfortunately, the school system's own interest in democracy was swiftly waning, particularly when it came to Communists (and homosexuals). In early 1940, New York State launched the Rapp-Coudert Committee to investigate the extent of Communist influence in New York public education. According to historian Marjorie Heins, the committee "honed [the] techniques that came to define Red hunting in the late 1940s and early '50s: equating communist beliefs with subversion, conducting inquisitions behind closed doors, and using secret information of sometimes dubious credibility to expose and stigmatize the people they named." The lead investigator of the committee, Robert J. Morris, would go on to head the incredibly powerful, incredibly dangerous Senate Subcommittee on Internal Security, which destroyed the lives of many suspected Communists (and some homosexuals) in the fifties.[73]

The same year that the Rapp-Coudert Committee was inaugurated, a Brooklyn woman named Jean Kay sued the Board of Higher Education in New York for hiring philosopher Bertrand Russell to teach at City College. Her case alleged that his views on free love and nonmonogamy, as well as that he "approved of homosexuality," would harm her daughter, who was a student in a public city school (although not the one Russell was to teach at). Kay won the case, and the judge declared Russell "morally unfit" to teach.[74] The message was clear: neither Communists nor queers were welcome in New York City's educational system anymore. Queer people were now persona non grata in the classroom, much as they were in bars (thanks to the end of Prohibition) and movies (thanks to the Hays Code).

The gay Communist professors at Brooklyn College soon came under the fearsome eye of the Rapp-Coudert Committee. Bernard Grebanier quickly agreed to turn over evidence. At first in a secret hearing, and then publicly, he named more than twenty other professors as current or previous members of the party—including David McKelvy White and Murray Young, both of who refused to testify or name names. Young struck back publicly, denying his membership in the party and saying that Grebanier's cowardly testimony was "typical of a man who, having been educated in the New York public school system, allows himself to be used to destroy it."[75] However, despite his testimony, Young was dismissed from his position, while Grebanier stayed on and had a long, lauded, and closeted career in higher education. In 1982, the city officially apologized and made restitution to Young's estate (and to nearly a dozen other professors). But by then, the damage was long done. The Communist Party faction at Brooklyn College was broken by the Rapp-Coudert Committee and would be a negligible presence in local and national politics thereafter. The English department's small knot of gay professors was simply collateral damage. Murray Young continued to teach in other schools as an adjunct and lecturer for the rest of his life. White soldiered on as a militant antifascist and Communist organizer, even though the party declared "degeneracy" (aka homosexuality) incompatible with being a Communist Party member in 1938.[76] By the end of World War II, the party was prepared to oust White over his sexuality, and he committed suicide in 1945, a fact that his family long tried to cover up.[77]

However, while politics consumed the gay professors at Brooklyn, as the thirties came to a close Harold Norse was pursuing that perennial college-student obsession: sex. After he and White parted ways, Norse met another gay Jewish poet at the Brooklyn College literary magazine, the young Chester Kallman. The two were near opposites: Kallman was tall, while Norse was short; fair, while Norse was dark; and well-off, while Norse was poor. Yet they were instantly drawn to each other. According to Norse, Kallman had "androgynous appeal: willowy grace combined with a deep, manly voice." He was thin, but unathletic, and Norse wrote that Kallman "disliked all physical exercise except cruising, which developed his calf muscles."[78]

For a year, the pair pretended to each other to be straight, before drunkenly hooking up on New Year's Day 1939. Kallman might have been closeted, but he was no stranger to sex with men. According to Norse, Kallman had "from the age of twelve molested adults in subway toilets" and had "at least a thousand and three conquests on his belt, which loosened so easily."[79] The two commenced upon a tumultuous relationship, where Kallman held all the power. Kallman introduced Norse to a cavalcade of Brooklyn's gay sex spots, such as the apartment of two middle-aged men with an open-door policy for the young and the beautiful. In return for sexually satisfying the hosts, the young men were fed, entertained, and given free rein to have sex with one another in a safe and semiprivate space—an arrangement that was similar to the way most gay brothels functioned at the time, only without the exchange of money. "In those late-Depression, prewar years . . . the number of young men we had was mind-boggling," Norse recalled.[80] Like many gay men of his generation, Norse remembered this period as allowing significantly more sexual freedom and experimentation among otherwise straight men. The Depression had put many young men on the road, tramping from one city to the next looking for work. The ramp-up to World War II drew thousands upon thousands of these men to Brooklyn, where they found jobs in war-related factories or were drafted into the Navy Yard. It was like World War I on steroids, as the streets of Brooklyn were flush with lonely men and boys, set free from any restrictions they might have previously known in small communities or while living near their families.

Norse and Kallman drifted apart largely because of those other young men (and, according to Norse, because of Kallman's casual cruelty). But they were still technically lovers on the momentous April day in 1939 when the pair went to see Christopher Isherwood and W. H. Auden give a reading in Manhattan—the first reading the two British authors ever gave together in the United States. Kallman and Norse were certain that the wry, celebrated British pair were homosexuals, so they hatched a plan: they dressed up, sat in the front row, and winked at the two authors throughout the talk. Isherwood noticed them; Auden didn't.

Isherwood gave Norse a card and told the two to come by the house where the pair were staying, but Kallman "borrowed" it from Norse and went on his own. Although at first Auden was disinterested, when he discovered that Kallman was well endowed (reportedly clutching his hands together in prayer and announcing, "Thank God it's big!"),[81] the two became lovers. Almost overnight, Norse was iced out; he and Kallman remained friendly, but Kallman's relationship with Auden rapidly became the primary love of his life.

At the time, Auden was renting a room in a tony section of Brooklyn Heights. But his relationship with Kallman created a problem. His landlady was already suspicious of Auden, and the last thing Auden wanted was Kallman coming around and causing a scene. The encroaching war had driven Auden from England, and he was looking for a place to call home, one where he could live (and write) freely and without stress. Thankfully, a good friend of his, the writer and magazine editor George Davis, had a solution. In a dream, he'd envisioned a house in Brooklyn where he and his friends could live together in a creative communal home. In 1940, Davis would make that dream come true at 7 Middagh Street in Brooklyn Heights, which would become an epicenter for global culture throughout World War II. As the Swiss author Denis de Rougemont put it, "All that was new in America in music, painting or choreography emanated from that house, the only center of thought and art I found in any large city of the country."[82]

Throughout the thirties, queer life in America had grown ever more visible, continuing a trend started by the pansy craze of the late 1920s. But the lightheartedness of America's early flirtations with queer people did not hold. "Awareness" quickly transitioned into "surveillance," and queer people went from "novelty" to "threat." Soon the press of fascism would unexpectedly and temporarily halt America's growing homophobia. As a result, the 1940s are a sharply divided decade in queer history: five years of comparative sexual freedom during the war, followed by an almost immediate crackdown. This homophobic postwar panic would be compounded in Brooklyn by a turn away from urbanism, which would tear apart the services, neighborhoods, and pro-diversity mentality of the city, all of which nurtured its queer residents. The wide gay world of the 1920s and '30s would be exposed as a fragile bubble, and when it popped, even the evidence of its ever having existed would be destroyed.

6. Brooklyn at War, 1940–45

In the early years of WWII, 7 Middagh Street, aka February House, was home to an artist commune that included Carson McCullers, W. H. Auden, and Oliver Smith. (*Photo courtesy of the Brooklyn Historical Society. North side Middagh Street East of Columbia Heights, 1940 ca., V1974.16.132; Edna Huntington papers and photographs, ARC.044; Brooklyn Historical Society.*)

The house at 7 Middagh Street was a gingerbread affair; a Georgian blend of brick and stone with a peaked wooden portico and Tudor trim surrounding the windows. Like the literary menagerie that inhabited it for the first half of the 1940s, 7 Middagh Street was fancier than its neighbors, which were squat three-story brownstones with no pretentions. The area had originally been residential, but now a small candy factory was nearby, as well as a convent and a fire station. The Depression had been hard on this part of Brooklyn Heights, and some of the older residences had been sliced up into boardinghouses or abandoned entirely. Seven

Middagh Street was built in the 1800s, when the Heights was a destination for well-off white families weary of life in the big city, but this block edged just too close to the water—money, like the tide, had long since receded. The house was in desperate need of repair, with a broken furnace and drafts whistling through all its windows. In a few years the building (and the entire block) would be demolished by Robert Moses to make way for the Brooklyn–Queens Expressway. But for now, big maple trees shaded the street in the summer, and in the winter, it was covered by fog and smoke off the river. Two blocks south was Hamilton Easter Field's former artist colony where Hart Crane once lived; two blocks west was the water. George Davis, the editor of *Harper's Bazaar* who discovered the house, told anyone who asked that it had come to him in a dream.

Inside, the house was a warren of many-size rooms—perfect for dividing up among its future inhabitants. A large parlor with a marble fireplace was on the first floor, and a kitchen and formal dining room down below. The other two floors were all bedrooms, which would soon be filled by some of the most famous artists in America and Europe. The first wave of residents would include editor George Davis; writer Carson McCullers; poet W. H. Auden; composer Benjamin Britten and his lover, the tenor Peter Pears; and burlesque star Gypsy Rose Lee. Among later residents were set designer Oliver Smith, married writers Jane and Paul Bowles, and the author Richard Wright and his family. Some of the better-known guests included Erika, Klaus, and Golo Mann; Christopher Isherwood; Jerome Robbins; Janet Flanner and Solita Solano; Denis de Rougemont; Salvador and Gala Dalí; Virgil Thomson; Aaron Copland; Leonard Bernstein; and Lincoln Kirstein.

Although he never lived there himself, Kirstein was instrumental in turning 7 Middagh Street into an urban commune. The house may have come to George Davis in a dream, but it also came with a price tag: $75 a month, plus a one-month security deposit. Davis couldn't even afford half that. The now thirty-four-year-old had been a literary wunderkind when his first novel, *The Opening of a Door,* was published in 1931. He'd caught the tail end of the Roaring Twenties in Paris, where he'd cruised for sailors with Hart Crane and hung out with Picasso on the Left Bank. But now, nine years later, he'd never been able to finish his second book. Instead, he worked as an editor for fashion magazines such as *Harper's Bazaar,* where he used his connections to fill the pages with some of the most new and exciting voices in fiction, such as his good friend (and fellow wunderkind) Carson McCullers.

Unfortunately, Davis didn't like office life; it interrupted the busy schedule of expensed lunches and late-night escapades that he argued were necessary to maintain the connections that enabled him to do his work. His employers often saw things quite differently, and the dramatic Davis was known to regularly threaten to quit—a threat his editor at *Harper's Bazaar* took him up on, just a few weeks before he had his dream about 7 Middagh Street. Out of a job, on the verge of being flat broke, Davis needed to find a way to make his dream come true, or else he'd be forced to leave New York and return to the family farm in Clinton, Michigan.

First, Davis approached Carson McCullers. The twenty-three-year-old author from Columbus, Georgia, had rocketed to the peak of the literary world with her first novel, *The Heart Is a Lonely Hunter*, which had come out earlier in 1940 and had been praised as an instant, groundbreaking classic. Readers both black and white were particularly amazed by the humanity she invested in her black characters, a rarity in novels by white authors at the time. But she was still the somewhat strange, sickly girl who'd always been an outsider in her rural Southern town, with her severe short bangs and her penchant for men's button-down shirts. Davis had taken her under his wing and introduced her to the kind of literary community she'd longed for. Often, the pair had talked about getting an apartment together, or a country home upstate near Davis's good friends the expat German artists Lotte Lenya and Kurt Weill, who had fled the encroach of fascism that was now filling New York with boatloads of European refugees every day. But this plan had one problem: McCullers's husband, Reeves. The two had married young, brought together by their literary aspirations and their dreams of a cultured life somewhere far beyond Georgia. They'd made a deal: Reeves would support them for a year while Carson wrote, and then they would switch places. But that plan had fallen by the wayside when Carson's career took off, and now the increasingly bitter Reeves was becoming an alcoholic anchor around her neck. After McCullers told Reeves about her attraction to the Swiss bon vivant Annemarie Clarac-Schwarzenbach, he'd slapped her, twice—"the first time I had ever been slapped in my life," McCullers wrote in her unfinished autobiography.[1] She knew she needed to leave their tiny Greenwich Village apartment, but the advance she'd received for *Lonely Hunter* was long gone, used in part to fund the pair's excessive drinking. She could pay some of the rent—perhaps even as much as $25 a month—but she couldn't help with the $150 down payment that was required to secure 7 Middagh Street.

So Davis called another old friend, the poet W. H. Auden. A few years earlier, Davis had been instrumental in wooing Auden and Christopher Isherwood to come to New York and allow *Harper's Bazaar* to publish their work. The three had remained close ever since, and it's likely that part of the reason Davis went looking for his dream home in Brooklyn Heights was because Auden already lived there. But Auden's apartment was expensive, and with the war in Europe the British poet was unable to get the proceeds from his book sales in England. (Instead, he directed his parents to donate them to charities that helped children escape London.) Worse, his landlady "had admitted to spending entire nights parked in her car outside the house, keeping an eye on the comings and goings of tenants whose activities had caused complaints."[2] In just the short while since Auden had met Chester Kallman, he'd had fallen hard for the young, arrogant, and enthralling student, and Auden didn't like the idea of his landlady watching them. The two made something of an odd pair: the withdrawn, sometimes sullen British poet who always looked rumpled, and the lithe, quick-witted Brooklyn student whom Auden referred to as his *"ange gauche,"* or "awkward angel."[3] But they would live the rest of their lives tightly bound to each other, if often in different countries, and almost never in the same bed.

Auden liked the idea of 7 Middagh Street. He could picture himself ensconced in one of its bedrooms, keeping his monastic writing schedule during the day and enjoying the freewheeling, gin-soaked conversation of Davis and McCullers in the parlor at night. He also liked being closer to the docks, where (before he met Kallman) he had cruised the waterfront bars for sailors. The whole city was on edge that year, as Hitler gobbled up more and more of Europe. Although America wouldn't officially enter the war until the bombing of Pearl Harbor in December 1941, the navy was already ratcheting up, and the bars of Brooklyn were once again flooded with young military men. Auden was faithful to Kallman (although the reverse was never true), but he still enjoyed spending an evening camping it up in rough dockside places such as the Bucket of Blood, which was "patronized by sailors, whores, stevedores, and transvestites" and was said to be one of George Davis's favorite haunts.[4] However, while Auden had slightly more income than either Davis or McCullers, even he couldn't pony up the $150 they needed to sign the lease.

Here Lincoln Kirstein came in. Auden was the kind of writer who attracted devotees. Not just young students such as Chester Kallman and Harold Norse, but men of wealth, power, and means. Men such as Lincoln Kirstein, who—when he wasn't out cruising on Sands Street—used his large inherited fortune to become a cultural macher in New York City. By this time, at just thirty-three years old, he had created the important literary magazine *Hound & Horn,* helped launch the Museum of Modern Art, convinced choreographer George Balanchine to emigrate from Russia, and cofounded the School of American Ballet. According to Sherill Tippins's fascinating study of 7 Middagh Street, *February House,* "Kirstein idolized Auden" and was also "thoroughly addicted" to Davis's "spellbinding and often salacious stories."[5] Compared to the amounts Kirstein spent on other projects, the $150 required to launch this strange and exciting residential experiment was peanuts.

Once the money was secured, the house came together quickly. Davis, McCullers, and Auden formed the core group and began to put the dilapidated house in order, with Auden acting as the master of the purse, collecting rent and making sure the bills were paid. Davis's decorating tended toward the old-fashioned, the campy, and the kitsch. Together, he and McCullers prowled the nearby second-hand shops on Fulton Street for "Edwardian pieces, Victorian porcelain hands holding roses, old-fashioned stationery scented and strewn with flowers, and lacy Valentines." Anaïs Nin would one day describe the house as looking "like a museum of Americana," though it's hard to tell if she meant it as a compliment or an insult.[6]

Shortly after the three moved in, another old friend of Davis's, the burlesque star Gypsy Rose Lee, became the fourth member of the household. Lee was fresh off her spectacular appearance at the 1940 New York City World's Fair, where *The New York Times* had declared her the "queen of the shedding sisters . . . tall, sleek and mischievous . . . a mighty fine girl."[7] After Mayor La Guardia's raids in the late 1930s had closed all of the real burlesque houses in New York, what remained was trying to go mainstream, and Lee was its presentable face. Just that year, she had purchased a town house in Manhattan, but it was primarily a home for her mother, with whom Gypsy had a fraught and sometimes violent relationship. Her mother (who was herself queer) turned the house into a rooming place primarily inhabited by queer women—as she did with several other properties Lee bought. For work reasons, Lee might not have been able to escape New York City entirely, but she was able to flee Manhattan. She hid her new location from her family so well, both her mother and sister believed that she never lived in Brooklyn.

But a celebrity of Lee's magnitude couldn't live in some dump. Flush from her star turn at the World's Fair, Lee provided Davis with $200 to finish repairs on the house and hire a maid. Only afterward would she move in, bringing along her trusted companion and cook, a black woman named Eva Morcur, whose delicious meals were an added bonus in the eyes of their many visitors.

George Davis had known Lee longer than any of the other residents of 7 Middagh Street. They'd met in 1925 when they were both kids with big dreams living in Omaha, Nebraska. Eight years earlier, Lee had started her career as a vaudeville chorus girl, backing up her sister, June. By 1925, when Lee was fourteen, she was still playing second fiddle and being dragged around the dwindling vaudeville circuit at the hands of their mother, the infamous Mama Rose, which is how Lee ended up in Omaha. Davis was nineteen and working as a clerk at a bookstore. Lee was an autodidact in all things; by this time, despite only infrequent and informal schooling, she was reading everything from Karl Marx to Giovanni Boccaccio. When Davis noticed her eavesdropping on his conversations with other patrons, he suggested she might enjoy Shakespeare's sonnets. Lee responded, "I don't care much about reading plays . . . being in the theater myself."[8] Davis explained they were poetry, and Lee bought the book on his recommendation. The two remained friendly ever after and reconnected in New York in the late 1930s. According to Sherill Tippins, Lee was struck by Davis's "instant understanding that her search had been not just for a book but for a different way to live, a different person to be."[9]

For Lee, that "different person" would be the intellectual bawdy queen, the brainy beauty. After her sister, June, ran off as a teenager, Lee was technically the star of her mother's show—but the show had become a smaller, more tawdry affair. By 1930, the vaudeville circuit they depended upon was dead, and at the Gayety Theater in Kansas City, Lee first stepped onstage as a burlesque performer. Although her earliest days in burlesque no doubt included full nudity and perhaps even simulated or real sex acts, by the time she was a star, she had perfected the mantra of "leave them wanting more." Sometimes she would remove only so much as a single glove over her entire routine. Her act at the 1940 World's Fair capitalized on this reputation. While performing, Lee recited a long poem about all the thoughts that were running through her head while she stripped, such as:

And when I display my charms in all their dazzling splendor
And prove to you, conclusively, I am of the female gender
I am really thinking of Elsie de Wolfe, and the bric-a-brac I saw
And that lovely letter I received from George Bernard Shaw[10]

While Lee seems primarily or entirely heterosexual (although also rather disinterested in sex and relationships that weren't connected to money), many rumors at the time said that she was either a lesbian or a female impersonator—hence the line about proving her gender. For those in the know, the poem also contained references to a number of well-known queer people, including the "mother of interior decorating," Elsie de Wolfe (who had been involved with the queer circle of actresses in the early 1900s), gay British authors Noël Coward and Oscar Wilde, and bisexual Italian actress Eleonora Duse. It also referenced several figures whose sexuality was openly speculated about, such as novelist George Santayana and playwright George Bernard Shaw.

By November 1940, Davis, McCullers, Auden, and Lee had gotten 7 Middagh Street into livable shape. As all but Lee shared February birthdays, a visiting Anaïs Nin christened their new home February House. As Thanksgiving approached, the final pair of the first wave of inhabitants, the musical British couple Benjamin Britten and Peter Pears, were preparing to move in.

Britten and Pears were perhaps the oddest addition to February House's menagerie. They were no stranger than the other residents, but they had a British properness to them—Britten in particular—that made them fade into the background, where the rest of the household always seemed larger-than-life. Britten was but twenty-six years old when he moved in, and he was already well on his way to becoming one of the most celebrated opera composers of the twentieth century. Pears was thirty, and though he was a wonderful vocalist, he "was clear about his own position as the junior partner," both in their relationship and in the world of music.[11] Britten was quick, small, and often ill; Pears was taller, fleshier, and slightly more grounded in the world. When the two were together, Britten told a friend, "I become so shy & retiring," and that part of his personality would show during their months at February House.

Auden and Britten were good friends and had worked together on a number of artistic projects, and it was Auden who invited the pair to move in. Like Auden, Britten was low on money because of the war; shortly before he moved to 7 Middagh Street, he directed his sister to cash in his life insurance policy. From the start, Britten and Pears found their residency at February House trying. "Living is quite pleasant here when it is not too exciting," Britten wrote to a friend shortly after moving in, "but I find it almost impossible to work."[12] For a young man who seemed to be constantly in the thrall of new inspiration, with music virtually pouring from his fingers whenever he sat down to write, this was maddening. Pears felt similarly, describing the house as "too wild, too uncertain . . . it didn't suit us."[13] Years later, other residents would describe the pair as reticent and incommunicative. Although they would live in February House for months, they would frequently leave for the weekend or for longer jaunts. Of all the residents of February House, they seemed to have touched and been touched by the experience the least.

With the house now full, a Thanksgiving feast was held to celebrate the new home. The guests were an eye-popping list of European and American cultural stars: the queer German siblings Erika, Klaus, and Golo Mann (who had been stripped of their German citizenship by the Nazis in 1936); their friend (and Carson McCullers's obsession) the Swiss journalist and traveler Annemarie Clarac-Schwarzenbach; the "Dean of American Composers," Aaron Copland (who was also queer); most of corps of the Russian Ballet; Auden's lover, Chester Kallman, and his father; and the American author Richard Wright, whose novel *Native Son* was one of the biggest literary successes of the year.

Dinner, according to McCullers's autobiography, started off on a bad note. Unaccustomed to being a host, and never at home in the kitchen, she bought only a tiny turkey to feed all of the guests. Luckily, Davis stepped in and saved the day, wrestling up a proper-size bird from who knows where. After dinner, they retired to the parlor for brandy, music, stories, and cigarettes. Davis, in particular, had a reputation as a raconteur—one of the reasons Lincoln Kirstein provided the funds for the house in the first place. It is easy to imagine Davis, fey, slight, and animated, leaning against the grand piano that a friend (fashion icon Diana Vreeland) had donated to February House, giving one of his campy monologues about the joys of Brooklyn cruising:

> *My dear, when I spotted this gorgeous hunk of seafood in a Sand [sic] Street bar I said to myself "Miss Davis, you have met your piece of trade for life . . . so get to work, girl, and literally charm the pants off your future husband. And that's what your mother did. He never said a word—how could he, poor dear? Your mother was blindingly brilliant, as usual. Well missy . . . he just listened in his strong silent manly way . . . mmm, the very thought of him [shriek]! Sooo at some un-god-ly hour your mother guided him through the unbroken ranks of tiara-studded queens camping shoulder to shoulder—Scylla and Charybdis they should*

call that joint—and we tip-toe through the juleps right out of there when
suddenly your mama . . . well, dear, you know, finding herself alone in the dark
with this big muscular brute—di-vine!—gets shivery second thoughts . . . tsk
tsk, this could be a homicidal maniac, a mad queer basher for all she knows. Sooo,
"Mademoiselle Davis," she says, "Miss Bazaaaar!" get hold of yourself girl . . . are
you out of your cottonpickin' mind? Have you forgotten the first law of cruising?
Never . . . never . . . [shriek] . . . never-lose-control! Just talk the big hunk out
of his skivvies before he gets any bright ideas. And, honey, that's just what your
mammy does as we stagger through the deserted streets—not too steady on our
pins—towards my bohemian bordello . . . your mother talking for dear life . . .
next thing she knows her legs are in the air![14]

That Thanksgiving, however, any stories being told were soon interrupted by
the Klaxon of the nearby firehouse—a suggestion of adventure that neither Carson McCullers nor Gypsy Rose Lee could resist. The two had quickly become
close, often cuddling in Lee's bed over sherry or one of Lee's homemade apple
strudels. Arm in arm, they raced out into the Brooklyn night, and while they
looked for the fire, McCullers had a breakthrough in the plot of her next book,
The Member of the Wedding: her main character, Frankie, was "in love with the bride
of her brother."[15]

It's unsurprising that this queer revelation would come to McCullers while
she lived at February House, or while in the presence of Gypsy Rose Lee. According to McCullers's biographer Virginia Spencer Carr, "Carson loved [Lee] . . .
with Miss Lee, life was light and bright. Neither of them would have had it otherwise."[16] Around the statuesque, nearly six-foot-tall Lee, McCullers felt less like
the gangly, awkward woman-child she often considered herself. In turn, McCullers seemed to bring out whatever latent nurturing instincts Lee had (as happened
with many people who spent time around the sickly writer).

Although she wouldn't stay there long, Brooklyn was undoubtedly a positive
influence on McCullers. As she wrote in an essay for *Vogue,* "Brooklyn, in a dignified way, is a fantastic place . . . one of the things I love best about Brooklyn
[is] everyone is not expected to be exactly like everyone else."[17] This appealed to
McCullers because even in Manhattan she was an odd duck; the writer Janet Flanner would later say that "Carson stood out with New Yorkers, even, as an eccentric of the first water."[18] In Brooklyn, McCullers found community, not just in

February House, but among the older denizens of the borough, whom she found delightfully quirky, as full of personality (in a Yankee way) as the Southern eccentrics she had grown up with. According to her biographer Carr, McCullers "wanted to study the city, take its pulse, and, like her idols, Walt Whitman and Hart Crane, fuse herself to it."[19] And to walk in their footsteps meant being part of life in Brooklyn.

Like many a queer Brooklynites before and after her, McCullers took particular joys in Sands Street. As she wrote in *Vogue:*

> One of the most gaudy streets I know stretches between Brooklyn Bridge and the Navy Yard. At three o'clock in the morning, when the rest of the city is silent and dark, you can come suddenly on a little area as vivacious as a country fair. It is Sand [sic] Street, the place where sailors spend their evenings when they come here to port. At any hour of the night some excitement is going on in Sand Street. The sunburned sailors swagger up and down the sidewalks with their gals. The bars are crowded, and there are dancing, music, and straight liquor at cheap prices. . . . In one bar, there is a little hunchback who struts in proudly every evening, is petted by everyone, given free drinks, and treated as a sort of mascot by the proprietor. There is a saying among sailors that when they die they want to go to Sand Street.[20]

Years later, that hunchback would be the inspiration for McCullers's novella, *The Ballad of the Sad Café.*

Away from her husband, Reeves, McCullers had space to pursue the intense emotional relationships with women that formed the core of most of her life. That role was taken by Mary Tucker, her first piano teacher, while growing up in Georgia. In Brooklyn, there was Annemarie Clarac-Schwarzenbach, Gypsy Rose Lee, and the German writer, actor, and activist Erika Mann; later, McCullers would develop life-sustaining connections with her psychiatrist (Dr. Mary Mercer), and a French neighbor named Marielle Bancou. A briefer infatuation with the handsome butch theater producer Cheryl Crawford also occurred while McCullers lived at February House; however, according to her biographer Carr, "It was discomfiting for Carson to realize she was once again attracted to a female. Surely it was the devil at work in her, she told [Newton] Arvin."[21] In general, Carson seemed to be attracted to women who were older, androgynously masculine, and who threw themselves into their lives and art with a gusto she could relate to.

While these relationships had erotic and physical elements, most McCullers scholars agree that none of them were ever consummated sexually. According to Carr, this probably had something to do with her marriage, as "Reeves could put up with his wife's frequent crushes on women with stoic resignation so long as they stopped short of the bed."[22] Reeves himself might also have been bisexual, and the pair had an intense (and eventually unhealthy) connection with a gay composer named David Diamond, whom Reeves temporarily lived with while he and McCullers were separated. McCullers often said that everything in her books had happened or would happen in some sense, and that her novel *Reflections in a Golden Eye*—partially about a closeted gay man living on an army post in Georgia—was inspired by things Reeves had told her.

Intriguingly, author Sarah Schulman has conjectured that McCullers's queerness may have been located more in her gender identity than in her sexuality. As Schulman wrote in *The New Yorker*:

> I started to notice that McCullers had issues with her gender. The first evidence was the most superficial. Her given name was Lula, but she took on her middle name, Carson, reminiscent of the American cowboy Kit Carson. She wore men's clothes, and was often photographed in a suit. Her main protagonists were young, boyish girls with men's names: Frankie and Mick. In fact, Carson invented this American prototype of the queerish tomboy girl . . . [and] she did once tell [Truman] Capote "I think I was born a boy."[23]

As Schulman points out, even that quote is far from proof of anything—many women have had similar thoughts. But taken together, all of these queer details create a portrait of a person whose nature was deeply at odds with the prevailing expectations of American womanhood in the 1930s and '40s. Psychologists were only just beginning to define the idea of "gender identity" as separate from "sex," and they mostly focused their work on people whom we would today call transgender women. Transgender men, such as that long-ago Brooklyn resident Elizabeth Trondle, were still isolated and underdiscussed rarities.

However, while living in February House might have provided emotional sustenance, queer space, and literary inspiration for McCullers, the actual *living* was hard on her, and she would stay for only a few months before illness required her to return home to Georgia. Over the next few years, she would return for frequent visits and occasional stays of up to a few months, but her drinking was out of control and other residents remembered her as difficult to interact with. Gypsy Rose Lee would also leave February House after less than a year, having been lured to Chicago to help run and headline at a new venue called the Theatre Cafe.

So around the start of 1941, the housemates needed to find people to take over the third floor, which had been split between Lee and McCullers. February House was already infamous, and the line of would-be residents was long. Many artists fleeing the Nazis spent time at 7 Middagh Street. In part, this was because Klaus Mann conceived the antifascist literary magazine *Decision* at their dining room table, with editorial assistance from McCullers, marketing advice from Davis, and Auden on its board of advisers. That put February House on the global map for the displaced intelligentsia of Europe. The next new residents, however, would come from much closer afield.

Paul and Jane Bowles were living at the Chelsea Hotel in Manhattan when they were invited to move in. Like Auden himself, Paul Bowles was something of a project for Lincoln Kirstein, and he urged the Middagh Street residents to allow the Bowles to jump the queue for admission to February House. They were all well familiar with Paul, who had been a frequent visitor when he lived in a small, unheated studio in an even shabbier part of the Heights. The tall sandy blond was a striking figure, often decked out in immaculate three-piece suits and carrying a silver art deco cigarette case. His wife, Jane, was "an impish twenty-three-year-old" who "loved parties and was known for flitting from one man's lap to another."[24] Although both would later achieve fame for their writing—Jane for her 1943 novel, *Two Serious Ladies,* and Paul for his 1949 novel, *The Sheltering Sky*—at the time Paul was primarily known as a composer, and Jane as his wife. By February 1941, just in time for Jane's to become another of the February birthdays in the house, the two were ensconced on the third floor of 7 Middagh Street. They would last about two months.

Three interrelated issues quickly drove the Bowleses from February House. First, their relationship was fraught. They both had affairs outside their marriage (primarily with people of the same sex), and though those were allowed, they often caused tension. Some scholars have gone so far as to describe both of the Bowleses as "essentially homosexual."[25] They married hastily, largely because Jane's mother refused to remarry until she knew Jane herself had settled down, and because they both delighted in shocking their friends. Yet the two had an intense connection that went far beyond the sexual. Both had a surrealist and absurdist outlook on life, which they brought to February House. Their guests included the painters Salvador Dalí and Pavel Tchelitchew, who painted a giant disturbing mural on the parlor wall. But the couple's strange private behavior, however, was what caused issues with their housemates. Their interactions were loud and disturbing, and the sounds of their elaborate (and at times violent) sexual role-playing would often drift through the building, barely muffled by the threadbare velvet drapes that adorned McCullers's old room. One such game

> centered on Paul's portrayal of Bupple Hergesheimer, a man-sized parrot, "monstrous in his behavior," who responded to Jane's efforts to put him back into his cage with weird, spontaneous eruptions of "Bupple" or "Rop."[26]

These games could go on for hours. But even noisier—and to both W. H. Auden and Benjamin Britten, more annoying—was Paul's work. Since the age of twenty-one, he'd been composing major works for the stage, and he would frequently collaborate with artists such as Orson Welles and Tennessee Williams. This, obviously, required a piano. Britten found the music distracting from his own work, while Auden found it simply insufferable. Auden demanded that Paul move his piano to the low-ceilinged, dimly lit, dusty basement. Paul refused, George Davis backed Auden, and the piano was quickly moved.

Thus from the get-go, Paul Bowles and Auden had a sour relationship. But the third reason for the Bowleses' quick eviction centered on the relationship between Auden and Jane. Jane and Auden got along famously, with Jane even acting as his amanuensis. For two years, she'd been sporadically chipping away at the surrealist novel that would become *Two Serious Ladies,* and working with Auden—or perhaps just the way in which he took her literary aspirations seriously—spurred her to return to it with renewed vigor. Paul, already angry at Auden, found his relationship with Jane to be an affront, and it deepened the animosity between the two men. In April 1941, Auden demanded that Paul give up his room to some visiting friends. Paul refused, and Davis and Auden kicked Paul and Jane out of February House. Although frequently in the same place at the same time, Auden and Bowles "did not speak again for twenty years."[27]

However, one other good thing did come from the Bowleses' brief tenure in February House: Paul's cousin, the twenty-two-year-old fledgling scenic designer

Oliver Smith, was invited to fix up the attic and create a room for himself. Smith was a complete unknown, but "his leading-man looks, excellent literary taste, and air of languid sophistication . . . won [him] a place as the much-loved baby of the family."[28] George Davis was particularly impressed with Smith's gorgeous watercolors of Brooklyn's harbor, which Smith painted while looking out the attic window. After being fired from *Harper's Bazaar,* Davis was hired as literary editor for *Mademoiselle,* where he brought on Smith as an occasional illustrator. Unlike his cousins, Smith blossomed during his time at 7 Middagh Street, turning the vast river of artists who flowed through the house into a network of collaborators. Via Pavel Tchelitchew, Smith got his first theatrical work, creating sets for a ballet called *Rodeo,* whose score was written by another habitué of February House, Aaron Copland. But Smith's next project would make his name and set his course for a lifetime of theatrical success: the 1944 Broadway smash hit (and subsequent blockbuster film), *On the Town.* Like his work on *Rodeo,* Smith's part in creating *On the Town* can be traced directly back to his time at February House.

On the Town began as a ballet called *Fancy Free,* conceived for the Ballet Theatre (now the American Ballet Theatre) by choreographer Jerome Robbins and composer Leonard Bernstein (both queer men whom Smith met at Middagh Street). The play told the story of three young sailors on shore leave in New York City during the war. While the show was nominally set in Manhattan, it was inspired by the bars on Sands Street. The musical ran for more than 450 performances, and one of the songs—"New York, New York"—would become a classic. Smith, credited as both scenic designer and producer, made so much money that (according to a letter Carson McCullers wrote in 1945) "now suddenly he is wallowing in wealth. Two weeks ago he couldn't pay George the rent."[29]

Ballet Theatre was so impressed with Smith's work that they named him co-director of the company in 1945, a post Smith held until 1980. The film version of *On the Town,* which starred Gene Kelly and Frank Sinatra, was a huge hit when it came out in 1949, winning the Academy Award for its score. After that, Smith would buy a mansion in Brooklyn Heights, which for years he shared with a young Truman Capote. He would go on to create the sets for some of Broadway's most enduring classics, including *Guys and Dolls, West Side Story, Oklahoma!,* and *Porgy and Bess.* Toward the end of his life, after he had won "six Tonys, five New York Drama Critics Awards, and the Sam S. Shubert Award for Achievement in the Theater," Smith informed a journalist that although *West Side Story* was set in

Manhattan's Upper West Side, it was actually inspired by "the time when he and a younger Jerome Robbins walked under the Brooklyn Bridge and down by the docks. . . . Consequently, the set for that show is really 'more Brooklyn than Manhattan. But don't tell anyone.'"[30]

Although Smith is often left out of discussions of the cadre of queer men who created many of the biggest Broadway hits of the 1940s and '50s, at the time he was clearly considered an instrumental collaborator—and February House was instrumental in making those collaborations come together.

However, not all of the residents of February House greeted Smith's arrival with joy. Benjamin Britten and Peter Pears were already the odd ones out at 7 Middagh Street. Although they were artists, they were not the kind that enjoyed the all-hours socializing and giddy squalor of the other February House residents. As Oliver Smith began refurbishing the attic, the noise he made—on top of the chaos of his cousins—was finally too much for the British couple. What had started as a grand experiment in artistic communal life was rapidly beginning to feel like living in an asylum. They had put up with bedbugs and fleas, circus performers and surrealists, but they couldn't abide the distractions preventing them from doing their best work. In the summer of 1941, Britten "admit[ted] to himself that the sort of wild ride on which Auden had taken him was not his style."[31] When the couple was invited to take up residence in California with some musician friends from England, they jumped at the chance.

In many ways, the story of 7 Middagh Street is emblematic of queer life during World War II—a brief, white-hot efflorescence that would burn fast and wink out just as suddenly. Of the initial residents, by the summer of 1941 only George Davis and W. H. Auden remained. The tenor of the house had changed remarkably in that time, from freewheeling to free-for-all. Without Gypsy Rose Lee, there was no more Eva Morcur to cook for the residents. Without Britten and Pears, no one complained when the parties went all night. After Britten, Pears, and the Bowleses left, February House would dwindle in importance—especially once Auden left that summer.

While Auden had found the general idea of February House exciting, the actuality of it never lived up to its potential. He and Benjamin Britten collaborated on the operetta *Paul Bunyan,* with Britten writing the score and Auden the libretto, but the work was critically panned when it premiered in May 1941. Auden's poetry writing was more successful; he completed much of his 1941 book, *The*

Double Man, while living at Middagh Street. But the chaos of his love life, not his work or home situation, was what ultimately caused him to flee Brooklyn for Ann Arbor, Michigan, that summer.

Auden, despite his occasionally libertine ways, had a deep Anglican streak in him. From the beginning, he believed himself to be married—in the eyes of God, if not the law or the church—to Chester Kallman. Early in their relationship, "he even wore a gold-band wedding ring."[32]

To anyone who knew Kallman, however, this idea was laughable. In 1939, when his relationship with Auden began, he was merely eighteen years old, a callow college student swimming in the sea of eligible young men who were just beginning to flock to Brooklyn—a wild mix of soldiers and sailors from all around America, and refugees from all across Europe. Some were searching for connection and comfort, others for a way to forget what they had seen or what they were soon to face. Sex was everywhere.

At first, Kallman tried to keep his indiscretions relatively secret, at least from Auden, but he would soon flaunt them openly. By the end of 1941, he had no qualms in writing to Auden about his escapades, such as how

> *just the other night I picked up a 6 ft 2 ½ in merchant sailor from Brooklyn. Wildly attractive, young, strong, perfectly built, and large. I was all prepared for an absolutely relentless fucking—but—as it turned out in the end, that is what I had to provide him with.*[33]

What caused Kallman to be so open about his later indiscretions? One of those many sailors who landed on Brooklyn's coast as part of the flotsam and jetsam of World War II, an Englishman named Jack Barker, almost broke Auden and Kallman apart (with Kallman nearly getting killed in the process).

Despite a rather patrician upbringing as the son of an English lieutenant general, Barker was an explorer from a young age. One acquaintance in Brooklyn described the muscular, handsome sailor as "young, bonny, and yearning for adventure . . . also bisexual."[34] Born in 1915, he shipped out on his first boat at the age of nineteen and wouldn't settle down again until much later in life. His experiences on commercial vessels across Europe, Australia, and in the Middle East and North Africa broadened his horizons and exposed him to all manner of sexual practices. As a young man in Egypt, for instance, Barker encountered a British doctor who was "keeping statistics of Arabic decadence by measuring the rectums of all his boy patients"—a decidedly *British* form of decadence, thinly veiled in racist science (similar to that practiced by R. W. Shufeldt, Loop-the-Loop's doctor in the 1910s).[35]

In his 1962 autobiography, *No Moaning There!,* Barker held back about his male lovers. Reading between the lines, however, some of his stories have obvious queer overtones, such as that of his intense friendship with an Indian-British student and dancer named Edalji Dinshaw, who also was painted in the nude by Pavel Tchelitchew, and who makes a brief appearance in Thomas Painter's list of men that he connected to Alfred Kinsey. In his book, Barker spends many paragraphs describing Dinshaw, telling of "an elfin face . . . of extraordinary beauty," and waxing rhapsodic about Dinshaw's "golden brown skin, large, gentle lustrous eyes fringed with long, curling lashes, and perfect features."

However, while Barker held back about his sex life with men, he did at least describe the homosocial world of life at sea, telling stories of men dancing with one another on deck, and sharing prostitutes while dockside. When he returned to Glasgow after a long sail, he recalled being told by another sailor that "after ninety days, you can do what you like with the cook."[36]

In 1938, Barker was living in Lapland, trying to start a reindeer farm. He'd sensed that Europe was on the verge of a "conflict that would devastate the whole civilized world" and had at first hoped to escape it by running north of the arctic circle. But as England called home its young men to war, he couldn't resist taking sides. As he recalled, "I was so violently anti-Nazi that I would undoubtedly have emerged from any lair at the outbreak of the war and drifted into it."[37] He was uncharacteristically silent about his actual work for the war effort, ending his memoir right at the start of 1940. But according to Auden scholar Nicholas Jenkins, he "was a member of the crew on a merchant ship making semi-official, and often very dangerous, voyages on behalf of the British Government."[38] According to shipping manifests, Barker sailed on a ship called *Argos Hill,*[39] which was bombed by German fighter planes at least once during the war.[40]

The *Argos Hill* first brought Barker to Brooklyn on December 12, 1940. In his pocket, he had a letter of introduction from the British poet Stephen Spender to his compatriot W. H. Auden. It seems that sometime between farming reindeer and fighting Nazis, Barker had had an affair with Spender. Spender wrote about it in an unpublished poem in his diary from 1939, in which he called Barker "Jack

Tar," and fantasized about his "muscles strained against the rope," the "fragments of sky" in his eyes, and his "navel chiseled in an abdomen of stone." In the diary entry, Spender jotted "rewrite this," but he never did.[41]

The letter of introduction to Auden was worth its weight in gold to an ambitious and adventurous young man such as Barker. According to Barker, "For me, Wystan was the greatest English-speaking poet alive."[42] Auden offered to put him up at Middagh Street for a time, where he quickly met and fell in lust with Chester Kallman. The two began a torrid affair, without Barker ever knowing about Auden and Kallman's preexisting relationship. Perhaps Kallman assumed that because Barker was shipping out shortly after, no one needed to know. But when Barker returned in the spring of 1941, now believing himself to be in love with Kallman, things came to a head.

On the very day he returned to Brooklyn, his cheerful reunion with Kallman was ruined by the revelation of his relationship with Auden. Barker "was horrified and insisted that either Wystan be told or it must end at once."[43] Kallman somehow convinced Barker to remain silent, but either Auden winkled it out, or George Davis let it slip.

This was the first of Kallman's affairs that Auden discovered, and it drove him mad with jealousy. He wasn't just furious with Barker, he was convinced that the English sailor had somehow connived Kallman into being unfaithful. Over and over, in person and in letters, Auden begged Barker to at least tell him that Kallman had been the "innocent" in the relationship, and that this was his first and only such indiscretion.[44] Unable to further break the heart of a man he idolized, Barker lied and took all the blame.

Perhaps suspecting the truth of the situation, however, Auden couldn't let it be. Thoughts of Kallman and Barker plagued him night and day. Toward the very end of his time at February House, he even wrote a poem about it, which seemed to equate the unhappiness of his relationship with the deflated stature of 7 Middagh Street, as its speaker contemplated how he was "Caught in the jealous trap / Of an empty house," whose creaks, leaks, and drafts all seem to ask "what have I done?"[45]

Those close to Auden knew that he had a rare, but mercurial temper, which occasionally showed in flashes of rage, often over minor things. Barker was no minor thing. Suddenly unable to take it anymore, Auden decided to kill Barker—but Barker was out at sea. With no other target for his anger, Auden crept into his bedroom at 7 Middagh Street, where Chester Kallman lay sleeping, wrapped his hands around his lover's neck, and attempted to strangle him to death.

From here, stories diverge: some say Kallman fought him off and fled out the door; others, that Auden's rage broke as soon as Kallman woke, and Kallman pushed him aside and went right back to sleep. Either way, the episode had a lasting effect on Auden. He couldn't stop loving Kallman—who, for all his faults, seemed devoted to the older poet (if not sexually faithful)—but Auden could direct the nature of that love. According to Auden, from that point on, though their lives would remain intricately bound together, they never again had sex. Perhaps at least dimly sensing the severity of the infraction of his affair with Barker, Kallman finally broke off the relationship—which was not a great sacrifice because Kallman already planned to leave Brooklyn for graduate school at the University of Michigan in the fall. Auden decided to follow him and accepted a teaching position in literature at the school. Although other artists would continue to live there for brief stretches, the queer heyday of February House was mostly over by the fall of 1941, after just a little more than a year.

As for Barker, in a final twist of the knife, Kallman later fobbed him off on another young man—the very man whom Auden had started sleeping with after his sexual life with Kallman ended. The move seemed designed to ensure that the poet and the sailor would never be friends, and in that Kallman succeeded. Auden, until the end of his life, believed Barker to be "evil." Barker, in turn, would later say, "It was Chester's nature to create jealousy, misery, and rage in his lovers."[46] In all Barker's subsequent transatlantic crossings, he seems to have eschewed Brooklyn entirely. After the war, he would return to Manhattan and open a fish-and-chips shop, before settling down in England and marrying a much younger woman.

Barker is emblematic of the many foreign sailors who arrived in the port of Brooklyn, much like Emil Opffer before him, bringing adventure and a sense of sexual availability to both men and women. In his essay *A House on the Heights*, Truman Capote (who lived in Brooklyn throughout the fifties), waxed rhapsodic about these men, writing:

Every kind of sailor is common enough here, even saronged East Indians, even the giant Senegalese, their onyx arms afire with blue, with yellow tattooed flowers, with saucy torsos and garish graffiti (Je t'aime, Hard Luck, Mimi Chang, Adios Amigo). Runty Russians, too—one sees them, flap-flapping in their pajama like costumes. But the barefooted sailors on the beach, the three I saw reclining there, profiles set against the sundown, seemed mythical as mermen: more exactly, mermaids—for their hair, striped with albino streaks, was lady-length, a savage fiber falling to their shoulders, and in their ears gold rings glinted. Whether plenipotentiaries from the pearl-floored palace of Poseidon or mariners merely, Viking-tressed seamen out of the Gothic North languishing after a long and barber less voyage, they are included permanently in my memory's curio cabinet.[47]

But at the end of 1941, after the Japanese bombed Pearl Harbor and the United States officially entered World War II, the number of foreign sailors would be as nothing when compared to the number of young, adventurous, sexually open American sailors thronging the streets of Brooklyn. New York City was *the* port of call for the European theater of the war: "More than 3 million men shipped out from New York Harbor, and at the height of the war, a ship left every 15 minutes."[48]

Brooklyn was a huge part of this effort. Starting quietly in 1938, the Brooklyn Navy Yard had begun expanding, purchasing the nearby Wallabout Market (home to some seven hundred merchants), which enabled it to build two additional dry docks and expand the two existing ones. The massive military complex now covered some 225 acres, including five miles of paved streets, a power plant, a radio station, and over thirty miles of railroad track. Down at the other end of Brooklyn, the Coast Guard purchased 125 acres to build the Sheepshead Bay Maritime Service Training Station, which trained over thirty-five thousand men every year of the war.[49] Women also served in the navy in World War II, through the Women Accepted for Volunteer Emergency Service (or WAVES) program. However, they trained separately from the men, on the Hunter College campus in the Bronx, and had no institutional presence in Brooklyn.

To support this military effort, an incredible array of civilians and ancillary projects was also necessary. By 1942, the Brooklyn Navy Yard was employing more than thirty thousand civilian workers (a number that rose to seventy thousand by the end of the war). In Fort Greene, near where poet Marianne Moore still lived, the city constructed the "ultra-modern Fort Greene Housing Project," which was to give homes to the families of some three thousand of those workers, many of who had traveled to Brooklyn for their jobs. These were some of the first projects built by the New York City Housing Authority. In a trend that would accelerate after the war, more than thirty thousand city-owned Brooklyn tenement units—mostly housing lower-income people—were destroyed, in part to make way for this new construction.[50] This was an early form of the kind of "urban renewal" project that would have devastating effects on the social fabric of Brooklyn postwar. But for the moment, the only thing on everyone's minds was surviving World War II, and other concerns were largely pushed aside.

According to contemporary reports, many of the sailors who passed through New York City were queer, or at least open to the idea. It was commonly stipulated (among those in the know) that being in the war would lead directly to experience with, or at least knowledge of, homosexuality. As Thomas Painter, former member of the Committee for the Study of Sex Variants, wrote:

> It is interesting to speculate on the sociological effects of this war on the problem in which we are interested [NB: homosexuality]. Millions of men who had never and would never have heard of it will have been introduced to it, directly or indirectly. Boys who would have stayed at home as quiet farm boys or middle class youths in small towns, now in the Navy, will have been fellated or pedicated, and this education will be even more thorough and all embracing than that accomplished by the Depression, because this will touch all classes of youth, not only the poor. And those who have not actually done it will hear about it so casually, frequently and intimately from others that it will seem like an ordinary phenomenon rather than the Nameless Vice it used to be (or used to be supposed to be—reading about [homosexuality] in the Nineties is quite revealing). And then also when they get home and read Time or the Saturday Evening Post nowadays they will find the word printed for all to read—homosexual. It may even get into the modern dictionaries. . . . It seems very doubtful that this war has created many new [homosexuals], just many new bisexuals.[51]

The military was not unaware of these facts. Homosexuality was considered a disqualifying condition, and investigating the sexuality of new recruits became a regular part of Selective Service interviews. The military wanted to keep out (obvious) homosexuals, but they didn't want to lose any able-bodied "normal" men who might be tempted to dodge the service by claiming to be gay. Some 16 million Americans—10 million of them draftees—would serve in some capacity in the war. In the navy, an astonishing 35 percent of them were teenagers. According to estimates made by historian Allan Bérubé in his book *Coming Out Under Fire*:

The History of Gay Men and Women in World War II, "At least 650,000 and as many 1.6 million male soldiers were homosexual."[52] The military draft boards were thus in desperate need of some experts, people who could separate the straight wheat from the gay chaff. Twelve days after the bombing of Pearl Harbor, those experts appeared in the form of Alfred Gross and George Henry, from the Committee for the Study of Sex Variants.

On December 19, Gross wrote a letter, at the direction of Henry, to Major Frank E. Mason, a top NBC executive and special assistant for public relations to the secretary of the navy. Gross detailed that through the research of the CSSV, he and Henry had realized that "naval personnel seem exceptionally choice objects" to gay men, and that this was a "tacitly accepted phenomenon on the part of the public authorities." Furthermore, their research also showed that being gay often allowed one to transcend "ordinary social restrictions" and interact with other gay men from wildly different backgrounds. Given that it was common knowledge that among the Nazis were many homosexuals, Gross suggested

> building up a force of patriotic homosexual men who were rejected from service. . . . I am thinking of men of two sorts—patriotic men who would serve through motives of national service, and the lower "stool pigeon" type of male prostitute who would probably have to be paid for services rendered. . . . I send you this, then, by direction of Dr. Henry, as a proffer of our services to the Government in the emergency, and to say that we will be glad to confer with you or any officers of the Intelligence Service to whom this might make some sense. . . . We have contact with several trustworthy patients . . . whom I am sure would be willing to be of use.[53]

Coming from Gross, this sounds like a pie-in-the-sky plan. But the idea seemed to move quickly up the chain of military command, soon landing on the desk of John C. Wiley, who had been tapped to run the Foreign Nationalities Branch of the Office of Coordinator of Information, which was an early predecessor to the CIA. In an internal memo to Wallace Phillips, a member of the Office of Naval Intelligence, Wiley praised the work of the CSSV and recommended a "careful study" of Gross's suggestions, writing, "The idea of using homosexuals for the purposes of political and military intelligence, should definitely be taken seriously."[54]

How much further down this road the navy went is unknown, but by July

1942, the Selective Service in New York City was regularly sending recruits to be evaluated by Gross and Henry. Meanwhile, the Payne Whitney Clinic—where these evaluations, like the ones conducted for the CSSV, occurred—had discovered that Gross was conducting many of the interviews himself, with no supervision from Dr. Henry. Perturbed by this (and the mounting costs of their X-rays, lab usage, space needs, etc.), clinic administrators attempted to force Henry and Gross to leave. This prompted a swift outcry from the military. On July 31, 1942, the chief medical officer for the Selective Service in New York City wrote to the clinic, saying he "took it for granted that nothing will be done to disturb the fine working, mutually satisfactory conditions between us and Dr. Henry."[55] The Payne Whitney Clinic instantly backed down, assuring the colonel that it had *never* intended to do such a thing.

According to Thomas Painter, who seems to have kept tabs on Gross even after leaving the CSSV:

> [Gross] is the man who decides who is a homosexual and who is not—and Henry rubber stamps it. This racket flourished most highly during the war, when Gross (technically, Henry) became the man to whom all New York draft boards sent (officially) all doubtful cases of self-declared, or suspected, homosexuality for diagnosis. His (Henry's) word was final . . . apparently, [he] has good close connections with the District Attorney, Dept of Corrections, and the F.B.I.[56]

As the gatekeeper for military service, Gross appears to have knowingly allowed some gay men to serve and given some heterosexual men a way out. Some members of the military seemed aware that homosexuals were slipping past the Selective Service and even argued that they should be allowed to serve, so long as they remained deeply closeted. As the authors of the handbook *Psychology for the Fighting Man* wrote, "If they are content with quietly seeking the satisfaction of their sexual needs with others of their own kind, their perversion may continue to go unnoticed and they may even become excellent soldiers."[57]

Apparently, the need to keep their "satisfaction" quiet also extended to those homosexuals working *with*, rather than *in*, the military. The relationship of the Selective Service, Gross and Henry, and the Payne Whitney Clinic seems to have fallen apart in 1943, when a young resident doctor discovered that Gross was attempting to date two of the patients passed on from the military. This time, the

Selective Service did not come to the pair's defense, and the Payne Whitney Clinic quickly forced them out.

So who were the queer men who made it past Selective Service and into the military? Dr. Robert Latou Dickinson, now eighty-two years old, said that Gross told him that only "one out of four of the actual [homosexual] applicants" were detected by the Selective Service and sent to him for examination. From his vast knowledge of NYC's gay community, Gross estimated that three-quarters slipped by entirely undetected.[58] Yet for a wide variety of reasons, these men's stories are rarely told. Some never thought of themselves as queer, while others never came out. Some were dishonorably discharged by the military for their sexuality and hid that they had ever been in the service, rather than reveal having received a "blue discharge" (so named for the color of paper it was printed on). As for the remainder, even if they were out, they were rarely asked about their experiences as queer people, and their thoughts, memories, and life stories were never recorded.

However, one young sailor by the name of William Christian Henry Miller, better known as Bill, was the rare exception whose life was well preserved—and

an incredible life it was. According to numerous sources, Miller was an inventor, model, kept boy, advertising executive, furniture designer, visual merchandiser for the Lord & Taylor department store, amateur sexologist, and "one of the most gorgeous men in 1940s Manhattan."[59]

Miller was born into a middle-class family in South Orange, New Jersey, in 1921. An excellent student, he graduated high school at the age of sixteen and turned down scholarships from both Wesleyan and MIT in favor of a vocational education in industrial design at the Franklin School of Professional Arts in Manhattan. Although possessed of many talents, he was unclear exactly what

William (Bill) Miller was an inventor, model, Coast Guard sailor, and participant with Alfred Kinsey's sex research. (*Box 46, folder 6, Christian William (Bill) Miller photographs and papers, Coll2012-003, ONE National Gay & Lesbian Archives, Los Angeles, California.*)

to do with himself—a running theme in his life—and thought learning a trade would prepare him to enter college later. But when he graduated from the Franklin School in 1941, war was imminent, and he thought it more important for "young men to direct their attention to the Air Corps than to architecture."[60] Unfortunately, his eyesight wasn't good enough for him to become a pilot, and instead he joined the Coast Guard Reserve. Although one of his earliest lovers, a college student and dancer named Otis Bigelow, recalled that Miller was stationed at the Brooklyn Navy Yard, he likely did his first actual training down in Sheepshead Bay, Brooklyn, where the Coast Guard was centered.[61]

Tall, ruggedly handsome, and square jawed, he filled out his Coast Guard uniform like the archetype on a navy recruitment poster. Although he would later describe himself as "about as worldly as Snow White" at that time, he seemed well aware of the effect that he had on men (and, later, women).[62] In the book *The Gay Metropolis,* his boyfriend Bigelow is quoted as saying that even fifty years later, he still remembered the moment they met: "A Frank Sinatra recording of 'I'll Be Seeing You' was playing on the phonograph. We went out and had dinner. . . . I was in love."[63]

At the time, Bigelow was dating an older man named George Gallowhur, a striking blond captain of industry, who'd invented the first successful suntan lotion. Gallowhur demanded one chance: a dinner where he could meet Miller and compete for Bigelow's affection. Dinner came and went, and Gallowhur lost. A month later, Bigelow returned to college, and Miller shipped out to Perth, Australia—or so Bigelow thought. After months of moping around, refusing other men, a scorned would-be lover told Bigelow, "Bill has been living in Turtle Bay with George Gallowhur since about three days after you left."[64]

Gallowhur would be the first of many older admirers who paved Miller's way in the world. Gallowhur brought Miller into his company, where Miller began working on a formula for insect repellent. Soon after, however, Miller *did* ship out to Australia, although not for long. When the navy contacted Gallowhur for help creating a portable desalination device for sailors to carry should they be shipwrecked or lost at sea, Gallowhur seems to have pulled some strings and had Miller shipped back to New York to work on the project.

Miller would spend the rest of the war working on various projects at Gallowhur Chemicals while still also serving in the Coast Guard. The Sunstill, as the desalination device came to be known, was hugely successful. By the end of

1943, Miller, who specialized in working with plastics (which were then exciting new marvels of technology), would create an inflatable boat "designed to weigh only a few pounds and fold into a small suitcase when deflated," and also a lightweight plastic sunshade to replace the clunky pith helmets used in the tropics.[65] But his most successful invention, according to *Time* magazine, was a chair made of metal mesh with a plastic inflatable seat over it, which the magazine described as looking surreal, yet feeling practical and comfortable.[66]

Gallowhur most likely facilitated Miller's introduction to the crème de la crème of Manhattan gay society. By 1943, Miller was regularly exchanging letters and gifts with the artist Paul Cadmus, who called him "the most beautiful man I have ever met."[67] In 1944, Miller and Gallowhur would exchange letters with Monroe Wheeler, a friend to both Marianne Moore and the denizens of February House, who was then the director of exhibitions and publications at the Museum of Modern Art. MoMA was interested in exhibiting Miller's folding boat in their fifteenth-anniversary show. Miller wrote Wheeler to invite him to "spend a few minutes this Friday morning in our laboratory, where we are working on the first full-scale inflated chair, and have lunch afterwards."[68] Lunch must have been a success, because both the boat and the chair were featured in the exhibition (and the chair—and Miller—would soon be photographed for *Vogue*). Wheeler struck up a close friendship with Miller, as did both of Wheeler's boyfriends, the photographer George Platt Lynes and the author Glenway Wescott. For the rest of the decade, Miller would regularly model for both Lynes and Paul Cadmus, as well as occasionally for a variety of other queer artists, including gay Russian entomologist/surrealist painter Andrey Avinoff, and bisexual painter and photographer Jared French.

In the late 1940s and throughout the 1950s, Miller would become another of Alfred Kinsey's sexological informants, like Thomas Painter. He sent Kinsey long letters about his various sexual escapades in New York and around the world, such as "a wonderfully successful Gang Bang (or Community Fling, or Cluster Fuck) I gave here on December 10 for Tennessee Williams . . . and a hand-picked group of relaxed and handsome young men."[69] Miller further related to Kinsey that in the fourth or fifth hour of the party one of the members fisted another. As Miller had never before seen this done he told Kinsey he thought it might be of interest.

A substantial amount of the material Miller sent to Kinsey came from his time as a kept boy to another wealthy older man, Dr. Herschel Carey Walker, who in-

vited him on a sex tourism trip around the world in 1948. Telling Monroe
Wheeler about his decision to accept the offer, Miller wrote, "If I travel with him
everybody in New York will thrill to say as soon as they can get it blurted out
that I have a 'sugar-daddy' and all the rest . . . but I can't let such talk stop me."[70]
For at least the next year, Miller traveled through Europe, North Africa, and
Southeast Asia, picking up local men, having sex in the newly unearthed pyra-
mids in Egypt, and occasionally working as a prostitute for men other than Carey
(who primarily seemed to want Miller as a procurer, wingman, and model for
pornographic photos and films).

However, Bill Miller was far from the only World War II military service
member involved with sex work during or after the war. For those with a taste
for men in uniform, Brooklyn offered innumerable delights. While some preferred
the mixed environments of the bars on Sands Street, for those who wanted a surer
thing, several places were well known where men of means could meet the men
of their dreams—at least for a night. Former CSSV member Thomas Painter knew
of at least three such "peg houses" in Brooklyn, which he visited regularly in the
early 1940s. Each functioned slightly differently and had a slightly different clientele (both in the johns and the trade). In general, each house had a procurer-in-
charge who recruited the young men, who in turn treated the place like something
of a clubhouse. They would relax there, eat, sleep, play cards, and wait for the
johns to show. At many of the houses, johns were charged an entry fee, and any
further deals or exchanges of money were left up to the individuals involved. At
others, the procurer took a stronger hand, introducing johns and clients, and getting a cut of the money exchanged.

One of Painter's good friends was a procurer who lived in Brooklyn and ran
a bordello on Third Avenue in Manhattan, working under the name Matty Costello
(or Dolores, when in drag). According to Painter, although it frequently moved
(as did all of the peg houses, to stay ahead of the cops), Costello's bordello was
always on Third Avenue and "goes back to the dim past. . . . [It] was flouring when
I first made my debut in New York homosexual circles—1934."[71] Through Painter,
Costello was connected with the CSSV, and the committee included Costello in
their book, *Sex Variants,* under the pseudonym Victor R. While they included
Costello in their list of homosexual cases, from the interview it's clear that Costello
identified as a woman and had sexual experiences (for fun and profit) with both
men and women. For that reason, I use female pronouns for Costello.

The CSSV's take on an effeminate, unashamed sex worker was cruel and exposed just how unscientific their work could be. They described the then-twenty-three-year-old Costello in derogatory terms, saying she had a "dwarfish physique" and "a weak, girlish face with an embarrassed smile that . . . makes him appear to have low average intelligence." They considered her "a person of meager ambition" and "a defeated person." However, they also included verbatim a large section of Costello's own accounts of her life, giving an unvarnished look into the experiences of an early twentieth-century madam from Brooklyn.[72]

In the book, Costello described some of her early sexual experiences, often with sailors, and often starting (or ending) at Coney Island. She also explained how she got her start as a procurer, stating:

> For a few months I entertained and got money from sailors in Brooklyn. Most of the time I got them drunk. It was a place where only boys and sailors went. It was very notorious. The boys painted up and it was just like a male whorehouse. It was very popular.

In the slang of the day, Costello got her start at a "molly house," which was not the same as the "peg houses" she eventually ran. At molly houses, the sex workers wore what we might call "light drag": perhaps makeup and a wig with a boy's outfit, or no makeup, but their own long hair and a revealing woman's shift. At a peg house (or as Costello calls it, a male whorehouse), the sex workers dressed as men. After a few months working at the molly house, Costello told the CSSV that she

> met a sailor who liked me and I went home with him. . . . At his suggestion we started a male whorehouse. We ran this together until two years ago and then we split up. . . . Since then I've been running the place alone. . . . I have eight or ten boys working for me. They average twenty years of age and they are tall, strong, and heavily built. Few of them are homosexual and they have relations with men in order to earn money. I get the boys by cruising. . . . When I go out to pick up people, I use cosmetics, anything that doesn't show too much—lipstick, powder, sometimes mascara and eyebrow pencil if I think it's necessary. . . . I get in a conversation with a likely boy, explain the racket to him, tell him what money it's possible to make, and take him on trial. If he is satisfactory, I usually keep him a few months or until the novelty wears off.

According to Thomas Painter, Costello's brothel catered to a high-quality clientele, and frequent visitors included songwriter Cole Porter, silent-film star
Ramón Novarro, author Christopher Isherwood, actor Monty Woolley, the "male
Greta Garbo" Nils Asther, and three of the denizens of February House: Gypsy
Rose Lee, W. H. Auden, and George Davis. Painter and Davis hated each other
(perhaps because they were interested in the same men). Painter described Davis
as "a horrid queen . . . a snob, bore, and a malignant faggot."[73] In his unpublished
autobiography, Painter said that Davis was one of Costello's "most frequent customers," and that Costello (as a good host) would attempt to keep Davis and Painter
from being at the brothel at the same time.

However, the single most famous—or rather, infamous—house of assigna-
tion in Brooklyn (and, by the summer of 1942, in all of America), was an incon-
spicuous two-story redbrick town house at 329 Pacific Street, a run-down block
near the border between Brooklyn Heights and downtown Brooklyn. The proprietor, a fifty-five-year-old, "moon-faced" Swedish immigrant, Gustave Beekman,
specialized in providing wealthy men with members of the armed services. He
had previously run a similar house a few blocks closer to the water at 235 Warren
Street, but had relocated after being busted in a police raid in November 1940.
At that time, he was charged with running a disorderly house, fined, and quickly
released. However, when the police raided his establishment on Pacific Street on
the evening of March 14, 1942 (accompanied by members of the Office of Naval
Intelligence), they would uncover a scandal that would rock the nation, consume
newspaper headlines for months, and get hotly debated on the floor of the US Senate. Or perhaps it's more accurate to say they would invent one. But it would be
Walter Winchell, then the gossip columnist for the *New York Daily Mirror,* who
would give this strange episode in Brooklyn history its enduring name: the Swastika Swishery.

The initial story, which was primarily reported in the *New York Post,* went something like this: Beekman ran a "house of degradation" where German spies hired
American servicemen to pump them over pillow talk for information about troop
movements. From there, the story quickly spiraled. Not only were there spies at
Beekman's house, a notorious "Senator X," who was well known as a closeted homosexual and opposed America's entry into World War II, was also a regular habitué
of Beekman's. By early May, Beekman wasn't just accused of hosting any old spy,
rather, he was catering to "one of Hitler's chief espionage agents in this country."[74]

For all of April and May, papers kept readers riveted with headlines such as "Service Men Lured to 'Den' Called Spy Nest,"[75] "Senator Linked to Spy Nest Which Lured Service Men,"[76] "Den Keeper Withholds Source of Cash,"[77] and "Leibowitz Pushes Spy Ring Probe: Tells Convicted Morals Offender to Talk or Get 20-Year Term."[78] News bulletins eagerly broadcast every new tidbit of information in the case, including the four separate (and contradictory) official statements Beekman gave to the police and the FBI.

The senator in question was soon revealed as David Ignatius Walsh, a Catholic "confirmed bachelor" from Boston, who—although liberal on many social issues—was a strong isolationist, believing America had no place in the affairs of Europe. *Time* magazine called his connection with the Beekman case "one of the worst scandals that ever affected a member of the Senate." When the Senate majority leader opened discussion of the issue on the Senate floor, he called the FBI's report on the case "disgusting and unprintable" and refused to have it entered into the Senate's official record. Another isolationist senator from Missouri called Dorothy Schiff, the publisher of the *New York Post,* an "old hussy" and demanded an investigation on the charge that she was part of a secret cabal that was trying to gin up public sentiment in favor of the war by making antiwar politicians look bad.[79]

To this day, numerous authors have speculated about what actually happened at Beekman's house in the middle of World War II, with most concluding that it was ultimately unknowable. However, Dorothy Schiff was so concerned that Senator Walsh might sue the *Post* over its reporting that she secretly commissioned a team of six private investigators and attorneys, led by Daniel A. Doran, to discover the truth. Their report, which took five months to prepare, ran over 150 pages and included everything from interviews with the major players in the case (including Beekman and all of his lawyers), to a detailed analysis of Senator Walsh's travel schedule for the times he was supposedly in Brooklyn. For years, this report has been publicly available, along with the rest of Dorothy Schiff's papers, at the New York Public Library, but no historians seem to have referenced it. As far as I know, I am the first to read its findings.

Local police had had Beekman under watch at least as far back as January 1942, having noticed an unusual number of sailors and soldiers coming and going from his building. In the two years since they had last busted Beekman, the war had begun, and no one wanted to arrest a bunch of men who might be needed in Europe or to impugn the morality of the military in general. So the police had no plans to raid his house until they were contacted by the Office of Naval Intelligence, which had secretly set up a spy post on the fourth floor of a nearby hospital, from which they were recording the license plate numbers of everyone who entered the building. The ONI wasn't interested in Beekman; rather, it was trailing William Elberfeld, a German national whom it believed to be a spy for Hitler. Together, the police and the ONI raided the establishment, arresting not just Beekman, but some of his clients (including noted composer Virgil Thomson), and some of the men who worked there.

One of the sex workers arrested was a Brooklyn merchant mariner named Charles Zuber, who was also one of Beekman's lovers. The assistant district attorney on the case, eager, perhaps, to make a name for himself, questioned Zuber at length about any particularly wealthy clients. The prosecution seemed convinced that Beekman couldn't be making much money from running a house of male prostitution, and so he had to have some other source of income—perhaps from Elberfeld or another spy. Zuber furnished the ADA with the name "Walsh," saying he believed the man to be a doctor. The ADA, aware of the long-standing rumors that Senator David Walsh was a homosexual, jumped to the conclusion that these two men were one and the same. He offered Zuber a deal: if he flipped on Beekman and testified against him on sodomy charges, Zuber would get off scot-free.

The ADA, or perhaps someone in his office, then passed the information about Walsh on to the judge in the case, Samuel Leibowitz. When Beekman was found guilty on charges of sodomy, largely thanks to Zuber's testimony, Leibowitz told Beekman that if he came clean about the extent of the spy ring, Leibowitz would be lenient; otherwise, Beekman was facing a twenty-year sentence.

According to the lead investigator hired by Dorothy Schiff, Beekman was "ingratiating, well-mannered, well spoken and plausible." He was also terrified and rather loose with the truth. He seemed willing to say whatever was necessary to avoid going to prison, which for a fifty-five-year-old homosexual whom the nation now believed to be a Nazi sympathizer might well have been a death sentence. Elberfeld had been a regular at Beekman's place, but he also ran a rival brothel in Manhattan and had no need to go to Brooklyn if he wanted to question sailors. Moreover, Beekman had banned him from his house around Thanksgiving of 1941, when Elberfeld told Beekman that Sweden was next on Hitler's list, and that after it was invaded, Beekman wouldn't be so "uppity-uppity."

The police literally tore apart both Beekman's home and Elberfeld's apartment and found nothing except a shortwave radio at Elberfeld's, which was technically contraband when owned by a foreign national. Elberfeld was placed on indefinite detention on Ellis Island—where he would remain for the rest of the war—but no charges were ever brought against him, and the police and the ONI no longer seemed interested in him at all. Instead, they leaned on Beekman to identify Walsh, once grilling him for over seven hours until he collapsed. A few of the men arrested in the initial raid were also asked about Walsh, with some saying he was there, others saying he wasn't, and a few saying they had no idea.

With no evidence other than a series of contradictory statements on whether Walsh had ever been at Beekman's home, there was no case. Yet the government still believed that Beekman was hiding some source of income, which Judge Leibowitz seemed to believe would have linked Walsh to the story. When Beekman refused to name his (nonexistent) financial backers, he received a twenty-year sentence to Sing Sing, the maximum-security prison in Ossining, New York.

By making a detailed analysis of Walsh's travel schedule, investigator Doran conclusively proved that Walsh could not have been at Beekman's establishment on any of the dates he was supposed to have been present. Moreover, Doran tracked down a Connecticut doctor, Harry Stone, a regular at Beekman's who bore a distinct resemblance to Senator Walsh. By presenting photos of Walsh and Stone to various witnesses (including Beekman), Doran concluded that Stone was almost definitely the man mistaken for Walsh. Yet no one seemed interested in using that evidence to exonerate Beekman, who would serve out the entirety of his twenty-year sentence before emerging from prison (where he was called "Mother Beekman"[80]) and disappearing from public records entirely. As for Walsh, although his fellow Senate members congratulated him on his aplomb during the entire affair, the airing of his gay laundry (plus, no doubt, his opposition to the war) seemed to sour voters on him. He was ousted from the Senate in 1946 and died the next year. After months of wild accusations, sting operations, and endless denunciations to the press, all the government got was the pointless destruction of the lives of two gay men and a witch hunt that sent innumerable others into hiding.

In a strange postscript to the case, many years later it would be revealed that the US government collaborated with the Mafia on counterintelligence initiatives during World War II. Toward the end of his life, Meyer Lansky, the Brooklyn Mafioso who rose to power during Prohibition, claimed that as part of this "Operation Underworld," his men had been asked by FBI director J. Edgar Hoover to investigate Beekman's establishment. Although this is completely uncorroborated, Lansky further claimed that after two of the men in the case were declared innocent, they soon mysteriously turned up dead. According to Lansky, "We knew those men were spies, and if the authorities weren't going to handle them, then Charlie's men probably settled the matter themselves."[81] Whom Lansky is referring to, and what actually happened to them, is one of the few enduring mysteries of the Swastika Swishery.

But if Beekman's house wasn't a den of Nazi spies, what was it actually like? According to one visitor, whose journal has been kept at the Kinsey Institute in Indiana University:

> His living room was warm and cozy. Young servicemen were sitting on sofas and easy chairs, relaxed and friendly. Coffee and snacks were being served, light banter went back and forth. We felt as if we had entered a happy family circle, George being Dad and Mom combined. He knew the boys problems, helped when he could, supplied shelter, food, and money, and was loved with the casual affection that children show their parents. He confided to us newcomers that this was a bad night, as all the boys had to report for duty; and soon they left, kissing George goodbye. When they had gone, he asked us not to be disappointed and named a "good" night for us to return, a night when several big ships were due in harbor. He then proceeded in a businesslike fashion to inquire about our tastes in servicemen. "What color of eyes and hair do you prefer?" he asked. "Do you like them tall, medium, or your own size?" All the details were jotted down in George's notebook. "Is there any nationality you like best?," and then he described how nationalities differ in anatomical as well as temperamental qualities. Even the branch of service was left to our choice, for George commanded an unlimited supply.[82]

Perhaps this sounds like an overly rosy picture; after all, would one of the johns know, or admit to knowing, the darker aspects of such a place? But the report commissioned by Dorothy Schiff at the New York Post largely substantiates this image of Beekman's house as a warm and even tender environment.

What Brooklyn looked like before the opening of
the Erie Canal. Francis Guy (American, 1760-1820).
Winter Scene in Brooklyn, ca. 1819-1820. Oil on canvas,
58 3/8 x 74 9/16 in. (148.2 x 189.4 cm). *(Brooklyn
Museum, Transferred from the Brooklyn Institute of Arts
and Sciences to the Brooklyn Museum, 97.13)*

Winslow Homer's Portrait of Helena de Kay (Gilder). 1872. Oil on canvas.
(Photo credit: Museo Nacional Thyssen-Bornemisza / Scala / Art Resource, NY)

Fulton Street before the "L" came, 1886. (*v1981.15.138; Ralph Irving Lloyd lantern slides, v1981.15; Photo credit: Brooklyn Historical Society*)

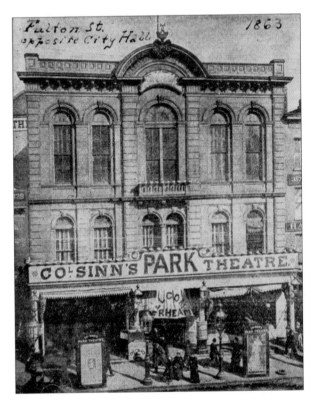

Colonel Sinn's Park Theatre, located at 381–383 Fulton Street, 1863. *(Photo from The New York Public Library)*

The Brooklyn Terminal, Brooklyn Bridge, c.1900. *(v1973.4.96; Postcard Collection, v1973.4; Photo credit: Brooklyn Historical Society)*

Mabel Hampton Rehearsing at Coney Island. *(Photo courtesy of the Lesbian Herstory Archives Educational Foundation, Mabel Hampton Collection)*

Photo of Emil Opffer. (*Courtesy of the*
Richard W. Rychtarik/Hart Crane Papers;
MSS 103; box 1; folder 68; Fales Library
and Special Collections, New York
University Libraries)

Marianne Moore and Her Mother,
Marguerite Thompson Zorach,
1925. Oil on canvas. (*National*
Portrait Gallery, Smithsonian
Institution © Estate of Marguerite
Thompson Zorach)

(above) *Stevedores Bathing Under Brooklyn Bridge,* Edward F. Casey, 1939. *(Courtesy of The Green-Wood Historic Fund)*

(left) *On "That" Street,* Charles Demuth, 1932. *(Photo credit: The Art Institute of Chicago/Art Resource NY)*

New *Broadway* ▾▾▾ *15 cents a copy*

BREVITIES

America's First National Tabloid Weekly

Third Sex Plague Spreads Anew!

Sissies Permeate Sublime Social Strata As Film Stars and Broadwayites Go Gay

Next Week : **"The American Jungle"**

Brooklyn Navy Yard Center Of Flagrant Camping For Gobs and Society Slummers

By JOHN SWALLOW MARTIN

During all the fairy round-ups of recent months there has been an undercurrent of Narcotic Squad investigations. The various raids in Bryant Park, which began earlier this year than last, have been accompanied by questions about "marahuana," the Mexican dopeweed favored by the underworld and especially by the perverts. One of the known peddlers was captured in Bryant Park, and sent away. Others, also known, are still at large, but under surveillance. "The Island" is said to have overflowed with degenerates, and to be permeated with "marahuana."

The Fleet's In

With the several raids staged at "Frank's Place" in Brooklyn, just back of the Navy Y. M. C. A., a plague-spot was discovered. Raided and closed several times, it has opened again, catering to the same patronage. The average citizen would scarcely believe his eyes had he been transported there as recently as the late spring, when the "fleet was in." Night after night, but especially on Saturdays and Sundays, anywhere from fifty to seventy-five sailors were there, and anywhere from fifty to a hundred men and boys, with painted faces and dyed tresses, singing and dancing. "High Society" dropped in, on "slumming" tours, of course. One recognized Mons. T——, the Scandinavian whose portrait has graced the society publications, and Adolphe D——, rich and fashionable, whose brother married the widow of one of the outstanding millionaires of America.

Way Out West

The hostesses, "Blossom" and "Violet," had their special following, and displayed a series of elaborate drags. Every other Sunday there was a "costume party," to the intense amusement of the gobs, all the way from "boots" (recruits) to "jimmie-legs" (masters-at-arms).

Sailors transferred from the Pacific Coast told strange and startling tales of their encounters with movie notables, especially the star who likes them "salty and sea-going." Earning thousands a week, he spends hundreds a week on the tattooed types. Brazening it out, he had himself

starred in a "navy" picture, enacting the rôle of a gob with many intimate little touches that delighted the water-tenders and "two-stripes."

Not only does one celebrity earn huge amounts through his picture acting, he has a profitable sideline in his antique-store. His own home is exquisitely fitted up, the "period" details being possibly over the heads of various associates. Nobody from the film colony moves in

(*Continued on page 12*)

AUTO GAG

The Absent Minded Motorist and the Balloon Tire

Read: "ON THE BANDWAGON" by R. J. D.

See Page 6

Back cover of the November 2, 1931, issue of *Broadway Brevities*. (*Photo courtesy of the collection of Will Straw*)

Coney Island cruising photo taken by Thomas Painter. *(From the Collections of the Kinsey Institute, Indiana University. All rights reserved.)*

(left) Anne Moses and unknown woman, 1928. *(Photo courtesy of the collection of Michael Levine)*

(below) Postcards from Robert Bonner's Heights Supper Club, c.1960. *(Courtesy of the author)*

As part of investigator Doran's research, he interviewed the wife and mother-in-law of Emanuel Bredel, one of the merchant mariners who worked and lived at Beekman's. Much like the Coney Island dowagers who didn't bat an eye at the gay men who took over the male beauty contest in 1929, these two women had a rather blasé attitude toward gay sex work. Bredel's mother-in-law, Mrs. Henrietta Levy, was a fifty-year-old Brooklyn matron. Levy said that Beekman "was very kind to Bredel and to her daughter Estelle," and that he visited them frequently at her home. When asked what she knew of the association between Beekman and Bredel, Mrs. Levy "smiled knowingly as she stated that she assumed that Mr. Beekman had picked up Bredel because he was a good-looking young sailor." Of homosexuality in general, Mrs. Levy told investigators that "people have certain ways of enjoying themselves and what business is it of yours or mine how they do this, just as long as they don't bother anyone."[83]

Mrs. Levy's daughter Estelle had, two years earlier, at the age of seventeen, married Emanuel Bredel and had briefly lived at Beekman's. Estelle said that her husband "had been in the Navy for six years and after he left the Navy he worked in the Brooklyn Navy Yard." However, when the Office of Naval Intelligence began hounding her husband (and all other known associates of Beekman's), Bredel was dismissed from his job and had to go back out to sea. Beekman, she said, was "a wonderful cook," and life at his house was "practically a steady party all the time." Estelle seemed to believe that only the johns were queer (as many of the men who worked as trade would agree), but she liked both the johns and the boys equally. "I would frequently sit around and watch the fags and queers," she told the investigators. "I got a great kick out of them."

The attitudes of both Levy women showed that even as the idea of homosexuality as a permanent orientation was taking hold in the country as a whole, many people still operated with older understandings of sexuality, which didn't preclude "normal men" from taking part in certain kinds of same-sex sexual activity. Their testimony furthers the idea that a more lax attitude toward (some kinds of) queerness still prevailed in some working-class communities in Brooklyn, if not in the editorial offices of the New York Post or on the floor of the Senate in Washington.

According to Thomas Painter and his network of male hustlers, the Beekman case had a chilling effect on gay brothels throughout New York. Not only was there more attention on their activities, but the lack of new housing construction

throughout the Depression, combined with the pressure of housing war workers, had made it nearly impossible for brothels to switch locations frequently—
their usual way of avoiding notice or police complaint. Within a year of Beekman's
arrest, all of the houses Painter had known had shut down. A few of the procur-
ers had even gone so far as to join the military, both to help the anti-Nazi cause
and to get out of town while the heat was on. The rest remained in the city, but
now functioned (on a much reduced scale) as a delivery service, where men could
call up and request to have an escort sent to them.

However, if 1942 saw a great reduction in the spaces where queer men could
meet, it also saw a great increase in spaces for queer women in Brooklyn. In August of that year, just a few weeks after Gustave Beekman was convicted, the
Brooklyn Navy Yard hired their first women to work in industrial jobs. As young
men shipped off to war by the tens of thousands, the home front suddenly accepted
the idea of women workers. Particularly for women of color and lower-income
women, not working was never an option. However, this work was typically in

Women contemplating the Sands Street entrance to the Brooklyn Navy Yard (c. 1942). (*Photo
courtesy of the Brooklyn Eagle Photographs—Brooklyn Public Library—Brooklyn Collection.*)

female fields such as teaching or domestic care, and it was often considered either temporary (until a woman got married), or an embarrassing necessity because a woman's husband couldn't support the family. But with the great labor shortage created by the war, America quickly came to embrace the Rosie the Riveter image of female employment as patriotic duty. Of the women who were employed in war-related work at the end of 1945, nearly 50 percent said that they hadn't wanted to work outside the home before Pearl Harbor—but a walloping 75 percent said they wanted to continue working now that they had begun.[84]

Brooklyn women were eager to do their part. According to Columbia University labor historian John R. Stobo:

> When openings for women in helper-trainee positions were announced [at the Brooklyn Navy Yard] the preceding winter, 20,000 applied. Of these the Yard examined 6,000 and found 3,000 to be qualified. The Labor Board then called in two hundred, sending about one-half to the shipfitters' shop. It was front-page news in the newspapers.[85]

While the effect these women had on the image of womanhood in America was incredible, it should be noted that their numbers—particularly in Brooklyn—were not as large as one might expect. According to the US Census, 27 percent of women were employed outside the home in 1940; by 1945, that number would increase to 36 percent.[86] Stobo goes on to write that of that original wave of female hires at the Navy Yard, only twelve were black, and that relative to other military operations, Brooklyn "hired the fewest women as a percentage of its total workforce."[87]

However, civilian war work soon followed suit, with the Todd Shipyard in Red Hook putting its first twelve women welders to work on October 6, 1942. They were called the Toddlers or welderettes, names as dismissive as they were affectionate. The shipyard promised them two things: "a basic 8-hour day" and "equal pay with men doing the same jobs."[88] The first was laughable. Almost no one in war-related work was working normal hours. But the second was true—at least for those women working at Todd; women working for the government at the Brooklyn Navy Yard remembered making much less than comparably employed men.

Anne Moses was one of those first women to walk into the boys club of the Todd Shipyard in 1942. Moses was a thirty-four-year-old butch with deep-set dark eyes, a wide nose, and the permanent hint of a smile on her face. She came from a large immigrant family: her father, Moishe Moishe, had emigrated from Romania to Brooklyn, where he worked as a tinsmith while raising eighteen children, nine boys and nine girls. As often happens with queer people who don't get married, Moses was the one who stayed at home, where she would remain, taking care of her mother until Anne was fifty-four (when she announced she was leaving to live with her girlfriend in Florida). War work—a chance to get outside the house, meet other women, and wear pants—must have seemed like an incredible opportunity, and she was willing to lie to make sure she got a job.

Moses had been the only one of her siblings who wanted to learn her father's trade. Although Moishe taught her how to solder and smith, it wasn't then an appropriate job for a woman. Instead, she kept his books and kept up her skills on the side, always the first one to climb up on the roof when something needed to be repaired. According to family lore, when the Todd Shipyard brought in that initial batch of women and non-draft-eligible men to consider for positions in 1942, the first question they asked was if anyone knew how to weld. Moses shot her hand up, figuring how different could it be from soldering? Metal was metal; heat was heat—she would work it out. She was hired on the spot and worked the next hundred days in a row before she got her first day off (when she and her girlfriends went to Coney Island).

At Todd, Moses learned to weld twenty-two-gauge galvanized steel, the kind that was required to build and repair the twenty-thousand-ton aircraft carriers—known as baby flattops—which were one of Todd's specialties. To keep themselves focused on their dangerous but repetitive task, workers held competitions such as "hammering the Axis," to see who could set the most rivets in the least amount of time.[89] Until the very end of the war, Moses would work at Todd. While there, she cofounded the Sparklers Letter Club, which established pen-pal relationships between current welders and the men who had been working in their same factories before shipping out. On October 7, 1943, the Toddlers threw themselves a one-year birthday party to celebrate a momentous occasion: they were "the first women to have completed one year of work in any ship repair yard in the country."[90]

We know all this because Moses was a prodigious scrapbooker, and we can thank her grandnephew Michael Levine for preserving her photo collection after she died. The hundreds of photos cover roughly three subjects—her family, mostly in Brooklyn; her work as a Toddler during the war; and what appears to be a tight-knit group of butch women. The earliest dated photos of these women come from 1926 to 1928 and appear to have been taken at a resort in Spring Valley, New York, just a little way outside the city in what would come to be known as the Jewish Catskills. In them, Moses is featured fishing, playing tennis and basketball, dressed as a pirate for a play, and shooting arrows. In one photo, she crouches low in a dark one-piece bathing suit, hair short and slicked back, fists raised. The caption reads *Benny Leonard's only rival,* a reference to the hugely famous Jewish professional lightweight boxer. In a few of the photos, she can be seen hugged up with a laughing woman with chin-length curly hair. In one, they share a swing. In another, Moses appears to be on her knees, proposing. And in a third, she is bent over the woman's lap, wearing a pair of high-cut shorts with big buttons up the side, as the woman spanks her. In later photos, probably from the mid-1950s, a few of these women seem to reappear, now all with short hair, baggy high-cut trousers, collared shirts, and sweater vests.

Also in the scrapbooks are numerous photos of Moses wearing heavy coveralls and a welder's mask with TODD emblazoned on the top. As a Toddler, Moses would have been expected to wear a hodgepodge of retrofitted men's protective gear: army cast-off pants and shirts, plastic helmets and breast covers, leather-sleeved coats, hairnets, and goggles.[91] This all-covering uniform was necessary to protect her from flying sparks, freezing weather, metal shrapnel, falling tools, and the thousand and one other hazards these women faced daily. Some of them

Anne Moses being spanked by unknown woman (c.1928). (*Photo courtesy of the collection of Michael A. Levine.*)

worked hanging off the sides of the giant ships, replacing battle-torn steel panels. Others wedged themselves into tiny compartments in the engine rooms, where it was next to impossible to avoid the flying sparks from their own blowtorches. Without protective gear—the kind that was generally only made for men, hence the need for army castoffs—their work would have been impossible.

In part because of the uniforms of these working women—and in part because of the fabric shortage caused by the war—a revolution was under way in women's clothing. Before the war, butch women such as Mabel Hampton and Vittoria Cremers faced public scorn and possibly even violence for wearing pants in public; afterward, trousers for women were suddenly fashionable. Lucille Kolkin, a shipfitter at the Brooklyn Navy Yard, recalled that wearing pants felt "romantic and exciting," but at first it was rare for the women to wear them outside work. Only over time, as their jobs became routine and changing into and out of their elaborate uniforms became exhausting, did women start to wear them home.[92]

Initially, factories were only interested in hiring young women with some kind of industrial background (such as Moses), but as the war went on, those restrictions loosened considerably. According to Mildred Justice, the personnel manager at the Todd Shipyard:

At first our age limit was twenty-one to thirty-five. Then we raised it to forty-five, and now there is no upper age limit. We have found from experience that many of the older women are stronger and can endure cold, bad weather better than some of the girls. We have a Danish woman welder who is fifty-three years old and she is one of our best workers.[93]

Although these women were of all ages and came from all walks of life, they did have some things in common. The majority of them were either unmarried, widowed, or their husbands were serving in the war. Few had young children. And they didn't have a problem doing work that was traditionally unfeminine. Many of them enjoyed the freedom to curse, earn their own money, wear comfortable clothes, and delay getting married. As Lucille Kolkin put it in an oral history she did with the Brooklyn Historical Society years later:

Those of us who worked in the Navy Yard must have had something a little bit different to begin with. . . . I mean, you wouldn't have taken the most feminine

*girl—she wouldn't have gone there. It was too dirty. You know. And that would
have bothered her. And that didn't bother me.*[94]

Just as Thomas Painter recognized that going off to war put straight men into
proximity with homosexuality—thus enabling them to understand and perhaps
even experience it—the same was true for women working in the factories. For
example, Bettie Chase was one of the twelve black women initially hired at the
Brooklyn Navy Yard. At twenty, she was straight, innocent, hardworking, and
short, which is what the yard wanted for its tack welders, who often had to work
hanging off the side of a ship or in cramped internal quarters. Fraternizing between the men and the women in the yard was frowned upon, but Chase remembered that she was particularly warned to steer away from any young man who
looked able-bodied but was 4F—meaning he had been rejected from the service,
presumably for being gay. Chase also heard rumors "that there was a woman that
[sexually] attacked a woman" in one of the bathrooms at the yard, which is why
she rarely went to them alone.[95] Learning about homosexuality, like wearing pants
and starting to curse, was just one of the many realities of working for the war
effort.

Unfortunately, although many oral histories and interviews have been done
with real-life Rosie the Riveters such as Chase, few of these addressed sexuality
(beyond straight marriage) openly or with any regularity. The only factory-working
Brooklyn lesbian to gain postwar prominence was the poet Naomi Replansky;
though her poetry speaks to what it was like on the floor of the Navy Yard during
the war, it doesn't provide insight into life as a lesbian at that time. And while we
have photos of Anne Moses and the women of her circle, their thoughts, experiences, and even names were never preserved. Thankfully, two early queer-history
projects—Len Evans's 1983, independently conducted oral history on the lives
of lesbians and gays during the 1950s; and Marcy Adelman's 1986 book, *Long Time
Passing: Lives of Older Lesbians*—both captured the World War II experiences of a
machinist and sailor named Rusty Brown. By combining the two documents, it's
possible to get a picture of the life that led one lesbian to become a factory worker
at the Brooklyn Navy Yard toward the end of the war in 1943.

Brown was born on a farm outside New York City, sometime around the turn
of the 1920s, just as Mabel Hampton was first treading the stage at Coney Island.
Brown's early childhood was hardscrabble and often dangerous, particularly once

her family moved to New York City. After she stowed away on a freight train to Washington, DC, at the age of eight, her parents placed her in the care of the Society for the Prevention of Cruelty to Children. The first day she walked through the door, one of the older girls yelled out, "Hey, we got another dyke." Although Brown didn't know the word, she somehow felt, instinctively, that the girl was right. "They said, do you let [boys] touch you? I said, 'The hell! . . . I'd break their arm if they tried it.' And [she] says, 'You're a dyke.'"[96]

"I breathed a sigh of relief," Brown told Evans. Inside, she realized, "I'm not alone, maybe I'm not crazy after all."

Brown went to school at the Five Points House of Industry, a vocational academy for wayward children. As a scholarly education, it wasn't great, but in lesbian experience, Brown said she graduated "cum laude." As she remembers, she was caught sleeping with "every girl over the age of twelve" and two of the teachers. Her family, afraid she would corrupt her younger sister, wouldn't let her return home, and Brown ended up a shoplifter, pickpocket, and occasional burglar. A few older women tried to convince her to go into sex work, saying that if she ever got hungry, to call them up. Brown responded, "I couldn't get that goddamned hungry." Around 1937, she was sent to Bellevue, where they planned to give her shock treatments to cure her "unnatural desires," but Brown stole a nurse's uniform and escaped.

While her family and the psychiatrists at Bellevue had problems with her sexual orientation, Brown remembered that, prewar, there simply wasn't the level of homophobia (or as she called it, "homophilia") that would be commonplace after the mid-1950s. "There wasn't this business of homophilia that there is . . . among straight people today," she told Evans. "I don't ever remember a person being beat up simply because he was gay." She was hassled occasionally, and there was a lot of ignorance, and there weren't a lot of lesbian-only spaces. But real fear and hatred of queer people, in Brown's experience, only started after the end of World War II.

After escaping Bellevue in 1939, Brown could sense that America was headed to war. But when she tried to enlist in the army, she was denied for two reasons: her placement in the SPCC as a child, which labeled her a delinquent, and a heart defect. Interestingly, she wasn't asked any questions about her sexual orientation or put through the same kind of antigay screening as male recruits. For her, like many other butches without a high school diploma, joining the military seemed to be her only option—nowhere, civilian side, would let her work with machines. Thankfully, after the army turned her down, she discovered she was eligible to be a civilian employee with the navy, which is how she ended up going to welding school in San Francisco. On the morning of Pearl Harbor, she was on a navy ship headed toward the Philippines, where she spent the first ten months of the war.

As it did for Jack Barker before her, life at sea exposed Brown to different sexual mores around the world. In Manila, she was a regular at a coffeehouse frequented mostly by queer women. As she described it in *Long Time Passing:*

> *You could tell when you walked in who was butch and who was femme. At some tables, one was butch and one was femme. At other tables the women were either all butch or all femme. . . . By sitting with the butches I'd find out who was going with who—I didn't want to get my head knocked off. I figured there was plenty of fish in the sea.*[97]

Brown told Evans that during her time in the Philippines, and later in Korea, she was surprised by "how many Asians I found were gay. . . . I had no problems finding companions wherever I went."[98] Later, when the navy briefly shipped Brown to London, she was excited to discover lesbian-specific bars, such as the Royal Queen and the Four Dices.

Afraid of getting drummed out of the service, Brown mostly avoided places where military members hung out—a common tactic used by queer people in the military, often resulting in increased isolation and a reputation for being unsociable, which in turn limited promotions. Brown found the military to be full of queers, but only at lower ranks. "There were millions of us, army, navy, marines, Coast Guard, air force," she told Evans. However, they were mostly "under the rank of major."

Queer people in the military, according to Brown, had two rules: "never hassle straight people, and don't mess with the people in your own outfit."[99] Despite her desire to avoid fraternization, Brown found herself in a relationship with another woman on her boat as it headed from the Philippines to Seattle. Her girlfriend was in the navy proper, which made it more dangerous for them, because "if word had gotten out, she would have been thrown out of the military."[100] Somehow, they kept their relationship a secret, which was difficult to do in the close quarters of ship life. Being responsible for repairs became a useful pretext for their affair. As Brown wrote:

> Since I was a mechanic, sometimes I'd say I was needed in the engine room—a big area with a main corridor with turbines out to the side. We would meet behind one of these turbines. We could never spare enough time to really have a sex act, which aggravated both of us. As it was, we were both taking a big chance. Mostly we just hugged and kissed and had a little foreplay. We never did get down to brass tacks.[101]

Some time around 1943, while Anne Moses was celebrating her one-year anniversary of becoming a Toddler, Brown began working at the Brooklyn Navy Yard. She didn't know of any lesbian-only spaces in the city—Brooklyn or Manhattan—at the time. She knew of a few mixed spaces, such as the Howdy Club, a holdover from the pansy craze where lesbian waiters in men's garb served food, and drag kings and queens onstage entertained a mostly straight audience. She enjoyed socializing with queer men and women at the same time, both because she liked queer people in general, and because if the place was raided, you could easily grab a guy and look like a straight couple. She would remain in New York for the rest of the war, and for large parts of the 1950s.

But though she would stay in Brooklyn, Brown had no way of knowing that on August 14, 1945, her entire life there would be upended. That day the Japanese surrendered, ending World War II. It would become a major—if rarely recognized—date in the history of queer people, the history of Brooklyn, and in particular the history of queer people *in* Brooklyn. What had seemed like a large and growing queer world would be exposed, almost overnight, as a fragile bubble. After 1945, the physical and mental suburbanization of America would rip right through the heart of queer Brooklyn (sometimes literally). As Brown remembered it:

> The war came to an end and our world started to collapse. I was working at the Navy base in Brooklyn when the Japanese signed the surrender; 150 of us were told that in two weeks our jobs would be through. The war was over, the military was all coming back (those that survived), and they were going to give them the priority on the jobs. I thought, "What the hell am I going to do now?"

That night, millions of people took to the streets to celebrate, thronging downtown Brooklyn and Times Square, but Brown was right to worry. With the end of the war, the celebrated image of Rosie the Riveter—the tough working woman in pants—would be jettisoned for the aspirational heterosexuality of Donna Reed and her aprons.

In 1945, 37 percent of women were employed outside the home. By 1950, that number would drop to 32 percent. Of the women who entered the workforce for the first time during the war, by then approximately 50 percent would no longer be employed. Even for women who remained working, there were significant changes. In particular, postwar "many women were forced out of high-paying jobs in traditionally male industries"—exactly the jobs that queer women such as Rusty Brown, Naomi Replansky, and Anne Moses had flocked to.[102] New jobs for women would primarily be in sectors that paid less and were considered acceptably feminine: clerical work, nursing, teaching, domestic care, and retail.

In the minds of many, queer American history is a straight line forever shooting upward, a march of incremental progress, where decades of closeted anger finally explodes into public view on the first night of the Stonewall Riots on June 28, 1969. The truth is much more complicated. What we know of as being "gay," "lesbian," "bisexual," or "transgender" didn't exist until the early twentieth century, but there was still a strong presence of men who loved men, women who loved women, and gender outlaws of all kinds. World War II exposed many people to the idea that these feelings meant you were a certain type of person, defined by your sexuality or gender identity. In the immediate aftermath of the war, a select few areas—the Castro in San Francisco, Greenwich Village in New York—would see an explosion of bars catering specifically to queer people. But just as Americans came to understand homosexuality at this time, they also learned homophobia. It's hard to hate what you cannot even name. After the war, "gay life" would become more isolated, more insular, and in some ways more dangerous—if also larger, more speakable, more visible, and eventually more politically potent.

Concomitantly, the suburbanization of American cities (and American aspirations) would begin to hollow out the urban cores where queer people had gathered since the end of the nineteenth century. Economic opportunity enabled queer life to flourish along the waterfront in Brooklyn's early history; looming urban decay would help to swiftly dismantle it. After World War II, Brooklyn's coast would become less and less important to the economics of the city and the country as a whole. As Coney Island, the Brooklyn Navy Yard, Red Hook, and Brooklyn Heights all began a long slide into economic instability, their nascent queer infrastructure would suffer and shrink. Organized queer life in New York City would be concentrated into smaller and smaller areas, and the vibrant queer histories of places outside Manhattan would soon be forgotten. Far from being a story of incremental progress, the story of queer Brooklyn between World War II and Stonewall is primarily one of separation, concentration, and ultimately decimation.

7. The Great Erasure, 1945–69

August 14, 1945, the day the Japanese surrendered, was a busy one for Bill Miller. In flowing blue script, he jotted down a whirlwind of appointments in his tiny pocket journal. He dropped off drawings for a new work project; met up with friends at Tony's, a popular gay bar on Fifty-second Street (known as Swing Alley for all its jazz clubs); and he was supposed to model for Paul Cadmus, but Cadmus canceled. Then at 7:00 p.m., when the announcement of the Japanese surrender went out over every radio station in the country, he threw on his sailor suit and rushed to Times Square, along with millions of other New Yorkers. *Life* magazine described the crowd as "ten New Year's Eves rolled into one."[1] Champagne bottles popped, car horns blared, and people tore phone books into impromptu confetti, which rained down from windows all over the city. The war was over, the soldiers were coming home, and nothing would ever be the same again.

For the most part, Miller's pocket diary is just a dry log of his daily activities. Even his sexual history (which he was keeping for Alfred Kinsey's research) is simply notched down in a tiny series of coded letters in the lower right corner of each entry. But on August 14 he recorded a rare outburst of emotion, noting, "Lunch Barclay Joe Marvel—hot!"[2] The Barclay was a high-class hotel, opened by the Vanderbilt family, just off Times Square. And Joe Marvel? Prior to the war, he was the assistant director of the Brooklyn Museum for eight years, where he organized the first show of Picasso in America, and the first performances of ballet ever at an American museum (no longer was ballet the province of rough workingmen's saloons, as it was when Ella Wesner got her start on the stage). In his spare time, Marvel was on the board of the National Urban League, worked with fashion designer Elsa Schiaparelli to create high-art anti-venereal-disease posters, and helped Margaret Sanger open her first birth control clinic, in the

Brownsville neighborhood of Brooklyn. As a conscientious objector during the war, Marvel was one of the only people allowed into Gestapo-controlled prisons in France, where he brought food and critical medical supplies to members of the Paris Underground.[3] After the war, he would become one of the few people in the country to work with returning gay veterans, which was probably the reason he had lunch with Bill Miller.

A few months after their meeting, Joe Marvel wrote a letter to his fellow members of the Quaker Emergency Service, an organization he had founded to provide assistance to conscientious objectors, war wives, orphans, and others affected by World War II. "With the beginning of the draft," he informed them, "a large number of young men were found to be disqualified for the performance of military duty by reason of psychiatric maladjustment"—the military's nom de guerre for homosexuality. "Inasmuch as there are practically no existing facilities for dealing with this small group of returning service personnel and draft rejects," Marvel suggested that the QES turn their efforts toward aiding these men.

Bill Miller, in many ways, was one of the lucky ones who didn't really need Marvel's help. He was allowed to serve in the Coast Guard as he wanted; once in the service, his sexuality was not discovered, or if it was, no one cared; he survived a war that killed nearly half a million Americans; and after it ended, he was eligible for benefits under the Servicemen's Readjustment Act of 1944—aka the G.I. Bill. The G.I. Bill did many things, such as authorizing $500 million to create a network of hospitals and medical coverage for veterans, and guaranteeing a yearlong stipend of $20 a week to any vet who was looking for work. It also provided college tuition benefits, starting at one full year (plus a living stipend) for anyone who had served at least ninety days, and growing from there depending on the length of service. After his time with the Coast Guard in Brooklyn was over, Miller used the G.I. Bill to enroll at Dartmouth, where he studied literature and had a brief, intense relationship with philosopher, inventor, and author Buckminster Fuller. Miller would be one of the 7.8 million World War II vets who would take advantage of the educational benefits of the bill in some fashion.

Many returning soldiers were not so lucky, as Joe Marvel must have known. The experiences of Marvin Liebman, a young Jewish soldier from Bay Ridge, were prototypical in this regard. Upon entering the Army, he had his first sexual experience with another man, and on a troop transport ship to Europe, he fell in with a large group of other queer soldiers. When a commanding officer discov-

ered Liebman's letters to one of those men—full of Dorothy Parker witti-
cisms and always ending on the line "Damn Miss Rose. I could spit."—Liebman
was publicly humiliated, tormented, and labeled a "New York Jew faggot."[4] He
was sent to an army psychiatrist, who laid out his bleak options: he could be declared straight and sent back to his regiment, where the men would likely make
his life hell; he could get transferred to a base in Bahrain, where troublesome pri-
vates were sent to work in 130 degree heat as punishment; or he could get a blue
discharge. Liebman took the discharge, lied to his family about the reason behind
it, and bought a secondhand army medallion that was given only to honorably
discharged soldiers, to serve as proof of his service. Shortly thereafter, he married
a woman, became a conservative Republican activist, and stayed in the closet
until 1990, when he was sixty-seven years old.

Men like Leibman who were punished for their sexuality took great pains to
hide their 4F status and their blue discharges, so it's not unsurprising that one of
the few well-known contemporary examples was fictional: Angelo Maggio, from
James Jones's 1951 bestseller, *From Here to Eternity*. Described as being "of Brooklyn immigrant Italian stock," and an "absolute hater of the Army," Maggio is the
closest friend of the novel's protagonist.[5] Although the book and resulting film
(which starred Frank Sinatra as Maggio) were heavily censored, Jones's original
text had Maggio explaining that he had sex with men for money, and that he in
fact liked Hal, his regular fairy. Maggio is ceaselessly harassed by a superior, which
eventually lands Maggio in the stockade, where he goes insane and is given a blue
discharge. Jones wanted to accurately portray the life he had witnessed in the
military, which included a lot of sex between men—some tender, some violent,
some paid. Jones protested the censorship of his book in a letter to his editor,
writing, "The things we change in this book for propriety's sake will in five
years, or ten years, come in someone else's book anyway . . . and we will wonder why we thought we couldn't do it."[6] It wasn't until 2011, however, that the
book was reissued with the gay content restored.

Upon receiving a blue discharge, many servicemen were forced to sign a paper stating, "I understand that I may be deprived of virtually all rights as a veteran under both Federal and State legislation; and that I may expect to encounter
substantial prejudice in civilian life."[7] This was a way of recognizing that even
though a blue discharge was not technically dishonorable, it was still treated that
way in practice, and it obviated the government's commitment to take care of

returning soldiers. During the war, military policy leaned toward rehabilitating homosexuals or finding ways for them to serve despite their sexuality, but afterward (when they were no longer necessary), they were explicitly banned from service. In peacetime, the dismissal rate for homosexuals would be nearly three times what it was during World War II—and during the Korean War dismissal numbers would again dip. Gays and lesbians were good enough to die as soldiers, but not to live as veterans. On average, two thousand members of the military were dismissed from service for homosexuality every year of World War II, and an unknown number received other-than-honorable discharges that were sexuality related in fact, if not on paper. The other group that disproportionately received these blue discharges were black men and women (most likely because a blue discharge didn't have the same high and specific misconduct threshold that it took to issue a dishonorable discharge, making it easier to use based on racism and personal opinion). Unlike Bill Miller, these veterans did not qualify for the educational or health benefits of the G.I. Bill. They couldn't use their service records in place of résumés, and when they were therefore out of work, they didn't receive a stipend. During World War II, nearly fifty thousand men and women would receive a blue discharge. Nearly 25 percent of those who received them were black service members, despite the fact that only 6 percent of the armed forces were black.[8]

Joe Marvel wanted to help these men—but how to reach them? Many didn't think of themselves as homosexual, and even if they did, there was no easy way to contact large numbers of queer people. Thankfully, Marvel soon encountered two individuals familiar to anyone researching homosexuality in New York City at this time: Alfred Gross and Dr. George Henry. After attending a semipublic meeting where the two men explained the work they had done at the Payne Whitney Clinic under the auspices of the Committee for the Study of Sex Variants and the Selective Service, Marvel suggested they join forces—and thus the Civil Rehabilitation Committee of the Quaker Emergency Service was launched. In the quiet, understated way he seemed to do everything, Marvel and the QES would provide lifesaving help to an uncountable number of gay men—hundreds certainly, thousands probably, and if you include the ripple effects of his work, tens of thousands. Ironically, that work would be embedded in a criminal justice system that would increasingly define homosexuality as a threat to society, and the

Civil Rehabilitation Committee itself would be used to paint queer people as sexual psychopaths.

Henry and Gross knew that the easiest way to reach gay men was via the police, who were busily arresting thousands of them every year, mostly in subway toilets, movie theaters, and parks. In 1945, for instance, a staggering 2,147 men were arrested for "disorderly conduct-degeneracy," aka soliciting for sex in a public place in New York City.[9] This represented a 100 percent increase over 1944. By 1948, that number would hit 3,289.[10] In Brooklyn, cops were quietly trying to stem a new tide of "sex degenerates" cruising in Prospect Park, a lush and wild landscape not far from the Brooklyn Navy Yard.[11] The city had also just reinstated a court specifically to deal with low-level arrests at Coney Island, including ones for degeneracy and cross-dressing. Times Square, Fort Tryon Park, the docks in downtown Brooklyn, Greenwich Village, the Bowery, Fourteenth Street, Harlem; the list of cruising grounds in the city was long, and the police were known to raid them regularly to meet arrest quotas, and occasionally to shake down "fairies" for money.

The public meeting where Joe Marvel met Alfred Gross and George Henry was also attended by Jacob Panken, a socialist reformer and New York City judge. Panken urged the men to use his name to develop a relationship with the courts. However, in a move that would ultimately prove disastrous, the QES ended up partnering with Justice Edgar Bromberger, the chief city magistrate of New York. Bromberger would provide the homosexuals; Gross and Henry would provide the expertise in treating them; and the QES would act as fund-raisers, organizers, and arbiters of disputes—of which there would be many.

From the beginning, the Quakers, the courts, and the queers had vastly different ideas of what the Civil Rehabilitation Committee was doing. Henry and Gross wanted to help gay men find some level of self-acceptance and avoid future arrest. Magistrate Bromberger wanted to isolate and cure these men of their deviance, and if a cure was not possible, to figure out why people became homosexual so that it could be prevented. The Quakers vacillated between these two poles, taking a little from each. Marvel didn't believe homosexuality could be cured, and he wanted to help these men, but he also believed that if children under the age of six could be reached, the knowledge gained through the Rehabilitation Committee could be used to prevent them from turning gay.

The QES assembled a team of psychiatrists, social workers, and religious figures, any or all of who could be called upon to work with a particular client. The
QES also brought in a wide array of consulting staff, including lawyers, nonprofit
leaders, and physicians. Their work touched men from every borough, and fit-
tingly, the committee did as well. Brooklynites involved included Frank Ortloff,
a lawyer who would provide legal guidance both to the committee and to its clients, and Leland Barnes, the director of social service at the Brooklyn Division
of the Protestant Council, who helped affiliate the committee with the greater
Protestant Church in New York.

In the committee's first full year of operation, they saw 414 men, or about
15 percent of those arrested for soliciting in 1946. The committee developed a
system whereby these men were evaluated before being sentenced by the court,
and if they were considered redeemable, they were given two years of probation
and required to report to the committee. The committee recommended probation for a number of reasons. First, jail time did nothing other than lock a man
away for a short while and probably cause him to lose his job, sending him spiral-
ing further down into dissolution. But simply paying a fine was too light of a slap
on the wrist to dissuade future soliciting. They believed probation would instill a
healthy dose of fear, "a reminder that society cannot tolerate the particular type
of sexual misconduct which brought these men to the notice of the court."[12]

What men were considered redeemable? First, although it was never stated,
the committee generally accepted only white men, later estimating that only
1 percent of their clients were "colored."[13] Given that black men, as well as gay
men, were more likely to receive blue discharges, this was a painful, racist
irony that left gay black men with few therapeutic options and an increased
likelihood of incarceration while removing their experiences from any reports,
findings, or recommendations that would come from the QES (or from any historians using their wealth of data to reconstruct the queer world of the late 1940s
and early 1950s).

All factions of the QES agreed that it was best to work with younger men who
had relatively stable lives, were employed or at least actively looking for work,
wanted the help they were being offered, and, most of all, weren't too effeminate
or vocal about being gay. Their program, groundbreaking though it was, emphasized respectability, and men who lacked an interest in hiding from the straight
world infuriated the committee. Take, for example, their thoughts on one "Pete

Maguire," a "blondined fairy . . . of the most extreme type." Maguire was arrested after a police officer, seeing that he was obviously gay, had spent the day
following him around the city, waiting for an opportunity to entrap and arrest
him in a subway bathroom. Yet the committee couldn't understand why he considered having to report to a probation officer for two years "irksome and mean-
ingless." The real problem, according to the committee, was that Maguire took
out his parental-abandonment issues on authority figures and could never get a
job because "a prospective employer would have to look at him but once" to know
he was queer. Maguire was "a complete social casualty" and "must be written off."[14]

However, for the men they would assist, the help provided by the QES was
often lauded as lifesaving. Alfred Gross told the chief probation officer of the courts
that the most significant contribution of their work was "the re-establishment of
the offenders' self-respect."[15] In the second year of its existence, the committee
began tracking voluntary visits by its clients. These surpassed the ones required
by the courts by a margin of almost two to one. At the end of the year, its office
was inundated with cards filled with gratitude for its work. The committee offered the first—and only—alternative-to-sentencing program in the country for
men arrested for their sexuality. In an unofficial capacity, they helped these men
get jobs, warned them against predatory lawyers, and even set them up on dates
with one another. They also taught many of these men (even the ones who were
married or who had attractions to women) that they were "homosexuals," not just
"normal men" who sometimes had sex with other men. Through the work of the
committee, the modern psychiatric model of sexuality would spread to working-
and middle-class communities around the city.

But after a year and a half, things started to go off the rails. The first sign of
trouble was a splashy, two-page article about the committee, published in Collier's magazine in February 1947. Titled "The Biggest Taboo," it began by praising
their work as a "brave venture," before distorting it out of all recognition. Collier's discussed their work entirely within the context of violent sex crimes and
fetishistic murders, and the "biggest taboo" they evoked was pedophilia, which
the article returned to over and over. "Without help," the author wrote, their clients "might sink into any one of the fierce distortions of the sex drive: not only
homosexuality, abuse of children, rape, and incest, but also such crimes as fire
setting, sadism, and murder."[16]

In the article, the differing opinions among the committee members were suddenly made clear. Whereas Gross told the author that his long-term goal was helping these men achieve self-respect, Magistrate Bromberger said that homosexuals "direct their activities toward those incapable of resistance" and "impose themselves on children." "From this point on," he said, their "path leads inexorably to crime." The article toyed with the idea of killing all homosexuals ("we have enough electric chairs"), before endorsing a solution from Samuel Leibowitz—the Brooklyn judge in the Swastika Swishery case—for the creation of an institution "midway between a jail and a hospital" where deviates could be kept until they were cured. "In some cases," Leibowitz pointed out, "that means the rest of their lives."[17]

Behind the scenes, things were even tenser. Henry and Gross wanted to expand their work to include giving free legal advice to men arrested for the first time, whether or not they were clients; Magistrate Bromberger and the Quaker lawyers objected. Shortly after the *Collier's* article was published, Gross wrote a stiffly worded letter to Marvel, noting that he was owed some $4,000 in back pay and questioning if the committee members thought "he is really worth what they are paying him—which is precisely nothing."[18] Clashes also occurred over entrapment, which Bromberger argued was a necessary part of police procedure, but both Marvel and Gross thought was illegal. Rumors started up that Gross was once again fraternizing with, and perhaps even dating, some of the clients. Bromberger soon became suspicious of what was *actually* happening at the clinic and made an unannounced visit, where he discovered that (once again) Gross was meeting with patients, not Dr. Henry. Bromberger immediately wanted Gross fired, which Henry resisted. The Quakers supported Henry, but instituted a humiliating policy whereby Gross was no longer allowed to handle the committee's money and had to request petty cash from Henry weekly.

By early 1948, the committee was on the ropes. In meetings with the entire group, Judge Bromberger suggested that the clinic leave its current home in the court on Mulberry Street because it sent the wrong message to prospective clients; in behind-the-scenes conversations with the Quakers, he revealed that the real reason he wanted the clinic gone was Gross. By May of that year, Henry and Gross had officially parted ways with the QES and the courts.

Unmoored but still committed to the work, the Quakers recruited Dr. Fredric Wertham, a German psychologist who had recently had success setting up a free psychiatric clinic for working-class African-Americans in Harlem. Under his auspices, a new venture was launched, confusingly called the Quaker Emergency Service Readjustment Center. Despite his lack of experience with homosexuality, by all accounts Wertham was dedicated to the clinic's work and resisted calls to criminalize or cure homosexuals. At first it seemed that he would act as a counterbalance to Magistrate Bromberger's vocal homophobia, but this was not to be. The court soon overwhelmed the clinic with cases, which were no longer limited to men arrested for soliciting, but included exhibitionists, Peeping Toms, rapists, pedophiles, prostitutes, thieves, runaways, check forgers, burglars, and drunks. Little by little, Magistrate Bromberger was forcing the clinic to conform to his idea that homosexuality and general criminality were linked. Soon, the clinic was seeing over a thousand people a year, far beyond its capacity, many of who had no interest in treatment. Although Dr. Wertham believed that no new sex crime laws were necessary, with the backing of Magistrate Bromberger, New York State passed a new law in 1950 that allowed for indefinite sentences for people convicted of sex crimes and required a psychiatrist's recommendation before release. As psychiatrists were rapidly teaching men who had sex with men that they were homosexual, they were also teaching the country that psychiatrists were the only ones who knew how to properly handle this problem. Meanwhile, the court increasingly leaned on the clinic to violate patient confidentiality, to provide recommendations for sentencing, and to allow court-approved researchers access to their confidential files—initiatives that Joe Marvel vocally opposed.

The clinic staff, lacking any expertise in sexuality, produced reports that became confusing and contradictory. On two back-to-back pages, they asserted that "exclusive homosexuality occurs in a relatively small percentage of cases," but also that most homosexuals were lying about having heterosexual sex. The staff believed that "homosexuality in men is nearly normal," but also that their goal was to cure their patients and render them heterosexual.[19] The volunteer psychiatrists recruited by Wertham were a motley crew. Some, such as Dr. Harry Benjamin, a pioneer in working with transgender individuals, had extensive experience in sexuality; others had crackpot theories such as that asking people to draw a tree would reveal when in their life they had experienced serious trauma, by the subconscious placement of knots at different points on the trunk. Some were downright dangerous, such as Rorschach expert Luise Zucker, who felt that her job was to make a client "understand, in as realistic a manner as possible, that he is lonely and dissatisfied, and that he is getting less out of life than others."[20]

Only by teaching homosexuals that they were miserable, she felt, could they get them to change.

These kinds of disagreements over the nature and treatment of homosexuality were common among early psychiatric practitioners, as they had been generations earlier among medical physicians. But in the homophobic 1950s, psychiatry as an institution quickly joined the chorus of official voices asserting that homosexuality was a fundamentally damaged and damaging condition. By 1952 the American Psychiatric Association would include homosexuality in their newly created *Diagnostic and Statistical Manual of Mental Disorders,* officially defining it as a mental illness for the first time. But the great experiment of the QES was already over by then, ironically destroyed by the very forces they were working to ameliorate.

The only thing that had been keeping their wobbly, disjointed alliance together was the behind-the-scenes work of the Quakers, particularly Joe Marvel, who spent his days fund-raising, organizing meetings, and getting the various parties to agree on basic operating issues. Without Marvel, the clinic would never have existed and could not continue—as they were to discover on a Thursday afternoon in March 1951, when he was arrested for soliciting sex from an undercover cop in a subway toilet.[21]

Dr. Wertham quickly wrote a letter to the judge testifying to Marvel's good character, and the charges were dropped, but the damage was done. Sudden accusations of fiscal and clerical impropriety were leveled at the clinic from Magistrate Bromberger's office. Within three weeks of Marvel's arrest, the courts had stopped sending clients to the clinic, and within four it was closed forever. Years later, Dr. Wertham would tell one of the volunteer psychiatrists that he had to close the clinic because "there were things going on which I'm sure you didn't know"—almost certainly a reference to Marvel's arrest.[22] The clients were abandoned, the volunteers were disbanded, and the New York City courts seemed to give up on understanding homosexuality at all. They stopped tracking degeneracy arrests separately from other kinds of disorderly conduct, and in 1954, working with the head of the Brooklyn State Hospital, they would refocus their psychiatric sex-related work on "sexual psychopaths"—a media-created panic that equated any sex-related arrest with violent assault and murder.[23]

In the aftermath of his arrest, Joe Marvel's wife separated from him, and he would soon retire due to "ill health" to a farm in Vermont, where he committed suicide in 1959. His *New York Times* obituary simply noted that the QES clinic handled "lewdness and other things."[24]

The great work started by pioneering lesbian journalist Jan Gay in the 1930s, which had sought to demystify queer people to bring about greater understanding, had finally sputtered to a halt, brought down by the very homophobia it fought to undo. Gay herself bounced through a dozen different jobs—including researcher, publicist, children's book author, and journalist—before settling down in Sausalito, California, where she lived with her partner until Gay's death in 1960. Never again would she research queer lives, but in a final poignant attempt to increase our shared knowledge of the world, she left her body to science.[25]

The same year that Joe Marvel was arrested, another queer Brooklynite by the name of Edward Sagarin would publish one of the most important early works of the newly fledged organized homosexual movement. Perhaps more than anyone else, Sagarin exemplified the double life of closeted men in the 1950s—so much so that he has often been referred to as the "Dr. Jekyll and Mr. Hyde" of early gay rights.[26] As Edward Sagarin he was a devoted husband and father living in a quiet residential area of Brooklyn, just off Prospect Park. Born in 1913, he had severe scoliosis and a hunched back. He studied chemistry and published a book in 1945 called *The Science and Art of Perfumery.*

However, as Donald Webster Cory, he was the author of *The Homosexual in America,* a point-by-point rebuttal of the homophobic myths, slanders, and rumors that were now commonly associated with homosexuality. As Cory, he argued that the opinions of an experienced homosexual were just as "essential as those of the psychiatrist, the jurist, or the churchman"[27] for understanding homosexuality. Although his book is deeply rooted in psychiatry, which led to many of its worst flaws, it struck back at the idea that the homosexual was a problem to be defined and fixed by others. He pointed out that most heterosexuals saw only a small slice of the homosexual population, and—like blindfolded men trying to explain what an elephant looks like—made erroneous assumptions based on their limited knowledge. The book discussed everything from Freudian analysis, to the American legal code, to queer practices among ancient civilizations. In a scholarly yet readable voice, Sagarin asserted that homosexuals were not sick, deranged, criminal, or emotionally stunted; rather, they were a despised minority deprived of their civil rights.

For this, he was hailed as a "mythic hero" by members of the nascent homosexual rights movement that was coalescing around the country.[28] The Mattachine Society, a gay men's civil rights group that was founded in California in 1950, would make many of these same arguments, and Sagarin would be one of the early members of the New York branch. Shortly after publishing his book, Sagarin founded a brief-lived social and civil rights organization called Homosexuals Anonymous, which ended up bringing him into dangerous contact with Alfred Gross.

After being asked to leave the Quaker Emergency Service, George Henry and Alfred Gross set up the George W. Henry Foundation, a small operation that ran out of a janitor's closet in a building on the Lower East Side. Almost entirely under Gross's direction, the foundation taught gay men "the delicate skills required to live" in the closet and worked within the Episcopal Church to advocate for more pastoral tolerance of homosexuality.[29] Gross walked an uneasy line, calling for less repression by the state and more understanding from the church, but also condemning gays who were too effeminate, too sexual, or too interested in organizing politically.

When Sagarin heard about the foundation's therapeutic work, he invited Gross to speak at a Homosexuals Anonymous meeting in 1952. Gross found the group, well—gross. They were drinking, socializing, camping it up, and organizing. He coldly informed the members, that the "'homosexual had no rights as such that the community was bound to respect,' and that they should be aware that homosexuals would be judged 'by the conduct of [their] worst members.'"[30]

Clearly, Gross considered those "worst members" to be the very men he was speaking to, and he left before their meeting was finished. We know all this because Gross then took it upon himself to report Sagarin and Homosexuals Anonymous to the FBI, with whom he apparently had an established relationship, most likely dating back to his work with the Selective Service. Although Sagarin wasn't arrested, the FBI kept track of him from this point on, and it's likely that the FBI's influence is part of the reason Homosexuals Anonymous quickly folded. Gross would continue his strange breed of counseling into the early 1970s, but it would become even less tolerant as years passed. In the preface to a faux-scholarly book on homosexuality in 1962, Gross would state that "homosexuality, with its lack of responsibility for the procreation of the species," was a factor in the decline of American civilization.[31] Despite all his work to help other gay men improve their self-esteem, Gross seemed to live his own life mired in self-loathing.

Unfortunately, Sagarin himself soon went down a similar path. As the 1960s wore on, he became more and more conservative in his outlook on homosexuality. In 1963, he coauthored *The Homosexual and His Society,* which argued that while some homosexuals might appear well adjusted, the vast majority were disturbed. He followed this up in 1964 with *The Lesbian in America,* in which he wrote, "Some lesbians see themselves only as victims of hostility; some onlookers and specialists see them only as disturbed. The truth would seem to be found in a combination of both."[32] After he got his PhD—as Edward Sagarin—with a thesis on the Mattachine Society, he publicly propounded that homosexuals were disturbed and needed therapy. In 1974, when he attacked the post–Stonewall Riots gay liberation movement during a panel at the American Sociological Society, Edward Sagarin was publicly outed as Donald Webster Cory, and he retreated from organized gay life and scholarship until he died in 1986.

Aside from Cory, a few other early homophile leaders also lived and organized in Brooklyn, like Curtis Dewees, a leader of the New York chapter of the Mattachine Society in the late 1950s and early 1960s. In 1950, Mattachine became the second gay rights organization founded in America (after the Society for Human Rights, a brief-lived Chicago-based group from the 1920s). In 1955, activists launched a New York chapter. Primarily an organization of white, middle-class men, Mattachine mostly pursued a political strategy of getting heterosexual experts to publicly declare that homosexuality was neither an illness nor a crime, in hopes that society at large would listen. They also organized gay men socially. In an interview conducted by Martin Duberman, Dewees recalled helping to establish Mattachine "discussion groups" around the city, including two in Brooklyn. "The Brooklyn one became quite large," he said, "so we broke them into a Brooklyn Heights discussion group and the Greater Brooklyn discussion group."[33] These groups served many functions, but they were mostly a place for consciousness-raising and the creation of a local queer community. Aside from Manhattan, Brooklyn was the only borough to have more than one group—and they were the only non-Manhattan ones to gain strong, loyal followings.

Dewees's self-published autobiography, *Memoirs of a Gay Rights Maverick,* also contains tantalizing hints of other brief-lived moments of gay social organizing in Brooklyn. Twice, he writes about living in semi-intentional queer spaces. From 1957 to 1960, he lived with his boyfriend Al de Dion (another Mattachine leader), at 331 Cumberland Street in Fort Greene, a half block from Marianne Moore's apartment. For $25 a month, the pair shared a cold-water flat, heated only by a fireplace in the living room, on the top floor of a four-story walkup. According to Dewees, "the entire building was gay except for the one other apartment on our floor. . . . The super was an early middle-aged guy on some kind of disability who picked up extra money making dresses for drag queens. . . . A very fat, feminine lesbian lived on the floor beneath us, with her tiny but very butch lover and a gay guy."[34] How they all came to share the same building, or whether the others stayed after Dewees left, remains a mystery.

After Dewees and de Dion broke up in 1960, Dewees bounced around a few Brooklyn apartments, until in 1965 he purchased a building on State Street, "on the fringes of Downtown Brooklyn." The area was rapidly gentrifying, with well-to-do Manhattanites snapping up and repairing buildings that had been abandoned due to suburbanization and white flight. Soon after Dewees moved in, he began renting rooms in his building to queer friends, and other gay men purchased a number of other buildings on the block. Within a few years,

half of the homeowners on the block were gay. . . . We formed our own little self-contained community. As everyone got to know each other, we began to give parties winter and summer for other like-minded block residents. . . . As we all fixed up our houses inside, we each agreed to paint our façades a different color, coordinating with the others. . . . In the summer, the sidewalk became our communal living room. There were almost always two or three outside gossiping, camping, or talking about some one's latest trick. The block was now so beautiful that it became a local tourist attraction, as it stood out in an otherwise drab neighborhood. People would drive cars by slowly on summer Sundays, to see the houses and their queer inhabitants socializing on the sidewalk. I soon became aware that gays were buying on surrounding streets and blocks as well.[35]

Both on Cumberland and State Streets, Dewees found (and helped to nurture) informal queer communities, the kind that leave little institutional evidence once they disappear, making it impossible to pinpoint exactly how, when, or why they began or ended. Dewees stayed on State Street until the early 2000s, by which point the rest of the block's queer community was long gone.

Around the same time he landed on State Street, Dewees parted ways with the Mattachine Society, as newer members became interested in more radical tactics. "When they started active demonstrations, I was not in favor of that. . . . I felt that was jumping ahead too fast,"[36] he told Duberman. Despite his early gay rights activism, Dewees had a conservative streak, and he eventually joined the Log Cabin Republicans, an organization for LGBT people in the Republican Party. The discussion groups he started foundered without him (except for one, the West Side group in Manhattan, which became an influential stand-alone organization). Future leadership in the Mattachine Society, and in the LGBT organizations that followed, would mostly be made up of Manhattanites.

Although the stories of Edward Sagarin, the Quaker Emergency Service, and the Mattachine Society in New York are filled with mistakes, infighting, and tragic ends, they at least represent some kind of recognition of the difficulties men who had sex with men were experiencing after World War II. For lesbians, no equivalent city-supported, religiously organized therapeutic program existed, nor any three-hundred-plus page book dedicated to their concerns. Nor was there any kind of G.I. Bill to help the women who lost their jobs when the men returned home from the war. If anything, the nation turned its energy toward convincing those women that their proper place was in the home, the kitchen, and the suburbs—leaving lesbians such as Rusty Brown to fend for themselves. The Brooklyn Navy Yard cut some sixty-five thousand workers in the year after World War II ended, beginning the decline of the entire area.[37]

Brown may have been fired from the Navy Yard at the end of the war, but that didn't stop her from wanting to be a machinist. She liked the job, and it was all she knew how to do. After a brief break to get her head sorted, she came up with an idea: using her grandfather's name, she headed to one of the civilian factories in Brooklyn. She was slim and small, and although she was around twenty-five years old, she managed to pass for a sixteen-year-old boy. By claiming to be too young to have been in the war, she avoided the awkward questions about her discharge papers that bedeviled the clients of the QES. Any healthy man of the right age who couldn't furnish his military record was automatically suspected of being a shirker or a Communist or a homosexual, and who wanted to hire one of those?

When they asked how she learned her way around a machine shop, Brown told the factory that her father had owned one. When they asked why she wasn't working with him, she said he was dead. Perhaps out of empathy for a poor, young Brooklyn orphan, they hired her. But keeping up her disguise was a constant challenge. "When I went to the bathroom, I'd go in to the one stall that had a door on it," she remembered years later. "I tried to go . . . as infrequently as possible."[38] After her shift, she'd go out with the other workers, who gave her man-to-man advice, which mostly boiled down to play the field and don't get married.

However, Brown couldn't pass as a boy forever—eventually, she knew, her lack of a beard would give her away. So she drifted back to the military and this time was allowed into the navy, where she shipped out to Korea around 1950. During World War II, homosexuality in the military had been kept mostly quiet, both by gay service members and by the military bureaucracy. But starting in the late 1940s, the military instituted lectures to warn all new recruits about the dangers posed by gays and lesbians. As Allan Bérubé described in *Coming Out Under Fire,* these talks were "vehemently antihomosexual" and warned women that "homosexuality threatened their ability to assume their proper roles in life as feminine women." Normal men and women were expected to police themselves and their surroundings for any trace of homosexuality and report what they found. Furthermore,

> *in order to "emphasize the seriousness of this business and the danger in associating with 'homos' in any way whatsoever," a 1948 Navy lecture linked grisly murders with homosexuality. "You read in the newspapers of fiendish and horrible sex crimes committed against men, women, and ofttimes, small children," the lecture explained. "Sometimes the bodies of these victims are horribly mutilated." In most every case, this kind of sexual perversion "can be related to homosexuality," and "ofttimes the person who commits such an act is found to be a homosexual."*[39]

The military, the courts, psychiatrists, and journalists now all spoke with one voice: a screeching Klaxon warning the world of dangerous queers.

Shipside in Korea, Brown heard rumors about military and government purges of homosexuals, headed by a vicious Senator Joseph McCarthy, but she didn't believe them. "That was a comedy. . . . Here he is, all this to-do about being a homosexual in Washington," she told an interviewer in the 1980s, "and there's millions of us wearing the military uniform."[40] But on leave, when she would return to Brooklyn, she realized McCarthy was no joke, and the homosexual panic he helped gin up—aka the Lavender Scare—was just getting started.

Around the time Brown shipped off to Korea, the Senate Appropriations Committee issued a report on the "employment of homosexuals and other sex perverts in government." Its purpose was to consider why their "employment by the Government is undesirable"—a clever way of ensuring it found the results its authors wanted. It claimed to have identified some 5,000 homosexuals in Washington, DC, 3,750 of who worked directly for the government.[41] It verified that 91 suspected homosexuals had already been fired from the State Department,[42] and by the end of 1950, over 600 employees would be forced out.[43] As the Korean War was ending in 1953, President Eisenhower signed Executive Order 10450, which banned anyone who might be a security risk from working for the federal government or for private contractors hired by the government. The list of potential security risks included alcoholics, neurotics, and homosexuals. However, while these purges were patterned on efforts made in the navy immediately after World War II, the idea that homosexuals posed a security risk was a conspiracy theory concocted entirely by the government. According to Allan Bérubé, top military officials gave "the security risk argument little credence."[44] The only instance Senator McCarthy could point to was that of an Austrian military official being blackmailed in 1912. To most of America, however, homosexuals and Communists were now lumped together as insidious forces out to destroy the American way of life.

Brown didn't have much trouble with the antihomosexual purges in the military, but when she hung up her uniform, things changed. She might have started off doing drag as a survival tactic, but she discovered she was good at it. So good that when a friend found out that she could also dance, he brought her on as his partner in a drag act, "doing a take-off on Ginger Rogers and Fred Astaire."[45] Brown soon became a professional drag king, often working down at Coney Island.

But the entertainment industry had been infected with McCarthyism as well. Although people today are more familiar with the blacklists of supposed Communists in movies and television, queer people were also targeted. "Producers got scared of who they hired in a show," Brown recalled. It wasn't just the visible talent who were in danger. "The director would ask certain pointed questions of just ordinary stagehands," she said, "for fear that if there was a stagehand that was caught, it could reflect on them."[46]

Brown managed to avoid the government, but the police were another matter altogether. "I had been arrested in New York more times than I have fingers and toes, for wearing pants and a shirt," she told historian Len Evans. As she explained:

You had to have three pieces of female attire. Now, let's put it this way. At the time I was young, I had nothing on top so what the hell was I going to put in a brassiere? I'm not exactly the type for lace panties. And if I'm wearing pants, I sure as hell didn't need a pretty coat. So there goes your three pieces of female attire.[47]

This "three-piece rule" is often cited by people writing about postwar New York, and by the folks who lived at that time, such as Brown. But no such law appears on the books. It seems likely that police policy specified wearing three pieces of clothing of the "appropriate gender" to avoid a cross-dressing arrest, since so many people reference it, but all the arrests relied on the same set of laws that had been used to police gender identity and sexuality for decades: the old masquerade, public nuisance, and disorderly conduct laws. Arrests were simply more frequent, in part because more women were wearing pants in general, giving gender-queer women *slightly* more room to express themselves on the streets (and thus making them that much more visible to the police). Although the laws hadn't changed, enforcement had.

Once, when Brown's partner convinced her to switch parts—to dress "appropriately" for their genders—Brown was arrested again, and this time thrown into the men's jail overnight, where she recalled the other prisoners screaming, "Bad enough you got us in this jail, you have to put this damn fag in here with us."[48] Too masculine for dresses and not allowed to wear suits, Brown seemed to have no way to win.

Working as a drag king brought Brown down to Coney Island, where she would meet the love of her life, a burlesque dancer named Terry. When Terry noticed Brown in the front row of Terry's show at Madam Tirza's Wine Bath, she sent a note inviting Brown to her dressing room afterward. "This chick has got to be straight," thought Brown.[49] But the two were together for the next twenty-eight years.

Coney Island burlesque star Madam Tirza, date unknown. (*Photo courtesy of the collection of David Denholtz.*)

Madam Tirza herself was a fascinating woman. According to another of her dancers, Mary Hood, Tirza was "a he-she, she-he . . . she'll either fall in love with a man or a woman."[50] If Tirza was out late the night before with a girl, Hood recalled, she or another of the backup girls would be Madam Tirza for a day, shimmying beneath a many-headed fountain of red-dyed water, surrounded by a phalanx of mirrors that turned one dancing girl into five.

Tirza had invented her wine-bath routine shortly before the war. While contemplating the beautiful Bethesda Fountain in Central Park one day, she realized how fabulous her act would look set inside it. So she hired an architect, who developed a prototype that weighed so much it was impossible to move. Frustrated, Tirza took a sledgehammer and refashioned it herself, just in time to get sponsored by a Chicago wine company and present her act at the 1940 World's Fair in New York (the same one that featured Gypsy Rose Lee). After that, Tirza was on the road for years, dragging along her twelve-hundred-pound wine fountain.[51] The tank required a lot of setup and maintenance, and the ranks of skilled workers had been badly depleted by the war, so Tirza became a member in good standing of the plumbers union, as well as a licensed trucker. She summered at Coney Island, where her act soon became a well-known draw. Later, Tirza would recall this time as the "best run" she ever had.[52]

After the war, however, Coney Island quickly began to hit the skids. In 1945, for the first time ever, its summer crowds were bested by Rockaway Beach, which had twice the number of visitors.[53] In June 1946, Tirza's Wine Bath—along with two other Coney Island burlesques—was temporarily shuttered by the city license commissioner, Ben Fielding. Tirza's mother, who helped with the show, shadily pointed out that even under the restrictive La Guardia administration (which had closed all the official burlesque houses in the city), Tirza had been allowed to operate. "I think Mr. Fielding is a very fair and square gentleman," she told a reporter, "even if we were allowed to continue under La Guardia's administration without a bit of trouble. Maybe we went a little further than we meant this time, thinking it was a Democratic administration and a little gayer somehow. But we guessed wrong."[54]

(*Gay* was already being used to refer to homosexual men by this time, and it still retained echoes of its earlier slang meaning, referring to female sex workers, but it's not clear in what sense Tirza's mother meant it here.)

By August of that year, the women's columnist at the *Star* newspaper noted that the city wasn't just going after the bump-and-grind joints. All of Coney Island seemed set in its sights. "Every day brings a new wave of censorship," she wrote. "Coney Island bath houses by the dozen have been closed in the clean up." The barkers, whose ballyhoos brought the rubes in to see the shows, were now forced to submit their scripts to the License Commission for advance approval.[55] Coney Island restaurants would be hit with numerous sanitary citations. Even the visiting crowds were suddenly subjected to increased scrutiny. Over six thousand people were ticketed in the first half of 1946 for such crimes as "undressing on the beach," "ball-playing," and "peddling." This was nearly a 40 percent increase over the year before.[56]

This wasn't just an attack on Coney Island, it was a growing war on poverty—or rather, a war on the poor and the places they congregated. Soon, Commissioner Fielding promised, "each of the city's 102 bathing establishments . . . will be the subject of unexpected visits by our department."[57] Coney Island bathhouses most likely came under particular scrutiny because both poor people *and* homosexuals could be found in them. Coney Island was rapidly losing its reputation as a destination for all New Yorkers and being reimagined, in the words of one city magistrate, as a "Devil's play pen," where "one million poor people swarm onto the beach."[58]

By 1949, the signs were serious that Coney Island was in trouble. The long-standing Mardi Gras festival was canceled that year, "a victim of economic pressure."[59] Luna Park, the famed amusement park that burned down in 1945, had been purchased by real estate speculator Fred Trump (father of President Donald Trump). Although Fred Trump planned in 1950 to turn it into a drive-in movie complex, eventually he built a parking lot instead.[60]

In 1952, the License Commission would again shut down Madam Tirza, and in 1953, put off by the dwindling crowds, the increase in petty crime, and the constant government harassment, none of the bump-and-grind shows even bothered to apply for a license.[61] As Tirza recalled, "Coney Island had deteriorated so badly I was afraid to open."[62] Around this time, she married a Coney Island local named Joe Boston, and the two spent the next thirty years together on the road. (As for Rusty Brown and Terry, they moved to California, where they lived together until Terry died, and Rusty remained active in queer life up through the late 1990s.)

In the face of this increased regulation, Brooklyn residents yet again showed a more blasé attitude toward sex at Coney Island than their Manhattan overlords. Under the headline "Poor Man Must Be Protected from Girls in Bath," one local wrote to *The Brooklyn Daily Eagle* to drily observe:

> *The poor man who cannot enter a New York night club with a well-stuffed wallet and a collar and tie—the same man, who simply can't resist the barkers appeal to 'hurry,' 'hurry,' 'hurry,' to see Tirza, should and must feel a deep sense of appreciation to our Acting Commissioner of Licenses for protecting his morals.*[63]

Newspaper articles tried to put a good face on the closings, insisting that "some merchants hereabouts say it's better for business," but Coney Island was inexorably dwindling away.[64] Boosterish headlines blared that Coney wasn't folding, but their very protests seemed to certify the exact thing they were trying to deny. "The Nickel Empire" was once a compliment to the pinnacle of New York attractions, but now it was a snide reference to how cheap and tawdry Coney had become.

What had happened? The answer, in two words: Robert Moses.

No history of twentieth-century New York City and its marginalized communities can avoid talking about Moses, the incredibly powerful city administration figure who almost single-handedly redesigned New York as a city for cars and the people who could afford them. At one point in his career, he held twelve simultaneous government positions (all appointed, none elected), including commissioner of the NYC Parks Department, chairman of the Triborough Bridge Authority, chairman of the Long Island State Parks Commission, chairman of the Mayor's Committee on Slum Clearance, and others. A short list of New York City projects that are wholly or mostly the work of Moses include the Throgs Neck, Whitestone, Henry Hudson, and Verrazzano Bridges; the Brooklyn–Queens Expressway, the Staten Island Expressway, and the Meadowbrook Parkway; the Brooklyn–Battery Tunnel; Idlewild Airport (now JFK); Lincoln Center; Shea Stadium; and much of the city's public housing.

Robert Moses obviously disliked Coney Island. In 1949, he said in a public meeting that he "wouldn't want to sink Surf Avenue on Coney Island, but just get rid of about a third of it." He imagined a clean, empty expanse of beach—much like the ones he had created on Long Island—where there were no "gadgets or catch penny devices." When he looked at the history of Coney, he said, "The trend is downward."[65]

In part, that trend can be traced back to Moses himself, who had been sur-
reptitiously eating away at Coney Island since the mid-1930s. In 1935, for example, Moses wanted twenty-five acres of land on Coney Island to build a park. The
land was in the hands of the Board of Education, which planned to build a "badly
needed school" for the local community.[66] When Mayor La Guardia had the te-
merity to suggest a mixed-use site, with a park on one side and a school on the
other, Moses savaged him in public, causing the mayor to back down. Moses got
his park, and Coney Island residents were forced to make do. In 1938, Moses—
again via the Parks Department—took control of the Municipal Bathhouse at
Coney Island. The year before, it had seen some 150,000 visitors, of who
approximately 7,500 were "charity admissions," who paid no fee. Seeing the great
need that the bathhouse was meeting, Moses turned it into a storage complex for
Parks Department equipment.[67] That same year, Moses succeeded in having ju-
risdiction over the boardwalk and beaches of Coney Island removed from local
borough-president control and placed under his aegis.[68] Although World War II
slowed him down, from this point on, it was only a matter of time before Moses
remade Coney Island to his wishes.

As Madam Tirza's history shows, many of the attractions at Coney Island were
temporary. Some returned every year, others were there for a while and then
moved on. Like the Brooklyn brothels, they depended on some turnover to keep
functioning. Moses saw in this an opportunity. By 1949, he estimated that through
his powers at the Parks Department, he had acquired about one-third of the land
along the boardwalk in Coney Island. The owners of these properties had slipped
into bankruptcy or simply skipped town when winter arrived, never paying the
debts they had accumulated. By buying up the properties, Moses could keep the
businesses empty, inexorably accelerating the decline of Coney Island, and thereby
allowing the Parks Department to gobble up more and more land. By 1952—Madam
Tirza's last year—he was ready to deliver his coup de grâce: a giant redevelopment that would turn Coney Island from a "noisy amusement area to a beautiful,
residential center with its buildings set in spacious, landscaped grounds."[69]

Publicly, he claimed that the redevelopment would provide the city with renewed tax revenue, without ever discussing how the freeways and parkways he
was building were creating a commuter class that left the city for the suburbs,
taking their tax money with them. He ironically insisted that he was protecting
Coney Island from "outsiders," who had abandoned the businesses he had pur-

chased.[70] Coney Island residents weren't fooled, however, and they protested vigorously against the redevelopment. In April 1953, the Coney Island Chamber of Commerce unanimously rejected Moses's plan. In particular, the members were concerned about the rezoning of major parts of Coney Island from business to residential or retail. Both designations would effectively outlaw the games, music halls, dance pavilions, bathhouses, and other establishments that made Coney Island the unique destination it had been for decades. However, their concerns were ignored, and the redevelopment moved forward.

Moses was eager to redevelop Coney Island for a few reasons. It was the only beach that was easily accessible by public transit, and he wanted to push city residents out to his farther-flung, car-accessible beaches. Also the city's "poorest residents happened to live" here already, making it an ideal spot, in Moses's mind, for high-rise public housing projects, which could contain a maximum number of poor people at the farthest distance from the city's core—aka Manhattan. And from his experience on the Mayor's Committee on Slum Clearance, Moses knew that poor communities were less likely to be listened to if they protested his plans.[71]

Coney Island had also accidentally got caught up in another of Moses's schemes. He loved bridges and hated tunnels, though the latter were cheaper to build and displaced fewer people. Instead of the Brooklyn–Battery Tunnel, he had wanted to build a bridge; when his plans were thwarted, he came up with a creative fuck-you to the city. In October 1941, he summarily began the destruction of the beloved New York Aquarium, which had been located in Battery Park, Manhattan, since 1896. He claimed—erroneously—that building the Brooklyn–Battery Tunnel would undermine its structural integrity. He proposed relocating the aquarium to Coney Island and pressured the mayor to spend $1 million on land for its new home. Moses claimed it would cost just an additional $2 million to build the new aquarium, and that the money would come from the New York Zoological Society (which oversaw the Bronx Zoo). In the end, it cost $11 million, all paid by New York City taxes. As Moses's biographer Robert Caro wrote in *The Power Broker*:

> The high admission fees Moses set for it insured that many New Yorkers were going to be able to visit infrequently if at all. The poignance of this situation was accentuated by the location of the Aquarium at Coney Island, the lone bathing beach reachable by public transportation and therefore the one to which, because of Moses' class-separating policies, the city's poor were herded.[72]

The old aquarium was free; despite claims from the city that the new aquarium would cost "considerably less than a dollar"[73] to visit, the admission price was set at ninety cents.[74] Since Moses started demolition of the old aquarium with no plans for a new one, New York City would spend sixteen years without an aquarium. Construction would take so long that for eleven of those years, Coney Island had twelve acres of desolate, unused land directly abutting the boardwalk. When it finally opened, Moses called the aquarium "the symbol of a new era," one in which they were "shrinking the amusement section to proper limits and getting rid of its worst manifestations."[75] In one last stab in the back to old Coney Island, Moses erected a quarter-of-a-million-dollar ramp from the subway station to the new aquarium, which was designed to "'funnel all' potential customers to and from the beach and waterside aquarium area and away from the amusement[s]."[76] What little of Coney Island Moses could not buy or bully into closing, he starved into submission.

Moses's plan had direct effects on the businesses of Coney Island that provided queer women with work, but its ripples would disturb the cruising grounds that gay men had established on the beach and in the bathhouses at least as far back as the 1920s. By 1949, when the mysterious author Swasarnt Nerf (Sixty-Nine) published *The Gay Girl's Guide* (the first gay guide to New York ever written), it listed only two places in all of Brooklyn: the St. George Hotel in Brooklyn Heights, and the beach at Coney Island, where "some of the lowlier faggots on occasion form a large party to take over a section."[77] Thomas Painter, now long separated from the Committee for the Study of Sex Variants, was one of those faggots, and he carefully tracked cruising culture at Coney in his letters to Alfred Kinsey throughout the 1940s and the beginning of the 1950s.

That Painter loved Coney Island is inarguable. When he first started going, men and women of all social classes and identities still crowded together on its beaches from Memorial Day to Labor Day, sometimes millions at a time. A group of Jewish matrons might sit under umbrellas just a few feet from a raucous collection of Italian-immigrant teenagers necking to Sammy Kaye on the radio singing "Careless Hands." Beachcombers made a living plucking dropped nickels and lost jewelry from the dunes. Young men impressed young women by doing acrobatics and weight lifting on the forgiving sand, and if they were lucky, they could retire to the cool shade beneath the boardwalk, where nameless, transient joints served soda, beer, and cheap beach food, in an atmosphere that Painter described as "sex, delinquency, sex, sordidness, and sex."[78] This was the dawn of the baby boom, when teenagers would begin to rule American pop culture, and nowhere in New York was this more evident than at Coney Island.

Painter's diaries describe three distinct but overlapping subcultures of Coney Island men who had sex with men, two that were evident by the late 1940s, and one that emerged later, in the early 1950s.

The first group consisted of men such as Painter himself: older homosexuals who were (at least to each other) fairly obvious about their desires and identities. Many of these men spent a great deal of time in the bathhouses, particularly the Washington Baths and Stauch's, which Painter described as "Times Square in Coney Island." These institutions were multilevel, formerly grand bathing pavilions, with restaurants, cafés, exercise equipment, pools, tanning salons, smoking areas, etc. Most were directly on the boardwalk, across from the beach, and many of them had their own stairs leading down to the sand. Under the boardwalk, they built rows of small pavilions, much like the changing rooms in department stores, where people could put on the bathing suits they had rented upstairs. It was still illegal in New York City to wear a bathing suit on the street, and though this law was routinely flouted, Robert Moses would increasingly use it to target poor people at Coney Island. Painter would refer to Moses as his "bête noire" for this very reason.[79]

Although Painter went to the bathhouses fairly regularly, usually to tan naked on the roof, he disliked the scene because "there were too many faggots."[80] Painter was rarely interested in having sex with other out gay men, particularly ones who were in any way "swishy" or effeminate. Also, other gay men represented competition for the younger, primarily heterosexual (or at least straight-seeming) men that Painter was after. And lastly, even just one too-obvious homosexual could put the kibosh on an afternoon of cruising by being too forward, too flaming, or too public about his desires, driving away the boys for whom same-sex activity was an afternoon of fun (and, often, profit), but not an identity they wanted to be publicly associated with. These young, white, working-class men, primarily from Brooklyn, made up the second subculture Painter documented.

Painter perfectly captured the tension between these two groups in a scene he described at the Washington Baths on July 4, 1947. It started when he noticed "a group of the young tougher characters," ranging from about sixteen to twenty-five, tanning on the roof. For a brief period, an "extremely obvious homosexual of middle age" chatted them up, and the group "kidded him and half tolerated him." Once he was out of earshot, however, things got interesting.

> When he had gone there was a flood of comment among the group, principally being a repetition of how if he had "started anything" or "made a pass" they would have picked him up and thrown him down the fucking stairs. . . . All disapproved of the matter and of fellation (being "blowed") . . . and made out as to how none of them had or would, except one who [allowed] as to how he might follow the person and get him to blow him, and they laughed loudly and said they wouldn't put it past him, he would fuck a snake.[81]

Being gay was disgusting, but getting an occasional blow job from a man still existed in a sexual gray area. As Painter discovered, many young Coney Island men had more open attitudes toward homosexual sex than did the majority of supposedly sophisticated Manhattanites. Painter usually referred to these young men as heterosexual, which some definitely were. But many seemed to live outside our modern idea of sexual orientation as a permanent and unwavering con-

The sunbathing roof deck at Stauch's bathhouse on Coney Island (c.1950). (*Photo courtesy of the collection of Hugh Hagius.*)

dition defined by the sex of the people to whom you are generally attracted. A lot of the youths were in it for the money, but they also seemed to enjoy it, and sometimes did it for free. As one of his young partners explained to Painter, "It does him no harm, is not unpleasant . . . so why not do it?"[82]

Painter was surprised to discover that so long as he respected their boundaries, these men often wanted to be friends, or at least friendly, unlike the professionals who worked Times Square. An astute observer of sexual mores, Painter pointed out in his diaries that the straight world was willing to tolerate an underclass of gay men and male sex workers if they kept their interactions to the "minimum required for [their] unnatural and obscene practices."[83] Friendship with a gay man endangered fragile heterosexuality as much as did gay sex. But parts of Coney Island still seemed to exist outside the rigid hetero-homo dichotomy that was taking over America. For Painter, not only did this present an opportunity for picking up the trade that he was attracted to, it also helped him feel better about himself. As he wrote to Kinsey:

> Remember how I used to say "Each and every homosexual is an individual tragedy." Well, that statement . . . was colored by the subjective. And I have changed. Some one . . . recently remarked to me that I seem to have made a good adjustment to my condition. (Especially since Brooklyn.)[84]

By the late 1940s, Painter perfected a method of cruising for these young men: asking them to model. This period saw an explosion in what were referred to as "strength and health" magazines, or what we would today call beefcake. For many of these working-class young men, the idea of being paid to have their pictures taken was an incredible opportunity—a way out of communities that were on a downward slide into poverty and dereliction. Painter was a hobbyist, at best. The only audiences for his pictures were himself, the men he photographed, and Alfred Kinsey (to whom he sent duplicates of nearly every photo he took). But professionals such as Lon of New York would help make some of these Coney Island boys into famous models, and soon they all knew that an older man with a camera was a sure sign of quick cash, and perhaps some sexual fun.

The vast majority of these guys were working-class Italians and Irishmen, or as Painter characterized them, men of the lowest social order. Many were friendly, some were dangerous, and a few verged on being sociopaths. In his diaries, Painter recounted being threatened, robbed, blackmailed, beaten, and (once) raped. Yet he also developed close friendships with many of these men—including some of the ones who robbed him. Of the men Painter kept in touch with, many married, a few found long-term boyfriends, some drifted off to the military or jobs in other states, and some continued hustling. A not insignificant number would go on to be models, movie stars, professional dancers, and Olympic athletes.

Rumors of hustling or queer desires have dogged many famous beautiful men, and it's retrospectively easy to dismiss them as wishful thinking, malicious gossip, or sexual boasting. But on Coney Island, Painter repeatedly picked up a teenager whom he described as "a Brooklyn Italian . . . well fed and well mannered . . . [and] incredibly, shockingly beautiful."[85] At sixteen, this boy seemed to have a better head on his shoulders than all the other hustlers combined. He was determined to get an agent and get to Hollywood. Thus, at first, he would only allow Painter to take clothed photos, then eventually nude ones, before finally allowing some limited sexual contact between them. Soon, the boy had attracted a stable of powerful, well-connected gay men, including a big-shot agent, who pointed out that, "Brando, Cary Grant, and others . . . had similar backgrounds [and] the general public doesn't know, will never know."[86]

Soon, the boy landed in Hollywood, where he became a star whose career would last well into the 2000s. Quickly, he realized that his years on Coney Island could become a liability, so he wrote a long letter to Thomas Painter.

> Dear Tom,
> I won't begin this letter in the usual fashion making excuses for not having written previously. . . . The story is, in brief, that I don't feel particularly comfortable with those photos in existence. . . . You could relieve the situation some by sending me the negatives of the photos I took with you. I don't doubt that you have kept your promise and not sold any, but one can never tell if they should be stolen or lost. I have no idea how many pictures you have, so if you should agree I can only trust you to send all of them. . . . [87]

This youth was one of the last "Great Beauties" that Painter encountered at Coney Island, as its sexually permissive scene would not last for long. Painter cruised there occasionally right after World War II, but the area really picked up in the late forties, when part of Coney Island became known as Muscle Beach, so named for all the "strength and health" boys who hung out there. It was one link on a chain of places where gay men and trade could still hang out together, similar to Sands Street, some parts of Harlem, Fourteenth Street in Manhattan, and a number of bars near Times Square.

The first sign that this sexual archipelago was under attack was a series of crackdowns in the Manhattan bars where gay men and trade gathered. In 1950, Painter wrote that his favorite such place, the Famous, had been declared off bounds by the military, effectively killing the flow of trade. Sailors and soldiers quickly shifted to other bars in the area, but these places "shoo out idling hustlers, [and] hesitate to serve Negros and queer looking queers."[88] In May 1951, Painter recounted the emergence of a number of Manhattan bars that catered *only* to homosexuals, but contrasted that with the closing of "queer-man bars," including the Famous, the Moss, Gilroy's, Perry's, and the Times Square. "There is not now, and has not been for almost a year," Painter told Kinsey, "a real rip-roaring queer-man bar in the old fashioned tradition."[89] The trajectory of homo-hetero separation, which had begun before World War II with the ending of Prohibition and the onset of the movie code, was accelerating. It would fold neatly into the mental and physical suburbanization of America that would come to dominate the culture in the fifties and early sixties.

Soon, Painter began sending chilling newspaper articles to Kinsey about gay men being murdered all around New York. Simultaneously, however, papers were painting homosexuality as "the real sex menace," in the words of *The New York Age*.[90] Echoing Magistrate Bromberger, journalists now routinely evoked the specter of queerness even in cases that had nothing to do with homosexuality. For instance, after four Brooklyn teens beat and murdered a man in a case that captured headlines for months, one psychologist—who had only ever seen photos of the boys—opined in the press that they were "probably homosexual."[91] Suggesting latent homosexuality was the perfect way for psychiatrists to claim a deeper understanding of human nature than laypeople, because their theories couldn't be disproven. Thus, psychiatrists burnished the reputation of their field at the expense of those they were purportedly out to help. Queers and Communists were now all-purpose bogeymen, to be summoned up whenever blame was to be assigned.

Attitudes at Coney slowly began to shift with the times. In 1951, for example, Painter told Kinsey about the harassment some of his regular models faced when they tried to pick up a few girls on the beach: "These two young, handsome, muscular youthes [sic] couldn't get a girl to speak to them, except to get told to 'go away,' 'get out,' and 'you fag,' 'you fairies.'"[92] That these men were masculine and interested in women no longer mattered the way it once did. *Any amount of queer experience instantly and irrevocably defined one as a homosexual.* By 1952, Painter's regular crowd at Muscle Beach had begun to disappear, heading instead to Robert Moses's newly created Orchard Beach, which was clean and lacked Coney Island's growing aura of poverty and sleaze. In June 1954, Painter told Kinsey that Muscle Beach was completely dead, the strength-and-health boys were all gone, and no new ones had come up to replace them. Another of his favorite cruising grounds, the area around Fourteenth Street in Manhattan (where once upon a time Jennie June had been the queen of the Fourteenth Street rialto) was similarly abandoned. Again, all the "queer-man bars" had been shuttered by the police, and the once semi-available street youth had coalesced into dangerous gangs that were more likely to kill a queer than service one. "So there we are at a series of dead ends," Painter wrote in 1954. "Times Square, the muscle boys, and 14th Street" were cruising grounds no longer.[93]

Arrests ramped up throughout the rest of the year. In September, Painter informed Kinsey of an "unprecedented" series of raids in the city:

> It started in the Square, continues there, goes on all over. . . . Over 700 (seven hundred) were arrest[ed] <u>last</u> week end—in all four burroughs [sic], from Coney Island to Van Courtland Park to the Rockaways: loiterers, drunks, bums, disorderly, "suspicious," panhandlers . . . included in the unsavory aggregation are "homosexuals." There is no explanation of how they were arrested, and what for—just for being (suspected of being?) homosexuals? IE looking like one? . . . The result on the Square is amazing—no hustlers, no faggots.[94]

This wasn't just an antihomosexual crusade; it was an attack on all kinds of public immorality, and in particular the kinds of "crimes" committed by poor people who lack private space: loitering, public drunkenness, panhandling, street hustling, etc. While this was happening in the cruising grounds of Times Square and Coney Island, the city launched Operation 25, which flooded Harlem with hundreds of additional beat cops in a similar attempt to harass or jail marginal communities out of public existence. In 1955, the police followed up with Operation Hazard, which poured battalions of cops into the Brownsville area of

Brooklyn, which had recently seen an influx of black residents. The theory seemed to be that the city couldn't get rid of homosexuals (or black people), but they could ensure that they stayed hidden as much as possible.

However, even in moments of great repression, queerness finds a way. As Painter was documenting the disappearance of the working-class, white queer-man scene at Coney Island, he found a new group blooming in its place: a queer Puerto Rican community that would briefly flourish at Coney Island in the early 1950s, right up until Robert Moses's plans for major redevelopment went into effect in 1954.

In 1920, there were just over 7,000 Puerto Ricans living in New York City; by 1950, there were over 180,000, many of who settled on Brooklyn's waterfront.[95] What caused this influx? To begin with, at the turn of the century the United States had seized Puerto Rico in the Spanish-American War, and in 1917, its people were officially declared US citizens. In 1900, the island was primarily rural, an agglomeration of small towns and individual farmers. Even by 1930, more than 70 percent of Puerto Ricans still lived in places with populations under twenty-five hundred people.[96] However, annexation into the American empire swiftly transformed local agriculture into a monoculture of giant sugar plantations, as American agribusinesses (and some Puerto Rican–owned ones) leaped to buy up land. Industrial farming techniques meant that these plantations employed vastly fewer people than the small farms they replaced, leaving many people with neither land nor jobs. In 1950, the unemployment rate in Puerto Rico was 10 percent[97]—more than double what it was in the rest of America.[98] After World War II, the mainland United States desperately needed workers, particularly in the booming field of housing construction, which was rapidly creating the idealized white world of suburbia. The pull of jobs—and the push of unemployment—created the perfect storm for a mass exodus from Puerto Rico.

In 1951, a few months after Thomas Painter first mentioned the declining white queer-man scene, he began to notice more and more Puerto Rican men hanging out at Coney Island. "Who cares," he told Kinsey, as "the more they come the prettier they seem."[99] By 1952, he informed Kinsey that the beach now had a primarily Puerto Rican area, much like the Italian area where he had first met his strength-and-health boys. This new group was centered around an area designated Bay 13, which was also where Stauch's bathhouse—the most popular among gay white men—was located. Soon, the area where the steps from Stauch's hit the sand would become a popular hangout for the Puerto Rican community, and in particular its queer members. Painter only fully realized this in 1954, by which point the majority of the new boys he was meeting at Coney were of Puerto Rican descent. At its zenith, the scene at the nameless "tavern" under Bay 13 was perhaps the most queer-friendly, ethnically mixed environment Painter had ever found. In his letters, he contrasted it with the Italian area he had once frequented and found the Puerto Rican one vastly superior. As he wrote:

> On week ends it is packed . . . almost like a subway car or a queer bar. The predominant customers are aged 23-15 . . . of both sexes even tho with a slight majority of males. They are of the lowest social level, a large proportion being obviously delinquents and semi-criminal. They are a complete mixture racially, but, as they are the lowest social level, the majority are Puerto Rican and Italians, Negroes (less than the proportion should be) and some blonds. The juke box blares continuously. Beer and soft drinks are guzzled, but many just hang around for the fun. . . . They loll on the tables in informal poses—feet on the table if you wish, including the girls. Introductions are not required. "Mingling" seems not banned. As to necking, you can do anything short of actual sexual intercourse, but there is less than you would expect (it is more comfortable on the sand of the beach, after all). If you are a boy obviously not old enough to buy beer an older boy buys it for you. Queer[s] stand around and ogle, while the regulars chat with and paw their boys. . . .
>
> The Italian place is similar except there are no queers, and one gets the impression of an intense, blaring heterosexuality and virility which would not tolerate it. There is no racial mixture, just Italian. . . . The sense one has of potential hostility (due to one's sexuality) and mere toleration of one's non-Italian-ness (due to one's being Nordic) make me nervous. In the P.R. place it is more relaxed, more tolerant, completely accepting.

Obviously, Painter was a more visible outsider in the Puerto Rican area, and his sense of safety and acceptance was influenced by his being a white man. Whiteness offered him no protection from the Italian youths down the beach, but probably mitigated any similar discomfort he might have felt in the predominantly Puerto Rican area of Bay 13. Still, his experiences suggest that this area was more accepting of sexual and racial diversity than anywhere else on Coney Island.

Unfortunately, the same forces that were pushing white queer people out of

Coney Island seem to have quickly pushed Puerto Rican queer men out as well. After 1954, as Painter documented in his diaries, their world no longer centered on Coney. Instead, he would meet most of them in the Lower East Side, Chelsea, South Harlem, and Puerto Rico itself. In a large oral history project conducted by the Brooklyn Historical Society with members of early Puerto Rican communities in Brooklyn, Coney Island wasn't even mentioned once.

A fire (probably arson) destroyed the Washington Baths in 1955, and although Stauch's would linger on as the last Coney Island bathhouse up into the seventies, it would no longer be a landmark on the map of gay New York. By 1958, when Ann Aldrich published *We, Too, Must Love,* a field guide to lesbian New York City, she would quote one lesbian as saying that at Coney Island "you feel funny if you're different."[100] By 1964, even the last of the famed amusement parks, Steeplechase, which had operated at Coney Island since 1897, would close, and in 1966, Fred Trump would throw a demolition party as he razed the site to prevent it from gaining landmark status.

Stauch's Bathhouse, abandoned (1984). *(Photo courtesy of the Brooklyn Historical Society. [Stauch Baths], 1984, v1992.48.1; Anders Goldfarb photographs of Coney Island, v1992.48; Brooklyn Historical Society.)*

Sometime in the early 1950s, it seems, Coney had completed its transformation from a sexually anarchic playground to a place where—as Martin Boyce, the Stonewall veteran, would later remember—gay people no longer dared gather in large public numbers. Another piece of queer Brooklyn had been wiped away.

The city didn't just build public housing at Coney Island around this time, it also developed large housing projects next to the Brooklyn Navy Yard; near where poet Marianne Moore still lived in Fort Greene; in downtown Brooklyn; around Red Hook; in the center of Brooklyn Heights; and over in Gowanus; all waterfront or waterfront-adjacent neighborhoods where low-income people (including many queers) had lived, worked, and cruised for decades. Although these developments were intended to help low- and median-income New York City residents, they would ironically play a critical role in destroying the social fabric of these neighborhoods and displacing existing working-class people. Without ever being singled out by name, the fragile queer communities of Brooklyn would be particularly assailed by city housing policy.

To the city government, the poor were abstract, fungible numbers, and removing a few thousand for a few years was the equivalent of a rounding error in a massively complex equation. As far back as 1934, the city housing administration had begun demolishing "slum" areas and placing crippling regulations on the buildings they left behind, destroying or causing to be abandoned an estimated forty thousand low-income residences by 1936 alone. Why? In an effort to force the city to build *better* public housing, of course, by creating a housing crisis. As one reformer put it, "From excellent and humane motives we have thus accelerated the housing shortage. . . . If we keep on this course we shall have the highest housing standards in the world, while a third of the population sleeps on park benches."[101] This was part of the reason why Brooklyn's brothels shut down after the war—the lack of housing stock made it impossible to stay one step ahead of the cops.

This destruction didn't start with Robert Moses, but he used the chaos it caused to his advantage once he took the helm. He sold his housing projects "as a putative destination for slum clearance tenants displaced elsewhere," but it rarely worked out that way.[102]

Take, for instance, the Farragut Houses, built on either side of Sands Street right where it intersected with the Brooklyn Navy Yard. In 1946, the city used eminent domain to take ownership of a twelve-block, eighteen-acre area that was home to an estimated eight hundred residences and two hundred businesses.[103] These were demolished to create eleven fourteen-story-high apartment buildings, surrounded by what was generously called "parkland," which mostly consisted of flat expanses of cement and fenced-off grass, without benches, amenities, trees, or amusements. One member of Moses's Parks Department would later claim about these newly constructed areas, "There is no room for trees, and even if there were trees, children would run into them and get hurt."[104] As early as 1943, one of the first executive directors of community planning for the New York City Housing Authority (NYCHA) warned that these so-called towers in the parks "might prove troublesome" because of the way they warehoused the poor and

The Farragut Houses, public housing units built where Sands Street once met the Brooklyn Navy Yard (1954). (*Photo courtesy of the Brooklyn Eagle Photographs—Brooklyn Public Library—Brooklyn Collection.*)

"should be abandoned," but they would be the norm in public housing for the next decade and a half.[105]

To accommodate the expected uptick in traffic caused by the Farragut Houses, large stretches of Sands, Nassau, and Gold Streets were widened, necessitating the destruction of even more of the bars and businesses that had once served sailors, sex workers, factory women, artists, and entertainers.[106] After construction began, *The Brooklyn Daily Eagle* published a "swan song for the Sands St of old," noting how all the businesses that had once made the area "colorful" were now gone.[107] Thereafter, the delights of Sands Street would never again be praised by queer Brooklynites.

In a conference extolling their virtues, the president of the Brooklyn Real Estate Board announced, "When the Farragut Houses are completed, the displaced tenants who qualify could be given first choice in the new buildings."[108] The operative words here are *qualify* and *could*. Spoiler alert: most of the old residents didn't qualify and wouldn't be given first choice—or any choice at all.

First off, in the intervening years between when they were kicked out and when new developments were completed, most former residents had moved and were probably not eager (or able) to uproot themselves again. Even had they wanted to, shortly after the houses were completed, NYCHA instituted a twenty-one-point moral code to keep out unwanted inhabitants, which would virtually guarantee that no former Sands Street residents could move in. Although never listed in name, queer people were particularly penalized under this code. Included on the list of undesirable qualities were:

- any court contact in the last five years (such as an arrest for cross-dressing or disorderly conduct);
- any "other than honorable" discharge from military service (such as a blue discharge for sexuality); and
- any history of mental illness that required hospitalization (an increasingly popular option for dealing with homosexuality after it was added to the psychiatric diagnostic manual in 1952).

Other parts of the code targeted poor people generally, banning anyone who had moved too frequently in the past, or who was considered to have poor housekeeping habits, or who lacked furniture, or whose conduct was considered "obnoxious" by NYCHA officials, or who possessed a highly irregular work history, or who had a history of trouble paying rent.[109] These policies were enforced in public housing in New York City until 1968.

In a separate set of policies, NYCHA set a hard income cap on tenants in these new buildings, which meant that as working-class families began to get their feet under them and earn more money, they were forced to move yet again. This created a revolving door of poverty and destabilized the communities that might have formed within the projects. Moreover, these new buildings were constructed with a belief that simply moving working-class people into modern homes would naturally help them climb the economic ladder. Thus, they did not include the "social services that characterized early public housing."[110] By the 1960s, NYCHA housing would become synonymous with poverty and crime. With the old residents gone, and the old buildings destroyed, the queer history of Sands Street was effectively erased—particularly once the Brooklyn Navy Yard shut down for good in 1966. The bustling two-hundred-acre campus that had housed and employed so many queer people over the last hundred years would be left derelict, until trees grew up through the buildings and you were more likely to find graffiti than people inside them.

Meanwhile, a very different set of housing policies was pushing middle-class (and less precarious working-class) white families out of the city, and into single-family homes in the suburbs. These included many of the same families that NYCHA administrators had imagined would move into their new public housing developments, which were intended at the start to be racially integrated communities for the striving classes. But racist suburban housing policies would ensure that only white families could escape the city's decaying urban core, thus creating what is popularly known as white flight. As a result, public housing became a way to warehouse poor people of color, while the suburbs became the white American dream.

In the decade after World War II, the federal government authorized billions of dollars in mortgage insurance through the Federal Housing Administration, which was designed to promote private home development by guaranteeing builders a return on their investment. Included in the G.I. Bill was a similar provision, designed to provide mortgages to veterans to enable them to "return to civilian life with a home of their own."[111] Much like NYCHA housing, these mortgages came with moral codes, which included "unsatisfactory domestic relationships" as a factor for denying a mortgage application.[112]

With the Veterans' Emergency Housing Act of 1946, priority in construction loans and scarce building materials was given to anyone building dwellings for married returning vets—which functionally excluded queer people. Despite the fact that 50 percent of veterans wanted to rent (presumably in the city) and not own a house in the suburbs, only 12 percent of the buildings constructed in 1946 and 1947 would be urban rental units.[113] Under these new policies, it was cheaper to build single-family homes in the suburbs than to build or renovate apartments in the city—and the real estate business followed the money. These new homes were so cheap to build, they could be offered to prospective buyers with no down payments, a much more attractive deal than the standard first-month, last-month, and security deposit that was required to secure a city apartment.

As a result, suburban development skyrocketed, peaking in 1950 when nearly 1.7 million single-family houses were built.[114] The most prolific developers in the country were the Brooklyn-based father-and-son team of Abraham and William Levitt, who used mass-production techniques to build whole towns in record time.

Their first "Levittown" was on Long Island, and it had 17,400 houses with eighty-two thousand residents. New York City families waited in line for days to purchase homes in Levittown, with fourteen hundred contracts being drawn up on a single day in 1949.[115] And each and every one of them was for a white family.

Levittown leases included a clause that read, "The tenant agrees not to permit the premises to be used or occupied by any person other than members of the Caucasian race."[116] However, this wasn't just a personal prejudice of the Levitts; it was a structural practice pushed by the government. The same Federal Housing Authority manual that listed "unsatisfactory domestic relationships" as a reason to deny mortgage applications also took into account whether the neighborhood had "inharmonious racial groups."[117] Integration was seen as a potential indicator of future community strife, which could in turn lead to defaulting on a mortgage. To qualify for FHA funding, most building developers simply didn't build any homes for people of color at all. Even when people of color had the money and the desire to leave the city, they thus rarely had the option to do so. Out (or too-obvious) queer people, particularly queer people of color, were left with even fewer options. They were considered unfit for the suburbs *and* for the projects, while their old neighborhoods had been destroyed to make way for both.

By 1950, suburbanization had become a crisis, leading *The New York Times Magazine* to publish an article with the blaring headline "The Suburbs Are Strangling the City." Its author detailed how "the outer neighborhoods of commuting New Yorkers—comprising 40 percent of the total population and increasing daily—are living on the lifeblood of the central city without contributing the nourishment necessary to sustain it," in the form of tax dollars.[118] Not only did they use all the elements of the city that dwellers of the five boroughs did—the police, the fire department, public transport, hospitals, parks, etc.—these commuters also required more and more car-friendly roads and parking lots. These would be provided by Robert Moses.

If you look at a map of modern Brooklyn, you'll see a ring of roads that separates the waterfront from the rest of the borough—primarily the Shore Parkway, the Gowanus Expressway, and the Brooklyn–Queens Expressway, along with on-ramps for the Verrazzano Narrows Bridge and the Brooklyn–Battery Tunnel. To a large extent, these roads made it possible for suburb dwellers on Long Island to work and play in New York City. They also completely cut off the waterfront from the rest of Brooklyn—and they were all built by Robert Moses between

1934 and 1960, or approximately the years when most of queer Brooklyn collapsed in on itself. To ensure that the flow of traffic was mostly one-way, enabling wealthier suburbanites to access the city, but not vice versa, Moses built the connecting highway on Long Island—the Southern State Parkway—with overpasses too low to accommodate the city's public buses.

The waterfront wasn't just becoming physically isolated; it was also becoming economically isolated. The development of container shipping in New Jersey in the early 1950s made it easier and cheaper to off-load ships there than in Brooklyn, in much the same way that the port of Brooklyn itself had eclipsed lower Manhattan in the late 1800s. When the St. Lawrence Seaway opened in 1959, it made the now-ancient Erie Canal—the critical artery that had connected Brooklyn shipping to the rest of the country for 130 years—obsolete. As the Seaway was being built, the Port of New York Authority estimated that it would annually divert 1.5 million tons of cargo away from Brooklyn; cost the city some additional $15 million in federal taxes for upkeep; wipe out the jobs of some four thousand Brooklyn longshoremen; and destroy or vastly scale back "hundreds of thousands" of other jobs that were dependent on shipping trades in Brooklyn.[119] This would help set the stage for the financial crisis that engulfed the city in the mid-1970s.

Together, these housing and transit policies radically altered the demographics of Brooklyn. While the population steadily declined through the fifties, sixties, and seventies, the borough went from 96 percent white in 1940 to 73 percent white by 1970. Between 1950 and 1960 alone, a record 856,000 people (or about 12 percent of the population) left New York City.[120] This intense churning tore apart the existing communities (including queer ones) that had developed in Brooklyn over the last hundred years of steady growth and prosperity. In the long term, new residents would establish their own queer institutions and locales, in such areas as Crown Heights (home to the Starlite Lounge, a bar for queer black Brooklynites for decades) and Park Slope (where a large lesbian community would form in the 1980s). However, the building up of a new community takes time, leaving a gap in history before these new institutions appeared. The only thread of Brooklyn's older queer waterfront-related communities that survived through these trying times was the oldest, most established, and wealthiest queer area in Brooklyn: Brooklyn Heights. Even the Heights, however, was not completely immune to the pressures experienced by the rest of the borough.

In 1945, Robert Moses attempted to send the Brooklyn–Queens Expressway (BQE) shooting through the heart of the Heights. In a rare setback for the master builder, his plan was opposed by residents, who called on allies all the way up to Eleanor Roosevelt to defeat the proposal. (A decade later, Moses would experience similar resistance in Manhattan, when urban-planning activist Jane Jacobs successfully opposed his plan to put a four-lane highway through Washington Square Park.) Instead, the BQE was shunted much closer to the waterfront. Moses then built an on-ramp that destroyed some of the area's most important queer history. In one vicious swoop, he knocked down 110 Columbia Heights—where Washington Roebling, Hamilton Easter Field, Emil Opffer, and Hart Crane had all resided—and most of Middagh Street, including February House. George Davis, the last of the original residents remaining, was finally compelled to leave Brooklyn. In 1951 he married his good friend Lotte Lenya, both as a way of taking care of each other and as a cover for his perhaps too-open lifestyle in previous decades, and he died of a heart attack in Berlin in 1957.

With the destruction of February House, Brooklyn Heights lost the reputation it had gained as an international destination for artists of all kinds. However, while it may have dropped off the mental map of the global queer intelligentsia, it continued to have a strong (if sub rosa) queer presence. In many ways, the Heights was the one place in Brooklyn where "Bohemians" could thrive even in straightened postwar circumstances—as Thomas Painter was shocked to discover when he moved into the storied St. George Hotel in 1953. Painter moved because his job with the city transferred him to the courthouse in Brooklyn Heights. He was excited to find that the area still had a mix of the run-down, the disreputable, and the genteel, telling Alfred Kinsey it was "like Greenwich Village" in the 1930s.[121] Painter liked living at the hotel because it was anonymous yet lively, making it easy to bring home tricks without putting himself in danger. Moreover, he quickly discovered that the hotel was a popular cruising ground, as it had been when Hart Crane and his friends lived in the area thirty years earlier. "Les fleurs du mal flourish in this hotel," he wrote with surprise, despite the fact that from the outside "it seems to be a terribly stuffy joint."[122] Given Painter's wide knowledge of queer New York, and his intimacy with members of February House, his surprise about the 1950s gay scene in the Heights suggests that it was already well hidden.

After the BQE was completed, Painter discovered that the Promenade, a long scenic walkway built to hide the BQE and provide Heights residents with a view of Manhattan, was quickly turning into a gay cruising ground. He groused that it was "pure homosexual," however, and lacked the trade that interested him.[123] According to Martin Boyce, the Stonewall veteran, the Promenade would be one of the few places in Brooklyn that still had a citywide gay reputation by the time of the Stonewall Riots in 1969.

Thomas Painter was still living at the St. George Hotel on the afternoon of March 7, 1955, when a city investigating committee grilled him about his work for Kinsey, and whether he was now or had ever been a member of the Communist Party. Although they didn't ask directly, he could tell they were trying to ascertain whether he was gay.[124] Within a year, he would be abruptly—and without reason—asked to leave his job at the court, becoming one of the innumerable hidden victims of Senator McCarthy's purge. Without a job keeping him in Brooklyn, he moved back to Manhattan, where the majority of the Puerto Rican men he now associated with were living. Brooklyn was no longer on his queer map either.

Yet queer artists were still to be found in the Heights. Just three blocks away from the St. George Hotel lived the married couple Willard Maas and Marie Menken, who created one of the first American experimental art films, *Geography of the Body,* in 1943. The pair was famously alcoholic, and although devoted to each other, they fought often—primarily over Menken's two miscarriages and Maas's bisexual philandering. Their fights would be immortalized in their friend Edward Albee's play *Who's Afraid of Virginia Woolf?.*[125]

Together, Menken and Maas created the Gryphon Group, an experimental film collective. Although Menken was the heterosexual of the pair, she had the larger effect on queer culture. A tall woman with a commanding presence, Menken began as a painter, but made her mark as a filmmaker. Her films were often nonnarrative and visually evocative, using collage, animation, stop-motion, and cut-up techniques. In the 1960s, she would become a mentor to two of the most important queer filmmakers of a generation: Andy Warhol and Kenneth Anger. In his book *Popism,* Warhol described Maas and Menken as "the last of the great bohemians."[126]

Anger lived with Maas and Menken for about three months in 1963, during which time he visited Coney Island and met an Italian biker gang. Anger was fascinated by their "hand-customized bikes" with incredible details such as "surrealist shark-like tail fins." He was also fascinated by their handsome leader, Bruce

Truman Capote in the backyard of Oliver Smith's Brooklyn Heights home. (*Photo by David Attie.*)

Byron. The bikers inspired Anger's film *Scorpio Rising,* which Byron starred in.[127] A film critic for *The New Yorker* called it "by far the best of the so-called underground movies."[128] But *Scorpio Rising* would be Anger's only film set in Brooklyn, and like Maas, Menken, and Warhol, most of his public, artistic life would happen in Manhattan, or outside New York entirely. The same was true for two other prominent Heights gay artists: Oliver Smith and Truman Capote.

In 1953, the same year that Thomas Painter moved into the St. George Hotel, set designer (and former February House resident) Oliver Smith purchased a gorgeous Greek revival mansion at 70 Willow Street. The luxurious yellow brick villa was nearly the oldest remaining home in the neighborhood. Perhaps to hark back to the harbor views he'd once had at 7 Middagh Street, Smith placed his studio in the attic. From 1955 to 1965, he rented out the basement apartment to his good friend Truman Capote, who likened its lush, secluded garden to his native Louisiana.

Here Capote would write both *Breakfast at Tiffany's* and *In Cold Blood,* as well as his 1959 essay for *Holiday* magazine, "Brooklyn Heights: A Personal Memoir." Famously, he opened the piece with the words "I live in Brooklyn. By choice." Like nearly every other artist who lived in the Heights, Capote extolled its long artistic and literary histories as some of the virtues that drew him to the neighborhood. However, he also worried about what we would today call its rapid and recent gentrification, writing:

Soon after the war, the Heights commenced attracting a bright new clientele,
brave pioneers bringing brooms and buckets of paint: urban, ambitious young
couples, by and large mid-rung in their Doctor-Lawyer–Wall Street–Whatever
careers, eager to restore to the Heights its shattered qualities of circumspect,
comfortable charm.[129]

Soon, disagreements between those new up-and-comers and the neighborhood's established queer residents would spill out all over the pages of the local
paper, the *Brooklyn Heights Press*. They revealed a gay community of surprising size
and acceptance for the era—one that would be almost completely forgotten by
the time of the Stonewall Riots.

It began in October 1962, when a Heights resident sent in an "omnibus" of
complaints to the *Press*. Point two on his list was "The Heights Peace Corps—
Homosexuals." The author complained that he had been reduced to taking
women with him when he went on his nightly stroll to protect him from advances by the "Princes of the Promenade." "When I go walking on a cold night—
alone—and one of those misbegotten pansies starts to try and find out if I am a
foot warmer," he threatened, "I'm going to belt him, or her, or it, right in the
chops!"[130]

In the next issue, multiple Heights residents responded in protest. Shockingly,
all of them signed their names, showing a surprising willingness to defend homosexuality in public. One writer urged the police to crack down on heterosexual
couples, who were frequently being seen "loving it up in a most flagrant and disgusting manner." A second said that the writer of the original letter is "on another planet" and recommended that he read the Constitution. A third suggested
he simply try saying "no."[131]

Responses continued in the next issue as well. This new round of letter writers wasn't just protesting the first letter, they were actually celebrating the
Heights's diversity. "You see every race and creed on these streets—but they have
something in common," said one, "taste and intelligence." It noted that the original letter writer had mentioned his Syrian heritage and suggested that his own
experiences with discrimination might open his eyes to the plight of the homosexual. A married father of two with many gay friends wrote that he was
"distressed by the uncouth condemnation of our Brooklyn Heights homosexuals,"

saying he found "most of them to be cultured, quiet, and amiable, a credit to our community."[132] No residents wrote to support the original author, or if they did, the *Press* didn't publish the letters. The next year, however, a less lopsided debate would take over the letter section, suggesting that even the Heights was getting less tolerant with time.

In the fall of 1963, the police began an extended crackdown on homosexuals in Brooklyn Heights, which eventually caused the closure of Tony Bonner's Heights Supper Club, a popular neighborhood restaurant. Tony Bonner had been a photographer during World War II, and afterward he settled down in Brooklyn, where he helped launch a couple of other restaurants, before going in with some backers to open the Supper Club at 80 Montague Street in 1950. The Supper Club would be the first gay bar in Brooklyn (and by this I mean what we would today think of as a gay bar, not the queer-friendly trade bars that existed in such places as Coney Island and on Sands Street).

The motto of the Supper Club was "Where it's never too late to dine," because although it opened at 3:00 p.m., it was known for its late hours. The fare was fancy for the day, heavy on seafood, with Asian and Italian influences. The rather intimate room was mostly given over to long rows of two-person tables. A decorative wrought-iron screen of lacy leaves acted as a proscenium separating the dining area from the small "cocktail lounge." Bonner had snagged the screen from the nearby Temple Bar Building when it was being reconstructed and installed it himself.[133] Candles were on every table, a tiny piano was next to the bar, and sprays of fake flowers were in the corners. During the day, it was a place to see and be seen for the neighborhood's society women.

It's impossible to say when exactly it became a gay bar, but a suggestive note in the *Brooklyn Heights Press* hints that it might have been around July 1953, when Bonner bought out his backers. As sole proprietor of the Supper Club, the unsigned article noted, he planned to "manage it in the manner to which his many friends have become accustomed."[134] Given the *Press*'s gay-friendly coverage, this seems like a nod to those in the know. On the one-year anniversary of becoming sole owner, Bonner celebrated with a champagne fountain and a twenty-six-dish buffet.[135]

Regardless of when it began catering specifically to gay men, the Supper Club was certainly an established gay bar by December 1963, when *The New York Times* reported that its liquor license had been revoked for being a "homosexual haunt" that had been "repeatedly raided by the police." The chairman of the State Liquor Authority (SLA) called the Supper Club one of the city's "notorious congregating points for homosexuals and delinquents." According to the SLA, the bar had a system of lights that were flashed on whenever a suspected police officer attempted to gain entry, to warn "the boys to stop dancing with one another."[136]

The *Times* article listed a number of areas in the city that were known for being thronged with "identifiable homosexuals." Although the article centered on a bar in Brooklyn, its author did not include the Heights, or any other neighborhood outside Manhattan, on this list of early gayborhoods.

These arrests were hotly debated in the *Brooklyn Heights Press*. Again, the first letter was a complaint. "Homosexuals project their 'femininity' to the nth degree on the street," the letter raged, before suggesting that all homosexuals were prostitutes and pedophiles, and congratulating the police on their efforts. The author made specific reference to the changing character of the neighborhood, writing "as for the homosexual in Brooklyn Heights, I consider him a menace— economically as well as morally. . . . In my seven years in Brooklyn Heights, I have seen it change from a fag haven to respectability and back again."[137] Another letter writer railed that society had become *too* tolerant of homosexuals, and that they were now repressing heterosexuals by existing in public. Tellingly, both of these letters went unsigned—as a series of *signed* responses pointed out in the next issue. One author mocked them as "individuals who are reluctant to accept public responsibility for their views," before stating that "the neighborhood has had a significant and growing homosexual population" since at least the time the BQE was built.[138]

The final word on the debate was an unsigned article by the *Press* editors, bluntly titled "Homosexuality," which avoided the moral and legal issues and focused instead on facts. "Despite the differences of opinions," they wrote, "no one denied that homosexuals in large numbers were frequenting several bars in the Heights." The editors' main complaint was that *The New York Times,* in "listing areas where homosexual colonization is high," had left the Heights off the list.[139]

Already, queer Brooklyn was being forgotten. Tony Bonner's Supper Club never reopened. In 1965, when a writer for the *Press* suggested banning Walt Whitman in schools because of his sexuality, protests would again flood the letters section—but none of them would mention the local gay community. In fact, after 1963, the issue of gays in the Heights seems never to be mentioned in the *Press* again. A 1969 gay guide to the city would mention two other bars in the Heights, but it seems that they no longer enjoyed the approbation, or even recognition, of the greater neighborhood.

By this point, most of the midcentury artists who had given Brooklyn cultural cachet before and during World War II were gone. Truman Capote moved back to Manhattan in 1965, as did the poet Marianne Moore in 1966. Willard Maas and Marie Menken remained in Brooklyn Heights, but their prestige had long since been eclipsed by that of their protégés, and they would die within days of each other right around New Year's Eve, 1971. Oliver Smith also stayed in Brooklyn, but he conducted most of his public life in Manhattan, and his mansion never became the kind of artistic commune he'd had in February House. By the time the Stonewall Riots rolled around on June 28, 1969, queer people remained in Brooklyn, but no part of Brooklyn—not the Heights, or what remained of Sands Street, or even Coney Island—was considered "queer" in the public imagination.

Queer Brooklyn could be likened to a canary in a coal mine—a small, fragile thing whose passing indicated larger dangers. Since 1800, Brooklyn had been on a growing, upward trajectory, but after World War II, its population shrank. From 1950 to 1960, it lost over one hundred thousand residents, and from 1960 to 1970, it lost twenty-five thousand more. And that's just counting the change in the total population, not the thousands of residents who left and were replaced. The waterfront, which had been the economic engine that enabled so many queer people to build lives in Brooklyn over the last hundred years, would cease to be the borough's defining element of prosperity. Although queer people would obviously continue to live and work in Brooklyn as they always had, a major moment of disjuncture was created in the infrastructure, loci, and visible evidence of queer people in the borough.

Around the time Bonner's Supper Club closed in Brooklyn Heights, the Starlite Lounge opened in Crown Heights, and slowly became an underground institution in the city's black queer community. In the eighties, Park Slope would be rechristened "Dyke Slope" thanks to the large number of queer women living there (and still today, one of the city's few lesbian bars, Ginger's, can be found in the Slope on Fifth Avenue). Williamsburg, a neighborhood just one stop from Manhattan on the subway, would become a hot spot for artists in the 1990s, some of them queer. These and other new queer institutions set the stage for Brooklyn to become the queer arts mecca it is today, but they were only dimly connected to the century of history that came before them, if they were at all. In the 1980s, when the queer magazine *The Advocate* published an article about queer Brooklyn, one Heights resident even went so far as to say that the gay history of Brooklyn Heights started in the 1960s—mistaking a midpoint for a beginning.[140]

These new communities were also disconnected from the queer world of Manhattan, which became more insular as the city (and country) became increasingly more dangerous for queer people. Brooklyn would no longer exist on the queer mental map of the city, at least for most people outside the borough. In the popular imagination, Brooklyn post-1950 was reduced from the "second city of the Empire" to Manhattan's rinky-dink sister—a place people came *from,* but never went *to.* When Brooklyn was represented, it was as poor, provincial, and resoundingly heterosexual, a world of mooks and molls, race riots, and insular Orthodox Jews. But mostly, it was just never talked about. Pick a random book about "New York City" history, and chances are, it will mention Brooklyn (or any borough other than Manhattan) sporadically if at all. The chance that it talks about the queer history of Brooklyn? Nearly zero.

But nothing lasts forever, even silence. If this history shows one thing, it is the resourcefulness of queer desire, which found ways to express itself long before America even had words for it. With the dawn of the new millennium, queer Brooklyn has rebounded with a fierceness and a cultural relevance that now threatens at times to outshine Manhattan. In 2011, the American Cultural Survey found that the area of New York City with the highest proportion of same-sex households wasn't Chelsea or Greenwich Village, but a ten-block area along the waterfront between Red Hook and Brooklyn Heights.[141] On television, NBC has a half-hour sitcom called *Champions,* which focuses on a young, queer boy of color being raised by his father and uncle, above the gym they own in Brooklyn. And in downtown Brooklyn, an organization called the Red Umbrella Project (which was founded by queer women) empowers and advocates on behalf of sex workers—not far from where Gustave Beekman's brothel was once raided during the Swastika Swishery.

New queer history is being written; old queer history is being restored to its proper place. Let us hope that this time, it is written in indelible ink; in sweat and blood; in hopes and tears; in letters one hundred feet tall that will never be forgotten.

epilogue

The first time I ever thought the words *queer* and *Brooklyn* in the same sentence, I was twenty-one years old. It was 1999, and I was headed into the city to go to a queer anarchist convergence, called Queeruption, which was being held in DUMBA, a queer collective home in Dumbo (a tiny sliver of a neighborhood squeezed between the Brooklyn Bridge and Vinegar Hill).

My family was from the Bronx, but I grew up in the suburbs. The only thing I knew about Brooklyn history was that in family lore, my great-aunt Maeve had moved there in the 1930s, despite my grandmother's warning that no one would ever visit her in Sunset Park. My grandmother was right; my great-aunt moved back to Gun Hill Road, and nothing more was said about Brooklyn until my older brother moved to Williamsburg in 1997. My personal queer map of New York City was a small right triangle, with the vertex around Christopher Street, and two perpendicular arms extending outward, one east, to trashy, punky Astor Place, where I got my tongue pierced on a wooden chair in the middle of the street; and one north, to Tunnel and Twilo and Roxy and Limelight, the vast mega-clubs that dotted the West Side of Manhattan, where I danced all night after sneaking out of my parent's basement.

I never made it to DUMBA that first night. Something went wrong with the F train, or maybe I just got lost. (Pre-smartphone, many of my plans in New York City quickly turned into accidental adventures.) But it forged in my mind a connection between Brooklyn and edgy queer culture. Over the next few years, I found my way back to DUMBA repeatedly, for parties, and film screenings, and concerts, and workshops on everything from safer sex to safer protests. At night, the neighborhood shut down entirely, and walking on some of its still-cobblestoned streets, hearing only the sounds that drifted in from the river, I found it easy to imagine myself in a long-ago Brooklyn . . . one I knew nothing about.

Shortly after 9/11, I moved to New York—to Brooklyn. Park Slope. My downstairs neighbors were a lesbian couple and their seventeen thousand dogs; our landlord lived next door and was slowly restoring two small buildings to period elegance. If he wasn't gay, he was the best Quentin Crisp impersonator I've ever met. In short order, I discovered the dyke bar (Ginger's) and the gay boy bar across the street, Excelsior. I heard that the Lesbian Herstory Archives were in a brownstone by the park, but I wouldn't have the chance to visit them for a few years. Somehow, accidentally, I'd landed in the middle of a gayborhood I never knew existed. From old-timers, I learned that Park Slope had been a lesbian haven since sometime around the late seventies or early eighties. Yet somehow, it was never mentioned on the lists of gay neighborhoods in New York, which were always only in Manhattan. I had a degree in feminist, gender, and sexuality studies, and a dawning realization that I knew much less about all of those things than I thought.

Over the next decade, I bounced around Brooklyn, always moving as the rents went up (and up, and up). Everywhere I went, I picked up scattered shards of queer history. A friend took me to Sunday-night karaoke at the Starlite, a queer-friendly POC bar in Crown Heights that had been around since the late sixties. Jennifer Miller, the former woman-with-a-beard at Coney Island, taught me both how to walk on stilts, *and* how the sideshow nurtured decades of little-discussed queer life. For a while, I dated a boy who lived in a boardinghouse in Brooklyn Heights, where each floor had a shared bathroom and kitchen. He'd heard stories that it had once been a gay brothel, but neither of us believed them until the day the heating broke, and in trying to fix it, the landlord discovered an ancient, tiny pistol hidden in his vent.

Rumors and avuncular older queers and disconnected bits of ephemera; bars and beaches and brothels—this, I learned, was what Brooklyn's queer history was made of.

In late 2010, I accidentally founded an organization called the Pop-Up Museum of Queer History. It started life somewhere between an art project and a party, an experiment to see what it would be like if a museum featured queer exhibits, made by queer people, in a queer space (my apartment), for a queer audience. When three hundred people showed up, I knew I'd touched a nerve;

when twelve cops surrounded the apartment with flashing lights and shut us down around midnight, I knew I had to keep going. I formed a collective to oversee the museum, and we began doing community-created historical exhibits in different locales around the country, such as New York, and Philly, and Bloomington, Indiana.

Given that we started in a loft in Bushwick, it seemed only natural to do a Brooklyn show. But when we talked to people about making exhibits, we hit a wall. Few people knew much about Brooklyn. At most, some knew a little of the recent history—perhaps that Jill Harris had become the borough's first out elected official in 1993, when she won election to the school board in District 15, which covered Park Slope and the waterfront of Red Hook. Or they had vague ideas—about lesbians at the Brooklyn Navy Yard, say, or gay men cruising in Prospect Park—but nothing definitive to build an exhibit around. In a city of 2.5 million people, settled over 350 years ago, Brooklyn's queer history seemed not to go back past 1940. Something didn't make any sense.

This is how *When Brooklyn Was Queer* began: from a paradox. Brooklyn has a vibrant queer present—undoubtedly, Brooklyn today is queer again—and it's next door to one of the epicenters of queer history in the United States. Were queers like vampires, incapable of crossing the East River, or what? I was certain there was queer history in Brooklyn; it was just a matter of finding it.

For the next few years, I picked up bits of Brooklyn history whenever they floated my way in my job as a journalist working on queer stories. One of the other Pop-Up organizers, an archivist named Rachel Mattson, suggested I look along the waterfront. This was the first major break in my research and helped frame everything that came next. Soon after, the New York Public Library granted me a fellowship to do this work in a more organized fashion, and suddenly I was writing a book for real.

Along the way, tracing this history has meant understanding some hard truths about the city I love. When I found fewer queer people of color than I'd expected, I looked at the demographic history of Brooklyn and realized I was seeing a long story of racism written in tiny percentages and redlined neighborhoods. But it's also meant finding spiritual ancestors I'd never known before, people such as Jennie June, Mabel Hampton, and Thomas Painter, who charted some of these same histories seventy-five and a hundred years ago.

This book almost certainly just scratches the surface of the real queer history of Brooklyn. I will have missed important stories and got other ones all cocked up. Generations of history have come and gone since Stonewall, and those deserve a book all their own. But then, queer history has always been piecemeal and canonless—a mutual endeavor of shared love. I look forward to the book that comes after this, and the one that comes after that, and the one that maybe you're going to write. I look forward to having a future where we also have a past, and I look forward to creating it with you.

acknowledgments

This book would not have been possible without the work of generations of historians, archivists, and tale-tellers who came before me. In particular, I want to thank Martin Boyce, George Chauncey, Rachel Corbman, Lisa Davis, David Denhotlz, Charles Denson, Martin Duberman, Avram Finkelstein, Hugh Hagius, Nicholas Jenkins, Charles Kaiser, Jerry Kalbas, Gerard Koskovitch, Michael Levine, Ken Lustbader, Rachel Mattson, Jennifer Miller, Jason Baumann Montilla, Joan Nestle, Gillian Rodger, Saskia Scheffer, Randy Sell, Al Stencell, Todd Swindell, Marvin Taylor, Bud Thomas, Jae Whitaker, Shawn Wilson, and Matt Young for their ceaseless assistance.

I also have to thank the patient and endlessly generous group of early readers and supporters who helped me guide this book along the way: Alexander Chee, Laleña Garcia, Garth Greenwell, V. Hansmann, Sassafras Lowrey, Nicole Pasulka, Sarah Schulman, Deborah Schwartz, Alejandro Varela, and Cookie Woolner. No single person has been more instrumental to making this book happen than Brian Ferree, my research assistant, sounding board, and all-around queer-man Friday.

Without the support of Louis Wiley Jr., the New York Public Library, the Martin Duberman Fellowship, the Queers Arts Mentorship Program, the New York Foundation for the Arts, Stephen Guy-Bray, and the many Patreons who support me online, I would never have been able to finish writing this book. As well, this project was developed in part at The Watermill Center during the 2018 Artist Residency Program. Without Robert Guinsler at Sterling Lord Literistic, no one would know this book existed, and without Karen Wolny, Sylvan Creekmore, and Martin Quinn at St. Martin's Press, you wouldn't be holding it in your hands right now.

I'm also incredibly indebted to the staff of the following archives, the guardians of the ephemera upon which this history is based: Kinsey Institute at Indiana University–Bloomington, Lesbian Herstory Archives, New York Public Library's Manuscripts and Archives Division, New York City Municipal Archives, Schomburg Center for Research in Black Culture, Fales Library and Special Collections at NYU, Tamiment Library and Robert F. Wagner Labor Archives at NYU, Columbia University Archives, Library of Congress, New-York Historical Society, Brooklyn Museum, Brooklyn Public Library, ONE National Gay & Lesbian Archives at the USC Libraries, National Security Archive, LGBT Community Center National History Archive, SF GLBT History Society, Stanford University Special Collections & University Archives, Swarthmore College Peace Archives, Beinecke Rare Book & Manuscript Library at Yale University, Boise State University Library, BLDG 92 at the Brooklyn Navy Yard, Archives of the Brooklyn Navy Yard Development Corporation, and Brooklyn Historical Society.

Finally, I want to thank my parents, my brothers, my extended family, my cats, and my partners Tim and Jason, for joining and supporting me every step of the way on this deep journey into Brooklyn's queer past.

notes

1. From *Leaves of Grass* to the Brooklyn Bridge: The Rise of the Queer Waterfront, 1855–83

1. "A volume of poems, just published," *Brooklyn Daily Times,* 1856, accessed from the Walt Whitman Archive on September 28, 2018.
2. Walt Whitman, *Life and Adventures of Jack Engle.*
3. Ralph Waldo Emerson, "The Poet," in *The Portable Emerson.*
4. Kenneth M. Price, *Walt Whitman: The Contemporary Reviews.*
5. Rufus Griswold, "Review of *Leaves of Grass* (1855)," *Criterion,* November 10, 1855.
6. "Mayor's Message," *Brooklyn Daily Eagle,* January 2, 1855.
7. Whitman, *Leaves of Grass.*
8. Whitman.
9. "The Erie Canal: A Brief History," New York State Canal Corporation, accessed May 26, 2017, http://www.canals.ny.gov/history/history.html.
10. Edwin Burrows and Mike Wallace, *Gotham: A History of New York City to 1898.*
11. Burrows and Wallace.
12. Joseph Alexiou, *Gowanus: Brooklyn's Curious Canal.*
13. Alexiou.
14. Alexiou.
15. "Mayor's Message," *Brooklyn Daily Eagle.*
16. Rebecca Dalzell, "The Whiskey Wars That Left Brooklyn in Ruins," *Smithsonian,* November 18, 2014.
17. Judith Wellman, *Brooklyn's Promised Land: The Free Black Community of Weeksville, New York.*
18. Robert Furman, *Brooklyn Heights: The Rise, Fall and Rebirth of America's First Suburb.*
19. Walt Whitman, *Notebooks and Unpublished Prose Manuscripts,* ed. Edward F. Grier.
20. Grier.
21. "United States Summary: 2010, Population & Housing Unit Counts," US Department of Commerce, September 2012.
22. Carla L. Peterson, "Answers About Black Life in 19th-Century New York, Part 2," *New York Times,* February 17, 2012.

23. Burrows and Wallace, *Gotham*.

24. William N. Eskridge Jr., *Dishonorable Passions: Sodomy Laws in America, 1861–2003*.

25. Emerson, "Poet."

26. Gary Schmidgall, ed., *Intimate With Walt: Whitman's Conversations With Horace Traubel*.

27. Schmidgall, *Walt Whitman*.

28. Peterson, "Answers About Black Life."

29. Wellman, *Brooklyn's Promised Land*.

30. Carla L. Peterson, *Black Gotham: A Family History of African Americans in Nineteenth-Century New York City*.

31. W. Jeffrey Bolster, *Black Jacks: African American Seamen in the Age of Sail*.

32. Bolster, *Black Jacks*.

33. Peterson, "Answers About Black Life."

34. Wellman, *Brooklyn's Promised Land*.

35. Wellman.

36. Gloria T. Hull, *Give Us Each Day: The Diary of Alice Dunbar Nelson*.

37. Gloria T. Hull, *Color, Sex, and Poetry: Three Women Writers of the Harlem Renaissance*.

38. Burrows and Wallace, *Gotham*.

39. Jim O'Grady, "In Rescued Letters, a Civil War Soldier from Brooklyn Faces Death," WNYC, May 5, 2015, accessed April 6, 2018, https://www.wnyc.org/story/150-years -after-civil-wars-end-recalling-soldier-brooklyn/.

40. Alba M. Edwards, "1940 Census of Population: Comparative Occupation Statistics for the United States, 1870 to 1940," Bureau of the Census, 1943.

41. Gilson Willets, "Artist Authors of Today," *Art Interchange* 35, no. 5 (November 1895).

42. James Grant Wilson, *The Memorial History of the City of New York*.

43. "For the Better Half," *Philadelphia Times*, July 30, 1894.

44. Darlis A. Miller, *Mary Hallock Foote: Author-Illustrator of the American West*.

45. "Amusements in Brooklyn," *Brooklyn Daily Eagle*, September 21, 1863.

46. "Another Feature of Metropolitan Life," *Brooklyn Daily Eagle*, November 30, 1863.

47. Vera Mowry Roberts, "Women Who Managed Theatres in Nineteenth Century America" (address at John F. Kennedy Center in Washington, DC, on April 26, 1992), accessed April 6, 2018, https://www.thecollegeoffellows.org/wp-content/uploads/2015/12 /RobertsVera-19th-Century-Women-Managers-1992.pdf.

48. Miller, *Mary Hallock Foote*.

49. Christine Hill Smith, *Social Class in the Writings of Mary Hallock Foote*.

50. Miller, *Mary Hallock Foote*.

51. Carroll Smith-Rosenberg, *Disorderly Conduct: Visions of Gender in Victorian America*.

52. Smith-Rosenberg.

53. Untitled article, *Brooklyn Daily Eagle*, April 21, 1895.

54. Letter from Mary Hallock Foote to Alice B. Stockham, 1887, Special Collections and Archives, Boise State University Library.

55. Smith-Rosenberg, *Disorderly Conduct*.

56. Smith, *Social Class*.

57. Miller, *Mary Hallock Foote.*

58. Richard Watson Gilder, *Five Books of Song.*

59. Smith-Rosenberg, *Disorderly Conduct.*

60. Smith-Rosenberg.

61. Smith, *Social Class.*

62. Smith.

63. E.P.D., "Views of Correspondents," *Brooklyn Daily Eagle,* January 25, 1867.

64. Letter to Washington A. Roebling, October 5, 1856, Special Collections and University Archives, Rutgers University.

65. Letter to Washington A. Roebling, Thanksgiving Day 1856, Special Collections and University Archives, Rutgers University.

66. David McCullough, *The Great Bridge.*

67. Eskridge, *Dishonorable Passions.*

68. "Our Civic Triumph," *Brooklyn Daily Eagle,* Thursday evening, May 24, 1883.

69. McCullough, *Great Bridge.*

70. McCullough.

71. Lewis A. Erenberg, *Steppin' Out: New York Nightlife and the Transformation of American Culture, 1890–1930.*

2. Becoming Visible, 1883–1910

1. Alexiou, *Gowanus.*

2. Edward Le Roy Rice, *Monarchs of Minstrelsy.*

3. "A Burlesque Prima Donna," *Columbus* (IN) *Republic,* November 30, 1883.

4. Foley McKeever obituary, *New Orleans Times-Picayune,* November 7, 1883.

5. "Ricardo," *Brooklyn Daily Eagle,* November 2, 1883.

6. "A Dead Minstrel," *St. Louis Post-Dispatch,* November 2, 1883.

7. "Ricardo," *Brooklyn Daily Eagle.*

8. "Dead Minstrel," *St. Louis Post-Dispatch.*

9. George Chauncey, *Gay New York: Gender, Urban Culture, and the Making of the Gay Male World, 1890–1940.*

10. Timothy Gilfoyle, *City of Eros: New York City, Prostitution, and the Commercialization of Sex, 1790–1920.*

11. Elizabeth Alice Clement, *Love for Sale: Courting, Treating, and Prostitution in New York City, 1900–1945.*

12. Gillian M. Rodger, *Champagne Charlie and Pretty Jemima: Variety Theater in the Nineteenth Century.*

13. "The Elephant in Brooklyn," *Brooklyn Daily Eagle,* December 9, 1861.

14. "Would a Stock Theatre Pay in Brooklyn?," *Brooklyn Daily Eagle,* November 20, 1882.

15. "Amusements," *Brooklyn Daily Eagle,* September 27, 1862.

16. *Brooklyn Daily Eagle Almanac 1890.*

17. *New York Clipper,* October 2, 1880.

18. "Ella Wesner Lies in Man's Garb," *New York Times*, November 14, 1917.

19. Rodger. *Champagne Charlie and Pretty Jemima*.

20. "The Gaiety," *Brooklyn Daily Eagle*, August 21, 1889.

21. Amy Werbel, *Lust on Trial: Censorship and the Rise of American Obscenity in the Age of Anthony Comstock*.

22. Gillian Rodger, "'He Isn't a Marrying Man': Gender and Sexuality in the Repertoire of Male Impersonators, 1870–1930," in *Queer Episodes in Music and Modern Identity*, eds. Sophie Fuller and Lloyd Whitesell.

23. Laurence Senelick, *The Changing Room: Sex, Drag, and Theatre*.

24. "Josie Mansfield and Ella Wesner," Oswego (NY) *Daily Palladium*, August 28, 1873.

25. Michael Leavitt, *Fifty Years in Theatrical Management*.

26. "Rumored Elopement of a Hotel-Keeper with Ella Wesner," *Chicago Tribune*, November 18, 1872.

27. "Josie Mansfield and Ella Wesner," Oswego (NY) *Daily Palladium*.

28. Lynn Abbott, *Out of Sight: The Rise of African American Popular Music, 1889–1895*.

29. "Amusements," *Saint Paul Globe*, January 19, 1892.

30. "The Slums of Brooklyn," *Brooklyn Daily Eagle*, January 25, 1896.

31. Kathy Peiss, *Cheap Amusements: Working Women and Leisure in Turn-of-the-Century New York*.

32. Mark Knowles, *Tap Roots: The Early History of Tap Dancing*.

33. Jayna Brown, *Babylon Girls: Black Women Performers and the Shaping of the Modern*.

34. Marvin McAllister, *Whiting Up: Whiteface Minstrek and Stage Europeans in African American Performance*.

35. "Coney Island Stampede," *Evening World*, October 13, 1894.

36. "College Boys at Coney," *New York Sun*, June 25, 1894.

37. "Doings of Stage People," *Colored American*, January 13, 1900.

38. "Miss Florence Hines," *Indianapolis Freeman*, September 10, 1904.

39. Kathleen Casey, "Cross-Dressers and Race-Crossers" (University of Rochester, 2010).

40. "Miss Florence Hines," *Freeman*.

41. "Florence Hines Dead," *Chicago Defender*, March 22, 1924.

42. "Two Beautiful Creoles Pull Hair," *Cincinnati Enquirer*, March 2, 1892.

43. Carl Rollyson, *Amy Lowell Anew: A Biography*.

44. Chris Rigby, "Ada Dwyer: Bright Lights and Lilacs," *Utah Historical Quarterly* 43, no. 1 (Winter 1975).

45. "Driftwood," *Theater Magazine* 6 (April 5, 1890).

46. Rigby, "Ada Dwyer: Bright Lights and Lilacs."

47. "Hard on Handsome Hal," *Saint Paul Globe*, September 1, 1890.

48. "At the Local Theaters," *St. Louis Post-Dispatch*, March 10, 1891.

49. "Will She Divorce Him," *New York Evening World*, June 9, 1891.

50. Harold H. Jenson, "True Pioneer Stories," *Juvenile Instructor* 63, no. 12 (December 1928).

51. "In the Theaters," Wilkes-Barre (PA) *Evening News*, October 2, 1909.

52. Helen Deborah Lewis, "Friends, Beloveds, and Companions: The Shadow Life of the Fin-de-Siècle American Lesbian Actress" (Tufts University, November 2011).

53. Mary Casal, *The Stone Wall.*

54. Sherry Ann Darling, "A Critical Introduction to *The Stone Wall: An Autobiography*" (Tufts University, May 2003).

55. "Her Own Sketch," *Buffalo Commercial,* December 5, 1900.

56. "The Tailor Made Girl," *Brooklyn Daily Eagle,* January 1, 1893.

57. "Her Own Sketch," *Buffalo Commercial.*

58. Casal, *The Stone Wall.*

59. American Newspaper Directory, 1886, https://archive.org/details/americannews pape1886newy.

60. Sarah Bernhardt, *My Double Life.*

61. "A Mad Marriage," *St. Louis Post-Dispatch,* February 1, 1888.

62. "A Mad Marriage."

63. 1900 Census Special Reports: Occupations at the Twelfth Census, Bureau of the Census, 1904.

64. "An Actress Who Has a Novel Way of Making Herself Conspicious," *Detroit Free Press,* April 24, 1892.

65. "Alice Mitchell Insane," *Brooklyn Daily Eagle,* July 30, 1892.

66. "The Trial of Alice Mitchell," *Brooklyn Daily Eagle,* July 24, 1892.

67. Untitled article, *Brooklyn Daily Eagle,* July 24, 1892.

68. "Griffo Gets One Year," *Brooklyn Daily Eagle,* August 13, 1896.

69. "Big Town 1898 Big Time," *New York World,* January 1, 1898.

3. Criminal Perverts, 1910–20

1. "Return to Raymond Street Jail," New York City Department of Correction History, accessed May 3, 2018, http://www.correctionhistory.org/html/museum/gallery/ray mondst/return2raymondst.html.

2. "Jail Does Need Repair but Not Rebuilding," *Brooklyn Daily Eagle,* March 20, 1904.

3. "Advocate Prison Ward in Brooklyn Hospital," *Brooklyn Daily Eagle,* May 21, 1911.

4. "Raymond Street Jail Is a Bastille," *Brooklyn Daily Eagle,* July 12, 1914.

5. "Jail Does Need Repair," *Brooklyn Daily Eagle.*

6. "Insane Persons Sent Straight to Flatbush," *Brooklyn Daily Eagle,* April 12, 1909.

7. "Artist and Architect Face Homicide Charge," *Brooklyn Daily Eagle,* January 3, 1910.

8. "Held for Coroner," *New-York Tribune,* January 3, 1910.

9. William N. Eskridge Jr., *Gaylaw: Challenging the Apartheid of the Closet.*

10. Chauncey, *Gay New York.*

11. Charles H. Mills, *New York Criminal Reports: Reports of Cases Decided in All the Courts of the State of New York Involving Questions of Criminal Law and Practice,* vol. 31 (Albany, NY: W. C. Little, 1915).

12. R. W. Shufeldt, "Biography of a Passive Pederast," *American Journal of Urology and Sexology* 13 (1917).

13. Shufeldt.

14. Ralph Werther, *Autobiography of an Androgyne*.

15. Chauncey, *Gay New York*.

16. Werther, *Autobiography of an Androgyne*.

17. "No Crime for Girl to Wear Trousers," *Daily Standard Union: Brooklyn*, August 28, 1913.

18. "Trondle Girl Sent to Bedford Reformatory," *Daily Standard Union: Brooklyn*, September 3, 1913.

19. "No Crime for Girl to Wear Trousers," *Daily Standard Union: Brooklyn*.

20. "Still Clings to Her Male Attire," *Daily Standard Union: Brooklyn*, August 30, 1913.

21. "Girl Masquerading Is Miss Trondle," *Brooklyn Daily Eagle*, August 29, 1913.

22. "Begs Trousers of President," *Sun*, 31, 1913.

23. "Is Bridget a Woman?," *New York Herald*, July 31, 1898.

24. "Prefers Jail to Skirts," *Evening Times-Republican*, May 31, 1911.

25. "Girl Prisoner Won't Reject Boy's Garb," *Brooklyn Daily Eagle*, August 30, 1913.

26. "No Crime for Girl to Wear Trousers," *Daily Standard Union: Brooklyn*.

27. Eskridge, *Dishonorable Passions*.

28. "Still Clings to Her Male Attire," *Daily Standard Union: Brooklyn*.

29. Brooklyn Folder, Committee of Fourteen Collection, NYPL, Box 24.

30. "Trondle Girl in Dresses," *Brooklyn Daily Eagle*, September 3, 1913.

31. "In Male Attire," *Brooklyn Daily Eagle*, September 4, 1913.

32. Bernard Talmey, "Transvestitism: A Contribution to the Study of the Psychology of Sex," *New York Medical Journal*, February 21, 1914, 362–68.

33. Talmey, "Transvestitism: A Contribution to the Study of the Psychology of Sex."

34. George Henry, *Sex Variants*.

35. Committee of Fourteen Bulletin #272, Committee of Fourteen Collection, NYPL, Box 87.

36. Committee of Fourteen Bulletin #471, Committee of Fourteen Collection, NYPL, Box 87.

37. Gilfoyle, *City of Eros*.

38. Mara L. Keire, "The Committee of Fourteen and Saloon Reform in New York City, 1905–1920," *Business and Economic History* 26, no. 2 (Winter 1997).

39. Committee of Fourteen Annual Report, January 8, 1912.

40. Margot Canaday, *The Straight State: Sexuality and Citizenship in Twentieth-Century America*.

41. George Bernard Shaw, "Common Sense About the War," *New York Times*, November 22, 1914.

42. Thomas C. Mackey, *Pursuing Johns: Criminal Law Reform, Defending Character, and New York City's Committee of Fourteen, 1920–1930*.

43. Brooklyn Folder, Committee of Fourteen Collection, NYPL, Box 24.

44. Brooklyn Folder.

45. "Sailor Boys Lonely; Won't You Aid Them?," *Brooklyn Daily Eagle*, August 6, 1917.

46. Investigator Report, Brooklyn Folder, Committee of Fourteen Collection, NYPL, Box 24.

47. "Weather Report," *Brooklyn Daily Eagle*, January 14, 1916.

48. *The People of the State of New York Against Antonio Bellavicini*, Case on Appeal, February 1, 1916.

49. Committee of Fourteen Bulletin #896, Committee of Fourteen Collection, NYPL, Box 87.

50. *People of the State of New York Against Antonio Bellavicini.*

51. *People of the State of New York Against Antonio Bellavicini.*

52. Committee of Fourteen Collection, NYPL, Box 13, Folder S.

53. Committee of Fourteen Collection, NYPL, Box 18, Folder M.

54. Committee of Fourteen Collection, NYPL, Box 29.

55. "Negro Saloonkeeper, Exonerated by Coroner's Jury, Set Free," *Brooklyn Daily Eagle,* September 30, 1910.

56. "Fail to Get Witnesses: Magistrate Reynolds Again Puts Over Case Involving 'Strong Arm' Squad," *Brooklyn Daily Eagle,* August 26, 1912.

57. Committee of Fourteen Bulletin #576, Committee of Fourteen Collection, NYPL, Box 87.

58. Committee of Fourteen Collection, NYPL, Box 13, Folder M.

59. US Census, 1910.

60. R. W. Shufeldt, *America's Greatest Problem: The Negro.*

61. Shufeldt, 124.

62. R. W. Shufeldt, "The Medico-Legal Consideration of Perverts and Inverts," *Medico-Legal Journal* 48, no. 7 (July 1905).

63. Committee of Fourteen Bulletin #160, Committee of Fourteen Collection, NYPL, Box 87.

64. Committee of Fourteen Bulletin #1293, Committee of Fourteen Collection, NYPL, Box 87.

4. A Growing World, 1920–30

1. "5 Cents to Coney Started Today," *Brooklyn Daily Eagle,* May 1, 1920.

2. "Many Feet Cut at Coney," *Brooklyn Daily Eagle,* June 28, 1920.

3. "10,000 Sleep on Beach at Coney," *Brooklyn Daily Eagle,* August 9, 1920.

4. Michael Immerso, *Coney Island: The People's Playground.*

5. Clark Kinnaird, "Diary of a New Yorker," *Warren Tribune,* June 12, 1928.

6. Peiss, *Cheap Amusements.*

7. Kevin J. Mumford, *Interzones: Black/White Sex Districts in Chicago and New York in the Early Twentieth Century.*

8. Oral history of Mabel Hampton, http://herstories.prattinfoschool.nyc/omeka/document /62, accessed on September 28, 2018.

9. Mabel Hampton oral history at the Lesbian Herstory Archives, http://herstories .prattinfoschool.nyc/omeka/document/81, accessed on September 28, 2018.

10. Mabel Hampton oral history at the Lesbian Herstory Archives, http://herstories .prattinfoschool.nyc/omeka/document/81, accessed on September 28, 2018.

11. Mabel Hampton oral history at the Lesbian Herstory Archives, http://herstories .prattinfoschool.nyc/omeka/document/78, accessed on September 28, 2018.

12. Mabel Hampton oral history at the Lesbian Herstory Archives, http://herstories .prattinfoschool.nyc/omeka/document/78, accessed on September 28, 2018.
13. Langston Hughes, *The Big Sea.*
14. Eric Garber, "A Spectacle in Color: The Lesbian and Gay Subculture of Jazz Age Harlem," accessed May 8, 2018, http://xroads.virginia.edu/~ug97/blues/garber.html.
15. Mabel Hampton oral history at the Lesbian Herstory Archives, http://herstories .prattinfoschool.nyc/omeka/document/81, accessed on September 28, 2018.
16. Mumford, *Interzones.*
17. Mabel Hampton oral history at the Lesbian Herstory Archives, http://herstories.prattin foschool.nyc/omeka/document/79, accessed on September 28, 2018.
18. LaShawn Harris, *Sex Workers, Psychics, and Numbers Runners: Black Women in New York City's Underground Economy.*
19. Cheryl D. Hicks, *Talk with You Like a Woman: African American Women, Justice, and Reform in New York, 1890–1935.*
20. Committee of Fourteen Bulletin #1522, Committee of Fourteen Collection, NYPL, Box 87.
21. Katherine Bement Davis, *Factors in the Sex Life of Twenty-two Hundred Women.*
22. http://herstories.prattinfoschool.nyc/omeka/document/79.
23. Joan Nestle, *"I Lift My Eyes to the Hill": The Life of Mabel Hampton as Told By a White Woman.* Author interview.
24. "To the Ladies of Montgomery," *Montgomery Advertiser,* November 13, 1879.
25. Amelia Klem Osterud, *The Tattooed Lady: A History.*
26. Edo McCullough, *Good Old Coney Island: A Sentimental Journey into the Past.*
27. "Old Cap and Zip Now Together May Answer 'What-Is-It,'" *The Richmond Indiana Item,* July 8, 1926.
28. "Today's Amusements," *Monroe Louisiana News-Star,* April 28, 1932.
29. Joseph Mitchell, "Lady Olga," in *Up in the Old Hotel and Other Stories.*
30. "Veteran Supplier of Sideshow Attractions Tells of Peculiarities of His Profession and 'Stock,'" *Baltimore Sun,* September 3, 1922.
31. Jimmy Durante and Jack Kofoed, *Night Clubs.*
32. Marilyn Thornton Williams, *"Washing the Great Unwashed": Public Baths in Urban America, 1840–1920.*
33. Immerso, *Coney Island: The People's Playground.*
34. "Floozies Forgotten in Male Beauty Contest," *Variety,* August 14, 1929.
35. Committee of Fourteen Bulletin, Committee of Fourteen Collection, NYPL, Box 87.
36. Sexual Perversion Cases in New York City Courts, 1916–1921, Committee of Fourteen Collection, NYPL.
37. Annual Report City Magistrate's Courts, City of New York, 1947.
38. Annual Report City Magistrate's Courts, City of New York, 1923.
39. Annual Report.
40. Hart Crane, *O My Land, My Friends: The Selected Letters of Hart Crane,* eds. Langdon Hammer and Brom Weber.

41. Crane.

42. Crane.

43. Clive Fisher, *Hart Crane: A Life.*

44. Fisher.

45. Fisher.

46. Crane, *O My Land.*

47. Crane.

48. Crane.

49. Fisher, *Hart Crane.*

50. Crane, *O My Land.*

51. Fisher, *Hart Crane.*

52. Honor Moore, *The White Blackbird: A Life of the Painter Margarett Sargent by Her Grand-daughter.*

53. "Young Brooklyn Artist Puts Work on Exhibition," *Brooklyn Daily Eagle,* March 16, 1905.

54. Fisher, *Hart Crane.*

55. Wendy Jeffers, "Hamilton Easter Field: The Benefactor from Brooklyn," *Archives of American Art Journal* 50, no. 1–2 (Spring 2011).

56. William H. Fox, "Men High in Art World Pay Tribute to Memory of Hamilton Easter Field, Artist and Art Critic," *Brooklyn Daily Eagle,* April 16, 1922.

57. "Hamilton Easter Field," *Brooklyn Daily Eagle,* April 10, 1922.

58. "H. E. Field Leaves $110,000," *New York Herald,* April 23, 1922.

59. Crane, *O My Land.*

60. Crane.

61. Frederic Haskin, "Bohemia's Moving Day," Appleton (WI) *Post-Crescent,* November 2, 1921.

62. "How Do Brooklyn Heighters Like Greenwich Villagers?," *Brooklyn Daily Eagle,* May 1, 1921.

63. Hunce Voelcker, *The Hart Crane Voyages.*

64. Voelcker.

65. Helge Normann Nilsen, "Memories of Hart Crane: A Talk with Emil Opffer," *Hart Crane Newsletter* 2, no. 1 (Summer 1978).

66. Letter from Hart Crane to Bill and Sue Brown, February 16, 1927, Hart Crane Papers, Columbia University Libraries.

67. Letter from Hart Crane to Mony Grunberg, October 20, 1931, Hart Crane Papers, Columbia University Libraries.

68. Hart Crane, *The Bridge.*

69. Robert K. Martin, "Crane's *The Bridge:* 'The Tunnel,'" *Explicator* 34 (1975).

70. Crane, *O My Land.*

71. Robert Silvers and Barbara Epstein, eds., "Edward Dahlberg on Hart Crane," in *The Company They Kept: Writers on Unforgettable Friendships.*

72. Yvor Winters, "The Progress of Hart Crane," *Poetry* 36 (June 1930).

73. Crane, *O My Land.*

74. Fisher, *Hart Crane.*

75. Letter from Peggy Cowley to Solomon Grunberg, date unknown, Hart Crane Papers, Columbia University Libraries.

76. Fisher, *Hart Crane.*

77. Chauncey, *Gay New York.*

5. The Beginning of the End, 1930–40

1. "The Dial Passes," *Minneapolis Star-Tribune,* June 7, 1929.

2. Marianne Moore, *Selected Poems.*

3. Linda Leavell, *Holding On Upside Down: The Life and Work of Marianne Moore.*

4. Leavell.

5. Leavell.

6. Leavell.

7. Marianne Moore, *The Complete Poems of Marianne Moore.*

8. "Marianne Moore Wins Dial Prize of $2,000," *New York Times,* December 23, 1924.

9. Leavell, *Holding On Upside Down.*

10. Marianne Moore, "The Plums of Curiosity," *Vogue,* August 1, 1960.

11. Leavell, *Holding On Upside Down.*

12. Kenneth T. Jackson, *The Encyclopedia of New York City,* 2nd ed.

13. Federal Highway Authority, "State Motor Vehicle Registrations, by Years, 1900–1995," accessed July 7, 2018, https://www.fhwa.dot.gov/ohim/summary95/mv200.pdf.

14. Federal Highway Authority.

15. Leavell, *Holding On Upside Down.*

16. Leavell.

17. Leavell.

18. Leavell.

19. Moore, *The Complete Poems of Marianne Moore.*

20. Moore, "The Plums of Curiosity."

21. Author interview, December 15, 2016.

22. Amy Sohn, "The Star-Studded Life of Ms. Dorothy Bennett," *JSTOR Daily,* April 6, 2016, https://daily.jstor.org/dorothy-bennett/.

23. Alexiou, *Gowanus.*

24. Sohn, "The Star-Studded Life of Ms. Dorothy Bennett."

25. Chauncey, *Gay New York.*

26. *Broadway Brevities,* November 2, 1931.

27. Thomas Painter Archive, Kinsey Institute, Box 3, Series II D. 2, Folder 1.

28. "Sinful Sands Street Really Just a Sissy," *Brooklyn Daily Eagle,* October 26, 1935.

29. "While Brooklyn Sleeps: Sands Street, the Sailor's Paradise," *Brooklyn Daily Eagle,* June 10, 1935.

30. "By the Way, by Maxwell Hamilton," *Brooklyn Daily Eagle,* March 15, 1939.
31. "Homosexual Resorts in New York City, as of May 1939," Thomas Painter Archive, Kinsey Institute.
32. Lincoln Kirstein 1931–1932 diary, Lincoln Kirstein papers, New York Public Library.
33. Chauncey, *Gay New York.*
34. Chauncey.
35. *Brooklyn Daily Eagle,* December 25, 1927.
36. Chauncey, *Gay New York.*
37. Mara Bovsun, "When Cops Raided NYC's Minsky's Burlesque for 'Incorporated Filth,'" *New York Daily News,* August 14, 2017.
38. Jennifer Terry, *An American Obsession: Science, Medicine, and Homosexuality in Modern Society.*
39. Mecca Reitman Carpenter, *No Regrets: Dr. Ben Reitman and the Women Who Loved Him.*
40. John C. Moffitt, "First Days Are Worst in Novice Nudist's Life," *Buffalo Evening News,* September 23, 1933.
41. H. Allen Smith, "Newspaper Man Invades Nudist Camp at Highland; Doffs Clothes to Reveal Its Secrets," Peekskill (NY) *Evening Star,* August 19, 1933.
42. Robert Latou Dickinson and Lura Beam, *The Single Woman: A Medical Study in Sex Education.*
43. Dickinson and Beam.
44. Robert Latou Dickinson Case History, Robert Latou Dickinson Collection, Kinsey Institute, Indiana University.
45. Terry, *American Obsession.*
46. Names Binder, Thomas Painter Collection, Kinsey Institute, Indiana University.
47. Henry, *Sex Variants.*
48. Heather R. White, *Reforming Sodom: Protestants and the Rise of Gay Rights.*
49. Proposal for Study of Homosexuality, G. W. Henry file, Payne Whitney Clinic.
50. Henry, *Sex Variants.*
51. Terry, *American Obsession.*
52. Henry, *Sex Variants.*
53. "Gross, Alfred," Names Binder, Thomas Painter Collection.
54. "Gross, Alfred."
55. Letter from Alfred Kinsey to Jan Gay, August 13, 1946, Jan Gay File, Kinsey Institute, Indiana University.
56. Jan Gay Collection, Kinsey Institute, Indiana University.
57. Dorothy J. Farnan, *Auden in Love: The Intimate Story of a Lifelong Love Affair.*
58. Roger L. Geiger, ed., *History of Higher Education Annual: 1990.*
59. Gerard N. Burrow, *A History of Yale's School of Medicine: Passing Torches to Others.*
60. "'Not Towers of Marble,' Sing Brooklyn College Students," *Brooklyn Daily Eagle,* May 14, 1932.
61. Robert Friend, *Shadow on the Sun: Poems.*
62. Jonathan Lewin, "When Hoovervilles Cropped Up in NYC amid the Great Depression," New York *Daily News,* August 14, 2017.

63. Harold Norse, *Memoirs of a Bastard Angel: A Fifty-Year Literary and Erotic Odyssey*.

64. Norse.

65. Norse.

66. FBI File on David McKelvy White, File #100-5685, report made by G. Allison Driskell.

67. FBI File on David McKelvy White.

68. Norse, *Memoirs of a Bastard Angel*.

69. Interview with Bernard Grebanier, April 24, 1974, Frederic Ewen Audiotape and Videotape Collection, Tamiment Library, NYU.

70. Eva Kollisch, *Girl in Movement: A Memoir*.

71. "Loyalist Veterans Assail Aid to Fins," *Philadelphia Inquirer*, December 24, 1939.

72. "George White's Son Back at Poetry Studies Again After Doing Bit in Madrid," *Cincinnati Enquirer*, November 16, 1937.

73. Marjorie Heins, *Priests of Our Democracy: The Supreme Court, Academic Freedom, and the Anti-Communist Purge*.

74. Heins.

75. "Red Teacher Incited Students' Outbreaks, Grebanier Says; Other Colleges in Probe," *Brooklyn Daily Eagle*, December 3, 1940.

76. "Queer Dialectics/Feminist Interventions: Harry Hay & the Quest for a Revolutionary Politics," Bettina Aptheker keynote given at the conference Radically Gay: Celebrating the Centenary of the Birth of Harry Hay. CUNY Graduate Center, New York, September 28, 2012.

77. Conversation with historian Matt Young, November 2, 2017.

78. Norse, *Memoirs of a Bastard Angel*.

79. Norse.

80. Norse.

81. Norse.

82. John Lahr, "The Gang's All Here," *New Yorker*, June 4 and 11, 2012.

6. Brooklyn at War, 1940–45

1. Carson McCullers, *Illumination and Night Glare: The Unfinished Autobiography of Carson McCullers*.

2. Sherill Tippins, *February House*.

3. Farnan, *Auden in Love*.

4. Irving Drutman, *Good Company: A Memoir, Mostly Theatrical*.

5. Tippins, *February House*.

6. Virginia Spencer Carr, *The Lonely Hunter: A Biography of Carson McCullers*.

7. Brooks Atkinson, "The Play," *New York Times*, May 20, 1940.

8. Karen Abbott, *American Rose: A Nation Laid Bare: The Life and Times of Gypsy Rose Lee*.

9. Tippins, *February House*.

10. Abbott, *American Rose*.

11. Neil Powell, *Benjamin Britten: A Life for Music.*
12. Letter from Benjamin Britten to Antonio and Peggy Brosa, December 20, 1940, *Letters from a Life: Selected Letters of Benjamin Britten,* eds. Philip Reed and Donald Mitchell.
13. Christopher Headington, *Peter Pears: A Biography.*
14. Norse, *Memoirs of a Bastard Angel.*
15. McCullers, *Illumination and Night Glare.*
16. Carr, *Lonely Hunter.*
17. Carson McCullers, "Brooklyn Is My Neighborhood," *Vogue,* March 1941.
18. Carr, *Lonely Hunter.*
19. Carr.
20. McCullers, "Brooklyn Is My Neighborhood."
21. Carr, *Lonely Hunter.*
22. Carr.
23. Sarah Schulman, "White Writer," *New Yorker,* October 21, 2016.
24. Tippins, *February House.*
25. Jeffrey Meyers, "The Oddest Couple: Paul and Jane Bowles," *Michigan Quarterly Review* 50, no. 2 (Spring 2011).
26. Tippins, *February House.*
27. Tippins.
28. Tippins.
29. Carson McCullers to Reeves McCullers, January 6, 1945, Harry Ransom Humanities Research Center, University of Texas–Austin.
30. Fran Schumer, "Broadway Magic: The Lyrical Visions of Oliver Smith," *New York Alumni News Magazine,* Fall 1990.
31. Tippins, *February House.*
32. Farnan, *Auden in Love.*
33. Chester Kallman to W. H. Auden, November 10, 1941, W. H. Auden Papers, Berg Collection, New York Public Library.
34. Farnan, *Auden in Love.*
35. Jack Barker, *No Moaning There!*
36. Barker.
37. Barker.
38. Nicholas Jenkins, "Jack Barker: 1915–1995," *W. H. Auden Society Newsletter* 14 (April 1996).
39. "List or Manifest of Aliens Employed on the Vessel as Members of the Crew," *Argos Hill,* December 12, 1940, National Archives and Record Administration.
40. Donald A. Bertke, Don Kindell, and Gordon Smith, *World War II Sea War: France Falls, Britain Stands Alone.*
41. Stephen Spender, *Letters to Christopher,* ed. Lee Bartlett.
42. Farnan, *Auden in Love.*
43. Norse, *Memoirs of a Bastard Angel.*
44. Farnan, *Auden in Love.*
45. Tippins, *February House.*

46. Farnan, *Auden in Love.*

47. Truman Capote, *A House on the Heights.*

48. Jordan G. Teicher, "Incredible Images Capture WWII New York," accessed February 16, 2018, http://www.slate.com/blogs/behold/2013/07/24/new_york_historical_society _exhibits_shows_new_york_city_during_wwii_photos.html.

49. Colonel John L. Beebe, "This Is Sheepshead Bay," accessed February 16, 2018, http:// www.usmm.org/sheepsheadbay.html.

50. "Fort Greene Houses Dedicated by Notables," *Brooklyn Daily Eagle,* September 10, 1942.

51. Letter from Thomas Painter to unknown individual, April 5, 1944, Thomas Painter Archive, Kinsey Institute, Indiana University.

52. Allan Bérubé, *Coming Out Under Fire: The History of Gay Men and Women in World War II.*

53. Letter from Alfred Gross to Major Frank E. Mason, December 19, 1941, declassified by NARS, August 24, 1994.

54. Letter from John C. Wiley to Wallace B. Phillips, January 15, 1942, declassified by NARS, August 24, 1994.

55. Letter from Samuel J. Kopetzky to Edward W. Bourne, July 31, 1942, George Henry Papers, Medical Center Archives of NewYork-Presbyterian/Weill Cornell.

56. Alfred Gross Names Binder Entry, Thomas Painter Collection.

57. Bérubé, *Coming Out Under Fire.*

58. Letter from Robert Latou Dickinson to Thomas Painter, January 17, 1943, Thomas Painter Collection.

59. Charles Kaiser, *The Gay Metropolis.*

60. William H. Miller Jr., *Dartmouth Alumni Magazine* article, March 1946, Glenway Wescott Collection, Beinecke Rare Book and Manuscript Library, Yale University Library.

61. Kaiser, *Gay Metropolis.*

62. Miller, *Dartmouth Alumni Magazine* article.

63. Kaiser, *Gay Metropolis.*

64. Kaiser.

65. Miller, *Dartmouth Alumni Magazine* article.

66. Henry Robinson Luce, *Time* 43.

67. Letter from Paul Cadmus to William Miller, December 1, 1943, William Miller Collection, Beinecke Rare Book and Manuscript Library, Yale University Library.

68. Letter from William Miller to Monroe Wheeler, March 1, 1944, William Miller Collection.

69. Letter from William Miller to Alfred Kinsey, January 1, 1953, William Miller Collection.

70. Letter from William Miller to Monroe Wheeler, September 4, 1948, William Miller Collection.

71. Matty Costello, Names Binder entry, Thomas Painter Collection.

72. Henry, *Sex Variants.*

73. Letter from Thomas Painter to Alfred Kinsey, January 30, 1950, Thomas Painter Collection.

74. "Senator Linked to Spy Nest Which Lured Service Men," *New York Post,* May 1, 1942.

75. "Service Men Lured to 'Den' Called Spy Nest," *Brooklyn Daily Eagle,* April 10, 1942.

76. "Senator Linked to Spy Nest Which Lured Service Men," *New York Post.*

77. "Den Keeper Withholds Source of Cash to Fete Soldiers, Says O'Dwyer," *Philadelphia Inquirer,* May 20, 1942.

78. "Leibowitz Pushes Spy Ring Probe: Tells Convicted Morals Offender to Talk or Get 20-Year Term," *Brooklyn Daily Eagle,* May 1, 1942.

79. "The Press: The Case of Senator X," *Time* 39, no. 22 (June 1942): 48.

80. "Sing Sing Prison list of foreign born prisoners," New York State Archives.

81. Dennis Eisenberg, *Meyer Lansky: Mogul of the Mob.*

82. Martin Duberman, *About Time: Exploring the Gay Past.*

83. Confidential report by Ted Thackrey re: investigation of Senator David Walsh, 1943, Dorothy Schiff Papers, New York Public Library.

84. "Women Workers in Ten War Production Areas and Their Postwar Employment Plans," US Department of Labor, *Women's Bureau Bulletin* no. 209, 1946.

85. John Stobo, "Preparing for War, 1937–1941, Part 4," accessed February 19, 2018, http://www.columbia.edu/~jrs9/BNY-Hist-Prep-War-4.html.

86. Michael S. Sherry, *In the Shadow of War: The United States Since the 1930s.*

87. Strobo, "Preparing for War."

88. "Mrs. Herrick Starts Job at Todd Yards," *Brooklyn Daily Eagle,* September 15, 1942.

89. "This Is a New Game at the Todd Shipyards," *Brooklyn Daily Eagle,* July 14, 1942.

90. Undated issue of *Wartime Keel,* Todd Shipyard bulletin, Anne Moses Scrapbook in Michael Levine's (nephew's) personal collection.

91. "Shipyard Gals Wear Rejected Army Pants," *Brooklyn Daily Eagle,* October 15, 1943.

92. Lucille Kolkin oral history, Brooklyn Navy Yard Oral History Project at the Brooklyn Historical Society.

93. "Shipyard Gals Wear Rejected Army Pants," *Brooklyn Daily Eagle.*

94. Lucille Kolkin oral history.

95. Bettie Chase oral history, Brooklyn Navy Yard Oral History Project at the Brooklyn Historical Society.

96. Len Evans interview with Rusty Brown, July 7, 1983, San Francisco GLBT Historical Society.

97. Rusty Brown, "Always Me," in *Long Time Passing: Lives of Older Lesbians,* ed. Marcy Adelman.

98. Evans interview.

99. Evans interview.

100. Brown, "Always Me."

101. Brown.

102. Claudia Goldin, "The Role of World War II in the Rise of Women's Work." NBER Working Paper No. 3203 (Also Reprint No. r1619). Issued in December 1989.

7. The Great Erasure, 1945–69

1. "Victory Celebrations," *Life,* August 27, 1945.
2. Bill Miller appointment book, Box 2, Folder 1, William Miller Collection, Yale University Library, Beinecke Rare Book and Manuscript Library.
3. Jeannette Edwards Rattray, "Long Island Book Column," *East Hampton Star,* October 7, 1943.
4. Marvin Liebman, *Coming Out Conservative.*
5. James Jones, *From Here to Eternity.*
6. Kaylie Jones, "Was a WWII Classic Too Gay?," *Daily Beast,* November 10, 2009, accessed March 6, 2018, https://www.thedailybeast.com/was-a-wwii-classic-too-gay.
7. Bérubé, *Coming Out Under Fire.*
8. Christine Knauer, *Let Us Fight as Free Men: Black Soldiers and Civil Rights.*
9. Annual Report City Magistrate's Courts, City of New York, 1945, New York City Metropolitan Archives.
10. Annual Report City Magistrate's Courts, City of New York, 1948, New York City Metropolitan Archives.
11. Memo from Joseph Leary, Active Lieutenant, Eightieth Squad, to Commanding Officer, Eighteenth Division, October 20, 1945, New York City Metropolitan Archives.
12. Report of Dr. George Henry, Consulting Psychiatrist, for the Year Ending 31 December 1946 to Chief City Magistrate Edgar Bromberger, Quaker Emergency Service Records, Friends Historical Library, Swarthmore College.
13. Note by Fredric Wertham, August 13, 1949, Fredric Wertham Collection, Library of Congress.
14. Report of Dr. George Henry.
15. Letter from Alfred Gross to the Honorable Dorris Clark, undated 1946, Quaker Emergency Service Records.
16. Howard Whitman, "The Biggest Taboo," *Collier's,* February 15, 1947.
17. Whitman.
18. Letter from Alfred Gross to Josiah P. Marvel, May 15, 1947, Josiah Marvel Collection, Friends Historical Library, Swarthmore College.
19. "QES Readjustment Center statistics 9/30/52," Fredric Wertham Collection.
20. Letter from Luise Zucker to Fredric Wertham, April 23, 1951, Fredric Wertham Collection.
21. Handwritten notes of Fredric Wertham, March 29, 1951, Fredric Wertham Collection.
22. Letter from Fredric Wertham to Richard Benjamin, November 1, 1956, Fredric Wertham Collection.
23. Edward S. Silver, Report by the District Attorney of Kings County, NY, for the Year 1954, New York City Metropolitan Archives.
24. "Ex-Quaker Aide Ruled a Suicide," *New York Times,* July 27, 1959.

25. "Jan Gay, 58, Author, Dies After Illness," San Rafael *Daily Independent Journal,* September 12, 1960.

26. Douglas M. Charles, *Hoover's War on Gays: Exposing the FBI's "Sex Deviates" Program.*

27. Donald Webster Cory, *The Homosexual in America.*

28. James T. Sears, *Behind the Mask of the Mattachine.*

29. White, *Reforming Sodom.*

30. Charles, *Hoover's War on Gays.*

31. Jess Stearn, *The Sixth Man: A Startling Investigation of the Spread of Homosexuality in America.*

32. Donald Webster Cory, *The Lesbian in America.*

33. Transcript of interview with Curtis Dewees. Martin B. Duberman, Box 146, Folder 5.

34. Curtis Dewees, *Memoirs of a Gay Rights Maverick.*

35. Dewees.

36. Dewees interview, Martin B. Duberman.

37. "Rooney Flays Brooklyn Navy Yard Layoffs," *Brooklyn Daily Eagle,* May 12, 1946.

38. Adelman, *Long Time Passing.*

39. Bérubé, *Coming Out Under Fire.*

40. Len Evans interview with Rusty Brown, July 7, 1983.

41. "Employment of Homosexuals and Other Sex Perverts in Government," Interim Report, Senate Subcommittee on Investigations, December 15, 1950.

42. "Homosexuals Seen Bad U.S. Security Risks," *Longview* (TX) *News-Journal,* May 25, 1950.

43. David K. Johnson, *The Lavender Scare: The Cold War Persecution of Gays and Lesbians in the Federal Government.*

44. Bérubé, *Coming Out Under Fire.*

45. Len Evans interview with Rusty Brown, July 7, 1983.

46. Evans interview.

47. Evans interview.

48. Evans interview.

49. Evans interview.

50. Mary Loretta Hood interview in the Coney Island History Project Oral History, accessed February 24, 2018, http://www.coneyislandhistory.org/oral-history-archive/mary-loretta-hood.

51. R. H. Gardner, "Wine, Woman, and a Thousand Pounds of Plumbing," *Baltimore Sun,* May 21, 1951.

52. A. W. Stencell, *Girl Show: Into the Canvas World of Bump and Grind.*

53. "Coney and Rockaways Row over Attendance," *Brooklyn Daily Eagle,* July 21, 1946.

54. "'Wine Bath' Ban Yields No Grapes of Wrath," *Brooklyn Daily Eagle,* June 26, 1946.

55. Alice Hughes, "A Woman's New York," *New York Star Press,* August 1, 1946.

56. "6,103 Tried at Coney," *New York Times,* July 31, 1946.

57. "Fire and Health Hazards Charged to 25 Concessionaires at Coney," *New York Times,* July 12, 1946.

58. "Coney Island May Be Poor Man's Paradise, but It's Just Devil's Play Pen to City Magistrate," *New York Times,* July 23, 1949.

59. "Coney Cancels Mardi Gras This Season," *Brooklyn Daily Eagle,* August 8, 1949.

60. William J. Phalen, *Coney Island: 150 Years of Rides, Fires, Floods, the Rich, the Poor, and Finally Robert Moses.*

61. "Coney Island's Only Girls on Beach Now," *Indianapolis News,* July 1, 1953.

62. Stencell, *Girl Show.*

63. James A. Mannix, "Says Poor Man Must Be Protected from Girls in Bath," *Brooklyn Daily Eagle,* August 18, 1952.

64. Coney Island Has Just as Much Hurly but the Burly Is Gone," *Niagara Falls Gazette,* July 1, 1953.

65. "Public Seen Tiring of Coney Gimmicks," *New York Times,* October 6, 1949.

66. Robert Caro, *The Power Broker.*

67. "Full Details on Coney Island Municipal Baths," *Brooklyn Daily Eagle,* December 27, 1953.

68. "The Improvement of Coney Island, Rockaway, and South Beaches," Department of Parks, City of New York, November 20, 1937, accessed March 11, 2018, https://archive.org/stream/improvementofcon00newy/improvementofcon00newy_djvu.txt.

69. "New Aquarium Seen Inspiring Coney Island's Rebirth as Model Home-Resort Area for Boro," *Brooklyn Daily Eagle,* December 10, 1952.

70. "Public Seen Tiring of Coney Gimmicks," *New York Times.*

71. Jonathan Mahler, "How the Coastline Became a Place to Put the Poor," *New York Times,* December 3, 2012.

72. Caro, *Power Broker.*

73. "Aquarium Opens June 6," *New York Times,* March 4, 1957.

74. "Crowds Tax Aquarium's Capacity on Its First Saturday," *New York Times,* June 10, 1957.

75. "Ground-Breaking for Aquarium Begins Dignified Era for Coney Island Area," *Brooklyn Daily Eagle,* October 25, 1954.

76. "City Rebuffs Ride Operators on Coney Ramp," *Brooklyn Daily Eagle,* November 19, 1954.

77. Hugh Hagius, *Swasarnt Nerf's Gay Guides for 1949.*

78. Thomas Painter to Alfred Kinsey, September 9, 1953, Thomas Painter Collection.

79. Painter to Kinsey.

80. Thomas Painter to Alfred Kinsey, July 8, 1948, Thomas Painter Collection.

81. Thomas Painter to Alfred Kinsey, July 4, 1947, Thomas Painter Collection.

82. Thomas Painter to Alfred Kinsey, December 30, 1951, Thomas Painter Collection.

83. Thomas Painter to Alfred Kinsey, August 1, 1954, Thomas Painter Collection.

84. Thomas Painter to Alfred Kinsey, April 16, 1951, Thomas Painter Collection.

85. Names Binder, Thomas Painter Collection.

86. Thomas Painter to Alfred Kinsey, December 7, 1953, Thomas Painter Collection.

87. Thomas Painter Collection.

88. Thomas Painter to Alfred Kinsey, May 28, 1950, Thomas Painter Collection.

89. Thomas Painter to Alfred Kinsey, May 27, 1951, Thomas Painter Collection.

90. "The Real Sex Menace: Society Ignores Problem as Harlem Faces 'Invasion,'" *New York Age,* January 7, 1950.

91. "Psychiatrist Says Sadistic Crimes Are on the Increase," Rockland County (NY) *Journal-News,* August 20, 1954.

92. Thomas Painter to Alfred Kinsey, June 9, 1951, Thomas Painter Collection.

93. Thomas Painter to Alfred Kinsey, June 22, 1954, Thomas Painter Collection.

94. Thomas Painter to Alfred Kinsey, September 1, 1954, Thomas Painter Collection.

95. Carmen Theresa Whalen and Víctor Vázquez-Hernández, eds., *The Puerto Rican Diaspora: Historical Perspectives.*

96. César J. Ayala, "The Decline of the Plantation Economy and the Puerto Rican Migration of the 1950s," *Latino Studies Journal* 7, no. 1 (Winter 1996): 61–90.

97. "The Status of Labor in—Puerto Rico, Alaska, Hawaii," Bulletin no. 1191, US Department of Labor, December 1955.

98. "The Measurement and Behavior of Unemployment," Universities-National Bureau, 1957, accessed March 8, 2018, http://www.nber.org/chapters/c2644.pdf.

99. Thomas Painter to Alfred Kinsey, September 9, 1951, Thomas Painter Collection.

100. Ann Aldrich, *We, Too, Must Love.*

101. Nicholas Dagen Bloom, *Public Housing That Worked: New York in the Twentieth Century.*

102. Bloom.

103. "For Better Housing," *Brooklyn Daily Eagle,* September 19, 1946.

104. "Parks Association Tours Brooklyn," *New York Times,* May 25, 1956.

105. Bloom, *Public Housing That Worked.*

106. "Street Widening Planned near Housing Project," *Brooklyn Daily Eagle,* August 14, 1947.

107. Margaret Mara, "Old Sands Street Rates Swan Song," *Brooklyn Daily Eagle,* April 14, 1950.

108. "George Currie's Brooklyn," *Brooklyn Daily Eagle,* April 30, 1947.

109. Bloom, *Public Housing That Worked.*

110. Alexander von Hoffman, "A Study in Contradictions: The Origins and Legacy of the Housing Act of 1949," *Housing Policy Debate* (Fannie Mae Foundation) 11, no. 2 (2000).

111. Kenneth T. Jackson, *Crabgrass Frontier: The Suburbanization of the United States.*

112. *Federal Housing Authority Underwriting Manual,* 1936.

113. "Construction and Housing, 1946–47," Bulletin no. 941, US Department of Labor.

114. Jackson, *Crabgrass Frontier.*

115. Jackson.

116. Philip S. Gutis, "Levittown, L.I., at 40: Once a Solution, Now a Problem," *New York Times,* September 21, 1987.

117. *Federal Housing Authority Underwriting Manual,* 1936.

118. William Laas, "The Suburbs Are Strangling the City," *New York Times,* June 18, 1950.

119. "Pros, Cons of Seaway," *Brooklyn Daily Eagle,* January 6, 1955.

120. Michael Oreskes, "Census Tracks Radical Shift in New York City's Population," *New York Times,* September 20, 1982.

121. Thomas Painter to Alfred Kinsey, August 21, 1953, Thomas Painter Collection.

122. Thomas Painter to Alfred Kinsey, January 18, 1954, Thomas Painter Collection.

123. Thomas Painter to Alfred Kinsey, June 23, 1954, Thomas Painter Collection.

124. Thomas Painter to Alfred Kinsey, March 7, 1955, Thomas Painter Collection.

125. Mel Gussow, *Edward Albee: A Singular Journey: A Biography.*

126. Andy Warhol and Pat Hackett, *Popism: The Warhol Sixties.*

127. Scott MacDonald, *A Critical Cinema 5: Interviews with Independent Filmmakers.*

128. William D. Romanowski, *Risky Business: Rock in Film.*

129. Truman Capote, "Brooklyn Heights: A Personal Memoir," *Holiday,* February 1959.

130. "Omnibus," *Brooklyn Heights Press,* October 4, 1962.

131. Letters to the Editor, *Brooklyn Heights Press,* October 18, 1962.

132. Letters to the Editor, *Brooklyn Heights Press,* October 25, 1962.

133. "Historic Wrought-Iron Grille Adds to Décor of Tony Bonner's Club," *Brooklyn Heights Press,* November 3, 1955.

134. "Bonner Purchases Hts Supper Club," *Brooklyn Heights Press,* July 24, 1953.

135. John W. Creighton, "Champagne Flows at Supper Club," *Brooklyn Heights Press,* July 22, 1954.

136. Robert C. Doty, "Growth of Overt Homosexuality in City Provokes Wide Concern," *New York Times,* December 17, 1963.

137. Letters to the Editor, *Brooklyn Heights Press,* September 12, 1963.

138. Letters to the Editor, *Brooklyn Heights Press,* September 19, 1963.

139. "Homosexuality," *Brooklyn Heights Press,* December 19, 1963.

140. "Bonnie Burke's Promenade Through Brooklyn," *The Advocate,* July 23, 1981.

141. Shane Kavanaugh, "Big Same-Sex District in Brooklyn Has Little Gay Vibe," *Crains New York,* April 24, 2011.

index

Page numbers followed by "p" indicate photographs.